The Contemporary British Society Reader

The Contemporary British Society Reader

Edited by

Nicholas Abercrombie and Alan Warde

Polity

Copyright © editorial matter and organization Nicholas Abercrombie and Alan Warde 2001
First published in 2001 by Polity Press in association with Blackwell Publishers Ltd

Editorial office:
Polity Press
65 Bridge Street
Cambridge CB2 1UR, UK

Marketing and production:
Blackwell Publishers Ltd
108 Cowley Road
Oxford OX4 1JF, UK

ISBN 0-7456-2262-3
ISBN 0-7456-2263-1 (pbk)

A catalogue record for this book is available from the British Library.

Typeset in 10 on 12 pt Sabon
by Best-set Typesetter Ltd., Hong Kong
Printed in Great Britain by TJ International, Padstow, Cornwall

This book is printed on acid-free paper.

Contents

Preface
How to use this book

The Contemporary British Society Reader is a compendium of sociological writing on key institutions and processes in Britain today. From it can be gleaned an understanding of a complex society, its structure and the prevailing trends which influence social life.

This book is a compilation of some of the best recent sociological analysis of the condition of Britain today. *The Contemporary British Society Reader* contains extracts from books and journals selected partly in order to give a wide coverage of topics central to sociology and partly to illustrate the power and variety of recent sociological research. Hence the book contains chapters which examine, for example, class, gender, ethnicity, mass media and education. The accounts report on the use of a range of different research methods – ethnography, in-depth interviews, observation and surveys. The chapters have been chosen for the high quality of their sociological analysis and their relevance to understanding social change. Most are based on recent empirical research and therefore able to capture in detail some of the more distinctive features of life in Britain at the end of the twentieth century. For the general reader, the selections may be read in any order. Readers with interests in particular topics should consult not only the chapter titles on the contents page, but also the list of key words associated with each chapter. The interdependence of social institutions means that, for example, a piece primarily about television viewing may have relevance for understanding the family, gender, generation and ethnicity. A desire to maximize this type of overlap has influenced the selection of material. In order to represent this overlap, readings are listed at the end of this Preface by topic area.

The Contemporary British Society Reader is also designed to be used in association with its companion volume, the third edition of *Contemporary British Society*, a text which offers a general introduction to the sociological analysis of British social institutions. The contents of the two books run in parallel, the excerpts in this book being ordered by their main topic into the same sequence as in *Contemporary British Society*. Therefore, anyone studying a particular topic can read both a summary of the general field and some associated original sociological studies. Such studies provide additional and more detailed information and analysis, and to that end the list of key words is a means for discovering the location of chapters on specific topics. However, they also give a feel for the texture of original sociological research and its analysis, the raw material of scientific investigation from which textbooks distil their summaries of current knowledge on particular issues. Textbooks, by their very nature, simplify: typically, description becomes general and generic, while debate and disagreement are minimized. The less refined form in which results are presented here captures more faithfully the character of sociological inquiry and investigation. *The Contemporary British Society Reader* gives the newcomer to sociology a taste of the excitement and complexity of original research and analysis.

The chapters in this reader are drawn from a range of sources, mostly ones published in the late 1990s. Because space is limited, the original source material has been reduced in length. An ellipsis within square brackets [. . .] indicates the excision of a small amount of text, primarily to eliminate superfluous references, thereby aiding the flow of the writing. Where more than one paragraph has been excluded, a line space appears above and below such ellipses.

Those inspired to read the full and unexpurgated version of the source material will find the necessary publication details clearly laid out in the Acknowledgements.

As we noted above, the readings that we have chosen cover a number of sociological topics. In order to help the reader who wishes to use the book to pursue a particular topic, the readings are listed below arranged by topic. The topics listed correspond to individual chapters in the companion volume, *Contemporary British Society*.

Globalization

Bennett on the relationship between global and local music making; **Roseneil** on the interaction between a local political protest and the global political context; **Bechhofer et al.** on national identity; **Dicken** on the global economy.

Economic organization

McNair on the changing political economy of the British press; **Hesmondhalgh** on the British dance music industry; **Dicken** on the global economy; **Gallie et al.** on changes in organizations; **McDowell** on aspects of financial services in the City of London; **Gewirtz et al.** on the privatization of economic organizations and the introduction of market processes within the school system.

Employment

Gallie et al. on changes in skill, occupations, organizations, managerial strategies, flexibility and unemployment; **Savage** on self-employment and occupational careers;

Devine on the underclass debate, inequality of income, poverty, unemployment and multiple deprivation; McDowell on managerial work and organizational cultures in banks in the City of London; Morris on unemployment, polarization and the underclass; Acker on teaching as a professional occupation.

Patterns of inequality and social mobility

Westergaard on the consequences of inequality of income and wealth for class differences; Savage on social mobility; Skeggs on working-class women and class identity; Independent Inquiry into Inequalities in Health on the relationship between inequality and health.

Social class

Warde on class differences in consumption habits; Westergaard on class inequalities, the decline of class and cross-class marriage; Savage on the middle classes, geographical mobility, self-employment and changes in careers; Devine on the underclass and its relationship to the working class; Skeggs on working-class women, respectability and distinction; McDowell on middle-class women working in the City of London; Sanders on partisanship and class dealignment in electoral politics; Mac an Ghaill on young middle-class rebels; Gewirtz et al. on the effects of the marketization of schooling on the prospects of children in working-class families.

Gender

Smart on conceptions of motherhood and fatherhood; Roseneil on a women's protest movement; Finch and Mason on gender differences in discharging obligations to family members; Gillespie on Punjabi boys' and girls' reactions to soap opera; Gallie et al. on changes in women's employment, flexibility and polarization; Devine on poverty, lone parenthood and deprivation; Skeggs on the cultural ambivalence of working-class women and their search for respectability; McDowell on gender divisions and women managers in the City of London and their encounters with masculinities and femininities; Morris on sexual divisions of labour, gender divisions, lone motherhood and the limits of welfare provision; Lury on shopping, domestic divisions of labour, gender divisions and femininity; Richardson on sexuality and citizenship; Norris and Lovenduski on political representation, party organizations and the small numbers of women members of parliament; Acker on gender divisions, labour market segregation and equal opportunities for women teachers; **Mac an Ghaill** on masculinity, peer group subcultures, youth and sexuality; **Thompson** on moral panics, homosexuality and AIDS; **Worrall** on gender and the criminal justice system; **Independent Inquiry into Inequalities in Health** on gender differences in health.

Ethnicity and racism

Bennett on the appropriation of black music by white youth in Newcastle; **Gillespie** on the meaning given by young Punjabis to television soap opera; **Virdee** on racial harassment; **Hetherington** on societal reactions to travellers; **Mac an Ghaill** on youth, ethnic divisions and national identity; **Independent Inquiry into Inequalities in Health** on ethnic differences in health.

Families and households

Irwin on changing family structure; **Smart** on fatherhood after divorce; **Roberts** on youth, leisure and identity; **Finch and Mason** on kinship and obligation; **Gillespie** on family, ethnicity and gender in Punjabi young people's response to television; **Morris** on household formation, sexual divisions of labour and lone motherhood.

Associations

Hetherington on the social relationships of travellers; **Finch and Mason** on relationships with the wider kinship network; **Phillipson et al.** on relationships between the elderly and their neighbours.

Leisure

Irwin for an account of the changing position of young people; **Bennett** on differences in the way that hip hop is interpreted by different youth cultures; **Roberts** on the relation of changes in the situations of young people to their lifestyles and identities; **Gillespie** on young Punjabis and television; **Hetherington** on Stonehenge as a space of consumption; **Skeggs** on working-class women and their quest for respectability through consumption; **Lury** on consumption, shopping and femininity; **Warde** on food and social class; **Bechhofer et al.** on identity in the context of national identity.

The media

Bennett on the different meanings given to hip hop; Hesmondhalgh on the British dance music industry; McNair on the changing British press; Gillespie on the manner in which a Punjabi community interprets *Neighbours*; Thompson on moral panics in the mass media and the representation of AIDS.

The state and politics

Roseneil on a local protest movement; Hetherington on protests associated with Stonehenge in the mid 1980s; Judge et al. on changes in the National Health Service; Bechhofer et al. on Scottish identity; Norris and Lovenduski on political representation, electoral bias, political elites and party organizations; Sanders on political parties, partisanship, electoral volatility and class dealignment; Richardson on citizenship and sexuality; Gewirtz et al. on the policy to privatize economic organizations and the quality of welfare provision in the educational sphere.

Education

Acker on school teachers and their careers; Mac an Ghaill on peer-group subcultures and schooling; Gewirtz et al. on working-class families, the marketization of education and the process of pupils transferring to secondary school.

Health

Judge et al. on attitudes to the National Health Service; Thompson on media representation of AIDS; Independent Inquiry into Inequalities in Health on the relationship between health and inequality.

Deviance, crime and control

Virdee on racial harassment; Hetherington on travellers and Stonehenge; Thompson on moral panics, deviance and the mass media; Worrall on juvenile delinquency and crime, punishment and the criminal justice system.

Acknowledgements

We are very grateful to a number of people who made suggestions of suitable readings for this book: Rosemary Deem, Sue Penna, Andrew Sayer, Keith Soothill, John Urry and Sylvia Walby (our co-authors of the companion volume, *Contemporary British Society*), Tony Gatrell and Sue Scott. Our thanks also to Pennie Drinkall, Judith Henderson, Alan Metcalfe, Dale Southerton and Ivo Vasilev who helped with the preparation of the manuscript. As always, we are very grateful to Polity Staff, Sophie Ahmad, Kathryn Murphy and Pam Thomas for their enthusiasm, professionalism and patience, and to Meg Davies for her efficient copy-editing.

The publishers gratefully acknowledge the following for permission to reproduce copyright material. Every effort has been made to trace copyright holders, but if any have been inadvertently overlooked, the publishers will be pleased to make the necessary arrangements at the first opportunity.

Extract 'A new geo-economy' from *Global Shift* by Peter Dicken, published by Paul Chapman Publishing 1998. Reprinted with permission of Sage Publications Limited.

Extract 'Rapping on the Tyne: white hip hop culture in Northeast England – an ethnographic study' from *Popular Music and Youth Culture* by Andy Bennett, published by Macmillan. Reprinted by permission of Macmillan Press Limited.

Extract 'Constructing National Identity: arts and landed elites in Scotland' by F. Bechhofer, D. McCrone, R. Kiely and R. Stewart, from *Sociology: The Journal of the British Sociological Association* Vol. 33, No. 3, August 1999. Reprinted by permission of Cambridge University Press.

Extract 'The Global Common: the global, local and personal dynamics of the women's peace movement in the 1980's' by Sasha Roseneil, from *The Limits of Globalisation* by A. Scott, published by Routledge, London, 1997. Reprinted with permission of Taylor & Francis.

Extract from *Restructuring the Employment Relationship* by D. Gallie, M. White, Y. Cheng and M. Tomlinson, published by Oxford University Press, 1998.

Extract 'Class in Britain since 1979: facts, theories and ideologies' by John Westergaard, from *Hitotusbashi Journal of Social Studies*, Vol. 25, No. 1, July 1993, pages 25–62. Reprinted with permission.

Extract 'The middle classes in modern Britain' by Mike Savage, from *Sociology Review* 5:2 published by Philip Allan Publishers 1995. Reprinted with permission of Philip Allan Publishers Limited.

Extract 'OPC Longitudinal Study 1991' Office for National Statistics. Copyright © Crown Copyright 2000. Reprinted with permission.

Extract from *Social Class in America and Britain* by Fiona Devine, published by Edinburgh University Press 1997. Reprinted with permission of Edinburgh University Press.

Extract from *Capital Culture: gender at work and in the city* by Linda McDowell, published by Blackwell Publishers 1997. Reprinted with permission of Blackwell Publishers.

Extract 'Work, gender and unemployment: a household perspective' by L. Morris, from *New Agendas for Women* published by Macmillan 1999. Reprinted with permission of Macmillan Press Limited.

Extract 'Racial Harassment' by S. Virdee, in *Ethnic Minorities in Britain* by T. Modood, and T. Berthoud, published by Policy Studies Institute, London. Reprinted with permission of Policy Studies Institute.

Extract 'Identifications of class: on not being working class' in *Formation of Class and Gender* by Beverley Skeggs, published by Sage Publications in 1997. Reprinted with permission of Sage Publications Limited.

Extract 'Demographic change and rites of passage: locating "new" life course transitions' from *Rites of passage, social change and the transition from youth to adulthood* by Sarah Irwin, published by UCL Press. Reprinted with permission of Taylor & Francis.

Extract 'The new parenthood: fathers and mothers after divorce' by C. Smart, from *The New Family* edited by E. B. Silva and C. Smart, published by Sage Publications, 1998. Reprinted with permission of Sage Publications Limited.

Extract 'Same activities, different meanings: British youth cultures in the 1990's' by K. Roberts, from *Leisure Studies*, 16, 1997. Reprinted with permission of Taylor & Francis.

Extract from *Negotiating Family Responsibilities* by Janet Finch and Jennifer Mason, published by Routledge, London, 1993. Reprinted with permission of Taylor & Francis.

Extract 'Older people's experiences of community life in patterns of neighbouring in three urban areas' by C. Phillipson, M. Bernard, J. Phillips, J. Ogg, in *Sociological Review*, Vol. 47, 1999. Reprinted by permission of Blackwell Publishers Limited.

Extract 'The British Dance Music Industry: a case-study of independent cultural production' by D. Hesmondhalgh, in *British Journal of Sociology*, 49:2, 1998 pp. 240–8. Reprinted with permission of Taylor & Francis.

Extract 'Before and after Wapping: the changing political economy of the British Press' from *News and Journalism in the UK* by B. McNair, published by Routledge, London, 1996. Reprinted with permission of Taylor & Francis.

Extract 'Economy and Extravagance' from 'Consumption, Food and Taste' by A. Warde, published by Sage Publications, 1997. Reprinted with permission of Sage Publications Limited.

Extract 'Neighbours and gossip: kinship, courtship and community' from *Television, Ethnicity and Cultural Change* by M. Gillespie, published by Routledge, London, 1995. Reprinted with permission of Taylor & Francis.

Extract from *Consumer Culture* by Celia Lury, published by Polity Press and Rutgers University Press, 1996. Reprinted with permission of Polity and Rutgers.

Extract 'Stonehenge and its festival: spaces of consumption' by K. Hetherington, in *Lifestyle Shopping: the subject of consumption* by R. Shields, published by Routledge, London, 1992. Reprinted with permission of Taylor & Francis.

Extract 'The new electoral battleground' by D. Sanders, in *New Labour Triumphs: Britain at the polls* by A. King, published by Chatham House Publishers, USA. Reprinted with permission.

Extract 'Supply and demand explanations' from *Political Recruitment: gender, race and class in the British Parliament* by P. Norris and J. Lovenduski, published by Cambridge University Press, 1995. Reprinted with permission.

Extract 'Citizenship and Sexuality' by Diane Richardson, in *Sociology* 32 (1): 83–100, 1998. Reprinted with permission of Cambridge University Press.

Extract 'Choice and class: parents in the marketplace' from *Markets, Choice and Equity in Education* by Gewirtz, Ball and Bowe, published by Open University Press in 1995. Reprinted with permission.

Extract 'Local student cultures of masculinity and sexuality' from *The Making of Men* by Mártín Mac an Ghaill, published by Open University Press, 1994. Reprinted with permission.

Extract 'Creating careers: women teachers at work' from *Curriculum Inquiry* by S. Acker, published by Blackwell Publishers, USA. Reprinted with permission.

Extract from 'Independent Enquiry into Inequalities in Health' published by HMSO, London, 1998. Reprinted with permission of HMSO, London.

Extract 'The NHS: new prescriptions needed?' By K. Judge, J.-A. Mulligan and B. New, from *British Social Attitudes: The 14th Report*' edited by R. Jowell, J. Curtice, A. Park, K. Thomson and C. Bryson, published by Ashgate Publishing Limited. Reprinted by permission of Ashgate Publishing Limited.

Extract from *Criminal Justice Matters*, No. 19, Spring 1995 pages 6–7. Reprinted with permission of The Centre for Crime and Justice Studies.

Extract from *Punishment in the Community: The Future of Criminal Justice* by Anne Worrall. Copyright © Addison Wesley Longman Limited, 1997. Reprinted with permission of Pearson Education Limited.

Extract 'Moral panics about sex and aids' from *Moral Panics* by K. Thompson, published by Routledge, London, 1998. Reprinted with permission of Taylor & Francis.

Changing Britain

Introduction

The abiding theme in the extracts included in this book is change in British society. They document the impact of globalization on economy and society, the changing character of social divisions, especially those of social class, gender and ethnicity, the dramatic alterations in the constitution of families and households, the growing diversity in cultures and the potential for new forms of politics. To an extent, change has generally produced greater diversity and fragmentation. But it is also important to stress that, although there is change, there is also continuity. Thus, the authors represented here demonstrate the persistence of such underlying structures of British society as social class, the institution of marriage and the state.

Globalization

It is often claimed that contemporary British society is being profoundly influenced by the forces of globalization. This is a term that describes not one single process but rather a phenomenon with several dimensions – economic, cultural, political, technological and even apocalyptic. Of these the most important is the economic. It is no longer easy to talk of a *national* economy (see **Dicken**) in which companies are identified with a particular country, the range of goods on offer is limited by a national taste and national governments can control economic activity within national borders. In a globalized economy, companies can operate on a world scale. They will promote and sell their goods and services worldwide, their ownership may be multinational, they will recruit staff from many countries, and have offices and plants in whatever countries suit their purpose. The consumer is faced with a bewildering variety of goods from every corner of the world and, indeed, it is no longer easy to say where any particular item is manufactured since so many goods, washing machines, cars or computers, for instance, are assembled from parts manufactured in different countries. National governments are faced by companies some of which may have turnovers larger than entire economies and which can relocate factories if government imposes a regulatory regime of which they disapprove. Vast international flows of money between foreign exchange markets can destabilize governments. As **Dicken** points out, economies have always been internationalized to some extent; trade has been international for a very long time and has needed a financial system to support it, for example. However, he distinguishes internationalization from globalization. The former refers to a simple extension of economic activities across national boundaries while the latter describes a process of functional integration of economic activities which are dispersed across the world.

The fact that the range of goods and services available in many countries is so international points to a cultural globalization. It is no longer the case that tastes are *nationally* circumscribed. The awareness of other cultures is fostered by tourism and the globalization of the mass media. People visit far-flung places and acquire different and varied tastes. They also learn about other cultures from the programmes broadcast by global media companies. This form of globalization has led to fears that, rather than encouraging diversity, the domination in music, television and radio of large media companies will standardize cultural experience; Western popular music and Hollywood films will come to be the only forms available and local cultures will be wiped out. Such a view underestimates the resilience of local cultures and, more subtly, the capacity for audiences to interpret what they see and hear in their own local way. For example, **Bennett** argues that, although hip hop is by now an international musical form, it has local variations and uses. In his study of hip hop on Tyneside, he finds performers adapting the form within the daily life of white, working-class young people using local accents and addressing local concerns.

As there are worries that local cultures will be subsumed into an American-dominated global culture, so also are there concerns that national identities will be eliminated. Again, this is to underestimate the resilience of the local and the interaction between local and global. It is argued that ethnic, religious and regional identities have flourished at the same time as global forces have become more powerful. **Bechhofer et al.** describe a tension between a state identity, such as 'British', and national identities such as Scottish, English or Welsh. The authors show how strongly a Scottish identity can be constructed even by people not born in Scotland.

The processes of globalization are clearly much helped by technologies of various kinds, many of which have developed during this century. People and things can be moved around the globe far faster and more cheaply than formerly. Perhaps even more significant are the rapid advances in computer and communications technologies which permit international flows of money or of media messages. Such technologies remove many of the barriers created by space and time. At the same time, the accelerating rate of technological advance creates global risks. For example, global climate change, which could have catastrophic consequences, is being produced by human interventions. Much of the period since the end of the Second World War has been dominated by the possibility of nuclear warfare. **Roseneil** demonstrates the relationship between global risks and local action. She shows how the Greenham Common peace camp in the 1980s mobilized women against the threat of international nuclear war. It was supported by networks that were both local and global, and the participants were motivated by the conviction that people had to confront global problems by acting locally.

Social divisions

Economic globalization impacts very directly on job opportunities in the UK. There has been considerable speculation about its likely effects on skills, training, contracts and job tenure. **Gallie et al.** provide empirical evidence regarding the spread of many of the supposed features of flexible capitalism. They identify a decline in the stability of employment since the 1980s, especially for men, and also an intensification of work, with concomitant increase in stress and insecurity. At the same time, most workers report that their jobs now require more skills than before. However, differences between men and women, and between employees in different social classes, seem not to have altered much.

Economic insecurity, arising from more precarious employment prospects during the 1980s, was accompanied by polarization of income. After several decades of gradual redistribution of income and wealth associated with the welfare state reforms after 1945, personal and household incomes in Britain became more unequal. For much of the twentieth century material inequalities were understood in terms of social class; the middle and upper classes were richer, better educated, in more rewarding and secure jobs and better able to pass on their privileges to their children than were the working class. Britain exhibited clear differences of class, identifiable through occupation, education, consumption habits and political affiliations. Class was a central division around which most sociological accounts of social structure revolved. Increasingly over the last twenty years the importance of class has been challenged. That challenge is the context of **Westergaard's** argument that income inequalities continue to map on to class positions, that the differences of condition of members of different classes are as clear now as in the past, and that many of the reasons adduced for predicting the decline of class are spurious. For him there remains a very small, powerful and cohesive upper class, a privileged managerial and professional middle class comprising about 30 per cent of the population, and the remaining majority whose condition is significantly less secure. However, even if the structure of class division persists, neither he nor any other sociologist would say that nothing has changed in recent years.

One of the most obvious developments has been the reduction in the number of male manual labouring jobs, which provided the basis for a shared working-class culture. Now, the bulk of employment is non-manual, in services rather than mining and manufacturing, and involves many more women and more people from minority ethnic groups. The sociological focus has thus shifted from the working to the middle class. **Savage** gives a synoptic overview of the structure of the contemporary middle class, identifying divisions within it, some groups being much better placed than others, and noting the importance of geographical mobility in the formation of classes. Another development much commented upon has been the emergence of an underclass in the late twentieth century. Whether the condition of poor people can be understood properly in terms of a shared class location has caused fierce debate. **Devine** reviews the debate and concludes that the sections of the population at greatest risk of poverty do not constitute a group with a shared culture of dependency on the state. Though we may not be able to identify a group with a shared culture shaped by poverty, evidence of other forms of shared class experience continues to surface. The distinctiveness of working-class conditions and practices is documented in several extracts (**Gewirtz et al., Independent Inquiry into Inequalities in Health, Mac an Ghaill, Warde**), but nowhere more poignantly than in the chapter by **Skeggs** which analyses the experiences of young working-class women. As she puts it, working-class women 'disidentify' with class; they seek to avoid being seen as working class, yet much of the way they organize their lives and reflect upon their circumstances reveals how class, intersecting with gender, figures in the creation of their personal identities.

One feature of recent social and political debate, and in turn of sociological concern, has been a deeper appreciation of forms of division other than class. In particular, gender and ethnicity are shown to be sources of unequal treatment. Inequality of opportunities for employment between men and women continues despite legislation which outlaws discrimination on the basis of gender. Many factors are responsible, ranging from routines for the socialization of children, through the sex-typing of jobs and biases in recruitment procedures, to a persistently unequal distribution of domestic responsibilities. Several chapters examine the channels through which gender inequalities are perpetuated. **Acker** shows that promotion in school teaching is skewed in favour of men and documents the ways in which, consequently, women think differently about their careers. **Norris and Lovenduski** consider whether the small proportions of women holding political office can best be explained by lack of resources, lack of motivation or anticipation of discrimination. **McDowell** isolates a further cause – informal interaction in the workplace which reinforces male advantage. As she shows, even highly paid and highly qualified women merchant bankers in the City of London find it difficult to cut an acceptable and comfortable path through the masculine culture of the organization employing them.

Gender inequality appears then not only in employment, but also in educational opportunities, social participation, political preferment and susceptibility to harassment and violence. Like **Devine**, **Morris** considers the connections between poverty and unemployment, but she concentrates on how the circumstances of unemployment and lone parenthood affect women. As she argues, structural change in the relationship between work, family and welfare provision is immensely important for our understanding of social divisions. One of the primary forces structuring social inequality is the state. The character of gender divisions varies considerably across Europe, for example, partly as a consequence of state welfare policy. The British state continues to emit contradictory messages. It encourages women's participation in the labour market. Yet it fails to ensure the provision of adequate supportive childcare facilities, without which, given their greater domestic responsibilities, women are disadvantaged in their careers and hampered in their attempts to care for children.

The expansion of welfare provision was, originally, primarily a response to class inequalities. The spread of citizenship rights – equality before the law, the vote, minimal social security – is one way of conceptualizing the spread of equality in Western societies. The post-war welfare state sought to guarantee some social and economic security, through health care irrespective of capacity to pay, through employment insurance, and so forth. These were measures particularly valuable to the least well off, to the working class who suffered poorest health and greatest vulnerability to unemployment. However, there is an equally compelling case that justice and fairness of treatment require that these guarantees be afforded to men and women alike, and also to particular minorities within society. Increasingly claims are being made for the equalization of rights along other lines of social division. **Richardson** points out that many people are denied full membership of the community because they lack some specific cultural attribute. People are often disadvantaged because they diverge from the majority by virtue of national origin or sexual orientation. These too are matters which require state regulation to prevent unfair discrimination or harassment. The chapter by **Virdee** documents the experience of harassment among minority ethnic populations in Britain, a product of continued racist intolerance which is perpetuated in part by the institutionalized racism of a key state agency, the police. State intervention remains ambiguous in its effects.

Thus can be seen change and continuity in the operation of social divisions in Britain. Class, gender and ethnicity are dimensions which do not simply differentiate experience, but which systematically give disproportionate levels of material resources, power and control to some sections of the population. Structural inequalities persistently affect British social institutions and cultural formations.

Family and household

At one time, perhaps as little as forty years ago, it might have been possible to say that households and families were more or less the same thing; households were made up of families consisting of once-married parents and their children. Such a stereotypical view of 'the' family continues to have power, as **Thompson** shows in his analysis of the reactions to the threat of AIDS. Over the past half-century or so, however, a number of far-reaching social changes have conspired to diversify households and to make the life-courses of individuals much more various; there is no longer a 'normal' or 'standard' family or household. As a result, the experiences of family life are less predictable, more uncertain and, to an extent, more insecure. Amongst the most important of these social changes are: a rising expectation of life, a larger number of single-person households, smaller families, greater numbers of single parents, delayed marriage, much increased cohabitation before, or instead of, marriage, and a steadily increasing rate of divorce.

The expectation of life has risen steadily since the end of the Second World War. Consequently, the proportion of the elderly in the population as a whole has increased. It also follows that married couples are potentially likely to spend much more time together without children in the household than they used to. Single-person households have become much more prominent in the last few decades in Britain; the proportion has risen from 11 per cent in 1961 to 26 per cent in 1991. Much of this change is due to the ageing of the population but some comes from a greater tendency for people to choose to live singly. Where households do consist of families, the size of those families is diminishing as couples decide to have fewer children or no children at all.

The institution of marriage is also changing as **Irwin** shows in her account of contemporary family formation. People are delaying getting married; the average age of marriage for men rose from twenty-four in 1950 to twenty-eight in 1995. The practice of living together without being married is becoming much more common. For example, half of the women marrying in 1987 had lived with their husband before marriage compared with 7 per cent of those marrying in 1970. One result of greater cohabitation is that more children are born outside marriage. In 1971, 9 per cent of births were to unmarried people; in 1996, 37 per cent were. At the same time, when couples do get married, the chances of their subsequently being divorced are rising. Of couples marrying in the year 2000, it is likely that about half will stay married to the same partner. However, divorce does not necessarily indicate that the partners concerned repudiate marriage as such. A substantial number, both men and women, remarry and the result is that family structures become complex. Children from more than one marriage may live together in the same household and parents will have emotional ties and practical obligations to children in different households.

Irwin suggests that it was plausible to argue in the 1960s and 1970s that there was a 'modern family' in that there was not a great deal of variation in the timing of major events in people's lives. However, diversification of experience has induced uncertainty which, in turn, alters behaviour. **Smart**, for instance, investigates the roles of motherhood and fatherhood after divorce. She argues that, during marriage, most fathers only relate to their children through the mother. The result is that divorce makes the continuing role of fatherhood very difficult. Fathers can no longer depend on the mother as an intermediary and mothers cannot rely on their ex-husbands to take on responsibilities which they had previously neglected. Some men respond to these changes by trying to preserve the balance between fatherhood and motherhood struck during marriage. Others, however, try to re-negotiate the relationship to create a new version of fatherhood.

Many of the changes that we have described have an impact on the experiences of growing up and of becoming adult. **Roberts** argues that there is greater variety of experience in all age-groups. There is no longer a normal trajectory for a young person. Youth has become prolonged as marriage is delayed and entry to the job-market is postponed. At the same time, there is greater diversity as many young people get married and obtain jobs at a relatively young age while others remain in education for several years. Young people's biographies have become individualized and uncertain as local job-markets change. These changes affect youth cultures which also have become more diverse; for example, a wider age-group is involved, groupings emerge around particular tastes in music or clothes, youth cultures are less male-dominated. However, **Roberts** is anxious to stress that, although there is change, there is also continuity. Actually, social class, gender and ethnicity continue to be the central organizing principles of young people's lives.

The same point about the significance of continuity can also be made in other contexts. There is contemporary debate about the importance of support for the elderly. It is often felt that changes in the family have meant that it is no longer possible for the elderly to be supported by their younger family members. **Finch and Mason** show, however, that flows of support between family members continue to be important. Amongst the people that they interviewed it was normal to help – emotionally, practically and financially – other family members. However, it was also difficult to detect any common patterns in the help offered and received. For example, it was not possible to predict what support might be given, or received, between two family members simply from knowing what their genealogical relationship was. Similarly there are no simple social class, gender or ethnic differences. **Phillipson et al.** concentrate on showing how the elderly continue to be supported by their neighbours despite the substantial social changes that have taken place in most cities. In the three urban areas studied, there were high levels of contact between older people and their neighbours. However, the relationship was not necessarily very deep, for neighbours tended to be the source of short-term emergency help. Longer-term commitment was provided by family or close friends.

Fragmentary cultures

In an earlier section, we discussed the possibility that the forces of globalization were producing a uniform and homogeneous global culture. In one sense such an argument seems plausible. Mass media companies are becoming larger and operate on a global scale. They appear, therefore, to be in a position to influence the cultural formations of very different types of societies across the world. This argument is supported by studies of media production which identify forces making for relative homogeneity of output. For example, **Hesmondhalgh** explores the organization of the dance music industry. Originally, the production of dance music was very decentralized with a large number of production companies and an audience which appreciated the authenticity of small-scale production and the variety and diversity that this made possible. However, he argues that it is difficult for small record companies to sustain themselves in the long term. Eventually they are forced into a relationship with a large company and the diversity starts to disappear. **McNair** similarly notes the constraints on diversity in the newspaper industry. Although technological changes and the destruction of union power have reduced the costs of newspaper production, the start-up costs of newspapers, particularly in marketing, are so high that only those who already have substantial resources can enter the industry.

However, it is more plausibly argued that there is considerable cultural diversity, even fragmentation, within most societies, let alone between societies. As we have seen in an earlier section of this Introduction, **Bennett** shows how an international form of popular music, hip hop, is taken up by different social groups on Tyneside in very different ways. Some insist on a kind of authenticity in which hip hop can only be understood as the music of oppressed black youth in America, while others think that it can be made to represent the wishes and desires of white youth in Newcastle. Such diversity of cultural response can be based on traditional social divisions which continue to be important, as we showed in the earlier section on social divisions. As we have already indicated, **Roberts** takes the view that, although youth cultures have become more diversified and fragmented, they are still fundamentally determined by factors of social class, gender and ethnicity. **Warde** shows that social class is a major determinant of food habits as measured by household expenditure on items of food, and treats this as an example of the way that consumption behaviour in general is an outcome of the unequal distribution of cultural capital. Interestingly, although the content of meals eaten by the British population changed during the 1970s and 1980s, social class differences were no less marked at the end of the period. **Gillespie** investigates responses to the television soap opera *Neighbours* by young Punjabi people in Southall, a part of London. Surprisingly perhaps, she concludes that there is a homology – a similarity in structure and behaviour – between the Southall community and the soap opera community. Gossip and rumour plays a significant role in both worlds and in Southall these factors are particularly powerful forms of social control. *Neighbours* gives the young people of Southall a way of talking about their community and its mores because they can relate the events of the soap to the events in the community. For example, the characters and plots of the soap opera allow the Southall teenagers to talk about the tension between Western and Indian values and to see ways of negotiating between them. The point, of course, is that the interpretation of *Neighbours* is determined by a particular ethnic experience. **Lury**, similarly, investigates how gender determines the culture of consumption practices. She notes that the burden of housework still falls on women, many of whom are at work. In many areas of housework, women appear to be consumers, as when they shop for the household. This is somewhat misleading in that they are also *producers* of cooked food or clean and tidy houses. In fact it is the men who are more nearly true consumers since they are rarely extensively involved in domestic production. In carrying out this role as domestic producers/consumers, women are encouraged to create some form of feminine self-identity for themselves.

A number of extracts in this volume therefore show how culture and identity are based on existing social divisions. It would be dangerous, however, to think that there are uniform class, ethnic or gender cultures. **Mac an Ghaill**, for example, shows how different groups of boys have different ways of learning masculinity. Even more radically, **Hetherington** argues that the role of traditional social divisions in generating and sustaining senses of identity and cultural belonging is diminishing. In his study of the travellers who used to gather at Stonehenge and other festivals, he suggests that there is a decline in the more ascriptive bases of lifestyle or identity, most notably, social class. In these circumstances, people look for alternative forms of identity and sociation. For the travellers these alternatives are organized around shared beliefs, styles of life and consumption practices. The result is a tribe-like grouping which tends to be unstable and requires considerable effort to maintain it. Consumption is particularly important in the creation of a sense of identity amongst the travellers. Their gatherings are, in many ways, celebrations of consumption. By this term, **Hetherington** does not simply mean shopping but rather the network of rituals, expressions of taste, beliefs and shared understandings that characterize consumption practices; consumption becomes an enactment of lifestyle carried out in places with particular meanings like Stonehenge.

Old politics, new politics and the state

Despite suspicions that the powers of nation states are diminishing in the face of the forces of globalization, they remain enormously consequential for the conditions of life of their populations. Acquiring control or influence over the powers of the state is the main objective of formal political activity in contemporary liberal democratic societies. Political parties, most obviously, are organized to compete for sufficient votes to obtain the right to claim legitimately to represent citizens in the making of policy, at various levels from the European to the local. The range of issues over which states have power are very considerable. Economic management, employment policy, foreign affairs, taxation, welfare provision, penal law and environmental regulation are but a few of the fields in which central and local government decisions affect social institutions and the quality of life. However, political parties and legislative bodies and their relationships with state agencies far from exhaust the terrain of politics. Political activity occurs in many other guises and at many different levels. The end of the twentieth century saw the emergence, some would say the return, to prominence of less formally organized, alternative expressions of political commitment. Whereas parties and governments are obliged to speak on behalf of the entire population in regard to all matters political, pressure groups and new social movements attempt to exert influence in relation to a particular range of issues. New social movements, like the environmental, peace and women's movements, have proved particularly important as agents of political change.

Access to powers of government are achieved formally and most directly through elections, for while there are many other channels through which interest groups, private organizations and campaigning groups seek to influence policy, it is the party or parties with an electoral majority who make new laws. General elections are thus major events in the political cycle. The 1997 election was particularly dramatic, because it produced a colossal majority for the Labour Party after eighteen years of continuous rule by the Conservative Party. **Sanders** offers an interpretation of the significance of the outcome for understanding changes in the party system and the structure of electoral support. He suggests that the extent of the swing to Labour might be interpreted as evidence of the increasing volatility of support for parties. The extent to which governments or parties faithfully represent the electorate is a perennial issue in political analysis. One aspect of the concern is whether, when parties achieve office, they implement the policies promised during their electoral campaigns. Another aspect is whether those elected comprise a sufficient cross-section of the population to represent properly the interests of all. Holders of political offices have for a long time been disproportionately male, white, middle aged and middle class. Despite public and legal concern about equal opportunities, this bias remains. **Norris and Lovenduski** offer an analysis of the processes through which party members offer themselves as candidates for office and the party machinery for selection accepts some and rejects others. A subtle interaction between the unequal distribution of personal resources, ambition and anticipation of likely success among potential candidates discriminates among the potential representatives of the electorate.

Single-issue campaigns and new social movements are typically less concerned with elections to office and the holding of formal positions, more with active involvement and moral persuasion. Their purpose is more diffuse – to influence policy-makers in part of course, but also to change people's minds, mobilize concern and recruit active support in such a way that personal convictions are affirmed and public opinion altered. This is broadly true of the women's peace movement as described by **Roseneil**. In recent years, much of this type of activity has revolved around constructions of identity and has involved claims for the recognition of rights of minority groups defined by criteria such as religious faith, minority national affiliation, lifestyle or sexual orientation. **Richardson** outlines some of the ways in which claims to equal citizenship have been registered by gays and lesbians, emphasizing the increasingly cultural element of political mobilization. Other forms and bases of cultural politics are described in chapters by **Bechhofer et al.** and **Hetherington**. This 'new politics' is associated with, and arises from, the differentiation and fragmentation of culture.

While governments have the capacity to use state legislative and executive power to affect institutional arrangements directly, they also have means to more diffuse influence. Control over the education system is a case in point. Government through the national curriculum insists on certain types of knowledge being transmitted to children, but schooling also transmits, less directly, social conventions and orientations to work. Educational arrangements also affect personal opportunities through the organization of the system of schools, which requires some form of allocation and selection for pupils. **Gewirtz et al.** examine parental involvement in the process of securing places for their children in secondary schools in London. The introduction of market discipline into the delivery of public services was a key Conservative policy in the 1980s, and to that end 'quasi-market' mechanisms were introduced to allocate pupils to secondary schools. The effect was to privilege pupils with parents who had skill and resources to obtain knowledge about the merits of different schools and who could effectively negotiate with head teachers. This was plainly to the advantage of middle-class children and might be expected in the long run to secure for them better futures. The internal organization of schools also has effects on pupils' development. The existence of pupil peer groups, and their capacity to generate sub-cultures within schools, has been recognized for decades. The particular forms that those sub-cultures take, and their impact on social relations outside school, varies over time, however. **Mac an Ghaill** describes the contours of such sub-cultures among young males, paying particular attention to the effects on the creation of masculine identities. Changing external circumstances (deteriorating job prospects and changes in the institutions of the family and sexuality), interacting with established divisions of class, gender and ethnicity, produce commitment to different models of masculinity. The organization of schools is also a function of the way in which teachers are deployed. The state still employs a substantial proportion of the British labour force. Not only does this enable government to influence wage levels in the economy, but it also, by virtue of demonstration to private sector organizations, makes it possible to improve conditions of employment, as for instance by insisting upon optimal implementation of health and safety or equal opportunities legislation. As **Acker** shows, the latter is not yet achieved, as demonstrated by the lower rates of promotion of women in the teaching profession.

Systematic inequalities between different social groups is also apparent in the field of health and health care. The **Independent Inquiry into Inequality in Health** documents inequalities of health by class, gender and ethnicity. It shows that although mortality rates have fallen, there has not been an equivalent reduction in morbidity, so that the extra years of life are likely to involve long-term illness. The National Health Service, like the education system, is a major object for the investment of public funds. When set up, it was a model of collective insurance against the uncertain risk of ill health, against which potential misfortune most people had insufficient income or wealth to protect themselves. A principle of equal and free health treatment accord-

ing to need was a major pillar of the welfare state settlement after the Se
War, a promise that social position would not compromise health. The N
since been highly popular among the population as a whole, and attempt
its role, for instance by requiring people to take out private medical insi
always met with considerable public opposition. **Judge et al.** examine public attitudes
which affirm continued support for the traditional structure of the NHS, but in a
context where people are very aware of the issue of the cost of modern health care.
The rationing of services is just one contentious issue about which they report on
opinions.

The state is also a principal agent for the maintenance of public order. Rates of
reported crime have risen steadily in recent decades and growing fear of being a victim
of crime has arisen on the political agenda. There has for long been debate about
whether punishment or rehabilitation is the appropriate response of the state to criminal activity and, as **Worrall** shows, penal policy tends to oscillate between these two
alternative philosophies. Governments introduce new systems of correction in order to
allay public concern and to try to find more effective means of treating offenders. In
such a vein, she suggests that, with respect to juvenile offenders, about whom most
alarm is normally expressed, the policies introduced in the 1980s resulted in a fall in
crime. That was, however, insufficient to quell moral panic about youth crime. Moral
panics are usually considered to be escalated by mass media such that they appear as
major threats to the whole society – despite, for example, the likelihood of being a
victim of crime being very unevenly distributed across the British population. **Thompson** examines the way in which the AIDS epidemic was represented in the mass media,
where the popular press identified gay men as primarily responsible. This served, as
do many moral panics, to focus attention on deviations from sanctioned and conventional family and sexual relationships. Though this particular episode cannot be
attributed to state agency, one activity of government is the attempt to mould values
regarding the family. However, the changing structure of the family and households
apparently dooms these attempts to re-establish the family values of the past, or
more generally to construct consensual order among an increasingly culturally diverse
population.

Conclusion

The extracts in this book provide a picture of a changing Britain. During the last couple
of decades the rhetoric of change has been very prominent. The political ideas of the
period were generated by the New Right, committed to reducing the role of the state,
expanding the operation of market mechanisms, releasing entrepreneurial energies,
encouraging self-reliance, individualism and personal ambition. The strategic achievement failed to match the rhetoric. The actual pattern of change is complex, for there
are many continuities as well as new developments. Living standards continued to rise
but inequalities increased. The manufacturing base declined along with many of the
institutions associated with an industrialized Britain, to be replaced with more flexible, but also more precarious, employment. Old social divisions persisted – even if
some of their effects, like those of class, were remarked upon less, others were more

frequently in the spotlight. Families continued to provide the main source of social and personal support, yet family relationships and household composition altered considerably. There was increasing cultural diversity, yet beneath the cultural mosaic could still be detected the social structuring principles of class, gender and ethnicity. Again, while new types of political mobilization captured the imagination and support of many, and new solidarities and commitments were established, the institutions of party government continued to exercise control and authority. The sociological writings collected together in this volume are testament to a complex combination of continuity and change in British social institutions at the end of the twentieth century.

Part I

Globalization

2

The Global Economy

Peter Dicken

Key words

Globalization, economic organization, global division of labour, internationalization of economic activities

In this extract Dicken gives an account of the forces working to create a global economy. Individuals are confronted by much more economic uncertainty which affects them as employees, particularly in greater insecurity of employment, and also as consumers offered an increasing variety of goods and services. It is widely accepted that these uncertainties are generated by international forces.

Dicken differentiates internationalization from globalization. The former refers to a simple extension of economic activities across national boundaries. The second is qualitatively different and refers to the functional integration of internationally dispersed economic activities. He contrasts the views of two groups of theorists, one of which argues that the world economy is no more global than it was at the beginning of the century, while the other suggests that a fundamental global shift has taken place, resulting in the powerlessness of nation states. Dicken himself takes an intermediate position, arguing that although we do not inhabit a fully globalized world, there are globalizing forces at work. For example, financial organizations operate globally, there is a more extended international division of labour and nation states have some difficulty in exercising full economic control.

Something is happening out there

The notion that something fundamental is happening, or indeed has happened, in the world economy is now generally accepted. As we look around us, all we seem to see is the confusion of change, the acceleration of uncertainty; feelings currently intensified by our proximity to the new millennium with all its promises – and threats – of epochal change. Television news reports and specials, press headlines and the like constantly remind us of our uneasy present and precarious future. Turbulence and change are, of course, nothing new in human affairs. But there is no doubt that the world economy, and its constituent parts, are being buffeted by extremely volatile forces. To the individual citizen the most obvious indicators of change are those which impinge most directly on his or her daily activities – making a living and consuming the necessities and luxuries of life. To those currently employed in a job, what matters is job security and the wages or salary received or anticipated. To those seeking a job, what matters is availability. On both counts, the situation seems to have become increasingly uncertain. In the industrialized countries, in particular, there is a real fear that the dual (and connected forces) of technological change and geographical shifts in the location of manufacturing and service activities are transforming the employment scene in adverse ways for many people, notably less educated and less skilled blue-collar workers although there has also been very considerable job volatility among white-collar workers as well. As consumers, the most obvious indicator of change is the vast increase in the number of products whose origins lie on the other side of the world but which are now either literally on our doorsteps (through superstores) or metaphorically in our homes (through the all-pervasive TV commercial). Whatever our particular position, however, we cannot fail to be aware that what is happening in our own back-yards is largely the product of forces operating at a much larger geographical scale.

The immediacy and longer-term impact of these major forces of change are enormously enhanced by the growing interconnections between all parts of the world. The most significant development in the world economy during the past few decades has been the *increasing internationalization – and, arguably, the increasing globalization – of economic activities*. The internationalization of economic activities is nothing new. Some commodities have had an international character for centuries; an obvious example being the long-established trading patterns in spices and other exotic goods. Such internationalization was much enhanced by the spread of industrialization from the eighteenth century onwards in Europe. Nevertheless until very recently the production process itself 'was primarily organized *within* national economies or parts of them. International trade . . . developed primarily as an exchange of raw materials and foodstuffs . . . [with] . . . products manufactured and finished in single national economies . . . *In terms of production, plant, firm and industry were essentially national phenomena*' (Hobsbawm, 1979, p. 313, emphasis added).

The nature of the world economy has changed dramatically, however, especially since the 1950s. National boundaries no longer act as 'watertight' containers of the production process. Rather, they are more like sieves through which extensive leakage occurs. The implications are far reaching. Each one of us is now more fully involved in a global economic system than were our parents and grandparents. Few, if any, industries now have much 'natural protection' from international competition whereas in the past, of course, geographical distance created a strong insulating effect. Today, in contrast, fewer and fewer industries are oriented towards local, regional or even national markets. A growing number of economic activities have meaning only in a global context. Thus, whereas a hundred or more years ago only rare and exotic products and some basic raw materials were involved in truly international trade, today virtually everything one can think of is involved in long-distance movement. And because of the increasingly complex ways in which production is organized across national boundaries, rather than contained within them, the actual origin of individual products may be very difficult to ascertain.

Something of this increased global diversity of production can be gleaned simply from examining the labels on products. Many labels are geographically misleading, however, particularly in the case of products consisting of a large number of individual components, each of which may have been made in different countries. Generally, the labels signify the country of the final (assembly) stage of production. But where are such products really made? Under such conditions what is a 'British' car, an 'American' computer, a 'Dutch' television or a 'German' camera? In today's global economy, some products can be regarded as having been made almost everywhere – or nowhere – such is the geographical complexity of some production processes.

What these developments imply is the emergence of a *new global division of labour* which reflects a change in the geographical pattern of specialization at the global scale. Originally, as defined by the eighteenth-century political economist Adam Smith, the 'division of labour' referred simply to the specialization of workers in different parts of the production process. It had no explicitly geographical connotations at all. But quite early in the evolution of industrial economies the division of labour took on a geographical dimension. Some areas came to specialize in particular types of economic activity. Within the rapidly evolving industrial nations of Europe and the United States regional specialization – in iron and steel, shipbuilding, textiles, engineering and so on – became a characteristic feature. At the global scale the broad division of labour was between the industrial countries on the one hand, producing manufactured goods, and the non-industrialized countries on the other, whose major international function was to supply raw materials and agricultural products to the industrial nations and to act as a market for some manufactured goods. Such geographical specialization – structured around a *core*, a *semi-periphery* and a *periphery* – formed the underlying basis of much of the world's trade for many years.

This relatively simple pattern (although it was never quite as simple as the description above suggests) no longer applies. During the past few decades trade flows have become far more complex. The straightforward exchange between core and peripheral areas, based upon a broad division of labour, is being transformed into a highly complex, kaleidoscopic structure involving the *fragmentation* of many production processes and their *geographical relocation* on a global scale in ways which slice through national boundaries. In addition, we have seen the emergence of new centres of industrial production in the newly industrializing economies (NIEs). Both old and new industries are involved in this re-sorting of the global jigsaw puzzle in ways which also reflect the development of technologies of transport and communications, of corporate organization and of the production process. The technology of production itself is undergoing substantial and far-reaching change as the emphasis on large-scale, mass-production, assembly-line techniques is shifting to a more flexible production technology. And just as we can identify a new international division of labour in production so, too, we can identify a 'new international financial system', based on rapidly emerging twenty-four-hour global transactions concentrated primarily in the three major financial centres of New York, London and Tokyo.

A 'new' geo-economy? The globalization debate

So, something is undoubtedly happening 'out there'. But precisely what that 'something' might be – and whether it really represents something new – is a subject of enormous controversy amongst academics, politicians, popular writers and journalists alike.[1] Box 1.1 provides a sample of quotations to reflect a spectrum of opinions. The first two quotations – by Cohen and Zysman and by Drucker – argue that fundamental, possibly irreversible, change has occurred in the world economy and that the result is a deep-seated shift in its structure and operations. But Reich and Ohmae go much further and assert that, in effect, we now live in a borderless world in which the 'national' is no longer relevant. It is this latter view which has become especially pervasive. 'Globalization' is the new economic (as well as political and cultural) order. We live, it is asserted, in a globalized world in which nation-states are no longer significant actors or meaningful economic units; in which consumer tastes and cultures are homogenized and satisfied through the provision of standardized global products created by global corporations with no allegiance to place or community. The global is, thus, claimed to be the natural order of affairs in today's technologically driven world in which time-space has been compressed, the 'end of geography' has arrived and everywhere is becoming the same.

Although the notion of a *globalized* world has become pervasive there are strong opponents who argue, in effect, that globalization is a mirage. According to this view – represented in Box 1.1 by the quotations from Gordon, Glyn and Sutcliffe and Hirst and Thompson – the 'newness' of the current situation has been grossly exaggerated. The world economy, it is argued, was actually more open and more integrated in the half century prior to World War One (1870–1913) in which there was

> unprecedented international integration. An open regulatory framework prevailed; short- and long-term capital movements were unsupervised, the transfer of profits was unhampered; the gold standard was at its height and encompassed almost all the major industrial countries by the period's close and most smaller agrarian nations . . . ; citizenship was freely granted to immigrants; and direct political influence over the allocation of resources was limited . . . Under these conditions, markets linked a growing share of world resources and output; exports outgrew domestic output in the core capitalist countries . . . and the migration of labour was unprecedented.
>
> (Kozul-Wright, 1995, pp. 139–40)

So, on the one hand, we have the view that we do, indeed, live in a new – *globalized* – world economy in which our lives are dominated by global forces. On the other hand, we have the view that not all that much has changed; that we still inhabit an *international*, rather than a globalized, world economy in which national forces remain highly significant. The truth, it seems to me, lies in neither of these two polarized positions. Although in quantitative terms the world economy was perhaps at least as integrated economically before 1913 as it is today – in some respects, even more so – the nature of that integration was *qualitatively* very different (UNCTAD, 1993b, p. 113):

Box 1.1   Some alternative views in the globalization debate

The world economy is changing in fundamental ways. The changes add up to a basic transition, a structural shift in international markets and in the production base of advanced countries. It will change how production is organized, where it occurs, and who plays what role in the process.

(Cohen and Zysman, 1987, p. 79)

The talk today is of the 'changing world economy'. I wish to argue that the world economy is not 'changing'; it has already changed – in its foundations and in its structure – and in all probability the change is irreversible.

(Drucker, 1986, p. 768)

We are living through a transformation that will rearrange the politics and economics of the coming century. There will be no *national* products or technologies, no national corporations, no national industries. There will no longer be national economies, at least as we have come to understand that concept . . . As almost every factor of production – money, technology, factories, and equipment – moves effortlessly across borders, the very idea of an American economy is becoming meaningless, as are the notions of an American corporation, American capital, American products, and American technology. A similar transformation is affecting every other nation, some faster and more profoundly than others; witness Europe, hurtling toward economic union.

(Reich, 1991, pp. 3, 8)

Today's global economy is genuinely borderless. Information, capital, and innovation flow all over the world at top speed, enabled by technology and fueled by consumers' desires for access to the best and least expensive products.

(Ohmae, 1995a, inside front cover)

Globalization seems to be as much an overstatement as it is an ideology and an analytical concept.

(Ruigrok and van Tulder, 1993, p. 22)

I would argue that we have *not* witnessed movement toward an increasingly 'open' international economy, with productive capital buzzing around the globe, but that we have moved rapidly toward an increasingly 'closed' economy for productive investment . . . The international economy . . . has witnessed *declining* rather than *increasing* mobility of productive capital . . . the role of the State has grown substantially since the early 1970s; state policies have become increasingly decisive on the international front, not more futile.

(Gordon, 1988, p. 63)

The system has . . . become more integrated or globalized in many respects . . . Nonetheless what has resulted is still very far from a globally integrated economy . . . In short, the world economy is considerably more globalized than 50 years ago; but much less so than is theoretically possible. In many ways it is less globalized than 100 years ago. The widespread view that the present degree of globalization is in some way new and unprecedented is, therefore, false.

(Glyn and Sutcliffe, 1992, p. 91)

We do not have a fully globalized economy, we do have an international economy and national policy responses to it.

(Hirst and Thompson, 1992, p. 394)

- International economic integration before 1913 – and, in fact, until only about three decades ago – was essentially *shallow integration* manifested largely through arm's length *trade* in goods and services between independent firms and through international movements of portfolio capital.
- Today, we live in a world in which *deep integration*, organized primarily by transnational corporations (TNCs), is becoming increasingly pervasive. ' "Deep" integration extends to the level of the *production* of goods and services and, in addition, increases visible and invisible trade. Linkages between national economies are therefore increasingly influenced by the cross-border value adding activities within . . . TNCs and within networks established by TNCs' (UNCTAD, 1993b, p. 113).

However, although there are undoubtedly global*izing* forces at work we do not have a fully global*ized* world economy. Globalization tendencies can be at work without this resulting in the all-encompassing end-state – the globalized economy – in which all unevenness and difference are ironed out, market forces are rampant and uncontrollable, and the nation-state merely passive and supine.[2] The position taken in this book is that globalization is a complex of inter-related *processes*, rather than an end-state. Such tendencies are highly uneven in time and space. In taking such a process-oriented approach it is important to distinguish between processes of *internationalization* and processes of *globalization*:

- *Internationalization processes* involve the simple extension of economic activities across national boundaries. It is, essentially, a *quantitative* process which leads to a more extensive geographical pattern of economic activity.
- *Globalization processes* are *qualitatively* different from internationalization processes. They involve not merely the geographical extension of economic activity across national boundaries but also – and more importantly – the *functional integration* of such internationally dispersed activities.

Both processes – internationalization and globalization – coexist. In some cases, what we are seeing is no more than the continuation of long-established international dispersion of activities. In others, however, we are undoubtedly seeing an increasing dispersion and integration of activities across national boundaries. The pervasive internationalization, and growing globalization, of economic life ensure that changes originating in one part of the world are rapidly diffused to others. We live in a world of increasing complexity, interconnectedness and volatility; a world in which the lives and livelihoods of every one of us are bound up with processes operating at a global scale.

However, although we are often led to believe that the world is becoming increasingly homogenized economically (and perhaps even culturally) with the use of such labels as 'global village', 'global marketplace' or 'global factory', we need to treat such all-embracing claims with some caution. The 'globalization' tag is too often applied very loosely and indiscriminately to imply a totally pervasive set of forces and changes with uniform effects on countries, regions and localities. There are, indeed, powerful forces of globalization at work – they are the central focus of this book – but we need to adopt a sensitive and discriminating approach to get beneath the hype and to lay bare the reality. Change does not occur everywhere in the same way and at the same rate; the processes of globalization are not geographically uniform. The particular character of individual countries, of regions and of localities interacts with the larger-scale general processes of change to produce quite specific outcomes. Reality is far more complex and messy than many of the grander themes and explanations tend to suggest.

Notes

1 The literature on this topic is huge and seemingly growing by the week. Major proponents of the globalization position include Reich (1991), Barnet and Cavanagh (1994), Ohmae (1985; 1990; 1995a,b). The underlying concept may be traced back to McLuhan's (1960) notion of the 'global village' but was explicitly introduced into the management literature in Levitt's (1983) paper on the globalization of markets. Strong counter-views are voiced by Gordon (1988), Glyn and Sutcliffe (1992), Hirst and Thompson (1992; 1996).
2 This argument is developed more fully in Dicken, Peck and Tickell (1997).

References

Barnet, R.J. and Cavanagh, J. (1994) *Global Dreams: Imperial Corporations and the New World Order*, Simon & Schuster, New York.

Cohen, S.S. and Zysman, J. (1987) *Manufacturing Matters: The Myth of the Post-Industrial Economy*, Basic Books, New York.

Dicken, P., Peck, J.A. and Tickell, A. (1997) Unpacking the global, in R. Lee and J. Wills (eds) *Geographies of Economies*, Arnold, London, Chapter 12.

Drucker, P. (1986) The changed world economy, *Foreign Affairs*, Vol. 64, pp. 768–91.

Glyn, A. and Sutcliffe, B. (1992) 'Global but leaderless'? The new capitalist order, in R. Miliband and L. Panitch (eds) *New World Order: The Socialist Register*, Merlin Press, London, pp. 76–95.

Gordon, D.M. (1988) The global economy: new edifice or crumbling foundations? *New Left Review*, Vol. 168, pp. 24–64.

Hirst, P. and Thompson, G. (1992) The problem of 'globalization': international economic relations, national economic management and the formation of trading blocs, *Economy and Society*, Vol. 24, pp. 408–42.

—— (1996) *Globalization in Question*, Polity Press, Cambridge.

Hobsbawm, E. (1979) The development of the world economy, *Cambridge Journal of Economics*, Vol. 3, pp. 305–18.

Kozul-Wright, R. (1995) Transnational corporations and the nation-state, in J. Michie and J. Grieve-Smith (eds) *Managing the Global Economy*, Oxford University Press, Oxford, Chapter 6.

Levitt, T. (1983) The globalization of markets, *Harvard Business Review*, May–June, pp. 92–102.

McLuhan, M. (1960) *Understanding Media*, Routledge and Kegan Paul, London.

Ohmae, K. (1985) *Triad Power: The Coming Shape of Global Competition*, Free Press, New York.

——(1990) *The Borderless World: Power and Strategy in the Interlinked Economy*, Free Press, New York.

——(1995a) *The End of the Nation State: The Rise of Regional Economies*, Free Press, New York.

——(ed) (1995b) *The Evolving Global Economy: Making Sense of the New World Order*, Harvard Business School, Boston, MA.

Reich, R.B. (1991) *The Work of Nations*, Alfred A. Knopf, New York.

Ruigrok, W. and van Tulder, R. (1995) *The Logic of International Restructuring*, Routledge, London.

3 | Local Interpretations of Global Music

Andy Bennett

┌───┐
│   **Key words**   │
└───┘

Popular music, hip hop, globalization, youth culture, ethnic relations, music scenes

The selection by Roseneil emphasizes the interaction of the global and the local. This piece by Bennett takes up much the same theme but in a quite different context. He formulates a position in the debate between cultural theorists who argue that globalization eliminates local cultural differences, producing bland and uniform music, film, television and literature and those who suggest the contrary, namely that there will always be local cultures and local reworkings of global cultural forms.

Bennett's article investigates the significance of a black musical form, hip hop, for white youth. He asks how music born amongst black Americans finds enthusiastic adherence among white youth in Tyneside. He concludes that there are, in fact, two quite different responses from young white people. The first comes from those who believe that hip hop can only be appreciated if one sees it as rooted in the experience of black Americans which is, at the same time, similar to that of the white working class on Tyneside. This group insists that hip hop has to stay authentic. Other white Tynesiders believe that hip hop does not have to be understood strictly as black American music but can be used legitimately to address the daily life of white working-class youth in Newcastle and can express local accents and concerns. Hip hop has become a global musical form. What has happened on Tyneside, however, is a local reworking of hip hop by white youth, but in more than one way. Furthermore, these local reworkings are generated by particular forms of local knowledge and experience.

[. . .]

Rappin' on the Tyne

Newcastle upon Tyne is a predominantly white, working-class post-industrial city in north-east England (see Colls and Lancaster (eds), 1992). Although small Asian and Afro-Caribbean populations do exist in Newcastle their influence upon the city's cultural environment, including the local music and club scene, has been nominal as compared to other British cities with larger ethnic minority populations (Hollands, 1995: 26; Bennett, 1997). This is also true of the small hip hop scene which has grown up around Newcastle, the neighbouring city of Gateshead and a number of outlying towns and villages, such as Blyth and Cramlington, this scene being dominated by white enthusiasts. As I will presently go on to discuss in more detail, the fact of white British working class youth appropriating African-American and other black musical forms is one which has long been addressed by theorists of youth culture and popular music. Significantly, however, there has been little attempt to study white appropriations of hip hop in the context of the UK.

My study of the hip hop scene in Newcastle was conducted using three principal methods of ethnographic research: semi-structured interviews, participant observation and focus groups. During the course of my study, which formed part of a larger research project on youth and music in Newcastle and Frankfurt, Germany,[1] I conducted around twenty 'one to one' interviews with local hip hoppers and ten focus groups (researcher-led group discussions) consisting of six to eight people. Both 'one to one' interviews and focus groups lasted about an hour and all were taped (with the consent of those participating). My route 'into' the local hip hop scene in Newcastle was largely facilitated by a local breakdancer who also worked as an instructor at a community dance project. Through this contact, who essentially acted as a gatekeeper, I gained access to or learned of key figures in the local hip hop scene, including Jim, the proprietor of a small independent rap music shop in Newcastle, and Ferank, a self-styled rap poet. I also accompanied my gatekeeper and a number of his dance students and other friends to around a dozen weekly 'hip hop' nights held in a bar in the centre of Newcastle.

[. . .]

Black music in the North-East

The north-east region of England has a long established tradition of appropriation from African-American music. During the 1960s, a Newcastle group, The Animals achieved international success with a style of music based closely on the urban blues of African-American artists such as Robert Johnson (Gillett, 1983: 269–72). Rhythm and blues continues to be immensely popular in the area with a large number of local 'R&B' groups performing in local pubs and clubs, while each August the County Durham town of Stanley plays host to an internationally renowned blues festival. Similarly, during the 1970s, a number of dance venues in smaller north-east towns featured 'Northern Soul' nights, an all-white 'underground' soul scene which centred around rare black soul imports from the US (Milestone, 1997). Significantly, in the case of north-east England, such white appropriations of African-American music and style have taken place without physical reference to a local black population. As such, the point raised above positing the issue of black 'association' as something which is actively constructed, and to some extent idealised, by white youth in their appropriation of black music and style, rather than as a structurally determined 'given' of such appropriation, is clearly illustrated. The consciously articulated nature of 'black association' in the north-east is further in evidence when considering the competing sensibilities which also characterise the local hip hop scene in Newcastle. At the centre of this scene a hardcore of hip hop enthusiasts share the belief that their intimate understanding of hip hop's essential 'blackness' as the key to its relevance for the white working class experience guarantees them a form of aesthetic supremacy over other local white hip hop fans who, according to this group, have no such understanding of the genre and thus no authentic claim to the title 'hip hopper'. Conversely, a number of other local hip hop enthusiasts firmly reject the notion that hip hop can be understood only in terms of its African-American context and attempt to rework it as a platform for the expression of issues which relate more directly to the day to day experiences of white working class youth. I want now to consider each of these responses to hip hop in turn and to illustrate how, despite their obvious ideological differences, they are both intimately bound up with the particularities of local experience.

'You into that "nigger music" then?'

In his study of the music scene in Austin, Texas, Shank (1994) draws attention to the important role played by local independent record shops in authenticating particular scenes by providing a space for like-minded individuals to meet, discuss their tastes in music and argue over the merits of particular tracks and artists, thus positioning themselves in relation to other music scenes located in the same city or town. In the context of the Newcastle hip hop scene, a comparable role is performed by 'Groove'. 'Groove' is a tiny independent record shop in the centre of Newcastle which deals exclusively in rap music; more specifically in US rap which is specially imported and, consequently, not readily available in the high street chain stores. The proprietor of 'Groove', a white Newcastle man named Jim, is a devotee of African-American rap music and hip hop culture. Having listened to soul music during his teens, Jim turned to rap as it became more widely available in Britain during the 1980s. 'Groove' has become something of a meeting point for those who believe, like Jim, that hip hop culture and rap music can only be understood in terms of their African-American cultural context. On the surface, the group of local hip hop enthusiasts who frequent 'Groove' appear to correspond unproblematically with the commonly expounded sociological thesis that African-American dance music is somehow able to connect with the experiential world of white working class youth in Britain.

[. . .]

Interestingly, however, when the wider cultural context of 'Groove' and those who frequent it is studied in more detail, it becomes evident that such a belief in the nature of hip hop carries a level of symbolic importance which goes beyond a shared sense of affinity with the African-American experience. Within the local Newcastle music scene, 'Groove' has a reputation for being one of the few 'specialist' record shops in the city. As such the shop enjoys something of an 'outsider' status. Indeed, as a local hairdresser and popular music enthusiast who is familiar with 'Groove' suggested to me one day as I sat in his chair: 'I can't see how he [Jim] makes any money from that business. It's more a labour of love for him really'.

In many ways the above observation constitutes a highly sensitive reading of 'Groove' and the type of cultural work which it performs. In the context of Newcastle, 'Groove', although ostensibly a business venture, at the same time plays host to a type of self-styled local hip hop elite in which an intimate understanding of hip hop's black roots is combined with a comprehensive knowledge of rap and what, on the basis of the group's understanding of the genre's cultural significance, counts as good or bad rap. This form of local 'cultural capital', into which the local reputation of 'Groove' is included, is then used as a way of articulating the group's difference from the 'new jacks', a term given to those who are considered to be hip hop 'tourists', that is, those who listen indiscriminately to rap music before moving on to a new trend. Thus, as Jim pointed out: 'These new jacks, you can spot them a mile off. They're just into hip hop 'cause it's trendy like. They come in here and they don't know what the fuck they're talking about. They'll buy about one record a month for a year or something and then get into something else, house or something'.

Marks has suggested that white appropriations of black musical forms are often symbolically transformed into 'badge[s] of exclusivity', particularly if such conspicuous displays of black taste on the part of young whites enable them to 'manifest their difference from the cultural mainstream' (1990: 105). Clearly, this observation goes some way towards explaining the shared sensibility of those local hip hop enthusiasts who frequent 'Groove' and their collective response towards the perceived fickleness of the new jacks' attachment to hip hop. Arguably, however, there is a further reason why these and other like-minded hip hop enthusiasts are so passionate in their symbolic association with African-American culture. Jones has noted in his own Birmingham-based research how young whites' 'displays of affiliation to black culture' resulted on occasion in them becoming 'the objects of a "deflected" form of racism' (1988: 199). In the social context of Newcastle, perhaps because of the city's predominantly white populace, such physical challenges to forms of black association occur more frequently. On one particular evening, I accompanied a group of local white hip hop enthusiasts, several of whom were regular customers at 'Groove', to a bar in the centre of Newcastle where a weekly 'hip hop' night was being held. On the way to the bar, the group, dressed in typical African-American hip hop style clothes, were subject to several shouts of 'wigger' and attracted comments, such as 'are you going to a fancy dress party?', from other young club and pub-goers.

[. . .]

This 'localised' response on the part of white youth to African-American hip hop style emphasises a further important point in relation to the localisation of hip hop. It is significant that in much of the work which focuses on non-US examples of hip hop, there is an implication that 'localisation' involves some element of stylistic and/or musical transformation in hip hop. Thus, for example, Mitchell argues that the development of an Australian hip hop scene has been 'given some degree of "official recognition"' by the release in 1995 of a compilation of rap tracks by Australian artists whose musical and stylistic direction indicates that the local hip hop scene 'no longer needs "supporting"' (1998: 9–10). It seems to me, however, that there is a danger here of essentialising the process of localisation so that it becomes synonymous with obvious innovation. In this way such an interpretation of localisation overlooks some of the more subtly nuanced properties of appropriation and transformation for which Robertson (1995) [. . .] coins the term *glocality*. Arguably then, the process of localisation, as this relates to rap and hip hop or indeed other forms of music and style, need not involve any obvious physical transformations of musical and stylistic resources but may, alternatively, rely on localised affinities which are experienced more at the level of the experiential and which, in turn, demand a more abstract form of analytical engagement with the situating properties of local environments. Thus, to return to the context of 'Groove' and those hip hop enthusiasts whose shared discourse of authenticity and integrity revolves around being a part of the ' Groove' 'scene', the local significance of rap and hip hop derives not from any physical reworking of the latter but more from a locally forged sense of affinity with African-American hip hop based upon a sense of its 'strength and intelligence' in comparison to what is seen as a fickle and undiscerning mainstream youth culture as this manifests itself in Newcastle.

A 'street thing'

A somewhat different, if equally fashioned, hip hop sensibility can be seen in relation to those individuals who make up what could be classed as Newcastle's *white* hip hop culture. For these local enthusiasts, hip hop's use as an authentic mode of cultural expression is not restricted to the form of felt association with the African-American experience shared by those individuals who frequent 'Groove'. Rather, there is a commonly held view among *white* hip hop enthusiasts that the essence of hip hop culture relates to its easy translation into a medium which directly bespeaks the white British working class experience. Thus as one self-styled white 'Geordie'[2] rapper explained to me:

> Hip hop isn't a black thing, it's a street thing y'know, where people get so pissed off with their environment that they have to do something about it. And the way to do it and get the word to the people is to do it creatively, be it writing on a wall or expressing it in a rap . . . or wearing baggy clothes y'know. It's all part of this one thing of going 'oh look man, we've had enough of this and we're gonna change it in our way'.

An interesting comparison here is a study of the hip hop scene in Sydney, Australia by Maxwell in which he observes that while Sydney hip hoppers' realisation of their scene involved taking 'the simulacrum of a culture which they had accessed through the electronic media' the physical realisation of this simulacrum brought it into contact with a new reality, one located in the streets and neighbourhoods of Sydney (1994: 15). In a similar fashion *white* hip hop enthusiasts in Newcastle are attempting to rework the hip hop genre so that it becomes a form of address which resonates intimately with the nature of their own particular local circumstances. I want now to consider two specific examples of the way in which hip hop has been taken up by white working class youth in Newcastle as a way of addressing issues encountered on a day to day basis in the city.

' 'Am that dreadlock hippy bastard that comes from the toon'

The above lyric is taken from 'Aa dee it coz aa can' ('I do it because I can') by Ferank, a Newcastle poet and rapper. Originally written as a poem, 'Aa dee it coz aa can' was later set to music and recorded as rap by Ferank, who also delivered an impromptu recital of his work on Channel Four's live coverage of the Glastonbury music festival in June, 1994. As with much of Ferank's work, this rap deals directly with his own experiences of living in Newcastle and is performed in a local Geordie accent, a feature which Ferank feels adds an important element of authenticity to his style. Thus, he argues: 'I'm not American, so it's pointless for me to do a rap in an American accent . . . Anyway, the Geordie accent that myself and other rappers up here are using is a dialect, just like patois, and so it should be used.' 'Aa dee it coz aa can', which is essentially a commentary on aspects of Newcastle life and the local Geordie culture, works at a number of different levels. Thus in one sense, the rap is intended to deliver a firm message to those living in other regions, both in Britain and abroad, whose impressions of Newcastle are dominated by the notion of the typical Geordie stereotype. Using his own starkly profiled local identity as a springboard, Ferank attempts to demonstrate, through the medium of his informed reading and poetical summary of the local situation, that the stereotypical image of the Geordie character is erroneous. Thus, as Ferank explained to me:

> I was tryin' to change people's perceptions of what they think o' Geordies. Flat caps and this Geordie pride thing which I don't feel. Eh, I'm proud o' where I come from and of the people that I care for and who care for me. But eh, there's a lot of malice in this town and a lotta people who need an education. And I'd like to think that I've had one of sorts, and I've always been from here. So it was kinda sayin' 'oh look man for fuck's sake, I might be from here but I'm not your typical Geordie!'. While I am . . . while I should be accepted as the most typical Geordie.

At the same time, however, 'Aa dee it coz aa can' also criticises the cultural conservatism which Ferank identifies with sections of Newcastle's population especially when they are confronted with someone who fails to conform with accepted conventions of appearance such as dress and hairstyle. Moreover, it is Ferank's opinion that such conservatism is destined to remain a part of the city's character for a long time to come as, from a very early age, children are indoctrinated by their parents into believing that those who are in some way 'individual' or 'eccentric' in their appearance or manner are misfits and should therefore be subject to a form of systematic stigmatisation. Again, as Ferank himself explained to me:

... when I'm out in the street I'll get someone pass a comment on how I look, within earshot of myself and they don't mind if I year. Y'know . . . and that's their attitude to everything here . . . Like I'll walk past kids in the street and they'll be with their parents and that and even the parents'll join in wi' like 'look at the state o' him, they look like bloody rats' tails in 'is hair'. Y'know, they're really blatant about it . . . These people need an education. You can't get away with that, you gotta expect a reaction. And they normally get one from me . . . They get it in a rhyme, they're there y'know. And maybe they'll see themselves and go 'oh hang on a sec . . . I need to think a little differently about what I'm sayin'.'

[. . .]

While Ferank describes his work as a form of protest against the conservatism which he encounters on the streets of Newcastle, there is a clear sense in which, at a deeper level, he is also exposing the contradictions inherent in the sensibilities of a local white youth culture which collectively appropriates black cultural resources while simultaneously stigmatising individual experimentations with black style as in some way going 'too far'. In considering the extent to which the style of contemporary white British youth is now influenced by African-American and Afro-Caribbean music and culture, Back has observed that 'Young white people may [now] have more in common with Bobby Brown than John Bull, with the result that it is impossible to speak of a black culture in Britain separately from the culture of Britain as a whole' (1993: 218). While this is most certainly the case, the fact remains that many young whites, especially those who live in predominantly white areas, maintain a double standard in which an acceptance of black music and style goes hand in hand with an intolerance of black minority groups. While Ferank, as a white 'imitator', remains untouched by the more brutal and disturbing aspects of such intolerance, the reactions of local white youth to his experiments with aspects of black style serve as a telling reminder of the considerable local variations which characterise racial tolerance and multi-culturalism in Britain.

The 'Broon Ale' ward

If the work of Ferank illustrates one of the ways in which hip hop is being modified by white youth in Newcastle so that it becomes a more localised mode of expression, other forms of distinctive white hip hop expression also exist in the city. Ferank is often to be heard performing his raps at a bar known as 'Mac's Bar', one of the few venues in Newcastle which provides an opportunity for local rappers to air their skill in a live situation. While much of Ferank's work is composed beforehand, many of the rappers who frequent 'Mac's Bar' engage in a form of rapping known as 'freestyle'. Basically, this involves taking a particular theme and verbally improvising a series of ideas and points of view around the chosen theme. This form of rapping has also become a primary way in which local *white* rappers address issues which are particular to Newcastle and its people. Indeed, in many ways 'freestyling' provides a more effective form of local address than written rap as it enables the rapper to engage in a relatively spontaneous form of discourse. Thus, snippets of local 'street' gossip and more widely acknowledged local themes and issues can be verbally woven together with pieces of local urban folklore to produce particularly pointed, hard-hitting and, on occasion, humorous cameos of local social life. The following account is drawn from a conversation with a member of a particular group of freestyle rappers who regularly perform at 'Mac's Bar':

> We used to use a lot of 'Americanisms' in our raps, but then when we stared comin' down here we heard pure Geordie rap. Like with Ferank . . . it was just like 'oh yeah check out Ferank's flow'. And then people'd be sayin' to us 'why don't you do a rap theme about like eh, like an American rap crew would do a song about Crack and about how it's affecting their city an' that?' An' we started thinkin' 'well aye why not, let's 'ave a go at doin' something about Newcastle Brown Ale' because there's lost of 'isms' for Newcastle Brown Ale. 'The Dog', 'Geordie into space', all these different names and it's . . . y'know all these different reputations it's got. They used to have a ward up at the General [hospital] which was the 'Broon Ale' ward. So we thought, 'yeah, that's the stuff we should be rappin' about'.

While the notion of a white Newcastle rap group rapping about the local drinking culture may initially seem rather comical it is important to understand the local circumstances to which the group is responding. Many young people in Newcastle, especially those with an interest in rap and other 'specialist' musics, such as techno, ambient and jungle, are growing increasingly cynical about the city centre pub and club scene and the aggressive, machoistic atmosphere which one often encounters there. Thus, in a very real sense, by rapping about the problems of excessive drinking and alcohol related violence, the white rap group quoted above are addressing an aspect of their local environment which, they feel, needs to be acknowledged and changed.

[. . .]

The obvious connection of such 'home grown' rap with the shared sensibilities of local hip hoppers is clearly evidenced by the particular type of listening sensibility which it appears to invoke in Mac's Bar. When the 'freestylers' take to the floor, usually towards the end of the evening, the audience, who have up to that point been lazily dancing to a mix of mainly US rap sounds, stop dancing and gather around the performers to listen to their raps. In doing so they are acknowledging the fact that the improvised stories which these local rappers are relating work out of a shared stock of local knowledge and experiences which are in many ways uniquely relevant to Newcastle and the surrounding area. In listening to the 'freestylers', regulars at Mac's Bar are receiving accounts of their *own* lives depicted via a form of quickfire verbal reference to locations and events, names and faces with which they are all intimately familiar. Again, this instance of local hip hop activity is indicative of the close links which prefigure collective notions of authenticity, identity and local experience in hip hop. When the Geordie rappers take to the floor, there is an obvious shift in the audience's response. From the point of view of the audience, the music ceases to provide purely a rhythm for dancing or a background noise over which to talk and becomes something to be listened to, something which actively involves them. In drawing around the stage to listen to the work of the Geordie rappers, members of the audience are collectively endorsing the more locally relevant focus of the work's message and thus acknowledging its particularised 'authenticity' for them.

Conclusion: Hip hop as a local construct

The purpose of this article has been to consider the appropriation and reworking of hip hop by white youth in north-east England. Focusing upon the local hip hop scene in Newcastle upon Tyne and drawing upon the results of empirical data collected from individuals within this scene, I have illustrated how the particular version, or versions, of hip hop culture created, together with the attendant debates as to which group of hip hoppers is authentically portraying the hip hop style, is underpinned by a stock of distinctive local knowledges. Thus, one particular group of local hip hop enthusiasts share in a sense of felt similarity between their own white working class identity and the African-American experience, this feeling, or rather the group's articulation of it, being the key to their use of hip hop as an authentic means of collective expression. This shared belief that theirs is the quintessential understanding of hip hop's relevance for the experiences of white working class youth is manifested in the form of self-styled hip hop elitism in which the group engages. In the absence of an established black population in Newcastle this group, by virtue of its comprehensive knowledge of African-American rap music and hip hop culture, aspires to become the symbolic embodiment of the *black* hip hop sensibility in the city. Having appropriated this role for itself the group then articulates its felt sense of cultural superiority by ridiculing the 'new jacks' and other allegedly inauthentic *white* hip hoppers while at the same time articulating its felt sense of blackness in a symbolic air of defiance against the perceived racism and small-mindedness of the 'town crowd'. At the same time, however, the lack of a substantial black presence in Newcastle has also facilitated the staging of an altogether different white response to hip hop in which other local hip hop enthusiasts, not content with forming a romantic association with the African-American experience, have advocated what they view as a more progressive role for the genre. Thus, these individuals have constructed their own notion of hip hop authenticity in which a form of address which deals more directly with the day to day experiences of the white working class 'Geordie' youth is a grounding characteristic.

Clearly then, when addressing the issue of hip hop and its significance as an authentic form of cultural expression, it is necessary to take into account the fact that the definition of such authenticity is inextricably bound up with the particular local circumstances in which hip hop is heard and collectively used by different groups of hip hop enthusiasts. If the music, images, and basic sensibilities of style contained within the hip hop genre, as this is marketed to consumers throughout the world, provide young people with a series of templates for social action, then the ways in which such templates are fleshed out depends very much upon the particular meanings and significance which these young people themselves attach to hip hop. As I have attempted to show here, such meanings and significance are, in every instance, generated by particular forms of local knowledge and experience.

Notes

1 I am currently writing a book based on this research to be published by Macmillan.
2 Geordie is a term applied to a native citizen of Newcastle upon Tyne (see Hollands, 1995; Colls and Lancaster (eds), 1992).

References

Back, L., (1993), 'Race, Identity and Nation Within an Adolescent Community in South London', in *New Community*, 19 (2): 217–33.
Bennett, A., (1997), 'Bhangra in Newcastle: Music, Ethnic Identity and the Role of Local Knowledge', in *Innovation: The European Journal of the Social Sciences*, 10 (1): 107–16.
Colls, R. and Lancaster, W. (eds), (1992), *Geordies: Roots of Regionalism*, Edinburgh: Edinburgh University Press.
Gillett, C., (1983), *The Sound of the City: The Rise of Rock and Roll*, 2nd edn, London: Souvenir Press.
Hollands, R., (1995), *Friday Night, Saturday Night: Youth Cultural Identification in the Post-Industrial City*, University of Newcastle, Department of Social Policy: Working Paper No. 2.
Jones, A., (1988), *Black Culture, White Youth: The Reggae Tradition from JA to UK*, London: Macmillan.
Marks, A., (1990), 'Young, Gifted and Black: Afro-American and Afro-Caribbean Music in Britain 1936–88', in Oliver, P. (ed.), *Black Music in Britain: Essays on the Afro-Asian Contribution to Popular Music*, Milton Keynes: Open University Press.
Maxwell, I. (with N. Bambrick), (1994), 'Discourses of Culture and Nationalism in Contemporary Sydney Hip Hop', in *Perfect Beat*, 2 (1): 1–19.
Milestone, K., (1997), 'Love Factory: The Sites, Practices and Media Relationships of Northern Soul', in Redhead, S., Wynn, D. and O'Connor, J. (eds), *The Clubcultures Reader: Readings in Popular Cultural Studies*, Oxford: Blackwell.
Mitchell, T., (1998), 'Australian hip hop as a "glocal" subculture', Ultimo Series Seminar, UTS, 18 March.
Robertson, R., (1995), 'Glocalization: Time-Space and Homogeneity-Heterogeneity', in Featherstone, M., Lash, S. and Robertson, R. (eds), *Global Modernities*, London: Sage.
Shank, B., (1994), *Dissonant Identities: The Rock 'n' Roll Scene in Austin, Texas*, London: Wesleyan University Press.

4 | The Framing of Scottish National Identity

Frank Bechhofer,
David McCrone, Richard Kiely
and Robert Stewart

Key words

Nationalism, identity, Scottishness, Englishness, national identity

---

In the opening to their article, Bechhofer and his associates note that, although the issue of national identity is investigated at the level of large-scale social structures, there have been few studies of the way in which individuals construct their sense of national identity. This is a particularly striking omission in the case of Britain, since there is an apparent conflict between state *identities like British (or from the United Kingdom) and* national *identities like Scots, Welsh or English. To remedy this defect, Bechhofer et al. conducted an interview-based study of members of the landed and arts elites in Scotland and of inhabitants of the town of Berwick-on-Tweed, chosen because it is near the boundary between Scotland and England. The result was a deliberately focused sample from two groups who were subject to heightened public awareness about issues of national identity.*

The authors' theoretical starting point in the extract is that any individual's sense of national identity is not fixed but is constructed and sustained by the mundane realities of everyday life. The national identity that anyone will claim will vary according to the context and the time, and depends on the way that others receive those claims. For Bechhofer et al.'s respondents, therefore, place of birth did not necessarily determine sense of national identity and over time this sense can change for any individual. In some families children will opt for the same identity as their parents while in others they do not. In making an identity claim some individuals implicitly or explicitly reject alternatives; they are constructing their own identity by contrasting it with other possibilities.

Bechhofer et al. distinguish identity markers from identity rules. The former are those characteristics that have symbolic importance in identity construction or

*recognition. Identity rules are those rules of thumb whereby, in particular circum-
stances, the markers are interpreted.*

[. . .]

We take as our starting points that:

- Individuals' sense of national identity is constructed in the processes of everyday life. It is not fixed and can change over space and time. National identities
  are not essential, given and unproblematic.
- Identity claims, which may be verbal but can also take other symbolic or behav-
  ioural forms, are made, sustained and modified by individuals in the course of
  the processes of everyday social interaction. In making a claim to a particular
  national identity, individuals frequently, explicitly or implicitly, reject alternative
  claims. Central to our argument here are the claims which they could credibly
  make and in different contexts might well make.[1] The claims an individual will
  make about their national identity cannot simply be 'read off' from those characteristics commonly perceived to determine their 'nationality' such as ancestry,[2]
  place of birth, place of residence, accent or even name. However, in the processes
  of social interaction, *others* will, initially at least, frequently attribute national
  identity to individuals on that basis.
- National identity is then the result of a continually negotiated process which
  takes place at the individual level, but is profoundly social. The claims an individual will make, let alone those which will be accepted, are socially structured
  and bounded. There are structural factors which create a *propensity* to make
  certain kinds of claim, and for these to be accepted or rejected.
- A person's sense of national identity is not in a perpetual state of flux. It is
  likely that at certain times and in certain places, national identity is highly salient
  and for quite lengthy periods entirely stable across a wide variety of contexts.
  Thus for instance, at times of national crisis such as war, the 'other', in contrast
  to whom national identity is defined, is so clearly delineated as 'the enemy'
  to unify most people in the 'nation' and overlay other 'national' allegiances.[3]
  We would expect that, in the Second World War, the idea of 'Britishness'
  was more unproblematic than during peacetime even among people who in
  less turbulent times would not have chosen this identity.[4] It is this stability at
  times when a national identity is highly salient which may mislead people,
  including researchers and other scholars, to underestimate the flexibility of
  national identities.[5]
- It is important to stress that at any particular moment in time and in specific
  contexts an individual may well regard her or his national identity as fixed and
  immutable. This is an empirical issue and such a belief cannot be contested by
  us as researchers. For most people most of the time their national identity is
  probably relatively unproblematic, albeit we lack the studies of general populations which would provide the necessary evidence. Our empirical evidence shows
  clearly, however, that *some* people are well aware that they *choose* to make particular national identity claims, that *some* make different claims in different contexts, and that *others* consciously articulate how their claims have changed over
  time and space. It is in the light of this evidence that we argue that national identity is not essential, given, unproblematic and unchanging. We cannot extrapo-
  late from the amount of flexibility in this group to the population at large,

but it is reasonable to argue on the basis of our work that even those who at a particular moment in time and in a particular context claim a national identity which they see as given and fixed, may yet at a later time and in a different context come to make a claim to a different national identity.

Some illustrative evidence

The nub of our argument then is that individuals' sense of national identity is constructed in the processes of everyday social life. It is not essentially fixed and can change over space and time. The claims an individual makes will often vary according to the context and over time, and according to the way in which they are received by others in different contexts and over time. Consider a quote from one of our respondents which explicitly refers to a changed national identity claim and the circumstances of the change.

> I've come to think of myself as British. If I'd never worked in Scotland I suspect I would say that I was English, but having worked in Scotland I'd say I was British. If I'd gone from London to work in France and somebody said, 'What nationality are you?', I would probably say I'm English. Now if they ask, I would say I was British. It's an appreciation that Britain exists, that there is Scotland. A lot of people working in London just never think about it, so they're Englishmen.

Not only does the respondent tell us that he has come to make a different claim in the Scottish context and as a result of living and working in Scotland,[6] but he quite explicitly suggests that it would also have been expressed differently in France where social interaction would be taking place in a quite different context.

As the next two examples (the first from a person born in England and the second from a Scot) show, a national identity claim can be made not just consciously but also manipulatively. Note also that, when doing this, the respondent takes care to ensure that there is no *a priori* reason to assume that the claim will be rejected by the others to whom it is made.

> When abroad I describe myself as British. In the UK, I regard myself as English, I'm pretty British actually rather than English. It's to do with having lived abroad on a number of occasions. It's very interesting to me the affection with which Scotland is held abroad, much more than England. That's something that I actually, sometimes quite shamelessly, play on. So hence, when I'm abroad people speak of me and I suppose I speak of myself as being British rather than English.

> It's to do with people's perceptions of you rather than my perception of myself. Of course there's always the Scottish trump card in that sometimes you go places where English people or British – British are very often conceived as being English anyway – English people are less popular, and I mean if you're Scottish, Scots people seem to be universally popular, so you can always play the Scottish trump card.

This second respondent's daughter was born in England, and the respondent commented on her national identity as follows: 'I think you can become Scottish to be sure. My daughter, for example, was born in Newcastle, but she won't let anybody know.' The daughter denies the Englishness that some people might 'read off' from her place of birth. In all our empirical work to date, place of birth has most commonly been perceived as the defining marker of nationality, albeit with some credence given to claims based upon ancestry or, perhaps slightly less enthusiastically, residence. However, in this case, the daughter obscures her place of birth in order to facilitate a claim to being Scottish, given that she undoubtedly perceives being Scottish to be a more positively received identity in this context. If challenged, she could, if successful in obscuring or downplaying the importance of her place of birth, attempt to support her claim by reference to the fact she resides in Scotland or that her father is Scottish. If pressed further she could argue that in her particular case, residence and ancestry should take precedent over what other respondents have referred to as 'accidents of birth'.[7]

The way in which national identity claims may change between generations is very illuminating and would merit further detailed study.[8] In the example above, the daughter claims the same national identity as her father despite the 'accident of birth'. In other instances, children of parents who claim English or British identity are said to opt for a Scottish identity which they claim and defend in various ways. In the following example (taking the parents' account at face value), at least one of the children is said to claim to be an Aberdonian on the basis of residence only, probably supporting the claim if pressed by appealing to the experience of being educated in Scotland. Such a claim might well be rejected by others if it were known that it rested on residence alone and this gives the marker of accent great importance. The younger child is said to class herself as an Aberdonian but to speak English and we may surmise that she would find it more difficult to sustain the claim, if indeed she makes it, than her sister.

Interviewer: What do you think the impact would be on your kids? I mean, do they speak with Aberdeen accents?
Wife: The eldest does.
Husband: The youngest was only ten months when we brought her up here and she speaks English.
Wife: Like me. But the eldest certainly. When we were selling this place and we thought about moving back down to England and we wondered whether that would be a wise move, 'Oh no, no. This is home.' She doesn't want to leave Aberdeenshire. They class themselves as Aberdonians, don't they?
Husband: Yes.
Wife: They think granny and grandpa speak funny. And Uncle Nigel, 'I can't understand a word he says, Mum.'

In another interesting example from the landed sample, place of birth takes precedence for the children over ancestry. The respondent said quite bluntly: 'I very much don't consider myself Scottish at all, whereas all three of my children were born in Scotland and they very much consider themselves Scottish'. If the children inherit the land, especially if they reside in Scotland, there is potential for their children in turn to appeal to ancestry ('my parents are/were Scottish'). In this way ancestry has been reconstructed, and the respondent's grandchildren may claim Scottish identity on this basis as many landowners do, even if not born or living in Scotland.

In making a claim to a particular national identity, individuals frequently, explicitly or implicitly, reject alternative claims. In differing contexts they may pursue a quite different course. They may reject the alternatives for a variety of reasons. Alternatives may simply not occur to them; our approach to the issue of national identity accepts entirely that for some persons their national identity is entirely unproblematic and taken-for-granted.[9] Indeed it would be strange if this were not so and Billig's important concept of 'banal nationalism' is again very relevant here. In our research, we have deliberately sought out contexts which reduce the likelihood of national identity being taken for granted. People may decide not to make a particular claim because they judge that in a particular context or at a particular time those to whom they made the claim would be likely to reject it. They may choose not to make a claim which would undoubtedly be accepted by the relevant others because they judge that it would in a particular context give offence or damage their interests. It would make the text well nigh unreadable were we to refer continually to 'choices to make a claim and choices not to make other claims of national identity', but where we refer to making claims it is important to bear in mind that choices not to make other claims are the reverse of the coin.

The following example shows the respondent, who would have been identified by others as English on the basis of various markers, clearly evaluating alternatives and choosing between them:

> I'm British on my passport. I regard myself as being British. I actually probably regard myself as European. That really gets me out of it!! I am by birth English but I don't think of myself in that way. If I am anything, I am a European / adopted Scot. If you saw me in a debating chamber in London then I am actually usually sort of fighting the Scottish corner. I am sort of Scottish by adoption and by thinking. That said, in four months time I may have a job in England and *I'll have to change because politically sometimes you do have to change.*
>
> (Emphasis added.)

The same sense both of the way national identity can change over time less instrumentally and of the importance of context is shown in the following quotation:

> I'm more Scottish since I've been an adult. I started to think about it maybe when I was mid-'20s, something like that. In recent times I've become more Scottish, because professionally I'm constantly put in the position of having to promote Scotland and promote Scottish arts, I'm constantly having to fly the flag. If I weren't in a job where I had to do that, I'm not quite sure whether I would be as Scottish as I am. This job has definitely made me feel more Scottish and more culturally responsible.

The quotation which follows is an example of a respondent rejecting a claim they would like to make because it would not be accepted by others:

> I feel more akin with the Scots than the British or the English. If somebody said to me what's your nationality, rather than saying English I will say British, or I'll put UK a lot of the time. What I feel, that's what you're asking, rather than I can say I am, is more Scottish than British but I could never say that I was Scots.

It is not possible simply to read off the claims an individual will make about their national identity from those formal structural characteristics such as place of birth which determine their 'objective' nationality, or from easily discernible personal characteristics such as accent, name or even dress. Nevertheless, in the processes of social interaction, *others* will, initially at least, frequently *attribute* national identity to individuals from just such characteristics. One of our respondents (X) described another as follows: 'I mean Y is almost a Scot, he's a Scottish background and a Scottish family, and I can't remember whether he was born up here or not but I think he really more or less counts as Scottish'. One might wonder why X had any reservations,[10] but Y does speak with an RP (received pronunciation) accent having been brought up in England and it seems likely that this accounts for the 'more or less'. However, X does see Y as more or less Scottish whereas Y, whom we also interviewed, made a less strong claim, despite being born in Scotland, telling us: 'I came from the South, but I was born here, my father worked here for twenty years, I've lived here since the 50s, and so I am in fact half-Scots.'[11]

Sometimes in a kind of first strike, people make a clear claim at the beginning of an interaction designed to avoid the attribution of an identity which they wish to reject. In the following quote it is interesting that the respondent not only avoids claiming British identity because of the risk of being thought English, but also takes advantage of the belief that others will then read off certain characteristics from the claim to be Scottish.

> When I do go abroad I can introduce myself as Scottish and people will know what that means and know what kind of person they expect me to be, but I think I couldn't say the same if I was to go over and introduce myself as British, I couldn't imagine, think what that means and people obviously normally assume that you are English and speak English and are referred to as English.

Most of the above quotations are drawn from members of the arts elite who by virtue of their structural position are very sensitive to the nuances of national identity claims, involved as they are in an area of Scottish life where debates about the nature of culture in Scotland, Scottish culture and the relation of the one to the other are common and sometimes acerbic. Given our research design, we can of course say nothing about how claims are received by the general public. However, very similar conceptual points about claims, choices and rejections could be made using quotations from the landed elite, albeit their very different structural position nuances the statements in rather different ways. For instance, some of them, especially the estate owners, feel a sense of class identity which makes them sensitive to the divisive dangers of either an English or Scottish identity and the inclusive political advantages of claiming to be British. In this context, British is also code for Unionist.[12] The argument is that land is neither Scottish nor English but British, and it matters not a whit whether land in Scotland is owned by English persons or vice versa. This is reinforced when land is, or has been, owned in both Scotland and England, which is not unusual. The crucial criterion determining who should hold land can then be defined as the way the land is managed. Thus one respondent says:

> But I'm not English and I think that's the key point. My immediate reaction is I'm British and theoretically[13] so are you. It's a wild and beautiful place and politics shouldn't have – I know politics gets in everywhere – but it shouldn't have any part to play. If we

run it responsibly, which we are, people should not care. It should be of no concern of what nationality one is whether you come from Glasgow or Southampton, as long as you are managing it responsibly.

Another respondent, originally from the United States, when asked if they were still seen as an American showed the same sensitivity to the ownership issue, along with an awareness of potential choice but expressed in this case in terms of formal nationality – the possession of a passport. It is likely that this person would have liked to claim Scottish identity but, realising the claim is likely to be rejected, expresses the feeling in these terms.

> Well I'm not American, I'm a British subject. Personally, I would not be comfortable owning this building were I not a national of this country. I do consider myself, if I had the choice between a Scottish or British passport, I would choose to have a Scottish passport.

The following lengthy quotation from another landowner shows very clearly that there may be a strong personal sense of a particular national identity and a wish to choose that identity, but that social interaction is crucial and a strategic choice has always to be made in the light of its likely acceptance:

Landowner: I've chosen this as the kind of people I like to live amongst, this is the kind of lifestyle I want, and I don't want to come up here and change it. 'Do we feel ourselves local?' I would like to think we did. I believe that you sort of move to an area and you're living in an area, you want to believe that you're part of that area and part of the community. This idea of you're English because your mum and dad decided to have you born in England, it doesn't wash as far as I'm concerned. I believe I'm Scottish, I think we should be classed as Scots. If you're living in Scotland that's what it boils down to, because you've made your own decision what you want to be, you want to be part of that community, then I can't see why you shouldn't – likewise, if I was in England and a Scottish chap came and lived next door and he wanted to join in and be one of us, I can't see why he can't be English really.

Interviewer: Do you see yourself as Scottish now then?

Landowner: Well, I personally do, yeah. But I wouldn't say to somebody, 'I'm Scottish'. I've been asked 'Are you Scottish?' – with my accent people would know I wasn't Scottish; well, I wasn't born in Scotland but I do choose to live here, and I would like to be classed and thought of as Scottish – it's a nice place and at my age I can make my own decisions and this is where I feel I really want to belong and I class myself as Scottish.

Interviewer: If I was to ask you if you saw yourself now as Scottish, English or British, which one would you say?

Landowner: I'd have to go for British I suppose really, you know to be fair to everybody, because British would cover the British Isles,[14] wouldn't it.

We are putting forward the argument that a complex process forms a person's national identity, whereby individuals make identity claims, be they explicit or very tentative, in differing contexts over time, and these claims are received in different ways, and in turn modified according to their reception. National identity is the result of this continually negotiated process. Clearly, only a very detailed study over a lengthy period could show this beyond any doubt but our interviews suggest that it is a reasonable inference from the data. Some of the earlier quotations refer to a changing sense of identity over time. The process is very apparent in the following quotation from another Highland landowner, born and brought up in England but with some Scottish ancestry. This respondent had earlier said, 'I would like to think that I was British because I'm terrified that we're going to turn our tiny country into an even smaller country by being foolish, and it doesn't really achieve anything for anybody.' This was a common view among the landowners who were primarily Unionist, but later the respondent said:

Landowner: I haven't given my true answers.[15] I'm going to come absolutely clean. I do actually consider myself a Scot. I might not have answered that ten years ago but obviously now, being very much involved up there, we both understand quite a lot of what goes on up there. One has a natural affinity to it and one sees the weaknesses between the two countries and one sees the difference between the two countries.

Interviewer: Did you see yourself as becoming a Scot in that sense? You said you wouldn't have said that ten years ago.

Landowner: Yes, I guess that's fair comment. Yes, I think one's sympathy is there and one understands that it is a totally different country. I'm not talking politically now because we're going to avoid that break up. But once you're across the border it is a different country. They are different countries with different values, different structure.

Identity markers and identity rules

In the previous section, we provided some illustrative evidence for our general approach. In this section, we introduce the concepts of identity markers and identity rules. Identity markers can be defined as those characteristics which are perceived to carry symbolic importance either as a signal to others of a person's national identity, or which might be mobilised by the individual themselves in support of an identity claim. Identity rules are the probabilistic rules of thumb whereby under certain structural conditions and in certain contexts, markers are interpreted, combined or given precedence one over another.

In the case of the landed and cultural elites in Scotland, natality, ancestry, place of residence, accent, name and appearance all figured as prominent identity markers. These markers can be applied with a fair degree of objectivity although accent, for example, may be less clear cut. Markers may however also be the result of judgements about attitudes or behaviour. These are often especially important in understanding why certain people coming into Scotland are labelled negatively as outsiders whilst others are less problematically accepted. In this latter case some come to be referred to as honorary or adopted Scots. The crucial markers here are perceived commitment, contribution and sensitivity on the part of these 'incomers' to the imagined community of Scotland.

The markers people use make it easier or more difficult for them to adopt a flexible and interactive approach to national identity. Sometimes, an individual's attachment to a particular marker prevents them from claiming an identity which another person with the same characteristics might choose. Markers can then be used in very different ways by different people and in different contexts.

Here are a few examples of the use of these various kinds of marker. Sometimes markers will be combined. For instance an appeal to ancestry may use natality as a marker as well as 'blood'. Ancestry and place may come together where people clearly feel a strong sense of geographical permanence, identification with and attachment to a place, which is reinforced by family connections over a long period. Sometimes markers are conflicting and will be interpreted differently by 'others' in varying contexts. This is where identity rules come into play.

Although I have very little English blood in me, I was born there and educated there and brought up there and I can't really pretend to be anything else.

(Natality)

I feel a sense of Scottish identity in so far as half my family comes from Scotland and so it would be wrong for me not to recognise and acknowledge that.

(Ancestry)

I have always thought of myself as Scottish, generations of my family have come from [place name] so it is fairly clear to me.

(Ancestry plus geographical permanence)

All my working life has been in Scotland, so in a way I'm as Scottish as anybody.

(Residence)

I would hope people would look at X and say he's chosen to live in Scotland, he likes living here, he wants to contribute to its culture, he's lived here for ten years, therefore he's as Scottish as anybody.

(Residence, plus commitment and contribution)

The conflict that arises for me is that I enthuse about Scotland, I've chosen to live here and I think that a lot of the English mentality is fairly ghastly. Then when I do speak though, I'm very obviously English. In many ways I would like my affection for Scotland to be reflected in the fact that I had a Scottish accent.

(Accent conflicting with residence and commitment)

English folk tend to stand out up here, you can spot it with their dress.

(Appearance)

Anyone coming from somewhere else to work here can become a Scot, but there is an act of commitment required, one that I don't believe all the people that occupy those jobs are willing to make. For a great many of them it is a staging post on the way up the career ladder.

(Residence plus commitment)

Some people who've come from elsewhere do become Scots. It's sympathy with the consciousness that exists. These people go 'I'm happy', 'I'm comfortable', 'I'm whatever' here, they're absorbed in the consciousness of what's happening here and they stay. If anyone can make a contribution, if anyone can help things develop, grow, mature, they're entitled. If they're taking away, if they are diminishing, if they're involved in a reductive process, then they're not entitled.

(Contribution)

Identity markers not only range from the objective to the subjective, but also may be more or less visible in the process of interaction. This becomes clear when one considers examples of people attributing national identity to others in a way which might seem odd if they had further information about them. Thus, for instance, a number of respondents who had been born in Scotland of Scottish families, but because of the way they had been brought up and educated had an 'English'[16] accent, were identified by others as English and deeply resented this.

Occasionally there are references in our interviews to people born in Scotland (and thus Scots by the most frequently used marker) whose behaviour leads to them being seen as outsiders and their Scottishness certainly devalued, possibly even denied. The following respondent is willing to attribute Scottish identity to those born in Scotland or living in Scotland. However, the comment implies that someone born in Scotland has by a combination of their residing outwith Scotland and their behaviour lost the right to be considered Scottish. The identity rules as applied by this respondent give primacy to contribution and commitment, which in turn is seen as implying residence.

The best definition of a Scot is someone who was born here or someone who lives here. Occasionally I sort of bristle when you hear Scots in London bleating, you think well they're in London, they're disqualified now. If they really want to put something into Scotland, they should be in Scotland.

[. . .]

Notes

1 At a more general level, people also reject alternative claims which they neither could nor would ever wish to make. A person's sense of national identity involves knowing what their identity is in contradistinction to what it is not. Making a statement of national identity is, almost by definition, to make a statement of what one is not, at any rate at that time and in that context.

2 Defined loosely as the 'nationality' of their parents, grandparents or even forebears going back for a couple of centuries or more. The attribution of identity or identity claims based on ancestry are of course themselves contestable.

3 This is one of the chief thrusts of Linda Colley's argument in her remarkable book, *Britons: Forging the Nation 1707–1837* (1992).

4 Interestingly, our own empirical evidence shows that those Scots in our landed sample who identify themselves as British frequently make reference to National Service, the Second World War and the Falkland War, or to the Empire and the colonies. This is in a context where the minority of Scots across the two samples, landed and cultural, identify themselves in this way.

5   The need in 'normal' times for nationalism to be continually and subtly reinforced is well discussed by Billig (1995), an author whose position has something in common with our own.

6   This is apparent from other parts of the interview.

7   This notion is interestingly reflected in our study in Berwick-upon-Tweed. Among some respondents great emphasis is placed on being a 'Berwicker', sometimes expressed as being born and bred in Berwick. The maternity facilities in Berwick-upon-Tweed lead to some births taking place outwith Berwick, occasionally even in Scotland rather than England. This forces some would-be 'Berwickers' to emphasise that they would have been born and bred in Berwick, were it not for this 'accident of birth'.

8   We did not collect this information systematically, but the issue was raised from time to time, especially among the landed group. Given the tendency to emphasise ancestry among the landed elite this is to be expected, but it also shows how the idea of ancestry can itself be reconstructed over time.

9   This it seems from our research is particularly the case for people born, schooled and having resided for a reasonable length of time in the one country.

10 The explanation may be that X places great weight on place of birth as determining national identity objectively, but given that he is uncertain on this point we believe that the accent was more likely to be the critical determinant.

11 The term half-Scots is interesting in itself. While it is unlikely that this particular individual would have done so, it would obviously be open to him in a different context to claim to be *only* half-Scots or half something else.

12 The term in this context means Union as opposed to any Home Rule whatsoever be it devolution or independence.

13 We may speculate on the use of the word 'theoretically'. Clearly the respondent is conflating citizenship, which for most people is not a matter of choice, with national identity because it suits his purpose as discussed above but also because he wishes to include the interviewer in a most interesting way. The interviewer was identified as coming from Glasgow and the respondent attributes to him, on the basis of accent as a marker, a Scottish identity. The respondent infers that the interviewer would make a claim to a Scottish identity and indicates that he would accept this claim (which had of course not been made) as reasonable, but wishes to point out that it could be challenged 'theoretically'.

14 This reflects the 'fuzzy' quality of the term 'British'. The lack of an adjective for 'relating to the United Kingdom' can lead to ambiguities.

15 We are well aware that this remark raises methodological issues. Undoubtedly, there are passages in the data where people modify or contradict previous statements and it is entirely possible that there are a very small number where the respondent was deliberately trying to mislead us. Of course, it could be argued that, if this were so, the way in which they chose to mislead us would itself be worthy of analysis, albeit the process would become very convoluted. However, we do not think that we need to be too concerned about this. We are as certain as it is possible to be that these are indeed a tiny minority. It is easy to be misled, but we formed the impression that people spoke very openly and frankly during the interviews, bordering at times on indiscretion when referring to others. However, if our approach to the issues of national identity is correct, then offering a view to our interviewers was to make a claim and we would expect that anticipation of the way the claim would be received would affect what was said. It is possible that this respondent had been reluctant to claim to consider himself as a Scot lest the claim be rejected. However, we made it quite clear that we had no preconceived ideas, and there is ample discussion of sociological research interviews generally which indicates that the interview is a very special form of social interaction. One of its strengths is that its one-off, entirely confidential nature allows the respondents largely to disregard the interactive consequences.

16   In Scotland, what is often described as a 'public school accent' would almost always be seen in this way; in some contexts RP (received pronunciation) would also be so described.

References

BILLIG, M. 1995. *Banal Nationalism*. London: Sage.
COLLEY, L. 1992. *Britons: Forging the Nation 1707–1837*. New Haven, Conn.: Yale University Press.

5

Local and Global Political Protest

Sasha Roseneil

Key words

Globalization, the women's movement, new social movements, peace camps, disarmament, political protest

---

There is a tendency in much recent sociological argument to see globalization as a process that sweeps all before it, rendering local differences unimportant. Roseneil argues for a more subtle approach which emphasizes the significance of an interaction between the local and the global.

In the early 1980s, when the Cold War was at its height, a women's peace camp was set up at Greenham Common in Berkshire where the United States Air Force had a base at which Cruise missiles with nuclear warheads were stationed. The camp, a protest against the siting of Cruise missiles in Britain in particular, but also against worldwide nuclear armament in general, was influential in the global peace movement and in feminist political organization as non-hierarchical, local, women-only and autonomous.

Roseneil argues that the events at Greenham Common demonstrate the interactions between personal, local and global processes. The women involved had powerful personal reasons for taking part in the peace camp and were impelled to participate by their fears about global nuclear war. They were also attracted by the nature of a localized feminist protest movement. The Greenham camp was supported by networks that were local, national and global. It was apparently a local protest but was against a local manifestation of a global phenomenon and had a global impact. The participants were motivated by the conviction that one had to confront global problems by acting locally.

[. . .]

The personal–local–global constitution of Greenham

The constitution of Greenham – the ongoing creation and re-creation of the camp and the wider women's peace movement over time – was dependent on personal, local and global processes, and on the interactions between these processes.

Like any form of collective action, Greenham was sustained over its eleven years of existence by the individual decisions of thousands of women to get involved and to stay involved. It was concern about the global politics of nuclear militarism which provoked the initial interest in Greenham of most of the participants. For many women who were mothers, this concern was focused on the future of their children or grand-children. For example:

> I had got involved because I did feel that the world was about to end if somebody didn't do something . . . I had these terrible dreams about what would happen if my children were at school and nuclear war broke out. My whole life was absorbed in this fear that my children, not even that they might die, but that they might actually live and I might be crawling around in some half-life state.
>
> (Simone Wilkinson, aged 38)

Other women, particularly younger women without children, experienced deep psychological stress about nuclear war, and feared directly for their own future.

> I felt like the world is going to explode at any minute and why am I going to college? I mean, why go on with your life in this normal way when you feel like the world is about to blow up?
>
> (Liz Galst, aged 20)

> I remember when Reagan was elected I was still at university and we had an End of the World party because that was how we felt. I mean everybody just got roaring drunk for two days because we really felt like that was it, that none of us were going to live to see the end of our twenties.
>
> (Helen Mary Jones, aged 23)

Thus, events on the global stage precipitated action because they were experienced in a personal way.

However, it was not only the global situation which impelled women to get involved with Greenham. To understand Greenham as created only from the negative impulse of nuclear fear is to miss the centrality of the positive pull exerted by the camp as a women-only protest and community. Expressive, affective and cultural factors drew women to Greenham and sustained them in their involvement; in other words, factors local to Greenham, rooted in the social organization of the camp and the experience of being part of it, were an important motivation for involvement. For example, a sense of ownership and real participation was experienced by many women because the camp was women-only, and the opportunities provided by this women's space for developing close friendships with other women were highly valued. Other women were specifically attracted to Greenham by the large number of lesbians who were living there and the possibility this offered of being in a community in which lesbianism was the norm. But above all, women chose to live at Greenham and to continue living there or visiting because it was enjoyable, and because they found it personally satisfying.

> My reasons for going were that I thought I ought to go, because I felt that other people were doing something that I ought to be doing and I shouldn't be leaving this to other women to do . . . But when I was there it was really different because I really loved it . . . I loved all the excitement and I loved to do all the actions and all that. It was great. And mixing with a big group of women which I'd not done before. I really had a good time and liked it and enjoyed it. And that's why I stayed.
>
> (Penny Gulliver, aged 22)

Greenham was a place where women were able to engage in transforming and consolidating their self-identity.

> The women weren't the only reason I was there, but they were certainly a big attraction [laughter . . .]. For the first time in my life I felt I'd found a place where I fitted in and whatever I was OK, and the same as the others.
>
> (Jinny List, aged 20)

> A hell of a lot of women grew through Greenham, in all sorts of ways. Your awareness of your own power and abilities. It broke our images of ourselves. We went with housewives' values, the values of real narrow-minded, narrow, narrow-minded women from the Rhondha, and we broke this image of what we were. And then anything was possible.
>
> (Christine King, aged 27)

Greenham was supported and sustained by networks of people, mostly but not exclusively women, which were national, local and global. Women went to live and to stay at Greenham not primarily from the surrounding area, but from all over Britain. Greenham was located close to the M4 motorway, allowing relatively easy access for those travelling from South Wales, the West Country, London, the Home Counties and the Midlands, and even for those coming from the north and Scotland, road connections were good.[1] The choice of USAF Greenham Common as a site for Cruise missiles had been made for operational reasons within the logic of global nuclear politics: good road networks would allow the movement of convoys of missile launchers about the countryside, in order to foil pre-emptive first strikes. However, this had the effect of locating Cruise in a place easily accessible to protesters living in the most populated parts of Britain.

Supporters often travelled hundreds of miles to visit Greenham for a few hours, bringing resources such as food, clothing, building materials, firewood and money, and for several years, there were hundreds of visitors to the camp each week. These flows of people around Britain not only provided essential woman-power and resources for the continuation of the camp, but also served to embed Greenham within the consciousness of the oppositional culture of the 1980s. Information and news about Greenham was carried by individuals from the camp to places throughout the country, bypassing the news media, which consistently produced inaccurate and hostile accounts of the movement (when it was not ignoring Greenham altogether).[2] Visitors to Greenham would report to their local CND group, trade union meeting, church group, Labour Party branch or women's group, and women who lived at Greenham travelled around Britain speaking at meetings of interested audiences. Money raised by Greenham support groups, women's peace groups and other organizations through local activities such as street collections and jumble sales provided the financial resources which bought food, materials for taking action against the base (such as bolt cutters, ladders, paint), paid for petrol and camp vehicles, and supported women from overseas who were living at Greenham.

Local support for Greenham was also crucial to its survival. In the early days of the camp, it was the local anti-nuclear group, Newbury against the Missiles, which provided the tents, sleeping bags and cooking utensils which made it possible for the camp to be spontaneously set up at the end of the walk from Cardiff. Over the years a network of people who lived within ten miles of the camp opened their homes to the women who lived at Greenham, offering hot baths and a comfortable respite from the rigours of outdoor living. Some invited women to stay when they were sick, others let women store personal possessions in their homes to protect them from confiscation during evictions. The Society of Friends in Newbury gave Greenham women free access to their meeting house, which enabled meetings to be held in warmth and comfort, away from the interruptions occasioned by visitors and police at Greenham. The local Quakers also installed showers and set up a small office for the camp in their meeting house, providing an essential telephone contact point. Whilst the number of local supporters was small, their regular letters to the local papers and the constant pressure they exerted on local councillors and on the local MP destabilized the hegemony of local hostility to Greenham, and gave Greenham some roots in the locality.

Although discussions of globalization have tended to focus on cities as global places (e.g. Harvey 1989; Lash and Urry 1994), the decision to site Cruise at Greenham made this rural space, four miles from the nearest (small) town, into a global locale. The US airforce was already stationed at Greenham, and the upgrading of the base to house Cruise brought hundreds more American service personnel and their families to the area. Then as the camp organized its first large-scale actions such as the blockades of Easter 1982 and the 'Embrace the Base' demonstration of December 1982, which attracted over thirty thousand women, the world's media focused on Greenham. Reporters and television crews from Europe, the USA, the Soviet Union and beyond went to Greenham to interview the women, and to film and photograph the camp. By the time the first missiles were installed in November 1983, people in countries as remote as Nicaragua and South Africa knew about Greenham.

Greenham was outside local culture, and largely separate from the local community. Its culture was profoundly other to the conservative, small town concerns of rural Berkshire. Greenham was cosmopolitan and looked outwards to a global community of anti-nuclear campaigners and feminists. The flows of women who came to Greenham from all over Europe, from Australia, the USA, Canada, some to visit, some to live, brought to the camp their previous experiences of political action and a range of political discourses and individual histories. In an environment in which the exchanges of stories and personal experience was much valued, the praxis of Greenham was created out of these different traditions. For instance, Australian women brought information about the connection between uranium mining and aboriginal land rights, and introduced aboriginal mythology; from this grew Greenham's use of dragon and serpent imagery. Women from the USA raised concern about US intervention in Central

America, which ultimately led to a number of Greenham women visiting Nicaragua, and to women from Nicaragua visiting Greenham. Women from overseas also 'carried Greenham home',[3] and spread the practices, ideas and actions of Greenham around the globe. Women's peace camps inspired by Greenham were set up in Australia, Canada, Denmark, West Germany, Italy and the USA.

Thinking globally, acting locally, globally and personally

The oft-quoted injunction of the environmental movement to 'think global, act local' demands that a global conscience should be enacted within a local context, and implicitly suggests that local actions can be of global significance. Greenham held a similar belief. The ethos which guided action at Greenham was one of personal responsibility. It was believed that every individual has a responsibility to act according to her/his conscience, and therefore should engage in action to oppose nuclear militarism. Underlying this was a belief in the importance of individual agency in the production, reproduction and transformation of society. It was held that the cumulative power of thousands of individual, local actions could have an impact on the global situation.

The global collective conscience of Greenham produced action directed at the specific location of Cruise missiles in Britain. Blockades of the base, and many thousands of incursions into the base, as well as the constant tacit protest enacted by the camp's presence outside the base, were all local actions of resistance against global power. Reaching the point at which they felt able to break the law, cause criminal damage, and defy the police, British soldiers and armed American servicemen, was, for most women, a difficult process of internal dialogue and self-questioning, within a context of discussion with others. The taking of action at Greenham which resulted in arrest and a court case, then often further underlined the global dimension of local and personal actions. In many of the thousands of court cases tried at Newbury Magistrates Court, women, usually defending themselves without a lawyer, would use international law, such as the 1969 Genocide Act in their defence.

Greenham actions were not just located at Greenham: Greenham women roved across Britain and beyond. 'Greenham women are everywhere' was a slogan coined early in the life of the camp, to suggest that Greenham actions took place beyond that one corner of Berkshire, and were not confined to women who lived at Greenham. Whilst there was, at various times, considerable tension about the label 'Greenham woman' and over the centrifugal pull of the camp, women's peace actions inspired by Greenham, and conducted by women who identified as 'Greenham women', took place all over Britain. Some of these were the actions of women who lived at the camp, but most were those of women whose primary commitment was to working in their home communities. It was particularly in taking action beyond Greenham that the project was pursued of 'making connections' between nuclear weapons, women's oppression and other forms of global injustice. Roving actions can be divided into two main groups: those that related directly to Greenham, but which took place away from the camp; and women's peace actions in the style of Greenham, but not concerned primarily with Greenham.

The first group of actions was directed mainly at raising the profile of Greenham or at taking the protest about Cruise to other locations. For instance in January 1983 women occupied the lobby of the House of Commons to demand that the issue of Cruise be debated. Local women's peace groups throughout Britain regularly held demonstrations in town squares, set up peace camps on roundabouts and engaged in dramatic street theatre, and mass blockades were held in London and other cities to protest against and publicize the exercising of Cruise missile convoys. In 1985 there was a walk to 'reclaim Salisbury plain' from military exercises; this passed over the firing range and the area in which convoys were exercised. This spreading of women's peace actions around Britain aimed to show how the problem of nuclear weapons was not confined to Greenham, but was an issue which affected everyone, everywhere.

Perhaps the most ambitious action in this category, and the one most clearly global in scope, was the court case brought in the New York Supreme Court by a group of Greenham women, their seventeen children and two US congressmen against Ronald Reagan, Defense Secretary Caspar Weinberger and US military chiefs of staff. The aim of this case was to get an injunction against the deployment of Cruise at Greenham, using international law and the US Constitution to argue that deployment was illegal.[4] The case attracted widespread support from the wider Greenham network and from the mixed peace movement in Britain and the USA, and for twenty-four hours on 9 November 1983 camps were set up at all 102 US bases in Britain in support of the case, as well as outside the White House and the Supreme Court in New York.

The second group of actions was inspired by the distinctive ethos and style of protest of Greenham but went beyond the issue of Cruise, often aiming to draw attention to the connections between nuclear militarism and other issues, some global, others more specifically British. For instance, on the occasion of President Reagan's visit to London (7 June 1982), women from the camp and from the wider Greenham network performed a symbolic die-in outside the Stock Exchange to highlight the huge profits made by the international arms trade. In March 1984, women demonstrated outside a seminar and sales conference for missile systems and technology, throwing red paint at the building in which it was held. Making links between militarism, the exploitation of animals in research and women's oppression there was also a women's camp at Porton Down (the chemical and biological weapons research establishment). To highlight the use of uranium mined in Namibia in the production of warheads for Trident nuclear submarines, a women's action was held at the British Nuclear Fuels plant, Springfields. Greenham women, working with Women against Pit Closure groups, also organized a series of women's walks from mining villages in South Wales to Hinckley Point nuclear power station, to demonstrate the relationship between the closing of coal mines, the expansion of nuclear power and the manufacture of nuclear weapons. The other major form of action in this category was the establishment of women's peace camps at other nuclear bases. Inspired by Greenham, there were, at different times, camps at military installations at Menwith Hill, Waddington, Morwemstow, Rosyth, Capenhurst, Fylingdales and Brawdy, amongst others, and blockades, fencecutting and incursions took place at these and other bases.

[. . .]

Conclusion

Greenham and the women's peace movement of the 1980s were embedded within processes of globalization. They were at the same time both the product of globalization and productive of globalization. Emerging as resistance to the global threat of nuclear war and the globalization of nuclear militarism, the movement was composed of global flows of actors, ideas and images, and it contributed to the creation of global identities and consciousness and to the formation of global networks of political activists.

This discussion of the interconnections between the global, local and personal dynamics of Greenham suggests that Greenham was a movement characteristic of high modernity. In an era of ever-increasing global interdependence and high-consequence risks, in which processes of individualization mean that these changes and risks are experienced intensely personally (Giddens 1991; Beck 1994), Greenham engaged in a collective challenge to what were perceived as the negative aspects of high modernity. But this challenge was inextricably bound up in those very processes of globalization, and was dependent upon them in its operation.

My focus on a social movement highlights the importance of attention to agency and human actors when considering globalization. The global–local–personal dynamics of globalization must be understood as social processes set in train and carried out by social actors, rather than just by the structures of the world economy, the inevitable development of technology or the power play of nation states. I have shown that social movements are not just constituted through globalizing processes, but actively contribute to them. Finally, this chapter has served to insert women as actors within the global–local–personal dialectics of the contemporary world.

Notes

1 Lash and Urry (1994) discuss the significance of the M4 corridor to economic development in the 1980s.
2 For discussion of the media reporting of Greenham, see Young 1990.
3 'Carry Greenham Home' was a song written for Greenham by Peggy Seeger.
4 The case was eventually dismissed in 1985. See Greenham Common Women Against Cruise Missiles 1984, Hickman 1986 and Young 1990 for a more detailed discussion.

References

Beck, U. (1994) 'The Reinvention of Politics' in U. Beck, A. Giddens and S. Lash (eds), *Reflexive Modernization*, Cambridge: Polity.

Giddens, A. (1991) *Modernity and Self-Identity: Self and Society in the Late Modern Age*, Cambridge: Polity.

Greenham Common Women Against Cruise Missiles (1984) New York: Center for Constitutional Rights, Legal Education Pamphlet.

Harvey, D. (1989) *The Condition of Post-Modernity*, Oxford: Blackwell.

Hickman, J. (1986) 'Greenham Women Against Cruise Missiles and others versus Ronald Reagan and others' in J. Dewar *et al.* (eds) *Nuclear Weapons, the Peace Movement and the Law*, Basingstoke: Macmillan.

Lash, S. and Urry, J. (1994) *Economies of Signs and Space*, London: Sage.

Young, A. (1990) *Femininity in Dissent*, London: Routledge.

Part II

Social Divisions

6

The Restructuring of Work since the 1980s

Duncan Gallie, Michael White, Yuan Cheng and Mark Tomlinson

Key words

Skill, occupational change, women's employment, organizational change, managerial strategies, flexibility, polarization of occupations, unemployment

Associated with transformations in the global economy, and the intensification of competition on an international scale, there has been much debate about the changing nature of work. The notion that work practices are, or should be, becoming more flexible in a period of flexible specialization, or 'post-Fordism', has attracted much attention. Gallie et al.'s Restructuring the Employment Relationship *is the most authoritative empirical study of the changing nature of work in Britain.*

Gallie et al. (1998) report on a programme of research, 'Employment in Britain', which set out to examine systematically change over time. Their book sought to test a number of speculative theories about changes in employment since the 1970s by comparing evidence from the 1980s with a newly commissioned survey, conducted in 1992. The survey explored 'the nature of, and patterns of change in, work and the employment relationship' and sought 'to assess the implications of the principal changes that are revealed for the subjective quality of working life and for work motivation' (p. 25). The principal issues concerned the effects of new technology, the impact of new managerial strategies, the consequences of more flexible contractual and working arrangements, job insecurity, the nature of work tasks, degrees of integration and involvement in work, and subjective perceptions of the contribution of work to well-being. These topics were explored using a national random sample survey of 3,869 employed people and 1,003 individuals who were unemployed. Respondents were interviewed between April and August 1992. The passage comes from the conclusion to the book where Gallie et al. summarize their findings in order to assess the empirical validity of some of the principal claims about the way that employment had changed since the 1980s.

They argue that the last decade has seen major changes in the nature of work, including a general tendency to upskilling. But at the same time there has been a decline in stability of employment, especially for men, and that this has produced an increasing sense of insecurity as well as stress associated with the intensification of work.

Interpreting restructuring

There can be little doubt from the evidence examined here that the spread of new technologies indeed had been spectacular. Within little more than half a decade, the proportion of employees working with automated or computerized equipment had risen from only 39 per cent to over half the workforce (56 per cent). While it had swept most rapidly through the higher skilled categories of the workforce, no occupational class was unaffected. And if men were more likely to be users of new technologies, change over time had been even more rapid in women's work. In contrast to the false prophecies of earlier decades, those who argued that a pervasive transformation of the technical infrastructure of the world of work was now underway were clearly correct.

Further, the evidence from the research points firmly in favour of the view that new technologies were associated with a rise in skill requirements. It was associated with higher demands by employers in terms of education and training even within occupational classes and those who had directly experienced the introduction of advanced technologies were more likely to report an increase in the skill demands of their job. Moreover, those who worked with advanced technologies were more likely to have seen their responsibilities for the work task increase than other employees. But this restructuring of work roles around new technologies was in no sense a deterministic outcome of the technologies themselves. Rather it reflected the interaction of new technical possibilities with managerial philosophies about appropriate methods of work organization. Most notably, employers appear to have responded in rather different ways to new technology depending on whether the workforce was male or female, increasing work responsibilities for men to a greater extent than for women.

The spread of advanced technology, then, does appear to have been associated with very positive changes in the nature of the work task and with higher levels of direct participation about relatively immediate work issues. However, in the wider context of the results, there must be doubts about the centrality that technology is often attributed in theories of change in the nature of work. It has already been seen that its implications for the design of jobs are contingent upon managerial choices about forms of work organization and that it is far from transforming the underlying employment relationship. But, in addition to this, it was only one of the factors that have contributed to the changing nature of work tasks and of the immediate work environment.

To begin with, the upward trend in skills appears to have been a much more widespread phenomenon than could be accounted for purely in terms of technological change. The overriding emphasis on the importance of technology for the nature of work derives from a historical period when the economic structure was dominated by manufacturing industry. The agenda of research has lagged well behind the transformations occurring in the real economy. One of the most important changes in the post-war era has been the shift in most advanced capitalist societies to economies based on the service industries. This has been accompanied by a profound shift in the underlying nature of work. The problematic of the alienation of the factory worker tied to the machine or the assembly line that dominated so much of the interwar and post-war literature is now beginning to look curiously dated.

In Britain in the early 1990s, only 6 per cent of employees were involved in assembly-line work, and only a further 11 per cent were primarily concerned with working with machines. Instead, the type of work that has grown in the wake of the expanding service economy is work that principally involves interacting with people. Our evidence indicates that just under half of the workforce (46 per cent) were predominantly involved in what might be termed people-work. This could take very different forms: it could involve caring responsibilities, selling products or services to people, or organizing people in their leisure and their work. But they pose radically different problems with respect to the experience of work to those of the repetitiveness and monotony of machine work. Moreover, it is clear that the performance requirements of people-work have been rising sharply in recent years, making this also a major contributor to the overall process of upskilling.

New forms of management

A second theme that has reappeared in many parts of the discussion is the nature and significance of managerial policies for regulating the workforce. The predominant post-war model, at least in the large-firm sector of British industry, had been based on the joint regulation of the conditions of employment through negotiation with trade unions. This was widely seen as implying a significant retreat in terms of traditional managerial prerogatives. Not only the terms of employment, but also the detailed organization of work, were increasingly subject to negotiation and agreement between management and shopfloor representatives. As shop-steward influence rose, many observers pointed to the decline of the power of supervision. Supervisors were reluctant to use disciplinary authority, when they were regularly bypassed by shop steward appeals to middle management. Rather management pinned its hopes on a policy of 'constitutionalism'. Where work roles were the outcome of joint regulation, it was more likely that they would be regarded as legitimate by the workforce. The economic and political conditions that had sustained this approach became increasingly precarious from the early 1980s.

But if the traditional system was clearly under attack, how exactly was it changing? A number of commentators pointed to the emergence of new systems of management, which emphasized more formalized, 'bureaucratic' procedures of performance assessment and career reward. The distinctive feature of this approach was that it involved a new emphasis on the direct relationship between management and the workforce, in contrast to the traditional pattern where relationships were mediated through the institutions of joint regulation. The importance of this was noted by writers from different intellectual perspectives: they were to be found in the ranks both of radical left critics of capitalist institutions and of authors of prescriptive guides to management practice. The latter found a common identity under the rubric of 'human resource management'. However, there was still relatively little evidence about the extent of such developments in Britain, let alone any empirical assessment of their implications.

Our evidence certainly indicated a hardening of employer attitudes to trade union influence. Whereas in the mid-1980s nearly two-thirds of employees (62 per cent) worked for employers that either actively encouraged or at least accepted trade union-ism, by the time of the survey in the 1990s, this had fallen to less than 47 per cent. It was not just that there had been an increase in establishments where there were no unions present; the more hostile attitudes of employers were evident even if the com-parison was confined to people in unionized establishments. There were good grounds for suspecting that employers were moving away from their reliance on joint regula-tion, with its implication of an arm's-length relationship with the shop floor, to more active forms of workforce management.

However, the research suggested that employers had followed quite diverse paths in seeking to strengthen their direct relationship with the workforce. Some had sought to increase the intensity of traditional forms of direct supervision, while others had adopted radically different strategies that involved giving greater discretion to employ-ees themselves and shifting to more impersonal forms of control. The fact that these diverse forms of control were closely linked to the presence of unions certainly sup-ports the view that they were an attempt by management to regain the initiative. But the pattern suggests a period of experiment with different types of policies by differ-ent types of employers, rather than the general endorsement of any specific new phi-losophy of management. But that said, there were clear signs of an increase in the types of practices commonly referred to as human resource management policies.

The literature on human resource management varies in its emphasis on 'individu-alistic' or 'collective' methods of developing a direct relationship between management and the workforce. In some versions, it is seen to involve encouraging collective par-ticipation at least in decisions about the relatively immediate work environment. However, the research found little evidence of a significant development of participa-tive procedures. Only a small minority of British employees (32 per cent) felt that they could have any significant say over changes in work organization and only half felt that they could exercise any influence at all. There was no evidence at all that such participation had increased over the decade. Indeed, the proportion feeling that they could exercise some degree of influence may have declined somewhat since the mid-1980s. It was true that advanced technologies appeared to be conducive to higher levels of participation, but this has been counteracted by other shifts in managerial thinking that have tended to de-emphasize the importance of wider involvement of employees in organizational decision-making. The types of performance-management system that have been becoming more common are primarily those based on more individualized relationships between management and employees.

One of the most notable features about the development of these policies was that they were very much focused upon higher-level employees. Our estimates indicated that whereas just over half of managerial and professional and lower non-manual employees were under what might be defined as a performance-management system, this was the case for less than a third of manual workers. Manual workers, on the other hand, were more likely to be subject to technical control systems, in which the constraints on performance were embodied in the machinery itself or in payment systems based on measured output. The trends with respect to increased direct super-vision were also strongly class stratified. In general, direct supervisory controls of everyday work performance were more likely to have decreased than to have increased for non-manual employees. However, among manual workers, direct supervision was more likely to have increased. In short, rather than the generalization of a new system of management across the workforce, our evidence suggests that employers were devel-oping class-specific policies that tended to reinforce the differentiation between cat-egories of employee.

[. . .]

Non-standard contracts and the polarization of the workforce?

It has been seen that the more 'integrative' forms of management policy, which have been the primary focus of discussion about changes in patterns of management, were in practice heavily centred on non-manual employees, in particular professionals and managers. This was a development then that tended to confirm earlier lines of social division in the workforce. A number of writers, however, have gone further than this in suggesting that recent trends have made divisions between different categories of employee even sharper. One of the major factors behind this increased polarization of the workforce is seen to be the expansion of non-standard forms of employment con-tract, in particular part-time and temporary contracts. The picture drawn contrasted a relatively stable and integrated stratum of higher-skilled employees on the one hand, with an increasingly insecure and flexible stratum of low-skilled employees on the other.

The issue is certainly an important one in that just under a third of all employees were on non-standard contracts. Our evidence confirmed that part-time and tempo-rary workers suffered from substantially poorer terms of employment. However, it did not support some of the conventional views of the nature of such work, and it under-lined the distinctiveness of these different labour market segments. Indeed, our results pointed to the need to distinguish clearly not only between the conditions associated with part-time and temporary work, but between different types of temporary work.

A first point to note is that the various non-standard contract workers varied very much in terms of their skill distribution. Women in part-time work were certainly in markedly less skilled jobs, whatever indicator one takes. They were also less likely than either men or women in full-time work to have seen an increase in the skill require-ments of their work. Indeed, they were disadvantaged on the more detailed skilled dimensions, even when allowance was made for the relatively low occupational class of their jobs. The low skill-level of the work was associated with little discretion over how the task was to be done and with work that was repetitive, lacking variety, and offering little in the way of opportunities for self-development. Although part-time employees in the public sector were rather better placed than their private sector equivalents, the overall pattern remains rather bleak.

However, this picture of the quality of the work cannot be generalized to all non-standard contract workers. Temporary workers on short-term contracts (less than a year) were much more evenly distributed over the skill structure, and were only slightly more likely to be unskilled than permanent employees. Those who were on medium-term contracts (one to three years), representing approximately half of all temporary workers, were at least as qualified as the permanent workforce. These medium-term 'contract' workers had shared fully in the process of upskilling, they were even more likely to have received training from their employer than permanent employees, and the quality of the jobs they did was just as high. These looked very much like 'entry' jobs into what was often quite high-quality work.

Second, the different types of non-standard contract offered specific types of flexibility. Neither female part-timers nor temporary workers were involved in jobs that could be defined as 'flexible' in any very general way. Indeed, there were several dimensions of flexibility on which both categories of non-standard worker were indistinguishable, or even less flexible than permanent workers. Part-time employees were less likely than permanent employees to switch between different types of work on the job and there was no difference in this type of 'task flexibility' between temporary workers and permanent employees. Both part-time and temporary workers were less likely to be on incentive or merit payment systems that related pay to performance. Finally, part-time workers were less likely than permanent workers to put in extra hours of work and temporary workers were no more likely to do so. Although both types of non-standard contract clearly offered employers particular types of flexibility, they were in other respects relatively inflexible working arrangements.

Third, there were marked differences between the various types of non-standard contract in terms of the likely difficulty of being able to move out of that position in the labour market. Part-time employees were clearly heavily constrained in their opportunities for getting promotion into better work. They were much less likely than full-time employees to think that they had any type of career ladder they could move up and they were far less likely to think they had a reasonable chance of getting promotion to a better job within their organization. This absence of serious career opportunities also characterized the jobs of short-term temporary workers. However, those on medium-term contracts were much more optimistic about their career prospects and indeed were as likely as permanent employees to think that they would get promotion in their current organization.

Finally, the different types of non-standard contract had very different implications for job security. There was no evidence to support the common view that part-timers had lower job security. Certainly they were less likely to be protected by employment protection legislation and they perceived this fact quite clearly. Our estimates suggested that only 53 per cent of part-time workers would have been covered by employment protection, compared with 71 per cent of women working full-time and 74 per cent of men working full-time. But, in practice, female part-time employees felt just as secure in their jobs as permanent employees. Moreover, an analysis based on people's work histories of the relative risks of becoming unemployed for part-time and full-time employees suggested that they were quite correct in this perception. It seemed likely that the lack of formal security of their position was counterbalanced by the fact that they tended to work in the more protected service industries (and quite substantially in the public sector services). In contrast, both types of temporary worker did clearly suffer from much higher levels of job insecurity, particularly those on contracts of less than a year.

While those on non-standard contracts shared the fact that they were in some significant respects disadvantaged relative to permanent full-time employees, they were highly differentiated in the degree, and in the particular types, of disadvantage that they experienced. Simply placing these employees together into an undifferentiated category of the 'peripheral' or 'flexible' workforce is to obscure the very distinctive character of these labour market positions, whether in terms of skill, promotion chances, or security.

The group that did come very close to the notion of a 'peripheral' workforce was that of employees on short-term contracts of less than a year, although even these workers were more evenly distributed across the different skill categories than is often suggested. This clear peripheral group constituted 6 per cent of the workforce. Longer-term contract workers, although also less secure, were in a more complex position. They were as skilled as the permanent workforce and a significant proportion saw their jobs as opening the way to a career path. A substantial proportion appear to have been in the position of trainees, preparing to enter relatively good-quality jobs. Part-time workers were particularly disadvantaged in terms of skill and promotion opportunities, but they had a relatively high sense of job security. Given their level of effective job security, it is far from clear that they can be meaningfully classified as part of a flexible or peripheral workforce. Overall, the pattern of differentiation was considerably more complex than is often allowed and our analyses showed how important it is to look at people's experiences as well as at formal contractual provisions.

Finally, although both temporary and part-time workers experienced clear (if rather different) disadvantages in aspects of their employment conditions, there was no evidence of polarization across time. Not only had these categories grown very little over the decade as a share of the overall workforce, but there was no sign that their employment conditions had become worse relative to those on standard contracts. Indeed, a notable finding was that the relative skill position of part-time workers (although not the responsibility they were allowed in their work) had improved. This reflected an increase since the mid-1980s in the proportion employed in lower non-manual work and a decrease in the proportion in semi- and non-skilled manual work. There also appears to been some degree of convergence in the job insecurity of temporary and permanent workers (in part as a result of the declining security of 'permanent' workers).

Unemployment and job security

An even more severe form of differentiation of life chances than that resulting from the diversification of types of contract came from the growth of job insecurity and unemployment. This was clearly one of the most fundamental changes in the character of the labour market, affecting those with so-called 'permanent' contracts. Our charting of the overall careers of the people interviewed underlined the rise in vulnerability to unemployment since the 1970s for both men and women. Indeed, it was striking that among the most recent birth cohort in the survey, 40 per cent of men and nearly 30 per cent of women had experienced a spell of unemployment.

There were, however, important variations in the overall experience of employment instability. The deterioration of the labour market appears to have been particularly

severe in its effects for men, particularly for young men. The position of men de-
teriorated with respect to all measures of stability. They were more likely to become
unemployed, they were less likely to be in stable employment in the sense of being
continuously in work, and they were less likely to have long-term employment with
any given employer. For women, although there was a rise in the risk of unemployment, there was at the same time an *increase* in their overall employment stability. This
apparent paradox results from the fact that they were less likely to withdraw from the
labour market to have children and that they made greater use of maternity leave.
Moreover, there was also an increase in the extent to which women remained in long-
term employment with particular employers, indicating that they were securing more
stable positions within organizations.

The factors affecting the risk of unemployment also differed in some important
respects between men and women. Perhaps the most striking difference was the extent
to which men were more heavily trapped by their previous educational and occupational backgrounds. Their degree of vulnerability was more strongly linked to family
background, in particular the extent to which they came from families where the
parents had encouraged education, and to the actual educational qualifications they
had acquired. The risk for men was also more closely related to the occupational class
of the jobs they had obtained (even taking account of early family circumstances).
While there was evidence that in recent years an increased proportion of the unemployed were coming from higher occupational classes, it was nonetheless clear that
it was still those in the manual working class that experienced the greatest risk of
unemployment.

These differences have to be seen in the context of the very high level of gender
segregation in the job market, with very different patterns in the development of job
opportunities for men and for women. In the male job market, the contraction of jobs
was above all in skilled and non-skilled manual work. Insofar as new job opportunities emerged, they tended to be in higher-level positions, which could be entered only
through the acquisition of formal educational qualifications. There was then a very
high educational penalty with respect to employment stability and transitions between
contracting and expanding areas of employment were very difficult to make.

In the female job market, in contrast, there was a major expansion even of the
number of non-skilled jobs (albeit often part-time) with the development of the service
sector. The class of previous job was then much less decisive in determining the availability of job opportunities. This may also account in part for the lesser importance
of education and family background for women's risk of unemployment. But, in addition to this, it must be remembered that in the service sector social skills were a considerably more important component of skill. Education is likely to be a weaker guide
to the level of social skill than it is to the technical skills needed in jobs primarily concerned with the production of information or objects.

But despite these differences, there was one very important feature common to the
experiences of job insecurity of men and women. For both, there was a clear process
of entrapment whereby once people became unemployed they were much more vulnerable to further spells of unemployment. Given that education and early family circumstances had been taken into account, it seems unlikely that this reflects individual
factors such as personality. Rather, the cumulative evidence showed that those coming
out of unemployment were generally forced to take jobs in a much less secure sector

of the labour market. They were excluded from more technologically advanced work environments (which were associated with greater job security), they were more likely to find themselves in temporary work, and they were more likely to be in jobs without trade union protection.

Moreover, it is clear that, even for those who did manage to stay in employment, the experience of unemployment had very severe long-term effects for their careers and for the quality of their work life. Those who had been unemployed were less likely to experience upward career mobility and they found themselves in jobs where there was less chance either to exercise or to develop their skills. Unemployment was not then a transitional experience, merely moving people from contracting to expanding areas of the economy. It left an enduring mark on people's work careers – greatly increasing the risk of future unemployment, making it more difficult to move to better jobs, and confining people to relatively poor-quality work. Further, the increasing risk of unemployment left its mark even on those who had not been directly affected, as was evident in the widespread worries about job security among those in employment and the fact that the greatest change in recent years in people's job preferences lay in the increased importance they attached to having a secure job.

[. . .]

Employment change and social divisions in the labour force

The discussion up to this point has largely dwelt on the general trends with respect to work and employment. But this leaves the question of whether specific social groups may have been rather differently affected by these patterns of change. [. . .] The most general issue is whether there has been any marked tendency for convergence or divergence in work experiences.

Gender and employment

One of the most notable findings of the research was the very sharp rise in women's commitment to employment over the decade. Whereas in 1981, women had been quite clearly less committed to remain in employment irrespective of financial need, this difference had entirely disappeared by the 1990s. Moreover, this change did not reflect a sharp polarization of the trends in work motivation between women in full-time work, who were becoming more highly integrated into the workforce and women in part-time work whose commitment remained marginal. Rather the rise in employment commitment was even more marked among women part-timers than among full-timers, leading to increased homogeneity in women's attitudes to work. It is clear that the period witnessed a major and very broad cultural shift in the significance of employment in women's lives.

Yet, while women's commitment to work has become very similar to that of men, the results of the research underlined the continuing extent of gender inequality in employment and labour market experiences in the 1990s. A comparison of the measures of the skill position of men and women showed that women were far more likely to be in low-skilled occupations where there were no requirements for qualifications, training, and experience on the job. They were also less likely to have benefited from the opportunity to increase their skills on the job in recent years. These marked skill disadvantages were reinforced by the fact they were given less scope to take decisions about how to do the work. Women's skill disadvantage was not simply a result of their distribution by occupational class; rather, with the exception of those in professional and managerial positions, it was evident within each occupational class.

But what had been the pattern of change over time? Had the trend been towards growing polarization between men's and women's skill levels, as some have suggested, or has there been convergence? If one turns to comparison over time, there is substantial evidence that the gender gap for skill is being closed. The same trend emerged on each of the indicators of skill. The signs are that the process of convergence has occurred through cohort replacement. It was notable that the younger the age group, the smaller the skill gap. Indeed, in the youngest age group (those between 20 and 25) the gender gap had reversed: it was now women rather than men who were in the more highly qualified jobs. This parallels the increasing superiority of girls' educational attainment over the same decade.

Once more there was no evidence that this reflected any growth of differentiation between different types of women's work. It has been suggested that, while more highly qualified women in full-time work may have been able to improve their position, this has been counterbalanced by a deterioration in the work situation of those in less skilled positions, especially those in part-time work. It was certainly the case that women in part-time work scored lower on all of the skill indicators than other women and this remained true even if one took account of occupational class and age. However, taking the trend over time, the evidence indicates that the 'skill gap' for part-timers has narrowed *even more* than for other women. Indeed, much of the relative improvement in the skill position of women over the decade is attributable to the changing position of part-timers, who had been increasingly recruited into intermediate rather than non-skilled class positions.

But while women's skill position clearly improved, this was not the case with respect to the decision-making discretion they were given in the job. For men, the rise in levels of skill had been accompanied by greater responsibility on the job. But comparisons over the decade showed no relative improvement in women's task discretion. However, in this respect, there were variations by occupational class. Among women in professional and managerial jobs, there was a narrowing of the gap between men and women, whereas this was not the case in other class positions. This provides some support for the view that the qualification lever has been particularly important in improving women's work status in higher occupations. The discrepancy between the trends in skill and discretion was particularly sharp among women in part-time work. Although part-timers had seen a marked improvement in their skill position, there was even some evidence of a decline in their task discretion. The difference in men's and women's experiences of responsibility on the job was also evident with respect to new technology. New technology had the same effect for men and women in enhancing skill levels, but it was only for men that it led to an increase in the scope for taking decisions on the job. The evidence converges to suggest that employers have continued to adopt gender-specific organizational policies that have operated to women's disadvantage.

However, there was one major respect in which women appear to have been at a relative advantage to men. Whereas men's employment stability has declined sharply over the decades, women's employment has become more stable. Women have experienced an increase in their vulnerability to unemployment, but this was less marked than for men. In terms of the continuity of their work careers, it was overshadowed by the decline in the time they spent out of the labour market and by the increased use of maternity leave. Moreover, for women there has been a rise in the proportion with long-term relationships with particular employers, whereas for men there has been a decline. The stability of women's employment position was particularly brought out in the examination of part-time work. Even though this type of employment had much poorer legal protection than full-time work, in practice employment security appeared to be just as great. The fact that women enjoyed greater protection from the sharp deterioration of the labour market in the 1980s and early 1990s must be related in part to the high degree of gender segregation of the occupational structure. Women's work was heavily concentrated in the expanding service sector and they benefited from a greater availability of job opportunities.

Overall, the pattern suggests that the decade saw a much deeper degree of integration of women into the employment system. Their commitment to employment became indistinguishable from that of men, there was marked convergence in skill levels, and they experienced higher levels of employment stability. These patterns were not confined to a particular sector of women's work, but appear to have been very wide-ranging. The main respect in which there was no evidence of improvement was that of responsibility on the job. While employers have made increasing use of women's skills, they have been reluctant to extend to them the level of trust in decision-making accorded to male employees.

There was, moreover, a price that women paid for their increased integration into employment. They were more likely than men to have suffered from work strain in the sense of mental and physical fatigue. This may have reflected the increased demands on them in work or the problems of reconciling these work demands with their continued prime responsibility for child-rearing and domestic work. While they had a similar level of organizational commitment to men, they were more likely to be absent from work. It was, moreover, notable that work strain had a much stronger relationship to performance, absence, and leaving intentions for women than for men. All the signs point to the fact that the change in women's employment position has substantially increased the pressures they face and that there remain major difficulties in satisfactorily reconciling the demands of family and employment.

[. . .]

Towards a new model of employment?

Finally, what are the implications of the different elements of our analysis for the broader picture of change in work and employment relations? A number of analysts have argued that the present era has been witnessing a profound change in the nature of work and the employment relationship, representing a rupture from the 'Taylorist' or 'Fordist' models that dominated the immediate post-war decades. The new era would be one in which a reskilled workforce would experience more satisfying work, higher levels of task discretion, greater autonomy from managerial control, higher levels of employee participation, and relatively secure employment. There would be an effective convergence on the type of employment relationship that has characterized the professional.

Our research has certainly confirmed that the decade has seen major changes in the nature of work in Britain and a marked restructuring of employment relationships. However, [. . .] the evidence for a major change in the nature of employment relationships was much less convincing. The first area in which our evidence conflicts sharply with these 'optimistic' scenarios of change is with respect to the organizational control of work performance. As part of their vision of the emancipation of work, they posit that a key trend is a shift from 'control' to 'commitment' as the underlying mechanism for ensuring high levels of work performance. Our evidence indicates that this provides a far too simple, and ultimately a misleading, description of the processes that have been occurring. Certainly, there is evidence that management has been developing new policies for regulating the employment relationship, which in part have the purpose of making employees more committed to their organizations. However, these were also systems designed to achieve more effective control of work performance, in a situation in which work processes had become more skilled, more complex, and less transparent. Managerial control of work performance had become more sophisticated, but control and its effects remained fundamental aspects of employee experience. Further, contrary to the assumptions of those who argue for a qualitative change in relationships, there was no evidence of an increase in the participation of employees in organizational decision-making. Rather it has been seen that the effective level of participation may have declined over the decade.

Taking the overall picture, the striking fact remained the low level of commitment of employees to their organizations.

[. . .]

Finally, despite the marked rise in skill levels and improvements in the quality of work, there persisted major differences in experiences between sectors of the workforce. Our evidence did not support some versions of the polarization thesis. For instance, while there were major differences in the employment conditions of 'regular' and 'non-standard' workers, there was no evidence that these grew greater over the decade and in some respects differences diminished. There was also no evidence of an overall sharpening of gender inequalities in employment. Rather it was a decade that saw a considerable enhancement of women's integration into the workforce, although with persisting gender differences in task discretion and material rewards.

However, the experiences of the workforce remained deeply divided along class lines. It was those in higher and intermediate class positions who primarily benefited from the positive changes to the quality of employment. They were much more likely to have experienced upskilling and hence more intrinsically interesting work. They certainly paid a price for this in terms of increased work effort and work strain. But the principal costs of change, namely the severe distress linked to unemployment, fell on the manual workers. The employment structure, then, continued to generate fundamental differences in people's life chances.

While it appears correct, then, that 'Taylorist' conceptions of work (to the extent that they prevailed historically) are now in the process of being superseded and that employers are placing a new emphasis on raising the skill levels of the workforce, the changes that have been taking place in the employment relationship are much less dramatic. The structures of control of work performance are being modified, but control remains pervasive and possibly more intense in the pressures it brings to bear on work effort. Far from converging on a 'professional' model of the employment relationship, the terms of employment remained fundamentally differentiated by class.

7

The Persistence of Class Inequalities

John Westergaard

Key words

Class inequality, inequality of income and wealth, social class, gender and class, decline of class, consumption cleavages, cross-class marriage

This extract, from a series of lectures by Westergaard, argues against 'revisionist' theories which contend that class has lost much of its social, political and socio-logical importance. Westergaard provides evidence of increasing inequalities of income and wealth between 1979 and 1991 and suggests that the patterns can be accounted for in terms of class, much as they could throughout the previous fifty years. He contests accounts which maintain that other types of division – age, household type, gender or consumption pattern – have replaced class position as the principal axis of material inequality. In parts of his paper not reprinted here, he insists that while there may have been a decline of political activity explicitly revolving around class, this is not the consequence of reduction in class inequal-ities of income, opportunity or power.

[. . .]

A longer version of the argument in this chapter appeared as Part III of John Westergaard, *Who Gets What?* (Polity, 1995).

I. Class structure in the 1980s and '90s: the facts of widening inequality

Theme

This chapter is about a puzzle. [. . .] The *facts* about class – in Britain and a number of other western countries – show that inequality has widened quite dramatically since about 1980. But, over just this same period, fashionable *theories* and influential *ideologies* have appeared to say almost the opposite. While rich and poor have in fact grown further apart, predominant ideology has set out to dismiss this; and both predominant ideology and leading social theory have come to argue that it does not matter anyway. Whatever the facts of class inequality, so it is now fashionable to argue, such facts do not matter much because class itself does not matter much any longer. If we are to believe the commentators, the politicians and the academic theorists who have set this tone in current debate, then class inequality has lost social force; it has lost moral force; it has lost political force.

[. . .] I shall try to do three things. First, I want to challenge these class-denying theories and ideologies, by summarising the firm facts which weigh against them. Second, I want to untangle the false assumptions which go into those theories and which have helped, as I see it, to blind theory to fact. Third and last, I want to consider some of the social reasons and forces behind today's class-denying ideologies.

[. . .]

The concept of class

I need to make a preliminary comment about what I shall mean by 'class.' I take the term for my purposes here to signify a set of social divisions that arise from a society's economic organisation. People, then, may be said to be in different classes in so far as they occupy – and in so far as they generally continue to occupy – distinct and unequal places in that economic organisation. And this in turn means places in the orders *both* of production *and* of distribution. [. . .]

In my conception, then, class structure is first of all a matter of people's circumstances in life as set by their unequal places in the economic order. In that sense, so I shall show, class structure has recently hardened in Britain. Thereafter – but only thereafter – comes the question of whether, and how, this hardening of class-as-*category* may translate into sharper political or quasi-political *group* divisions. It will be part of my argument that fashionable class-denying theory and ideology commits two errors, among others. It blurs the distinction between the two issues of economic category-existence and of political group-formation. And it naïvely infers, from new complexities of political group formation, an erosion of economic-categorical class which is, quite plainly, contrary to fact.

The historical background

In order to show just how contrary to fact this inference is, let me start with a short sketch of the history of class inequality in Britain: before the changes from the 1980s, and back to the 1940s. I take the 1940s to begin with, because that decade was something of a turning point. World War II and its end brought a new socio-political settlement, in Britain as in many other countries. Under first a coalition government, and then a Labour government which at the time met only limited resistance of principle from the Conservative opposition, policy was directed to 'social reconstruction.' This meant two things especially. One was Keynesian-guided public management of the economy, to help growth and to keep both business profits *and* labour employment high. The other was extensive reform of public welfare provision, which was intended to guarantee everybody a basic low-minimum income, even if unemployed, sick or retired; to give all children free schooling to the best level of their individual abilities, and help towards higher education for the most able; and, most radically perhaps, to make medical care a free public service for all citizens. Some bits and pieces were added to the reform package in the next three decades; a few were taken away; and, from around 1960 especially, governments of both main parties came on the whole to take a more active part in steering the economy, by way of attempted 'corporatist' cooperation with business and trade-union leaders, in the hope of sustaining economic growth while holding back price and wage inflation. As in other countries, the ups-and-downs in these three-cornered relationships between state, capital and labour made for tensions of class structure, and for disputes over shares in the national economic cake. But in Britain, at least, tripartite corporatism made for no significant and lasting new change; and the main features of the 'class compromise' of the 1940s stayed in place until the 1970s.

This was evident in the effects on patterns of class inequality. Those effects were two-fold. One effect came at the start, in the 1940s. This was to change the pre-war shape of things to some new advantage for ordinary workers, for the poor, and for trade unions. Organised labour gained new muscle in the labour market, and more voice in public affairs. Extreme poverty became rarer – and also less visible – than before the war. Inequalities of real income between classes, and between different levels within classes, became smaller. But the second point about the effects is that this change of balance came only once: it did not prove a continuing trend. [. . .] Once then set in a new and more moderate shape than before the war, class inequalities of 'category' in life circumstances showed no further significant compression over the 1950s, '60s and '70s. (See in general Westergaard and Resler, 1975.) Ownership of private wealth was still highly concentrated in the mid-'70s, for example, with just 5% of the adult population holding nearly 40% of the full total, and very much more of personally-owned shares in business capital. Inequalities of real income overall, and between different class- and occupational-groups, stayed fairly steady in relative terms over these three decades; and taxation by itself did little to change the pattern, mainly because progressive income tax was countered by regressive tax in less direct forms (Westergaard and Resler, 1975, Part 2). Welfare benefits did boost real incomes proportionately more for the poor than for the rich; but studies in 'rediscovery of poverty' from the 1960s on showed many people still living on the margins of, or even below, the officially guaranteed minimum level (Townsend, 1979). And the reforms of educational provision – first in the 1940s, with a second set in the 1960s – proved, against all these continuing inequalities, to have little force to reduce class disparities of individual opportunity (Halsey et al., 1980; Goldthorpe, 1987). Even differences in the risks of death between people of different classes stayed broadly constant in relative terms (Townsend and Davidson, ed., 1982).

The word '*relative*' here is important. These thirty years or so were years, generally, of economic growth. So the very continuity of pattern to the class structure, after the shift in the 1940s, meant that most people had some share in this growth: most people, at all levels, found their conditions and chances in life improving in *absolute* terms, at much the same rates across the structure of class. It is on this count especially that things have changed, and the class structure has hardened, since about 1980. [. . .] In the course of the last 10–15 years, in summary, the pattern has shifted from constancy of inequality in a context of broadly shared rise in living standards, to widened inequality in a context of economic growth now far more uneven both in pace and in distribution of its benefits.

The shift from about 1980: causes

I need to say just a little at this point about the causes of this dramatic change. There are two sets of immediate causes: economic on the one hand, and political on the other. The first set has involved a series of shifts in economic structure, world-wide and increasingly visible since the mid-1970s. Growth has become more uneven, both over time and across the globe. The older 'imperial' capitalist economies of the west have faced increasing challenge from Japanese, and now also from other East-to-South East Asian, business enterprise. Changes have accelerated in the patterns of division in production, and in markets for finance and services, for commodities and labour. Developments in the transnational organisation of capital have continued to outstrip, by far, the still largely nation-bound organisation of political processes and collective labour defences. In one form of summary: if Kondratiev's analysis from 1925 (see Tylecote, 1992) offers any guide, much of the world moved into the downward phase of a long-term wave from the mid- or late-1970s; and recovery is still uncertain.

For many and complex reasons, the British economy has been particularly exposed to risk from all this. So reactions in British politics and policy have shown a distinctively sharp edge of their own, though there are many parallels to draw with developments in other western countries. It is, of course, shifts of politics and policy that make up the second – and by far the most direct – set of causes. Those shifts were marked especially (though not only) by the British general election of 1979, when a government led from the radical-right flank of the Conservative Party came to office – and has stayed in office, even after a fourth election in 1992, and after Mrs Thatcher's replacement by Mr Major as Prime Minister before then. That is why my title for these lectures sets 1979 as a watershed year. And it was a watershed because, for the first time in some 35 years, there was now a government seriously and openly committed to challenging the socio-political settlement of the 1940s – to taking apart the 'class compromise' associated with postwar social reconstruction.

[. . .]

The *effects* of the change for class structure itself proved stark. The policies instrumental to those effects were of two kinds, to summarise simply. On the one hand, policy since 1979 has been directed to widening the scope for private business initiative in freed markets. The main means to this have included: legal curbs on trade union power; thinning out previous measures for protection of low-paid labour; deregulation in other forms; privatisation of once-public enterprises; reductions in direct taxation to foster initiative; and a general reliance on market competition for growth and for industrial discipline. On the other hand, and in parallel, radical-right policy has sought to hold back public expenditure – so in particular to trim down public welfare provision (though, significantly, *not* to dismantle it wholesale); and to encourage use instead of private provision – hence consumer-choice according to purse – in such fields especially as housing and retirement pensions, to a degree also in medical care.

Testing the effects on class structure

It should be no surprise that the effects have been dramatic for class structure – that is, I mean here again, to sharpen the pattern of class-as-category in respect of the inequalities in people's economic circumstances of life. This *should* be no surprise, because policy was now deliberately aimed to increase economic inequality. True enough, this has been an instrumental aim rather than an end-in-itself. The ultimate ends of the shift in policy have been to promote long-term economic growth; and to extend individual choice and personal responsibility. But new policy has been explicit in seeing increased disparity of individual outcomes – increased disparity of earnings, profits, pensions, real incomes overall – as a necessary means to those ends. [. . .]

I have first to test the arguments against the facts. The first test, obviously, concerns what has happened to the *distribution of real incomes*. Let me start here with earnings from employment; and I take wages and salaries from full-time employment, because the figures for that are comprehensive. [. . .] They show that, over the ten years from 1980 to 1990, earnings among the top-tenth of white-collar employees rose in real terms by about 40%. Increases were proportionately smaller for nearly every step down the pay-ladder: for manual as well as non-manual employees, for women as well as men. Even the best-paid tenth of blue-collar workers saw their real wages rise at only about half the top white-collar rate. And against the latter 40% or so increase, the blue-collar median wage rose by little more than 10% over the full ten years; while the poorest-paid tenth among blue-collar men gained hardly anything in real terms. These are plainly divisions by class in a very familiar sense; and the class gaps have widened right across the range.

Let me take next the distribution of gains and losses from changes in taxation together with changes in public welfare benefits. A comprehensive estimate for much the same period, here 1979 to 1989, shows *some* net gains for most households. [. . .] But it shows *no* gains for many of those households with only basic state pensions or unemployment benefit to live on; and these, of course, are people who were generally at low levels of the labour market when, earlier, they did have work. By contrast, of the aggregate net gain from changes in tax-and-public welfare over the ten years, nearly half the total (46%) went to just the richest tenth of all households. Most of the rest went to those in the next few deciles down. And the entire 60% of households from above 'middle income' to the very poorest got, between them all, only a 20% share in this distribution of the proceeds from re-gearing of the public money system. One-fifth only to the poor and middling three-fifths together, little short of half to the one-in-ten best-off – this, or something like it, is a recurrent pattern of experience in the 1980s.

Now put all this, and also property-incomes, together to get a picture of what has happened to shares in real income from *all* sources. [. . .] During the 1980s, real incomes rose for the richest 20% of households by about 40%. But they rose much less for others: by only 10%, at best, even for many 'middle-income' households (the sixth decile down). And the poorest 10–20% of households either gained still less, or their real incomes actually dropped below the levels of the late 1970s. In summary, two facts stand out. *First*, there has been a sharp new polarisation of incomes. Calculated after tax, the share of the poorest one-in-five of households in all income fell from 10% in the late 1970s to 7% in the late 1980s. The share of the richest one-in-five grew from 37% to 44%: now over six times the share of the poorest, and this after adjustment for differences in household composition. [. . .] But *second*, this did not mean that only the poorest lost out. At least right up to 'middle incomes', as I have shown, gains in real income were small [. . .]; and shares in the total of real income fell [. . .]. Substantial growth of affluence has been limited to people at or near the top. [. . .]

It is perhaps not surprising, then, that there has been evidence also of some widening of relative class differences in death rates over the period (Whitehead, 1987). But for my second main test, let me turn briefly to the *distribution of property*. Here, you might have expected some trend the other way. For government policy *has* favoured wider ownership of housing, and some wider ownership of shares in business through sale of previously public enterprises. But no: overall, stakes in private property of all kinds have in fact become more concentrated; not less. [. . .] So, for example, the richest 5% of the adult population owned 36% of all personal marketable wealth at the beginning of the 1980s; at the end of the '80s, their share was up to 38%; and excluding the value of housing their share rose from 45% (at the turning point of a previous downward trend) to 53% by 1989. Correspondingly, the tiny fraction of property owned by the poorest half of the population dwindled to little above vanishing point.

My third test concerns *individual opportunities in life: social mobility* by another name. The notion of free opportunity for all, according to personal talent and initiative, has certainly figured high among the aims proclaimed by radical-right government. And there have been some changes that could seem to point in that direction. The Conservative Party's leadership itself is now drawn from lower down the social scale than before: with 'petty bourgeois' family backgrounds, Mrs Thatcher and Mr Major are both examples of this. And it may be that new recruits to some parts of the City of London's high money-spinning financial business have been rather more mixed of social origin recently than before, though there are no statistics about this. But that, at most, is as far as it goes. Comprehensive studies of social mobility across the population as a whole, continued into the 1980s, have as yet shown no significant reduction of those relative inequalities of opportunity between classes which, for long, have sat side-by-side with a good deal of movement in life, and movement from one generation to the next. (See especially Goldthorpe, 1987.) And in one very important sense, individual opportunities have become drastically more restricted, especially towards the lower end of the class structure. Unemployment, of course, has been much higher in the 1980s-to-'90s than before. [. . .] The unemployed, and the long-term unemployed especially, come of course in disproportionate numbers from routine-grade and lower-paid jobs. So it is predominantly people in the downward reaches of the class structure who, far from gaining opportunities, have very tangibly lost them. [. . .]

II. Controversies about the social salience of class: revisionist theories

[. . .]

Demographic division

In summary, revisionist theory says that class division is fast losing salience because other divisions now over-ride it; or because class now divides only an isolated minority of poor people from a mass majority of affluent people. The two kinds of argument overlap and intertwine. But it will be simplest if I take the first kind first; and if I start there with arguments that postulate new divisions which may, loosely, be described as 'demographic' in kind (see especially Pahl, 1989).

In one form, this sort of argument says that, for economic inequality, division by age is now more important than division by class. In particular, so it is said here, old people make up a large proportion of the poor. The latter point is true: over 40% of the poorest one-in-five households in Britain, for example, comprise people retired from work (*Social Trends 1992*). But the *conclusion* does not follow. For one thing, from the 1980s on (the crucial period for the purpose of the argument), the relative share of old people in poverty has actually fallen, not risen. This is, quite simply, because the new harsh labour market has swollen the aggregate numbers of unemployed and low-paid employed people who are now poor. But more importantly, old age by itself does not bring poverty anyway: it does so only in circumstances which are set by class structure. The people who risk being poor when they are old are those, by and large, who have retired from *wage-earning jobs* – in Britain, often even from skilled jobs in blue-collar work, or from white-collar jobs in routine grades – because these jobs have given them few or no pension rights on top of the low minimum they get from the state. By contrast, people who retire from *salaried careers* get generous pensions; and their pensions, of course, are the higher, the nearer their careers came to the top of the occupational hierarchy. Pension arrangements remain, in fact, strongly class-divided. [. . .] Class inequality *after* working life matches – even tends to exceed – class inequality *during* working life.

[. . .]

There is [. . .] another line to this sort of argument. That line notes the steep rise in employment of married women, which has continued now for thirty years or more –

not least in Britain, where nearly three in every four wives of working age are in the labour market today. [. . .] The argument then goes on to assert that inequalities of income between families come now, not so much from the 'class' of work that earning family-members have, as from the effective number of earners in the family. It is especially decisive, so the argument here runs, whether the wife works full-time; or she works only part-time (as do about one half of all working wives in Britain); or she has no paid work at all. And, so the argument concludes, personal or family 'strategies' in life are coming to displace class in determining household income. (See Pahl, 1984; and especially Pahl, 1989.)

Again, however, the conclusion does not fit with the factual evidence. Of course, the number of earners does affect family income; but the result, if anything, is to strengthen the impact of class rather than to weaken it. (See Bonney, 1988a and b; also Dex, 1985.) *First*, to take the argument historically, paid employment among married women has increased more in the 'middle and upper' classes than in the working class. This is mainly because many working-class wives had some kind of paid work already earlier – at a time when most middle- and upper-class families still upheld the convention that wives ought to stay at home (cf. Westergaard and Resler, 1975, part 2, chapter 6). So new 'dual earning' has boosted middle- and upper-class household incomes more, over time, than it has boosted working-class incomes. *Second*, the result in fact is that – unlike in the past – dual earning is now rather more common among married couples in the middle and upper strata than among working-class couples. The differences are not very great; but their effect, once again, is to widen class disparities rather than to narrow them.

[. . .]

Gender division

To talk about women's employment is, of course, to begin to talk about the larger issue of inequality by gender. I now need to address this issue more directly. For it has been a major line of revisionist theory to postulate that class division is much less salient now, because gender division cuts across it. Inequality between the sexes is not new, of course. But, so the new revisionism says, gender inequality is the more visible and potent now, when women have increasingly challenged it; and when, especially, the great majority even of married women in Britain are in the labour market for most of their working-age lives – and there, all the more visibly, are exposed to practices and conventions that disadvantage women vis à vis men at all levels of the labour market. (For a symposium on the general issue of gender inequality in relation to class inequality, see Crompton and Mann, eds., 1986.)

The broad facts about women's disadvantages vis à vis men are not in dispute for my purposes here. One sign of them is that women, generally, have lower real and effective incomes than men. This reflects the multiple handicaps they suffer both in the labour market and outside it: handicaps from continuing job- and pay-restrictions, despite counter-legislation; and from continuing conventional definitions of women's roles as private and domestic par excellence, despite widening challenge. It also, perhaps curiously, reflects one *ad*vantage which women have over men. Women continue to die later. So, more women than men survive into old age; and in the working class, as I said before, old age continues to carry a high risk of poverty from lack of adequate pensions. But just as class inequality here interacts with gender inequality, so it does more widely. Division by gender is certainly a potent dimension of inequality. It is conceptually distinct from division by class, and certainly not confined to capitalist societies. But in practice the two twine together, to reinforce the effects of class rather than to go against them.

[. . .] Once in the labour market, women confront just the same inequalities of class as do men. Disparities of pay and conditions of work are, by and large, as sharp among earning women as among earning men, according to the 'class' of work done. Opportunities for advancement, and the risks of demotion, differ at least as much among women as among men, according to the individual's level of work and point of origin in the class structure. The difference is that, at every level, women are usually worse off than their male counterparts. Level for level of work, their pay tends to be poorer; their pensions, if any, tend to be much lower; their opportunities for careers are much more restricted; their confinement to routine-grade work, and their risks of demotion, are much greater; and they are far more liable than men to have part-time work only. [. . .] Yet none of this involves any sort of suspension of the force of class structure on economic life. The class structure of the labour market for women parallels that for men. It is in a sense the same structure except – crucially – that women are pressed into its routine-grade slots a good deal more than are men.

To sum up, you could put the point of logic I draw from these facts like this. When women have paid work, as most now do in Britain, they mostly find jobs well below the upper rungs of the class structure of work: still more so than do men. That signifies a continuing, though now somewhat easing, subordination of women to men. But it equally signifies a continuing structure of class. I have still, however, to put in one last link in my chain of argument. You may ask: what if the work that married women do should, in class terms, be unconnected with their husbands' work – or even tend to 'compensate' for it? What if wives in career posts are quite often married to men in blue-collar jobs; or vice versa? Then, surely, class inequalities would tend to even out, when measured by family circumstances?

The answer is quite simple: this can happen; but it happens only quite rarely. Thus, some two in every three wives who have 'service class' work are married to men who themselves are professionals, managers or the like; hardly any have blue-collar husbands. [. . .] Marriage between partners in wholly contrasting types of work – service versus core working class – is rare; and, in statistical terms, the employment class of wives correlates well with that of their husbands. (For the main data summarised here, see Goldthorpe, 1987; and Marshall et al., 1988; cf. also McRae, 1986.) There is, then, no general breach of class division on this score. Once again, inequality by gender interacts with inequality by class: the one has not displaced the other.

Other divisions

Revisionist theory points also to other divisions which are often now said to override class. About *ethnic* division – division by skin colour especially – I can be very brief here. People of black and brown skin are indeed distinctly handicapped in Britain today: there are new – and nasty – lines of racial inequality. But, to cut a long story short, those lines have in no way supplanted the lines of class inequality. For one thing, despite common discrimination against them, the 'coloured minorities' in Britain still stretch across too many occupations to constitute a single economic category. They are also culturally divided; and black-skinned people of Caribbean origin are more concentrated in lower-grade positions than brown-skinned people of South Asian and East African origin. For another thing, their numbers – some 5% of the total population – are in any case too few to give the British class structure that prominent imprint of ethnic division which is distinctive, say, of American, let alone of South African, class structure. (There is a large literature on this subject. For one cogent analysis, see e.g. Solomos, 1989.)

But revisionists have postulated yet a further kind of division which, they claim, increasingly puts old-style class division out of joint. This is division, so to speak, by patterns of consumption. The argument here is that, from the 1980s onwards, the real contrast in life circumstances now comes between a majority of people who have enough private resources to give them fair power over their own lives; and, on the other hand, a minority of people who lack such private resources, and instead have to depend on generally poor public provision. Revisionist theory in this manner has pointed, in part, to the growth of private pension schemes; of private health insurance on top of national health provision; of private motor-car ownership. But they have pointed particularly to the fast growth of *private ownership of housing*. (See especially Saunders, 1990; also Saunders and Harris, 1990; and Dunleavy and Husbands, 1985.)

Indeed, private ownership of housing spread still faster in the 1980s than before. Today in Britain, some two in every three households either fully own their own homes or are buying them on long loans; and the figure is above 40% even among unskilled blue-collar workers [. . .]. Yet the conclusion does not follow, in revisionist manner, that old-style class division is giving way to division between a majority of home-owners and a minority of tenants (mainly tenants in public housing). After all, relatively poor home-owners own relatively poor and low-price homes. They receive less tax-relief from the state to help them pay for their homes in consequence [. . .]. They are at higher risk of losing their homes when, as in recession, they cannot keep up the payments. In general, 'consumer power' from private resources remains highly unequal power, when overall private resources – that is to say, real incomes – remain highly unequal, and have grown more unequal over the years since about 1980. Consumer power, after all, is money power: quite simply, the rich and the comfortably off have much more of it than ordinary wage earners, let alone the poor who are out of wage work. Ownership of housing confers no general immunity from those wider disparities of 'consumer power'; and these disparities in turn continue, as before, to come from the structure of economic class. (For a study whose conclusions go against equation of home ownership with a postulated new consumer sovereignty, see Forest et al., 1990.)

[. . .]

References and sources

BAGGULEY, P. and MANN, K., 1992. 'Idle thieving bastards: scholarly representations of the "underclass." ' *Work, Employment and Society*, vol. 6.

BAUMAN, Z., 1982. *Memories of Class*. London, Routledge & Kegan Paul.

BONNEY, N., 1988(a). 'Gender, household and social class.' *British Journal of Sociology*, March.

—— 1988(b). 'Dual earning couples.' *Work, Employment and Society*, March.

CROMPTON, R. and GUBBAY, J., 1977. *Economy and Class Structure*. London, Macmillan.

—— and MANN, M., ed., 1986. *Gender and Stratification*, Cambridge, Polity Press. (On some of these issues, see also the debate in *Sociology*, vols. 17–19, November 1983–May 1985.)

DEPARTMENT OF SOCIAL SECURITY, 1990. *Households below Average Income*. London, Her Majesty's Stationery Office.

DEX, S., 1985. *The Sexual Division of Work*. Brighton, Harvester Press.

DUNLEAVY, P. and HUSBANDS, C.T., 1985. *British Democracy at the Crossroads*. London, Allen & Unwin.

ERIKSON, R. and GOLDTHORPE, J.H., 1992. *The Constant Flux*. Oxford, Clarendon Press.

FIELD, F., 1989. *Losing Out: the Emergence of Britain's Underclass*. Oxford, Blackwell.

FOREST, R., MURIE, A. and WILLIAMS, P., 1990. *Home Ownership, Differentiation and Fragmentation*. London, Unwin Hyman.

GALLIE, D., 1988. 'Employment, unemployment and social stratification'; in Gallie, D., ed. *Employment in Britain*. Oxford, Blackwell.

GAMBLE, A., 1979. 'The free economy and the strong state.' *The Socialist Register* (ed. R. Miliband and J. Saville). London, Merlin Press.

GOLDTHORPE, J.H., 1987. *Social Mobility and Class Structure in Modern Britain*. Oxford, Clarendon Press. (2nd edition, with C. Payne. 1st edition published 1980, with C. Llewellyn and C. Payne.)

—— LOCKWOOD, D., BECHHOFER, F. and PLATT, J., 1968–69. *The Affluent Worker* (three volumes). Cambridge, Cambridge University Press.

—— and MARSHALL, G., 1992. 'The promising future of class analysis.' *Sociology*, February.

HALSEY, A.H., HEATH, A.F. and RIDGE, J.M., 1980. *Origins and Destinations*. Oxford: Clarendon Press.

HALSEY, A.H., 1987. 'Social trends since World War II.' *Social Trends*, no. 17 (Government Statistical Service).

ed. 1989. 'Special issue: sociology in Britain,' *British Journal of Sociology*, September.

—— HEATH, A.F. and RIDGE, J.M., 1980. *Origins and Destinations*. Oxford, Clarendon Press.

HEATH, A.F. and McMAHON, D., 1991. 'Consensus and dissensus'; in *British Social Attitudes: the 8th Report* (ed. R. Jowell et al.). London, Social and Community Planning Research.

—— JOWELL, R. and CURTICE, J., 1985. *How Britain Votes*. Oxford, Pergamon Press.

JENKINS, S.P., 1991. 'Living standards and income inequality in the 1970s and 1980s.' *Fiscal Studies*, vol. 12.

JOHNSON, P. and STARK, G., 1989. *Taxation and Social Security 1979–89*. London, Institute of Fiscal Studies.

McRAE, S., 1986. *Cross-Class Families*. Oxford, Oxford University Press.

MANN, K., 1992. *The Making of an English 'Underclass'?* Buckingham, Open University Press.

MARSHALL, G., ROSE, D., NEWBY, H. and VOGLER, C., 1988. *Social Class in Modern Britain*. London, Unwin Hyman. (See also debate in *Sociology*, May 1990.)

MURRAY, C., 1990. *The Emerging British Underclass*. London, Institute of Economic Affairs. (This includes several papers critical of Murray's thesis: see especially the critique by A.C. Walker.)

PAHL, R.E., 1984. *Divisions of Labour*. Oxford, Blackwell.

—— 1989. 'Is the emperor naked?' *International Journal of Urban and Regional Research*, December.

SAUNDERS, P., 1990. *A Nation of Home Owners*. London, Unwin Hyman.

—— and HARRIS, C., 1990. 'Privatisation and the consumer.' *Sociology*. February.

SCOTT, J.P., 1982. *The Upper Classes: Property and Privilege in Britain*. London, Macmillan.

—— 1986. *Capitalist Property and Financial Power*. Brighton, Wheatsheaf.

SOLOMOS, J., 1989. *Race and Racism in Contemporary Britain*, London, Macmillan.

TAYLOR-GOOBY, 1991. 'Attachment to the welfare state'; in *British Social Attitudes: the 8th Report* (ed. R. Jowell et al.). London, Social and Community Planning Research.

TOWNSEND, P., 1979. *Poverty in the United Kingdom*. Harmondsworth, Penguin Books.

—— 1990. 'Underclass and overclass: the widening gulf . . .'; in Payne, G. and Cross, M., ed. *Sociology in Action*. London, Macmillan.

—— 1991. *The Poor are Poorer. . . .* Bristol, Department of Social Policy and Social Planning, Bristol University.

TOWNSEND, P. and DAVIDSON, N., ed., 1982. *Inequalities in Health*. Harmondsworth, Penguin Books. (This reprints, and adds an introduction to, the limited-circulation official report of a Department of Health and Social Security working party on 'Inequalities in Health,' submitted in 1980 to the Secretary of State by Sir Douglas Black as chair of the working party, Professor J.N. Morris, Dr C. Smith and Professor P. Townsend.)

TYLECOTE, A., 1992. *The Long Wave in the World Economy*. London, Routledge.

UNIVERSITY GRANTS COMMITTEE, 1989. *Report of the Review Committee on Sociology*. London, Universities Funding Council. (For a summary and commentary by two members of the review committee, see J.H. Westergaard and R.E. Pahl 'Looking backwards and forwards . . . ,' *British Journal of Sociology*, September 1989.)

WALKER, A.C., 1991. 'Poverty and the underclass'; in Haralambos, M., ed. *Developments in Sociology*, volume 7, Ormskirk, Causeway Press. (See also the note following Murray 1990, above.)

WESTERGAARD, J.H., 1992. 'About and beyond the "underclass".' (BSA Presidential Address), *Sociology*, November.

—— and RESLER, H., 1975. *Class in a Capitalist Society*. London, Heinemann. (Penguin Books, 1976.)

—— NOBLE, I. and WALKER, A.C., 1989. *After Redundancy*. Cambridge, Polity Press.

WHITEHEAD, M., 1987. *The Health Divide: Inequalities in Health in the 1980s*. London, Health Education Council.

See also the regular annual issues of *Social Trends* (Central Statistical Office, Government Statistical Service), London, Her Majesty's Stationery Office.

The Condition of the Contemporary Middle Classes

Mike Savage

Key words

Social class, middle classes, geographical mobility, social mobility, self-employment, occupational careers, political alignments

One of the most significant changes in the class structure in the past half-century has been the decline in the size of the working class and the growth of the middle class. This has been the basis for predictions about the diminishing importance of class for social and political practice. In the past most attention was focused on the conditions of the manual working class in the context of the political pressure for social reform that labour movements brought to bear. This led to comparative neglect of the middle class, despite its increasing social and cultural importance.

Savage considers the nature of contemporary middle-class work, culture and political orientations in the light of changes in the occupational structure. His is one of the clearest brief accounts of the anatomy of the British middle class. He argues that the old distinctions between blue-collar and white-collar work are no longer useful in understanding class divisions. He discusses different ways in which it is possible to map the boundaries of the middle class and considers the sociological implications. He then describes some key changes in the circumstances of different groups within the middle class, pointing in particular to the differences between managerial and professional workers.

Contemporary discussions of social class still tend to be couched within the theoretical frameworks laid down by Karl Marx and Max Weber in the late nineteenth and early twentieth centuries (see Scase 1992 and Edgell 1993 for recent examples). The world has, however, changed in significant ways since the days when they were writing. Perhaps most importantly, in the early twentieth century manual workers (in manu-

facturing and agriculture) formed the overwhelming majority of the working population, and it was therefore the character of the working class which held the attention
of sociologists and social commentators. Even down to the 1980s, much sociological
debate on social class has focused upon whether the working class has changed – think
of the discussion of the 'Affluent Worker' studies in the 1960s (Goldthorpe and Lockwood 1969), arguments about the way that consumption-sector cleavages were possibly dividing the working class (Saunders 1990) and, more recently, interest in whether
the working class is being divided into an underclass and a more prosperous group of
workers (e.g. Morris 1994).

However, as we approach the twenty-first century, the relevance of this focus is in
serious doubt. Since 1945, and especially in the past two decades, the number of people
employed in 'middle class' jobs has increased rapidly, so that any attempt to understand the social relations of modern Britain really cannot avoid seriously examining
the position and activities of the middle classes. It comes as something of a shock to
realise that there are now more university lecturers than coal miners! In 1991 29.4%
of those in the workforce worked in professions and management, a figure only mar-
ginally smaller than the 32.7% who worked as manual workers. If one were to include
the self-employed (10.7%) and the routine white-collar workers (27.2%) as part of
the middle class, we would have to conclude that the middle classes now comprise a
substantial majority of the employed population.

Thinking about the middle classes is therefore of fundamental importance for understanding contemporary social change, and in recent years a lively debate has taken
place on the significance of current trends for the way sociologists talk about social
class. Indeed, there is some suggestion that recent debates about the middle classes
have given a new lease of life to rather tired old debates about class (see notably the
papers in Butler and Savage 1995). In this article I shall point to some of the main
issues and findings from recent research.

Middle-class boundaries

Studies of the middle classes have always been bedeviled by the 'boundary problem'
(Abercrombie and Urry 1983), the problem of deciding which types of people can helpfully be seen as part of the middle class. In recent years a considerable amount of agreement has been reached on this tricky issue, however. Traditionally, the most common
way of differentiating the working classes from the middle classes was to claim that
the working class were manual workers, whilst the middle classes were non-manual
workers. This difference is occasionally referred to as the 'collar line', the distinction
between blue-collar (manual) and white-collar (non-manual) workers. Today, this
stress on the collar line has largely been discredited. It is generally agreed that many
routine white-collar workers (especially women) now have rather similar conditions
of work and remuneration to blue-collar workers, and cannot helpfully be seen as
being in a higher class.

The rise in employment in the service sector confuses the division between manual
and non-manual workers anyway, and it is possible to argue that many of the
most extreme forms of 'proletarianisation' – in the sense of poor wages, irregular

employment, and bad working conditions – are found amongst service workers. By the 1980s only 8% of British unskilled workers were employed in industry! Furthermore, it can be argued that many forms of supposedly 'working class' activity, such as trade union membership and industrial action, are now as strong, possibly stronger, amongst white-collar workers as they are amongst manual workers. In short, the idea of a 'collar line' being used to differentiate the middle from the working class has now been largely discredited.

The self-employed also pose interesting puzzles for thinking about the middle classes. Both Marx and Weber recognised the existence of the *'petit bourgeoisie'* as a distinct middle-class fraction, lying between workers on the one hand and large property owners on the other. Marx assumed that self-employed farmers, small business owners, small shopkeepers and so forth would increasingly be 'squeezed out' by the rise of large business. And indeed, for much of the twentieth century Marx's view seemed to be borne out, as the number of people working on their own account fell gradually, but steadily. However, there has been a remarkable turn-around in the past twenty years. Between 1971 and 1981 the numbers of self-employed bottomed out, at around 6.7% of those in the labour market; whilst in the years between 1981 and 1991 the numbers rose by a staggering 45%, to comprise over 10% of the workforce. The difficulty resides, however, in knowing what to make of this rise in numbers. Does it indicate a flourishing petty economy, and the expansion of opportunities for entrepreneurs? Or is there a bleaker portrait to be painted? Perhaps as workers have lost their jobs they have had to turn to self-employment as a last resort (possibly encouraged by Conservative government support of small business in the 1980s), with the result that this shift to self-employment masks the growth of marginal, insecure employment which can hardly be seen as middle class in any meaningful sense.

One way of considering which of these perspectives is correct is to see whether the self-employed tend to be a stable or unstable group. Do they continue in self-employment over a period of years, or do they tend to slip into more marginal forms of employment (or unemployment)? Recent research by Fielding (1995) examines what the self-employed in 1981 were doing ten years later in 1991 – and therefore allows us to consider whether self-employment was a temporary phase in a person's working life (see Table 1). Fielding shows that – rather against expectations – the majority of the self-employed in 1981 (67.2%, though a smaller proportion of women then men) who were still in the labour market in 1991 were still in self-employment. They therefore appear, on the whole, to comprise a relatively stable and secure part of the workforce. In fact this is a much higher figure than was found for the period 1971–81, where less than half the self-employed lasted the ten-year course (Savage et al. 1992). Around 12% of the self-employed had become unemployed by 1991, and a further 10% were working as manual workers. Putting these figures together suggests that, in general, the *petit bourgeoisie* are becoming a more secure, distinct and visible group in British society. This marks a very significant shift which reverses a long-term trend.

There is a further point to make here. In the past self-employment tended not to carry high status, and (with the exception of 'independent' professionals in legal or architectural practice and so on) most professional and managerial employees preferred to achieve rewards and standing by working for a large organisation. This seems to have changed, however. Considerable numbers of managers now seem to prefer to work for small firms or for themselves; and the proportion of managers moving

Table 1 │ **Social class transitions for men and women in England and Wales 1981–91**

A) MALES				Social class in 1991			
Social class in 1981	PRO	MAN	PB	PWC	PBC	UE	TLM
Professionals	63.45	18.63	4.01	4.04	6.56	3.31	100.00
Managers	13.91	54.16	11.58	7.41	8.12	4.82	100.00
Petit bourgeoisie	3.58	6.70	70.67	2.27	11.15	5.63	100.00
White collar	12.09	23.67	7.96	38.12	12.39	5.76	100.00
Blue collar	4.39	6.17	11.23	3.73	65.23	9.26	100.00
Unemployed	5.52	5.52	14.43	5.16	35.91	33.72	100.00
Education	13.90	8.30	6.08	16.50	35.90	19.32	100.00
Other	12.13	10.99	11.11	14.34	33.33	18.10	100.00

B) FEMALES				Social class in 1991			
Social class in 1981	PRO	MAN	PB	PWC	PBC	UE	TLM
Professionals	77.40	5.99	2.48	8.39	3.80	1.93	100.00
Managers	16.52	36.83	8.41	28.50	6.10	3.64	100.00
Petit bourgeoisie	7.03	7.51	48.41	24.38	10.33	2.34	100.00
White collar	7.24	9.65	4.32	62.30	12.54	3.95	100.00
Blue collar	4.55	3.18	3.35	22.66	60.00	6.26	100.00
Unemployed	11.78	5.68	4.70	35.78	24.98	17.07	100.00
Education	16.06	8.10	1.80	47.28	13.55	13.21	100.00
Other	11.39	5.31	7.21	44.81	25.60	5.69	100.00

Source: OPCS Longitudinal Study 1991 (Crown Copyright Reserved).

into self-employment rose considerably in the 1980s. Many areas of expanding self-employment were in 'glamorous' areas, such as consultancy work in financial services, or in 'hi-tech' industry. Some writers argue that many firms now prefer to contract services to outside consultants and agents rather than to carry them out in-house, with the result that the self-employed gain a further boost. Furthermore, it has become easier to have a 'business on the side', whilst continuing to be an employee (one survey reported in Savage et al. (1992) suggests that as many as one-third of managers in one firm had a side-business). In short, a group which had been regarded as recently as the 1970s as part of the 'traditional' *petit bourgeoisie*, a legacy of the past, seems to have found a new lease of life.

What does this mean for thinking about the size of the middle class? It seems sensible to see manual workers, the unemployed, and most routine white-collar workers as occupying largely working-class positions, which means that the majority of the population can still usefully be seen as working class (which comprises around 60% of the workforce). Nonetheless the middle classes employed in the professions, administration, management – and the self-employed – do now constitute a very sizeable proportion of the workforce. Let us now consider their sociological significance.

Thinking sociologically about the middle classes

Major issues of interpretation are posed by the changing positions of the professions and management – a group which accounts for nearly one-third of the workforce. The rise of people employed in these groups is striking. In 1971 10.2% of those in the labour market were employed in the professions; by 1991 this figure had risen to 15.2%. Comparable figures for managers indicate a rise from 7% to 11.3% over the same twenty-year period. What do these trends indicate for the shape of British society? Here a number of different theories have recently been advanced.

Perhaps the best-known account is the 'service-class' thesis, developed especially by John Goldthorpe (1982) and in a rather different way by Abercrombie and Urry (1983). Goldthorpe argued that professional, managerial and administrative workers form a distinctive social class, which separates them from all other social groups. He calls this class the 'service class' (or occasionally, and perhaps more helpfully, the 'salariat'). This term 'service class' can be confusing. It makes us think of workers in the 'service sector', such as catering. However, Goldthorpe uses a different definition which refers instead to workers who provide specialist 'services' (hence the title) to their employer. These services either involve providing specialist knowledge (in the case of professionals), or delegated authority (in the case of managers). In return for these specialist services these workers are granted special privileges, such as a high salary, job security, fringe benefits, and 'prospective rewards' – the potential for career development. Professionals and managers are relatively secure and privileged; and for this reason Goldthorpe argues that the service class will become a major conservative force in society as it seeks to defend and consolidate its own advantages. In short, the expansion of the 'service class' has helped bring about a new social group who can be expected to play a conservative role as bulwarks of the *status quo*, and the presence of this class will tend to damp down pressures for any fundamental social change.

In direct opposition to Goldthorpe's views is the work of some – mainly American – sociologists (notably Alvin Gouldner), who talk about the rise of a new class (occasionally called a 'professional-managerial class', or PMC) which stands outside traditional class divisions and is therefore able to sustain forms of social dissent and new ways of living. Gouldner (1979) argues that this 'new class', is able to generate a 'culture of critical discourse'. Other writers suggest that these new groups are bearers of 'post-materialist' values. Since they have 'solved' the problem of affluence, and no longer have to worry about such basic issues as feeding, clothing and housing themselves, their attention switches to other, more 'expressive', issues – such as ecology, personal wellbeing, better ways of living and relating – and so on. In short, the development of these professional and managerial groups is seen by Gouldner as a 'progressive' development, which augurs well for the future.

A third position is developed by Wright (1985), and Bourdieu (1984) and has been adopted by Savage et al. (1992) in their account of the middle classes in contemporary Britain. These writers argue that it is not helpful to talk about professionals and managers as a distinct class of their own, because there are in fact major divisions within their ranks. Perhaps the best known example of this view is Bourdieu's emphasis upon the differences between economic and cultural capital. Bourdieu stresses that some groups within the middle classes succeed by emphasising their cultural distinction and taste which, amongst other things, allows them to succeed in the education system and therefore gain qualifications to move into professional jobs. Other members of the middle classes (for instance, managers who work their way up from the shop floor), however, do not do well at school and succeed for other reasons.

Bourdieu emphasises the conflicts between the 'cultured' and the 'moneyed' groups which this can lead to. Savage et al. (1992) draw upon this framework to argue that in Britain there are major long-standing divisions between managers and professionals which, if anything, are becoming rather more distinct. Managers are becoming rather marginalised; whilst professionals have been able to defend their existing privileges and find new areas to deploy their expertise, by selling their services on the market. Savage et al. (1992) suggest growing tensions and conflicts within the middle classes as they struggle to improve their position.

Before evaluating these different views, it is noteworthy that none of them draws directly on the 'classical' class theory of either Marx or Weber. The pedigrees for each of these theories is hybrid. This does suggest that as the middle classes increase in size, so the sociological debates themselves shift. Let us now consider which of these theories offers the best way of understanding the contemporary middle classes.

How are the middle classes changing?

There is now a substantial body of research devoted to exploring various facets of middle-class life. Here I only have scope to deal with a few of the salient issues.

Traditionally both professionals and managers tend to have enjoyed predictable, secure careers in large bureaucracies. The idea of the organisational career refers to the way that these middle class employees could expect to work their way up a job ladder within a large firm or within a public organisation. Such employees often strongly identified with their employer, who in turn 'cocooned' their salaried workers with generous pension and fringe-benefit systems. However, the idea of predictable job movement in the course of one's career has radically changed in recent years. Professionals and managers alike are increasingly paid on the basis of their performance, and payment is also increasingly arranged on an individual basis and is subject to renegotiation.

A good example of these changes is in banking. Until the later 1980s bank managers were paid a salary which reflected their seniority in the bank and the size and importance of the branch or unit they were employed in. Salaries (for junior managers) were negotiated between unions and management, and contained an incremental component, which meant that they automatically rose each year. In the later 1980s the banks began to change this system. Managers' salaries were determined in part by whether they were able to achieve targets (for instance, a certain level of sales) which were set annually. Automatic increments, paid regardless of performance, were largely abandoned. A considerable number of managers, especially those over the age of 50, also lost their jobs during the recession of the early 1990s. Cases such as this are not unusual. Throughout much of the public sector, similar innovations – which question the security and privileges of senior staff – were introduced. Some local authorities, for instance, employed their chief executives on five-year renewable contracts.

These developments suggest that Goldthorpe's view of the 'service class' as characterised by 'prospective rewards', which stands above the rough-and-tumble of the labour market, is today misplaced. One might also suggest that an emphasis upon the way these groups have 'solved' their economic problems is also misleading. In fact, increasing levels of labour market insecurity may well have accentuated the struggle of middle-class employees to look after their own position!

This increasing instability means that professionals and managers now have more mobile and uncertain careers than hitherto. The significance of increasing levels of job mobility have been much debated in recent work. Goldthorpe (1982) has argued that job movement between professional and managerial positions indicates that the two types of worker are part of a common class. Savage et al. (1992) by contrast, emphasise that it is unlikely for professionals to become managers and *vice versa*, and that job insecurity has very different implications for the two groups.

Considerable evidence has now accumulated which suggests that the careers of managers have changed markedly. During the 1980s and 1990s many firms have cut management jobs (see Scase and Goffee 1989). Organisations have increasingly recruited managers from outside, rather than promote their own staff. Surveys of managers in private industry suggest that until the 1970s around 40% of managers had only ever worked for one firm. By the 1980s only between 10–20% of managers had worked for one firm. Fielding (1995) has shown that no less than 24% of managers in 1981 actually moved down the social ladder by 1991, indicating increasing proportions of instability. The comparable figures for professionals were much lower, at 14%. It has also shown that a significant number of managers have been able to move into professional employment (see Table 1). Table 1 also shows that substantial numbers of managers were downwardly mobile between 1981 and 1991. Over 20% of male managers in 1981 had moved to routine white-collar work, manual employment or unemployment by 1991. For women managers, the figure is an astonishing 38.2%. In short, it would appear that, although the managerial wing of the middle classes may have grown in size, it has become a rather insecure group. The professional middle class, by contrast, is rather more stable, with markedly lower rates of downward mobility for both men and (especially) women.

There is also evidence that professional and managerial groups have rather different cultural outlooks and political viewpoints, though much further research remains to be done here. One interesting example of fragmentation concerns the residential preferences of the middle classes. For much of the twentieth century the middle classes were an archetypically suburban class, and many aspects of middle-class identity were forged out of common residential patterns. From the 1960s social scientists began to detect that growing numbers of the middle classes were attracted to what has been called the 'rural idyll', as many professionals and managers have moved into the countryside. Indeed, one recent research project suggests that as many as two-thirds of migrants to selected rural areas are from the middle class. However, by contrast, there is also a contrary movement, whereby some parts of the middle classes have moved back to the cities – a process known as 'gentrification'. During the 1980s it became fashionable for members of the affluent middle classes to move to central urban

Table 2 | **Occupational divisions within the salariat 1987**

	Conservative	Alliance	Labour	Other		
Public sector	40	32	26	2	100%	(212)
Private sector	57	29	13	2	101%	(281)
Specialists	44	31	24	2	101%	(266)
Technocrats	56	29	14	2	101%	(287)
Welfare and creative	32	33	34	1	100%	(162)
Business and administrative	58	28	12	2	100%	(391)
Economically inactive	63	26	9	1	99%	(299)

Source: 1987 cross-section survey.

locations in London (such as Islington) and other large cities. Middle-class lifestyles appear therefore to have fragmented.

Finally, let us consider the case of politics. Goldthorpe argues that the service class is increasingly conservative, whilst the 'new class' theorists point to its radical potential. Research on political alignments suggest that the political alignments of the 'salariat' have actually changed little, despite the major political upheavals of recent years. Around 50–55% appear to identify with the Conservative party and around 22% with the Labour party. There are also significant differences within the 'service class' (see Table 2). Public-sector workers tend to be more left-wing than private-sector workers. Welfare and creative workers, such as journalists, teachers, artists and so on are distinctive in being relatively left wing – Table 2 shows that in 1987 these groups were more likely to vote Labour than Conservative. The highly educated appear to be more left-wing than the less highly educated, a fact which appears to endorse the 'new class' idea, at least for some fractions of the middle classes.

Conclusions

Let us return to the theoretical accounts of the middle classes. Goldthorpe's arguments about the 'service class' do appear to ignore the multiple axes of division within the middle classes, which I have briefly highlighted here. On the other hand, 'new class' ideas do not take account of the fact that only a small proportion of the middle class – the highly educated, people working in the arts and higher education etc. – appear to exhibit much 'culture of critical discourse'. So it would appear that an emphasis upon fragmentation is the most useful, though we need to know more about the sources of such division.

Further, it is important to recognise the way that different types of class position are linked by mobility chains. The fact that around 60% of the workforce are in working-class positions and 40% in middle-class ones should not blind us to the fact that many people move between such positions. Look at Table 1 again. Of all the routine male white-collar workers in 1981, over a third had moved into management or the professions by 1991 – though the figures for women are noticeably lower. There is also evidence that people from the middle classes are downwardly mobile. The processes facilitating and constraining mobility are therefore of fundamental importance for thinking about the meaning of class today. And, it might be added, given that gender, race and ethnicity appear to be important forces affecting mobility, it may be suggested that class cannot be seen as standing totally apart from these other social forces.

One final point is this. It should not be thought that the rising number of people in 'middle class' jobs means that class itself is less important. What we have seen is the erosion of the 'collar line' as a meaningful axis of social division. However, it would appear that the expansion of professional and managerial employees has led to new types of conflict and division. As traditional 'middle-class' privileges are called into question, and middle-class employees need to compete more intensively in the labour market, they are forced to engage in 'positional' conflicts to market themselves and their skills. The important conclusion is to suggest that even if it is true that the middle classes are forming a larger proportion of the workforce, this does not mean that we live in a more stable or harmonious society.

References

Abercrombie N. and Urry J. (1983) *Capital, Labour and the Middle Classes*, Unwin Hyman.

Bourdieu P. (1984) *Distinction*, Routledge.

Butler T. and Savage M. (eds) (1995) *Social Change and the Middle Classes*, UCL Press.

Edgell S. (1993) *Class*, Routledge.

Fielding A.J. (1995) 'Migration and middle class formation in England and Wales 1981–1991' in Butler and Savage (eds).

Goldthorpe J. (1982), 'On the service class: its formation and future', in A. Giddens and G. MacKenzie (eds), *Social Class and the Division of Labour: Essays in Honour of Ilya Neustadt*, Cambridge University Press.

—— (1987) *Social Mobility and the Class Structure in Modern Britain*, Oxford University Press.

—— and Lockwood D. (1969) *The Affluent Worker in the Class Structure*, Cambridge University Press.

Gouldner A. (1979) *The Future of Intellectuals and the Rise of the New Class*, Macmillan.

Morris L. (1994) *Dangerous Classes*, Routledge.

Saunders P. (1990) *A Nation of Homeowners*, Unwin Hyman.

Savage M., Barlow J., Dickens P. and Fielding A.J. (1992) *Property, Bureaucracy and Culture: middle class formation in contemporary Britain*, Routledge.

Scase R. (1992) *Class*, Open University Press.

—— and Goffee R. (1989) *Reluctant Managers*, Unwin Hyman.

Wright E.O. (1985) *Classes*, Verso.

In Search of a British Underclass

9

Fiona Devine

Key words

Underclass, inequality of income, poverty, unemployment, lone parents, working class, dependency culture, multiple deprivation

The notion of the underclass has a history which can be traced back to Victorian times. The concept has aroused much controversy. It was revived and re-entered British political discourse in the 1980s. There are several competing definitions of the underclass, some technical, some essentially polemical. The version which has aroused most political controversy is one which suggests that there is a significant minority of the population who share a common culture characterized by lack of motivation to gain employment and willing dependence on the state for subsistence. To portray people in this way is to suggest that they are personally responsible for their own unemployment, poverty and exclusion, rather than the unfortunate victims of structural economic change and inadequate institutional solutions to social problems.

Devine offers a cogent review of the debate about the British underclass. While recognizing multiple deprivations among the poor, deriving primarily from unemployment and lone motherhood, she argues that sections of the population at greatest risk of poverty do not constitute a group with a shared culture of dependency on the state. This extract provides evidence on the condition of the poor and the unemployed, their attitudes, social connections and political leanings.

[. . .]

Who are the poor? Examining the composition of the poor by family status, the evidence shows that couples with children constituted the largest group in poverty in

Table 1 | **Unemployment rates by ethnic group, age and sex, 1989–90**

	Age 16–59/64			Age 16–24			Age 25–44			Age 45–59/64		
	All	M	F	All	M	F	All	M	F	All	M	F
All origins	8	8	7	11	12	10	7	6	7	7	7	5
White	7	8	7	10	11	9	7	6	7	6	7	5
Total ethnic minority	13	14	12	19	20	19	11	11	11	12	13	10
Afro-Caribbean	14	16	13	23	24	23	12	11	12	11	15	6
African Asian	9	8	10	12	9	15	7	6	8	13	11	17
Indian	11	11	12	16	18	13	10	9	11	11	11	13
Pakistani	22	22	25	30	31	30	18	18	18	22	21	–[1]
Bangladeshi	24	24	–	19	15	–	23	26	–	33	33	–
Chinese	7	9	4	7	–	–	9	12	4	2	2	–
African	14	15	13	27	28	26	10	13	7	11	7	–
Other/Mixed	10	9	12	13	14	11	10	8	14	6	5	7

[1] Sample size too small.
Source: Jones (1993), Table 5.1, p. 124.

1989. In terms of economic status, it is the retired (where the head/spouse is aged 60 or over) who are the group of people living in poverty. However, looking at the risk of poverty by family status and economic status provides a different picture. In terms of family status, it is lone parents who are at the greatest risk of poverty (50 per cent). In terms of economic status, it is the unemployed and their families who experience the greatest risk of poverty (Oppenheim 1993: 43). Also, the poor have become more likely to be single parents and/or unemployed over time. The overwhelming majority (90 per cent) of lone parents are, of course, women (Glendinning and Millar 1992). Afro-Caribbean women are a large proportion of single parents but they have a high level of employment in the labour market (Bartholomew 1992; Jones 1993). The brunt of unemployment has been born by white men but a disproportionate number of ethnic minorities – notable Pakistani and Bangladeshi men – have experienced unemployment (as Table 1 shows) (Brown 1984; Jones 1993; Ward and Cross 1991). Finally, poverty and unemployment are highest in Northern Ireland, Scotland, the North and Wales and in the inner cities such as London, Liverpool and Manchester (MacGregor and Pimlott 1990; Willmott and Hutchinson 1992). Effectively, therefore, those who experience the greatest risk of unemployment are a very similar group of people isolated in the inner cities of America and Britain.

The growth of poverty in the early 1980s led to increasing controversy over 'the creation of a permanent underclass of the poor' (Pond 1989: 76; Brown and Scase 1991). The concept of the underclass was not entirely new to Britain (see Katz 1989 and Morris 1994 for full historical reviews). Giddens (1973; 1980) defined a growing underclass, dominated by women and ethnic minorities, concentrated in a secondary labour market of low-paid jobs, subemployment and unemployment (Giddens 1980: 112). He predicted the rise of conflict especially ethnic confrontation, given that ethnic minorities were denied access to the exercise of 'citizenship rights' on a par with white workers in the economic and political sphere (Giddens 1980: 218). Similarly, Rex and Tomlinson (1979), in their survey of Handsworth in Birmingham, documented the multiple disadvantages of a predominately black underclass in the education, labour and housing markets in comparison to the white working class. They also found evidence of increased radicalism – disaffection with society and conflict with the police (Rex and Tomlinson 1979: 224) and events in the 1980s – notably, the riots in Toxteth (in Liverpool) and Moss Side (in Manchester) – appeared to confirm their predictions of increased ethnic conflict (Rex 1986; 1988 and see his earlier predictions of 'urban riots', Rex and Moore 1967). However, Gallie (1988) cast a sceptical eye over these arguments. While not denying the multiple disadvantages which ethnic minorities face, Gallie concluded that there is a high degree of internal differentiation in patterns of employment and unemployment among ethnic minorities which has militated against collective action and, on the whole, ethnic minorities have been integrated into working-class organisations such as the trade unions and the Labour Party (Gallie 1998: 468; see Jones 1993). Distinct cultural and socio-political community groups have not led to national collective organisations which have usurped other forms of political mobilisation along class lines. The notion of an economically and socially distinct ethnic minority underclass, therefore, was undermined.

The debate on the underclass, however, enjoyed renewed momentum following Murray's account of the emerging British underclass (first published as a specially commissioned article for the *Sunday Times* (1989) and subsequently re-published by the Institute for Economic Affairs (IEA)(1990)). Describing himself as 'a visitor from a plague area come to see whether the disease is spreading', Murray (1990: 3–4) argued that, 'Britain does have an underclass, still largely out of sight and still smaller than the one in the US. But it is growing rapidly. Over the next decade it will probably become as large (proportionately) as the United States' underclass. It could even become larger'. Again, Murray described an underclass of working-aged healthy people distinctive in terms of their behaviour: namely high rates of illegitimacy, rising crime and drop out from the labour market. He noted, for example, that illegitimacy (concentrated in the lower classes) had risen from 10.6 per cent in 1979 to 25.6 per cent in 1988. Murray blamed the rise of liberal society – softer penalties for crime and the loss of social stigma associated with illegitimacy – and the benefit system which had bred a dependency culture as the main causes of the underclass. Again, he emphasised that all these social problems were interconnected, and that incremental changes would not solve the problem. He advocated 'authentic self-government' if Britain is to avoid the bleak outlook he predicted (Murray 1990: 34–5). Five years later, Murray (1994) reiterated his main predictions. On the basis of rising illegitimacy, for example, he predicted the rise of a 'new rabble' as lower-class communities would degenerate into more crime, more abuse, more child neglect and so on undermining the social order of civil society (Murray 1994: 21–2). Once again, he called for the reduction in welfare – including economic penalties on single women who choose to be pregnant – as a way of reducing the growing underclass in Britain.

[. . .]

Murray's thesis was also subject to fierce criticism (Brown 1990; Walker 1990; Deakin 1990; Alcock 1994; David 1994; Slipman 1994). Critics argued that the concept of the underclass was theoretically ill-defined and empirically imprecise (Brown and Scase 1991; Dean and Taylor-Gooby 1992). The analysis of single mothers, for example, overlooked the fact that the majority (75 per cent) of them were married before and only a quarter were single never-married mothers (Brown 1990: 43; Ermisch 1990; Hardey and Crow 1991). It also overlooked the fact that single mothers are less economically active than married mothers (49 per cent compared with 66 per cent in 1990) because they do not have childcare support. Nor is part-time employment a feasible option for those supporting a family on their own (Bartholomew et al. 1992). It was also noted that Murray's argument was tantamount to 'blaming the victim' for their poverty and distinguishing between the deserving and undeserving poor. Such a discourse, it was noted, has a 'long undistinguished history' in Britain (MacNicol 1987) and parallels were drawn with the 'cycle of deprivation' thesis promulgated by Keith Joseph in the 1970s. In an evaluation of the thesis, all the evidence suggested that poverty *per se* rather than the attitudes and behaviour of the poor accounted for the transmission of economic and social disadvantage from one generation to another (Brown and Madge 1982; Coffield et al. 1981; Rutter and Madge 1977). Bagguley and Mann (1992: 124) argued that the concept of the underclass 'is a set of ideological beliefs held by certain groups among the upper and middle classes (which) helps them sustain certain relations of domination of class, patriarchy and race towards the unemployed, single mothers and blacks through the formation of state welfare policies'. Dean (1991: 33) also concluded that the underclass thesis has been used for 'dramatic effect' in an analysis of economic and social trends in the 1980s and 1990s.

Westergaard (1992; 1995) also concluded that the concept of the underclass was a 'colourful shorthand' of these trends which has been put to rhetorical use (Westergaard 1992). He levelled two further criticisms at the British version of the underclass thesis. First, he was critical of the crude dualistic model of the labour market which underpinned the thesis. Echoing Gallie's criticism of Giddens, Westergaard rejected the argument that employment opportunities have been structured to create a privileged elite on the one hand and a reserve army of labour on the other. Despite the popularity of the distinction between primary and secondary workers (Atkinson and Meager 1985; Hakim 1987), the empirical evidence suggests that employers have not actively recruited core and peripheral workers in response to increased competition (Hunter and MacInnes 1992; McGregor and Sproull 1992). Rather, the labour market is segmented along much more complex lines as the result of employer strategies, trade union action, the state and institutional factors (Burchill and Rubery 1989; Rubery 1988). Second, Westergaard (1992: 578) argued that the identification of the underclass rests on its separation from a classless majority 'included in society by broad common participation in rising prosperity' which is highly problematic. The data on income distribution shows that substantial gains which were made by the top earners have not been shared equally by those further down the occupational ladder. The growth of low pay in the 1980s and 1990s is stark, for example, when the statistics show that in 1992 the poorest tenth of men working in manual jobs earned 62.8 per cent of average (median) earnings compared with 68.3 per cent in 1979 (*The New Review* 1992). The boundary between the underclass and the prosperous middle mass, therefore, is far from clear. Westergaard (1992: 580) concluded that 'there is no such sharp, single line towards the bottom of the pile; and some lines of division appreciably further up have become all the more pronounced with the concentration of gains towards the top'. The evidence on wealth and income distribution and a range of other indicators showed that class inequalities had deepened rather than been eclipsed.

Against the background of high unemployment in Britain, a wide range of empirical research published in the 1990s has directly or indirectly challenged the underclass thesis with reference to the unemployed and long-term unemployed (Allatt and Yeandle 1991; Dean and Taylor-Gooby 1992; Jordan et al. 1992; McLaughlin et al. 1989). Allatt and Yeandle's (1991: 121) study of the young unemployed and their families in Newcastle-upon-Tyne in the North East found that young people were desperate to work because of the scarcity of jobs. They found little evidence of family breakdown since the family played an important role in helping the young unemployed to 'survive' their experiences and maintain their hopes and expectations for better times. It was a source of strength in sustaining the threatened values of hard work, rewards and justice (Allatt and Yeandle 1991: 140). Jordan et al.'s (1992) study of low-income families in Exeter in the South West found little evidence of extensive criminality among the unemployed either. While there was some 'bending of the rules' of the benefit system, there was a strong moral code as to why they engaged in informal work and the extent to which they did so. That is, they justified small amounts of undeclared cash work with reference to their family responsibilities in periods when their financial circumstances were especially dire. McLaughlin et al. (1991) also found that claimants were not passive victims, happy to accept their dependency on the welfare state, but active in their resilience and resourcefulness in coping with the circumstances in which they found themselves. Finally, in their study of social security claimants in Kent and South London, Dean and Taylor-Gooby (1992) found that the harsh conditions for claiming 'compounded the strains upon the expectations of social security claimants' (Dean and Taylor-Gooby 1992: 123). They found that 'the social security system does not foster a dependency culture but it constructs, isolates and supervises a heterogeneous population of reluctant dependants' (Dean and Taylor-Gooby 1992: 125).

Drawing on a local survey in Hartlepool in the North East, Morris (1995) also rejected the underclass thesis. Examining the employment histories of her predominately working-class sample, Morris and Irwin found a variety of relationships to the labour market – long-term unemployment, temporary bouts of employment and unemployment and relatively secure employment – not encapsulated in the concept. There was no clear division between the employed and unemployed (see also Harris 1987; Payne and Payne 1993). That said, they found that there was a tendency for skilled workers (especially those with credentials) to have chequered careers while skilled workers (without credentials) and unskilled workers were prone to long-term unemployment. They concluded:

> If long-term unemployment is a feature of this class position it seems inappropriate to assign them to a separate class location, that of the underclass. To separate those affected from their position when in work is to disguise the source of their vulnerability.
>
> (Morris and Irwin 1992a: 411)

Irwin and Morris (1993) also found little evidence of a dependency culture among the female partners of the sample who had little opportunity to earn a wage sufficient for household maintenance. Examining the social segregation of the long-term unemployed, Morris (1992) found that employment and unemployment was concentrated among family, friendship and neighbourhood networks. Given that informal means of getting a job were paramount (most notably from someone in employment), the long-term unemployed were disadvantaged in the job search process. Thus, rather than exhibit any specific cultural predispositions towards work, it was informal patterns of association which determined success or failure in the search for employment. Similarly, Morris and Irwin (1992b) found evidence of informal exchange with kin and friends across all employment status groups thereby undermining the notion of cultural distinctiveness still further. Overall, Morris (1995: 132) concluded that the residual concept of the underclass 'runs the risk of defining unemployment as in some sense separate from class' and excludes rather than includes the unemployed in the analysis of social class.

Finally, survey data from the Social Change and Economic Life Initiative (SCELI) (especially the 1986 Work Attitudes Survey and 1987 Household and Community Survey) indicate that the concept of the underclass is problematic in relation to the unemployed. Gershuny and Marsh (1993: 66) found that there has been 'a substantial growth in the social stratification of unemployment'. That is, unemployment is increasingly associated with manual working-class men and especially young manual workers in the 1970s and 1980s (see also Ashton 1986). They found no evidence of an 'unemployment underclass' of people permanently out of the labour market. However, they found that unemployment is concentrated among a small group of people in distinctive geographical and occupational locations. In this respect, the rise of unemployment has witnessed the emergence of 'unemployment careers' (Gershuny and Marsh 1993: 113). Turning to attitudes to work, Gallie and Vogler (1993a: 124–6) found that the unemployed are more committed to employment than those in work. Two-thirds (66 per cent) of employees and the self-employed would continue working even if there was no financial necessity compared with three-quarters (77 per cent) of the unemployed. There was some variation between the different types of the unemployed ranging from 81 per cent among claimant seekers to 82 per cent among non-claimant seekers to a drop of 64 per cent among the non-seekers. However, the non-seekers were found to be older workers with problems of ill-health and younger mothers without adequate childcare support (Gallie and Vogler 1993a: 152). They also found that attitudes to work did not determine the position of the unemployed and nor did they determine how long it took them to find work. Gallie and Vogler concluded:

> Rather our evidence points to the importance for job chances of the availability of particular types of work, of the resources which can be provided by the household to facilitate job search, and of the structural misfit between the low qualifications possessed by the unemployed and the sharp rise in qualifications required by the changing nature of work in industry.
>
> (Gallie and Vogler 1993a: 152–3)

There was no evidence of a distinctive culture, therefore, among the unemployed which might contribute to their predicament.

Evidence was found to show that a husband's unemployment does have an effect on his wife's participation in the labour market. Davies et al. (1993) found that women married to unemployed men are often unemployed themselves so that the couple is dependent on the state. They found that married women are likely to give up work after approximately a year when their husbands would transfer from insurance-based unemployment benefit to means-tested benefit. It is at this juncture that what amounts to a tax on the wife's earnings becomes very high. However, the incidence of 'cross-couple state dependence' is confined to areas of high unemployment where the prospects of re-employment are not very high. Long-term rather than short-term unemployment, in other words, is anticipated. The system of social security, therefore, did influence labour market behaviour in this respect (Davies et al. 1993: 184). Gallie and his colleagues (1993a: 262) found no evidence of a 'withdrawal into passivity and social isolation' in terms of patterns of leisure and sociability among the unemployed. They found comparable leisure patterns between the employed and unemployed although the unemployed did substitute expensive for less expensive leisure pursuits over time. There were some differences between the patterns of sociability between the employed and the unemployed but the differences were in terms of its nature rather than its extensiveness. As Morris (1995) also found, the unemployed were restricted to social networks whose other members were also unemployed. Gallie et al. (1993a: 263) concluded, 'They therefore had weaker social support systems to help with both psychological and material problems. These networks may be a significant factor locking the unemployed into a situation of labour disadvantage.'

Finally, the extent to which the underclass might be described as politically distinctive needs to be considered. Previously, Gallie (1988) had argued that the unemployed do not have a distinct socio-political identity. The experience of long-term unemployment is one of considerable financial deprivation which 'engenders a loss of sense of self-efficacy' (Gallie 1988: 471). This view was confirmed by Bagguley in a case study of an unemployed workers' centre in Brighton, who argued: 'Whilst the politically quiescent unemployed express a series of ideological beliefs to a limited degree, most important is the informed and rationalised fatalism about the efficacy of collective action. This is the major reason for the contemporary quiescence of the unemployed' (1991: 203). Similarly, Heath's (1992) analysis of the British Election Studies found little evidence of distinctive political attitudes and behaviour among the unemployed.

[. . .]

Overall, therefore, the evidence suggests that there is a distinct group of people who have suffered the burden of unemployment and its associated poverty. The experience of unemployment increases the chances of further experiences of unemployment although that is not to say that a group of people are permanently out of the labour market. They often face cumulative disadvantages in terms of health, housing, psychological depression and so forth. However, there was little evidence to suggest that the unemployed are responsible for their predicament as implied by exponents of cultural explanations of the underclass. Their attitudes do not explain why they have been unable to find work. Most of the claimant unemployed were found to be actively seeking work and remarkably flexible about what job they would take. Gallie and his colleagues concluded that the unemployed do form a distinctive group at the bottom of the class structure who suffer from multiple deprivations but it is not their fault that they are at the bottom. The results, Gallie et al. suggested:

that people may be caught in a spiral of disadvantage in which small events may have large repercussions. Through an initial accident of job loss, a person may get trapped in a cycle of further unemployment. Unemployment frequently leads to depression, family break-up, and social isolation, which in turn makes the next job more difficult to find. After the event, we may identify a group with a distinct life-style at the bottom of the heap, but they were not destined to be there, and under different labour market conditions . . . they would not have been there.

(Gallie and Marsh 1993: 30)

The concept of the underclass, therefore, has not proved a useful instrument for understanding the position of the poor in the class structure. What the evidence does show is that the life-chances of members of the working class – to some extent between skilled and unskilled workers – have polarised in the last twenty years.

[. . .]

References

Alcock, P. (1994) 'Back to the future: Victorian values for the 21st century', in C. Murray (ed.) *Underclass: The Crisis Deepens*, London: Institute for Economic Affairs.

Allatt, P. and Yeandle, S. (1991) *Youth Unemployment and the Family: Voices of Disordered Times*, London: Routledge.

Ashton, D. (1986) *Unemployment Under Capitalism: The Sociology of British and American Labour Markets*, Brighton: Harvester.

Atkinson, J. and Meager, N. (1985) *Changing Working Patterns*, London: NEDO.

Bagguley, P. (1991) *From Protest to Acquiescence? Political Movements of the Unemployed*, London: Macmillan.

—— and Mann, K. (1992) 'Idle thieving bastards? Scholarly representations of the "underclass"', *Work, Employment and Society*, 6, 113–26.

Bartholomew, R. et al. (1992) 'Lone parents and the labour market: Evidence from the Labour Force Survey', *Employment Gazette*, November, 559–79.

Brown, C. (1984) *Black and White Britain: The Third PSI Survey*, Aldershot: Gower/PSI.

Brown, J.C. (1990) 'The focus on single mothers', in C. Murray (ed.) *The Emerging British Underclass*, London: IEA.

Brown, M. and Madge, N. (1982) *Despite the Welfare State*, London: Heinemann.

Brown, P. and Scase, R. (eds) (1991) *Poor Work, Disadvantage and the Division of Labour*, Milton Keynes: Open University Press.

—— (1994) *Higher Education and Corporate Realities*, London: UCL Press.

Burchill, B. and Rubery, J. (1989) *Segmented Jobs and Segmented Workers*, Social Change and Economic Life Initiative, Working Paper Number 13, Oxford: Nuffield College.

Coffield, F. et al. (1981) *A Cycle of Deprivation?*, London: Heinemann Educational Books.

David, M. (1994) 'Fundamentally flawed', in C. Murray (ed.) *Underclass: The Crisis Deepens*, London: Institute for Economic Affairs.

Davies, R.B. et al. (1993) 'The relationship between a husband's unemployment and his wife's participation in the labour force', in D. Gallie et al. (eds) *Social Change and the Experience of Unemployment*, Oxford: Oxford University Press.

Deakin, N. (1990) 'Mr Murray's ark', in C. Murray (ed.) *The Emerging British Underclass*, London: Institute for Economic Affairs.

Dean, H. (1991) 'In search of the underclass', in P. Brown and R. Scase (eds) *Poor Work, Disadvantage and the Division of Labour*, Milton Keynes: Open University Press.

—— and Taylor-Gooby, P. (1992) *Dependency Culture: The Explosion of a Myth*, Hemel Hempstead: Harvester Wheatsheaf.

Ermisch, J. (1990) 'Divorce: economic antecedents and aftermath', in H. Joshi (ed.) *The Changing Population of Britain*, Oxford: Blackwell.

Gallie, D. (1988) 'Employment, unemployment and social stratification', in D. Gallie (ed.) *Employment in Britain*, Oxford: Basil Blackwell.

—— and Marsh, C. (1993) 'The experience of unemployment', in D. Gallie, C. Marsh and C. Vogler (eds) *Social Change and the Experience of Unemployment*, Oxford: Oxford University Press.

—— and Vogler, C. (1993a) 'Unemployment and attitudes to work', in D. Gallie et al. (eds) *Social Change and the Experience of Unemployment*, Oxford: Oxford University Press.

—— (1993b) 'Labour market deprivation, welfare and collectivism', in D. Gallie et al. (eds) *Social Change and the Experience of Unemployment*, Oxford: Oxford University Press.

Gershuny, J. and Marsh, C. (1993) 'Unemployment in work histories', in D. Gallie et al. (eds) *Social Change and the Experience of Unemployment*, Oxford: Oxford University Press.

Giddens, A. (1973) *The Class Structure of the Advanced Societies*, London: Hutchinson.

—— (1980) *The Class Structure of the Advanced Societies*, 2nd edn, London: Unwin Hyman.

Glendinning, C. and Millar, J. (1992) *Women and Poverty in Britain*, 2nd edn, Hemel Hempstead: Harvester Wheatsheaf.

Hakim, C. (1987) 'Trends in the flexible workforce', *Employment Gazette*, November, 549–60.

Hardey, M. and Crow, G. (1991) *Lone Parenthood*, Hemel Hempstead: Harvester Wheatsheaf.

Harris, C.C. et al. (1987) *Redundancy and Recession in South Wales*, Oxford: Basil Blackwell.

Heath, A. (1992) 'The attitudes of the underclass', in D.J. Smith (ed.) *Understanding the Underclass*, London: PSI.

Hunter, L. and MacInnes, J. (1992) 'Employers and labour flexibility: the evidence from case studies', *Employment Gazette*, June, 307–15.

Jones, T. (1993) *Britain's Ethnic Minorities*, London: PSI.

Jordan, B. et al. (1992) *Trapped in Poverty: Labour Market Decisions in Low Income Households*, London: Routledge.

Katz, M. (1989) *The Undeserving Poor*, New York: Pantheon.

McGregor, A. and Sproull, A. (1992) 'Employers and the flexible workforce', *Employment Gazette*, May, 225–53.

MacGregor, S. and Pimlott, B. (1990) *Tackling the Inner Cities*, Oxford: Clarendon Press.

McLaughlin, E. et al. (1989) *Work and Welfare Benefits*, Aldershot: Avebury.

MacNicol, J. (1987) 'In pursuit of the underclass', *Journal of Social Policy*, 16, 293–318.

Morris, L. (1992) 'The social segregation of the long-term unemployed in Hartlepool', *Sociological Review*, 38, 344–69.

—— (1994) *Dangerous Classes*, London: Routledge.

—— (1995) *Social Divisions*, London: UCL Press.

—— and Irwin, S. (1992a) 'Employment histories and the concept of the underclass', *Sociology*, 26, 401–20.

—— (1992b) 'Employment and informal support: dependency, exclusion or participation', *Work, Employment and Society*, 6, 185–207.

Murray, C. (1990) *The Emerging British Underclass*, London: Institute for Economic Affairs.

—— (1994) *The Underclass: The Crisis Deepens*, London: Institute for Economic Affairs.

Oppenheim, C. (1993) *Poverty: The Facts*, London: CPAG.

Payne, J. and Payne, C. (1993) 'Recession, restructuring and the fate of the unemployed: evidence in the underclass debate', *Sociology*, 27, 1–22.

Pond C. (1989) 'The changing distribution of income, wealth and poverty', in C. Hamnett et al. (eds) *The Changing Social Structure*, London: Sage.

Rex, J. (1986) *Race and Ethnicity*, Milton Keynes: Open University Press.

—— (1988) *The Ghetto and the Underclass*, Aldershot: Avebury.

—— and Tomlinson, S. (1979) *Colonial Immigrants in a British City*, London: Routledge and Kegan Paul.

—— and Moore, R. (1967) *Race, Community and Conflict*, London: Institute of Race Relations.

Rubery, J. (1988) 'Employers and the labour market' in D. Gallie (ed.) *Employment in Britain*, Oxford: Basil Blackwell.

Rutter, M. and Madge, N. (1977) *Cycles of Disadvantage*, London: Heinemann.

Slipman, S. (1994) 'Would you take one home with you?', in C. Murray (ed.) *Underclass: The Crisis Deepens*, London: Institute for Economic Affairs.

Walker, A. (1990) 'Blaming the victims', in C. Murray (ed.) *The Emerging British Underclass*, London: Institute for Economic Affairs.

Ward, R. and Cross, M. (1991) 'Race, employment and economic change', in P. Brown and R. Scase (eds) *Poor Work, Disadvantage and the Division of Labour*, Buckingham: Open University Press.

Westergaard, J. (1992) 'About and beyond the "underclass": some notes on influences of social climate on British sociology today', *Sociology*, 26, 575–87.

—— (1995) *Who Gets What?*, Cambridge: Polity.

Willmott, P. and Hutchinson, R. (1992) *Urban Trends 1*, London: PSI.

10 | Women at Work in the City of London

Linda McDowell

> **Key words**
>
> Middle class women, gender divisions, management, financial services, organizational cultures, City of London, masculinities, femininities, embodiment, self

Financial services have been a major growth area in the economy in the last two decades. The City of London, the hub of British finance capital, has experienced rapid and radical transformation. The background to this transformation is examined in detail in McDowell's Capital Culture, *a book which goes on to study the nature of work in merchant banks in the City of London. Merchant banking offers extremely well paid employment to very highly qualified personnel. McDowell was particularly interested in the way that young women sought to develop careers in investment banking which, until the liberalization of regulations in the 1980s, had been conducted almost exclusively by men. The extract reports findings from in-depth interviews about the experience of professional women workers in this lucrative and competitive occupation in the early 1990s. The chapter discusses the performance of gender at work. Our abridgement has excluded material on the indignities associated with dealing with sexualized talk and behaviour, on the importance of dressing appropriately even though it was almost impossible to find appropriate garb, and on the problems of participating in workplace conversation that was predominantly about male topics – 'bats, balls and bullets' as McDowell refers to it. She proceeds to argue that there are few roles available to women within the organizational culture and few positive images of women. There are, however, some signs of change.*

Introduction

[. . .] The type of person who is recruited to a British merchant or investment bank is likely to be confident and outgoing with a good brain validated by a good degree from a good university. The women as well as the men, indeed perhaps even more so than the men, are apparently self-confident and 'pushy', and in general from an upper-middle-class background. So what happens to these young people when they enter their respective banks? Do the young women find themselves equally valued in the so-called 'new' City, where more open or 'American' attitudes might lead to challenges to the elitist 'English' social practices of the City? Or do they find themselves up against the barriers that face many women in professional occupations in a range of large organisations (Davidson and Cooper, 1992)?

There is now an enormous literature, some but not all of it feminist, which documents the ways in which institutional mechanisms, procedures and everyday attitudes position women within organisations so that their 'Otherness' is emphasised. Not only do women not fit the idealised image of a rational male worker, at least as far as senior positions of responsibility and status are concerned, but the very structures of organisations are based on masculinised assumptions – about the timing of work, the structure of tasks and ways of doing things, schemes of appraisal and promotion. [. . .] I look in detail at the social construction of self in everyday interactions inside organisations – in this case merchant banks.

The drama of work and the construction of self

Analyses of gendered organisations have a lengthening history from Kanter's (1977) classic study onwards (Cockburn, 1991; Knights and Willmott, 1986; Marshall, 1984; Savage and Witz, 1993; Witz, 1992; Wright, 1994). Kanter's work is notable for its comparison of men and women – a crucially important approach that apparently was forgotten by many successors who, although interested in gender divisions, interviewed only women. Despite their recognition of gender as a social construction reinforced in everyday interactions, later analysts ignored the gendering of men and the variety of masculinised behaviour, instead seeing masculinity as a singular oppositional category against which to compare the 'difference' of women. A common feature of these 'gender and organisational culture' studies is their characterisation of the position of women as performers in a drama. The ways in which women are made to feel out of place or like bit players have been outlined and the limited number of acceptable roles or scripts available to women attempting to fit into the masculinised performance of work have been detailed.

[. . .]

I explore the ways in which the changes in the nature of service sector work and in organisational structures affect and are reflected in changes in gendered self formation. Micro-scale practices in the workplace – the focus of what follows – connect to the enormous technological and organisational changes in the production and marketing of services, as well as to societal changes in ideas about gender relations. [. . .]

First, I show how women as a group are out of place in the workplace, marked by their gender and their bodies as 'natural' and so as unsuitable participants in the rational, cerebral world of work. As earlier studies of gender and organisations have suggested, the options for women in the workplace seem to be limited to a small number of variations on their sexual and/or familial roles, or an attempt to produce a gender-neutral performance in a parody of accepted masculine norms of workplace behaviour. But [. . .] the shift towards interactive work has altered the relationship between embodiment, the self and the ideal worker. In the new service sector occupations which are increasingly dependent on selling information and advice, the personal performance of workers, their ways of being and doing, are part of the service that is sold. This is leading to the 'feminisation' of all workers in the sense that bodies and personal appearance have become an integral element of workplace success. The old bureaucratic notion of the successful worker as disembodied brain-power, of a rational decision-maker who thinks and then acts, is being challenged. This necessitates a re-appraisal of workplace attitudes and behaviour by many men and may reposition women in a more powerful place.

A second significant aspect of these new forms of work [. . .] is a blurring of the distinctions between work and leisure (Du Gay, 1996; Leidner, 1993). My respondents often referred to work as 'enormous fun', suggesting that 'you have to have a certain love for it. There are people here who really do have a passionate love for being here' (man, 29, assistant director, Merbank). The blurring of these boundaries, between work and fun, waged labour and leisure activities, is also reflected in the new built environment of the City where, as the developers of the Broadgate Centre emphasised in their publicity material, the new buildings and the spaces around them are a 'total landscape of work and leisure'. Inside the workplace too, the lack of distinction is important. Many organisations now include sporting facilities in their redeveloped spaces, as well as atria and entrance lobbies to give new offices the feel of a hotel. This redefinition of the boundaries is leading to a greater emphasis on the cultural capital of workers, on attributes such as style and bodily form, on how they look as well as how they perform in the workplace. However, [. . .] the social construction of the female body as nature, not culture, for pleasure, not work, may continue to mark women as different from, and inferior to, an embodied but still ideally masculinised worker.

It may be, therefore, that the changing social characteristics of new service sector occupations are having a contradictory impact on women's position in the workforce. Certain aspects challenge their socially constructed inferiority whereas others reinforce it. In an investigation of these contradictions, in this chapter I keep a singular focus on 'woman', looking at the strategies that construct and place woman as the 'Other', different from an idealised masculine norm and so excluded from the still predominantly masculinised culture of merchant banks. Here I demonstrate the continuing strength of the binary distinction between masculine and feminine subjects or selves. [. . .]

Marked as 'woman' in the workplace

Drawing on the taped narratives, I first examined the range of ways in which the women I talked to suggested that they were marked as different from an idealised version of disembodied masculinity. All the remarks were made in the context of a general discussion about everyday working practices and were not elicited by direct questions about either embodiment or discrimination. My female interviewees openly discussed the ways in which they were reminded every day that they possessed a female body which classified them as inferior to men. They provided evidence of how the 'dynamics of desire and the pulses of attraction and aversion' identified by Young restricted the range of possible interactions with their peers, superiors and clients. From comments about size, 'attractiveness' and clothes, through sexualised jokes and gossip, to a range of behaviours verging on sexual harassment, the women I interviewed found that they were marked out and restricted to a small number of acceptable ways of presenting themselves at work.

[. . .]

Restricted roles: wife, mother, mistress, man?

[. . .] For women the images and roles that are available at work tend to be familial or sexualised. Pringle (1989), in her analysis of the roles secretaries are able to play, distinguished 'wives, mothers, spinster aunts, mistresses and femmes fatales' (p. 3). Marshall, focusing on women managers rather than secretaries, drew up a similar list – 'the positions of mother, seductress, pet and iron maiden' (and other variations on the same theme) (Marshall, 1984, p. 103) – whereas Davidson and Cooper (1992), in their study of women also in management positions, added the pet, the seductress and the honorary man to the scripts available to women. As the argument has been so well documented in numerous studies, it is hardly necessary to point out that many of these roles restrict women to servicing, nurturing and caring – apparently natural characteristics of an essentialised femaleness. It means that most professional women have to fight against incursions on their time, as supplicants assume too readily that women will be available to do a range of 'emotional' work at work.

One of the difficulties for women in male-dominated professional occupations is trying to find an image of a powerful woman which is not negative. Tannen (1994) suggested 'a whole menagerie of stereotypical images of women: schoolmarm, head nurse, headmistress, cruel stepmother, dragon lady, catwoman, witch, bitch' (p. 165) are the only powerful options. To the schoolmarm, nurse and headmistress we might add the nanny, matron and governess, all of whom are characters from the youth of the landed gentry and the prep school dormitory. These are images of women of discipline, forms of female authority that many bourgeois men are used to obeying, and it is interesting that some of the men whom I interviewed referred to senior women in these terms. Their 'public school' attributes are emphasised to construct them as a 'jolly good sort'. Mrs Thatcher, too, has been seen in terms of a school mistress or matron.

Julian Barnes, for example, commenting on Thatcher's second electoral victory, predicted four more years of 'the cold showers, the compulsory cod liver oil, the finger nail inspection, and the doling out of those vicious little pills that make you go when you don't want to' (*Observer*, 12 June 1983). (His comments perhaps reveal rather more about public school men than about Mrs Thatcher.) Anthony Barnett (1982), in *Iron Britannia*, explicitly compared Mrs Thatcher with a governess (p. 71).

An alternative, also pejorative image of a successful working woman is that of 'careerist', embodying an unspoken neglect of familial responsibilities or, worse, a selfish rejection of motherhood. The hysteria of the British press in their coverage of official figures for the birthrate, released in May 1995, which showed an increase (from 16 to 20 per cent) in women who will not become mothers, is indicative. Headlines about selfish, embittered careerists predominated. Some of my younger women respondents held rather similar views about successful women, echoing the comments of Marshall's respondents a decade earlier who feared that they would become 'hard' as they became older.

A young (28-year-old) woman in my sample reflects this view of older women in the City:

> Women in the City who are a generation older, and by that I mean women who are in their late 30s, perhaps tend to be much fiercer and harder and I put that down to the fact that when they joined the City the life was just so intolerable that they had to build themselves into some kind of Russian shotputter to make their point and, I mean, we've got someone in our department who's like that and she frightens clients . . . the clients appreciate how good she is but none the less she can't put things across in a particularly feminine fashion, or she feels she has to become a sort of pseudo-male to make a point.
>
> (capital markets, Bluebros)

And another woman (aged 30) remarked:

> Something that sticks in my throat a bit is people tend to sort of say so and so – she's a director at – I know quite a few people now that know of women who are directors in merchant banks but it's usually 'she's the director of so and so – tough cookie' [*with emphasis*] – the sort of inference that she's more, not even feminine, but that she's harder than hard to have got where she's got to.
>
> (analyst, Northbank)

For these women – irrevocably seen by both their male and female colleagues as 'dragons', fearsome models of female authority – other options seem to have been foreclosed but, as many feminist scholars have suggested, perhaps the only option for success in institutional structures dominated by masculinised assumptions and behaviour is to become an honorary man.

The honorary man – or not?

The relationship between a female body and lack of power is, of course, part of the reason why it has been argued that women are forced to act as if they were men to achieve success. For women in senior positions in merchant banks, their gender and appearance are at odds with the masculine nature of the occupation that they fill and the tasks that they perform. Similarly, the masculinist nature of everyday interaction in merchant banking, perhaps especially on the trading floor and in the dealing rooms, constructs women as the 'Other'. Acker (1990), Fine (1987) and Rhode (1988), among others, have argued from empirical analyses that many women, to achieve success in masculinist organisations, adopt a workplace performance that constructs them as honorary men. As Rosenberg et al. (1993) suggested, women in masculinist organisations behave 'as if the fiction of gender neutrality is a reality, as if gender is inconsequential to their careers' (p. 430) but don masculine attire and adopt masculine attributes to conform to the fiction.

Several women whom I interviewed argued that it was possible to become part of masculine culture, reporting that they felt that they had been accepted as 'one of the boys'.

> For most of the time I am an honorary man. They [her male colleagues] do treat me like an honorary male and that's what I prefer. It means that I can see the way they look on women. If I go out for a drink with them, then they will comment on anything that walks past in a short skirt, things that friends wouldn't say if I was there. I guess I'd rather be an honorary man than be on the other side.
>
> (salesperson, Merbank)

Many respondents, however, were sceptical of the success of this strategy.

> You can't go out and get ratted with the boys in the pub; it just won't work.

Other women recognised that:

> It's difficult, even demeaning, to try to be one of the boys. Don't play a man at his own game because I think quite frankly you'll fail if you try to do that.

Other research findings back up the sense of many of my respondents that there are problems involved in attempting to become an honorary man. Women who attempt to behave like men are often distressed to find not acceptance but distrust from their male peers. Barkalow (1990), for example, documenting her experiences as one of the first women to attend an elite US military academy, detailed the mistakes she made in an attempt to enhance her image in a male domain. She argued that women cannot become officers in the same way that men can but have to find another way to fulfil the masculinised requirements of a job without violating too many of the expectations of what and how a woman should be. One of my respondents explained:

> Men have a real problem with women who are unfeminine. If you hide your femininity entirely you get called a lesbian – they don't handle it very well. You can be tough but you have to maintain that edge of femininity somewhere.
>
> (female trader, Northbank)

This comment supports the contention of Spurling who, in a study of masculinity and femininity in an elite British university, came to the same conclusion: 'Women who imitate the masculine professional stereotype in male-dominated environments make their colleagues uneasy' (Spurling, 1990, p. 14).

As a male respondent rather condescendingly explained to me:

> There's a certain female type in the City; trying to be men, wanting to show themselves
> as that much more aggressive. I find it quite sad really. It more often backfires with col-
> leagues than helps.
>
> (manager, Northbank)

But many of the men whom I interviewed seemed to want it both ways. If a masculinised demeanour is regarded as inappropriate, some of the younger men felt themselves to be placed in a disadvantaged position because of those stereotypical feminine
attributes of caring and empathy. They suggested that femininity confers unfair advantages on women. In their comments, the discursive construction of feminine attributes
as natural was noticeable. Women were regarded as unfair competition because:

> Women are good at getting on with people. People tell them things.
>
> (male executive, Bluebros)

> Women may have a natural advantage, as the majority of clients are men, and clearly their
> PR skills and general warmth of approach is much better than a man's.
>
> (male manager, Merbank)

> There's a definite advantage to being a woman. Being feminine, even slightly sugar-coated,
> can be a great advantage both within the bank and with clients, because girls can manage
> to strike up an almost instant rapport, you know with their director and their clients.

And, what clearly worried him,

> I think it will influence the choice of promotion to a degree, as long as it's somebody who
> has the other skills.
>
> (male executive, Northbank)

So women seem to be in an impossible position. As female bodies they are out of place
at work, but should they manage to overcome the disadvantages of the masculinised
environment and achieve success, this is put down to the advantages conferred by a
set of naturalised female attributes.

The women, too, while understandably less positive about the advantages of femininity, accepted that becoming an honorary man was not a viable strategy. Thus, one
of the women who had 'made it' to director level was adamant about the failure of
the masculinised behaviour that she originally had adopted:

> Over the years I've come to the conclusion 'Why should I try to be a little man? I'm not
> a little man. It's not going to work. *I'll never be a man as well as a man is.*'
> (director, Northbank, my emphasis)

Herein lies the nub of the argument. Embodiment matters. As feminist theorists,
Threadgold and Cranny-Francis (1990) have pointed out that 'masculine and feminine
behaviours have different personal and social significances when acted out by male
and female subjects. What is valorised in patriarchy is not masculinity but *male
masculinity*' (p. 31, my emphasis).

Conclusions

This may seem a negative note and the end of the story. It is not. [. . .] Despite the effects of all the mechanisms that I have outlined above, there are two important factors that need to be taken into account in understanding the construction of gender in the workplace and its consequences for women. The first of these is a criticism. [. . .] Too many of the studies of gendered organisations rely on a single binary distinction between men and women. By establishing masculinity or masculinism as the norm, and so focusing on women as 'Other', the consequence is that the social construction of gender, what is often called 'doing gender' (West and Zimmerman, 1987), at work is ignored. [. . .] Instead of looking at how workplace interactions themselves gender women and men in multiple ways – some less, some more acceptable than others, some appropriate to one type of work or site of work and some, perhaps quite other ways of being female and male, to another type or site of work – the dominant model of disembodied rational masculinity that used to be so important in professional occupations is taken for granted. Those depressing sexual and familial or at best 'crazy outsider' or 'wicked witch' roles for women are compared against a singular hegemonic male model. It is increasingly clear, however, that it is important to examine how men as well as women 'do gender' in the workplace.

Second, insufficient attention is accorded in these binary models to the changing nature of work in advanced industrial societies. In the type of professional occupations that increasingly dominate service economies, new forms of working and new versions of workplace culture are challenging the old bureaucratic model of a professional organisation and automatic male dominance. As Brown and Scase (1994) illustrated in their work on recruitment, other 'ways of being' may now be more highly valued in organisations. Empathy, embodiment, feelings and team work rather than competitive individualism are the new buzz words of management science, and feminists have not been slow to point out that these characteristics are those traditionally associated with women. As I analysed the images and everyday behaviour of female and male bankers and talked to people about their bodily images, their clothes and diet, and the ways in which they presented themselves at work, it became increasingly clear to me that by focusing solely on women's bodies and comparing them to an idealised disembodied masculinity, I was missing part of the story. For merchant banking does not typify the type of masculinised bureaucratic work that organisational theorists and many feminists seem implicitly to be comparing to the feminised roles that they are analysing. Instead it is a world in which role-playing and drama, an embodied performance, is a key requirement for both men and women. Being an 'honorary man' was not the best strategy for women, nor even, at least in the classic disembodied bureaucratic sense, for many men in investment banking. [. . .]

References

Acker, J. (1990) Hierarchies, jobs, bodies: a theory of gendered organisations. *Gender and Society* 4, 139–58.

Barkalow, C. with Rabb, A. (1990) *In the Men's House: an inside account of life in the army by one of West Point's first female graduates*. Poseidon, New York.

Barnett, A. (1982) *Iron Britannia*. Allison and Busby, London.

Brown, P. and Scase, R. (1994) *Higher Education and Corporate Realities: class, culture and the decline of graduate careers*. UCL Press, London.

Cockburn, C. (1991) *In the Way of Women: men's resistance to sex equality in organisations*. Macmillan, London.

Davidson, M. J. and Cooper, C. (1992) *Shattering the Glass Ceiling: the woman manager*. Paul Chapman Publishing, London.

Du Gay, P. (1996) *Consumption and Identity at Work*. Sage, London.

Fine, G. (1987) One of the boys: women in male-dominated settings. In M. Kimmel (ed.), *Changing Men: new directions in research on men and masculinity*. Sage, Newbury Park, Calif.

Kanter, R. (1977) *Men and Women of the Organization*. Basic Books, New York.

Knights, D. and Willmott, H. (eds) (1986) *Gender and the Labour Process*. Gower, Aldershot.

Leidner R. (1993) *Fast Food, Fast Talk: service work and the routinization of everyday life*. University of California Press, Berkeley and Los Angeles, Calif.

Marshall, J. (1984) *Women Managers: travellers in a male world*. John Wiley, London.

Pringle, R. (1989) *Secretaries Talk*. Verso, London.

Rhode, D. (1988) Perspectives on professional women. *Stanford Law Review* 40, 1164–207.

Rosenberg, J., Perlstadt, H. and Phillips, W. (1993) Now that we are here: discrimination, disparagement, and harassment at work and the experience of female lawyers. *Gender and Society* 7, 415–33.

Savage, M. and Witz, A. (1993) *Gender and Bureaucracy*. Routledge, London.

Spurling, A. (1990) *Report of the Women in Higher Education Research Project*. King's College Research Centre, King's College, Cambridge.

Tannen, D. (1994) *Talking 9 to 5: how women's and men's conversational styles affect who gets heard, who gets credit, and what gets done at work*. Virago, London.

Threadgold, T. and Cranny-Francis, A. (1990) *Feminine, Masculine and Representation*. Allen and Unwin, London.

West, C. and Zimmerman, D. H. (1987) Doing gender. *Gender and Society* 1, 125–51.

Witz, A. (1992) *Professions and Patriarchy*. Routledge, London.

Wright, S. (ed.) (1994) *Anthropology of Organisations*. Routledge, London.

Young, I. M. (1990a) *Justice and the Politics of Difference*. Princeton University Press, Princeton, N.J.

—— (1990b) The ideal of community and the politics of difference. In L. Nicholson (ed.), *Feminism/Postmodernism*. Routledge, London.

—— (1993) Together in difference: transforming the logic of group political conflict. In J. Squires (ed.), *Principled Positions: postmodernism and the rediscovery of value*. Lawrence and Wishart, London, 121–50.

11 | Work, Gender and Unemployment

Lydia Morris

Key words

Unemployment, household formation, polarization, sexual divisions of labour, gender divisions, underclass, lone motherhood, welfare provision

---

The post-war welfare state was erected on assumptions of near full employment for men, the wages from whose jobs would provide, within the context of a conventional nuclear family, the resources to maintain a wife and children. Subsequent economic and social change has undermined this model. Higher rates of unemployment, more divorce and much higher rates of married women's participation in the labour market render problematic the basic premises of welfare provision. Policy makers are increasingly faced with households in which no-one is employed and in which the head of household is a lone parent. Such households, which are particularly prone to poverty, have often been granted little sympathy and have been the ones most likely to be identified as an underclass (see chapter 9 for a review of the underclass debate). The underclass has been characterized by its having become dependent on welfare provision and thus as prone to transmit a dependency culture to their children. Morris outlines some of the circumstances of unemployment and lone parenthood as it affects women. She argues that it is necessary to improve our understanding of structural change in the relationship between work, family and welfare.

The welfare state, the nuclear family and a traditional sexual division of labour were central building blocks of post-war British society. They constituted what may be thought of as a work–family–welfare nexus in which complementary social structures meshed with individuals' expectations of how life would and should be lived. Under the Beveridge Plan, social security for the working-age population was built around the expectations of secure employment for men, with unemployment no higher than 3 per cent. It also rested on the assumption that 'the ideal social unit is the household of man, wife and children maintained by the earnings of the first alone' (Beveridge, 1942), that those earnings would come from secure, long-term and often life-time employment, and that this 'breadwinner' role for the man would be supported by the domestic services of his wife.

The argument of this essay is that this work–family–welfare nexus has been gradually unravelling throughout the post-war period, with the most extreme aspects of change becoming apparent over the last 20 years. Very high levels of unemployment for men dominated the 1980s, and while there has been a considerable fall in the figures, this decline is at least partially explained by changes in the way they are calculated.[1] Furthermore, national trends mask stark regional inequalities, with many old industrial areas still showing very high levels of male unemployment. Meanwhile working life has become much less secure for many men, with redundancy an ever-present threat and increased 'flexibility' built around short-term contracts and precarious 'self-employment'. This drive for flexibility is apparent in other ways in women's working lives, most notably through rising levels of part-time employment. In fact, while there *has* been a challenge to traditional work roles for both men and women, with women's employment rising as men's was falling, this has not translated into 'role reversal' within the home. The pattern has rather been one of no-employment households and dual-employment households, and has implications which rebound on both the functioning of welfare and on structures of inequality. Finally, high and increasing levels of divorce and single parenthood have meant that the nuclear family household built upon a life-time partnership is no longer a taken-for-granted basis of social organisation.

Social polarisation

Of course, the effects of these changes are experienced differently for different households, and one of the clearest trends to have emerged is the pattern of 'social polarisation' in which work is concentrated in some homes and entirely absent from others. It has been noted in a number of area-specific studies (Pahl, 1984; Harris, 1987; Morris, 1995) that the employment status of spouses tends to coincide, such that when the man is unemployed then so too is his female partner. This is confirmed at national level by statistics throughout the 1980s (see General Household Survey) such that in 1989, for example, 70 per cent of the wives of employed men had jobs in contrast with only 28 per cent of the wives of unemployed men. The figures are no longer available in this form, but in a more detailed local study of Hartlepool (Morris, 1995) it was possible to isolate the *long-term* unemployed. This revealed a much sharper distinction between households, with only 13 per cent of the wives of long-term unemployed men holding jobs as compared with 71 per cent of the wives of men in relatively secure work.

To understand these results we need to look more closely at the trends in employment for women, and particularly for married women. Certainly, one notable feature of post-war society has been a gradual increase in women's workforce participation. Roughly expressed, women made up one quarter of the workforce in 1881, one third in 1966 and currently account for almost one half (see Dex, 1985; Labour Force

Survey). Participation has increased most markedly for women between the ages of 34 and 54, which also means amongst married women. There is a link to be made here with changing patterns of child-rearing; women have fewer children per family, return to work sooner after childbirth and also return to employment between births.

The role of part-time employment is extremely important in understanding these trends. Although in 1996 there were 10.4 million women in employment, almost equalling the 11.6 million men (Social Trends 27 1997, Table 4.2),[2] 4.5 million of these women were in part-time jobs, as compared with 0.8 million of the men. Male part-time workers were heavily concentrated among very old or very young workers, in sharp contrast with women. It is largely a growth in part-time employment over the last 25 years which accounts for the increase in women's employment generally, with part-time employment absorbing 23 per cent of women employees in 1973 but rising to 30 per cent in 1995 (GHS 1995, Table 4.6). Of course, much of the explanation for why women work full- or part-time relates to the presence of dependent children, with only 22 per cent of the mothers of these children working full-time, as compared with 38 per cent working part-time. The childcare effect should not be overstated, however, as 25 per cent of women in homes without dependent children also work part-time, as compared with 46 per cent working full-time. There are a number of likely factors at play here: other domestic and caring duties, personal preference and/or employer demand, for example.

The benefit disincentive?

Whatever the explanation, concentrations of women in part-time work have been seen as part of the explanation for a marked correspondence between male and female non-employment in couple-based households. The argument here is that the low amount of permitted earnings in benefit-dependent homes represents a disincentive to the wives of unemployed men, particularly if they choose or are confined to part-time employment. Indirect support for this view is found in work by Dilnot and Kell (1989) on Family Expenditure Survey Data; considering the *atypical* case of employed women who have unemployed partners, they found the majority to be working more than 30 hours per week. The focus of concern on the 'benefit disincentive' has, however, deflected more general interest in the differing potential employment profiles both of women with unemployed partners as compared with women whose partners are in work.

Fifty-five per cent of economically inactive women give looking after family or home as the reason for not working, compared with 7 per cent of economically inactive men, and only 4 per cent report a 'discouraged worker' effect which might, of course, include a financial disincentive (Social Trends 27 1997, Table 4.4). Indeed, a number of studies have found only a relatively small proportion of women's non-employment linked explicitly to a 'benefits effect' (see Irwin and Morris, 1993). Even accepting that disincentives may have a latent impact which is not necessarily acknowledged in women's accounts of their work decisions, there are a number of other factors that merit attention.

The principal question to be addressed is whether it is meaningful to compare women married to unemployed men with women married to employed men as if we are comparing like with like. Irwin and Morris (1993) explored this issue using data from the Hartlepool project referred to above. A sensitivity to *differences* between the two groups reveals that married men among the long-term unemployed will have a younger and larger family than their employed counterparts. This partly reflects a national tendency for the low skilled to have larger families and for long-term unemployment to be concentrated among younger workers. The pattern, of course, translates into heavier domestic and childcare responsibilities for the partners of the long-term unemployed. They are more likely to be mothers than the wives of employed men, and more likely to be mothers at a younger age.

Even holding these factors constant, women married to long-term unemployed men were more likely to cite childcare as a reason for not working. They are also more likely to be in the lower-ranking female occupations than the wives of employed men, and to have had more broken employment histories. One possibility is that when balanced against the low appeal of the poorly paid and unskilled work they are likely to command, then motherhood seems both more important and more appealing. It is in these circumstances that the low earnings allowance for benefit claimants may take on a particular significance, reinforcing women's commitment to their children. This finding may have an even stronger relevance for single mothers who have to contend with the additional demands of sole parenting weighed against unrewarding work.

'Scroungerphobia'

Another perennial issue linking benefit regulations and work incentives is the assertion that welfare has undermined *men's* will to work. However, alongside this view of the unemployed as habitually dependent lurks the suspicion that they are in fact working.

[. . .]

While ethnographic data on unemployment do reveal that some unemployed claimants take occasional opportunities for paid work, even official estimates of the numbers involved are no more than 10 per cent. Jordan et al. (1992) emphasise the enduring significance of work as a basis for identity and self-respect, noting: 'The men described themselves as active, needing to work to fulfil their personal needs as well as their roles as providers.' However, all writers stress the limited nature of the work available: 'Earnings tend to be occasional lump sums rather than regular weekly incomes and as a result although individuals have earned more than the legal amount in one particular week, over a longer period their earnings have often averaged out at less than this amount' (McLaughlin et al., 1989, p. 82).

Evidence of this kind points to an enduring need for the self-respect attached to work, and also the contradictions of a benefit system which wishes to preserve independence but stifles initiative in a climate in which regular employment for a certain section of the population has long been abandoned as a policy objective. A softer version of the 'work-shy' position is that workers are pricing themselves out of jobs and have an unrealistically high 'reservation wage', i.e. the lowest wage at which they would accept employment. Data on this issue are likely to be unreliable in that the stated wage at which a man will accept work will not necessarily correspond with a 'real' decision, especially given the significance of work as a focus for masculine identity. The problem anyway raises the question of minimum acceptable standards; does the obligation to accept available work extend to any work, whatever the terms and conditions?

One approach to the issue of reservation wages and low pay is the view that if benefits fall low enough, then the unemployed will start to accept jobs they would not previously have considered, and it will become financially viable for employers to create work which at higher wage levels would not have been possible. However, despite falls in the value of benefit in the 1980s (Micklewright, 1986), unemployment continued to rise, and meanwhile the unemployed became more impoverished in relation to the majority of the population. Any attempt to use reductions in welfare support as a means of driving people into employment calls up concern about the sharpening of inequalities, the relative poverty of the benefit population and their growing stigmatisation. This strikes a contrast with a view of the welfare state as the guarantor of social inclusion through 'social citizenship', defined by Marshall (1950) as full membership of the community. Hence, one argument might be that the welfare state has failed in its aim, that the commitment to full employment was never strong enough, and benefit levels were never high enough. An alternative position, however, suggests that the individuals affected are themselves implicated in the process of their own 'social exclusion', and this has been a central position in the underclass debate, explored below.

The underclass

The concept of the 'underclass' has more generally been used to suggest that there exists in society a group who have rejected the norms and values of mainstream society, and the evidence cited is state dependency, denial of the work ethic, the failure of morality and the rejection of family norms, often also argued to be linked with criminality (Auletta, 1982). A popular usage of the 'underclass' groups these disparate features together into a residual category, located 'outside' a society, which remains otherwise cohesive and free from internal challenge.

These arguments have been most fully developed in an American literature but have been applied in Britain in what may be seen as an exercise in conceptual containment. Rather than revise our understanding of social organisation to accommodate a number of rather complex changes, some explanation is sought which leaves the social world as we understand it more or less intact. The policy of 'Back to Basics' was a symptom of the same unease and search for containment. In particular, attention has focused on high rates of young male unemployment and rising single parenthood, both argued to be linked to aspects of welfare provision, and there has been some suggestion that the two phenomena are interrelated. Doubts have thus been raised about the stability of two key social institutions – paid work and the family.

[. . .]

Lone motherhood

The rise in lone motherhood is uncontested; between 1971 and 1995 married couple households fell from 92 per cent of homes with dependent children to 78 per cent, while lone mothers rose from 7 per cent to 20 per cent. The figures can be read in different ways, however, according to the way they are disaggregated. Some have argued (Buckingham, 1996) that single never-married mothers are now the largest group (8 per cent) as compared with divorced (7 per cent) and separated (5 per cent) lone mothers. However, these latter two groupings could be reasonably combined to make 12 per cent separated or divorced as compared to 8 per cent never married (GHS, 1995, Table 2.7).

Of all lone parents with dependent children 49 per cent rely on benefits and 37 per cent on earned income, as compared with 7 per cent and 88 per cent respectively for couple households. The figures look rather different for homes with only non-dependent children however, with only 10 per cent of the lone parent group dependent on benefits and 71 per cent on earned income, as compared with 3 per cent and 88 per cent respectively for couple households. Clearly responsibility for young children is a major factor in the working patterns of lone mothers, and even more so than for married mothers. Of all women with dependent children, 42 per cent of the married group work part-time and 25 per cent full-time, as compared with 24 per cent and 16 per cent respectively for lone parents (GHS, 1995, p. 44). Where the youngest child is over five years old the chances of working are twice as high as when the youngest child is under five.

The employment situation of single mothers is comparable to that of women married to unemployed men, though perhaps more intensely felt. In 1980 the introduction of a Tapered Earnings Disregard for lone parents replaced a low fixed-rate disregard above which earnings were deducted from benefits pound for pound. The expectation that this would increase lone mothers' labour force participation was misplaced (Weale et al., 1984), in that the manipulation of economic incentives had only minimal effects on decisions to take employment. Rather, decisions were based on a complex interaction of preferences; childcare constraints and job opportunities as well as financial rewards. With the introduction of Income Support in 1988 came a policy of special premiums for designated groups with particular needs. One such was single parents, but in 1998 this single parent premium was withdrawn from new or re-applicants, in favour of increased spending on childcare provisions in an attempt to drive single parents into work.

What model?

There are a number of possible responses to the debate about single parents. One would be to challenge the data. It is certainly the case that rates of *illegitimacy* do not in any direct way reflect the proportion of children growing up without two parents in their life. High numbers of births outside marriage simply reflect a decline in the formal institution of marriage, but tell us nothing about either long-term, marriage-like relationships, or patterns of parenting. Indeed, even household composition provides no *necessary* key to understanding the organisation of family life. It is perfectly feasible, and in the past was financially advantageous, for benefit-dependent couples to live apart but maintain a relationship of daily contact and commitment. This is not to argue that all single mothers are involved in some such arrangement, but rather to point out that this would still be consistent with the statistics which underpin arguments about a growing underclass linked to single parenthood.

While one response to the debate could be to suspect the data, another is to argue that high rates of divorce demonstrate that marriage is no longer necessarily viewed as a life-time commitment. Brown (1990) has suggested that marital, residential and child-rearing patterns are undergoing a revolution which is not confined to low-income groups but is a feature of society as a whole. Rates of divorce have risen steadily since 1961, while rates of first marriage have been falling since 1971, such that the nuclear family household cannot be taken for granted as the cornerstone of social organisation. Just as striking is the rise in the proportion of women who are childless by the age of 35; from 12 per cent of women born in 1944 to 20 per cent of those born in 1954 (Social Trends, 1997, Table 2.21). One possible interpretation of these trends could be a growing dissatisfaction among women with their traditional domestic and mothering roles – and an awareness of the detrimental effect they have on employment prospects.

There is now a generation of young women educated by feminism into an awareness of the disadvantages that traditional family life imposes on women. Those with reasonable career prospects will think carefully before entering into motherhood, while those for whom the future holds only unskilled, low-paid work may find motherhood more appealing. This latter group, however, is made up of women whose potential partners bear a disproportionate risk of unemployment. This may deter either partner from embarking on a marriage, or may disrupt the relationships of those who do – in either case contributing to the rising numbers of single mothers.

[. . .]

The sexual division of labour

In relation to the underclass, single mothers and social inclusion, perhaps there is an argument to say that traditional gender roles have been undermined; that a majority of women are now in paid employment and single mothers should be no exception to this trend. Here we must consider the employment options which are generally available to low skilled women in Britain and which account for the rise in recent years of married women in the labour force. Wages available to most women are not adequate for family maintenance (Brown, 1990), especially where employment opportunities are concentrated in part-time work; work constructed on the assumption of women's domestic role. The corollary of this is that many married women are working for a secondary wage, viable only because there is another wage in the household; not only for a secondary wage, but in secondary employment: low-paid, insecure and designed for cheapness and disposability. For many women, paid employment, together with mothering obligations, still requires some kind of dependency – whether it be on the state or on a husband.

Thus the gender-related issues which arise from the debate about the 'underclass' partly stem from unresolved questions about the sexual division of labour in society. Women's position in the household, and particularly the situation of single mothers, raises a number of problems for conceptions of social inclusion. As welfare dependants they become stigmatised members of the underclass, failing in their role of socialisation. Their weak position in the labour market, which is partly a result of gender segregation, means they are for the most part unable to earn sufficient to be self-supporting, and full-time employment would anyway conflict with their mothering role. It is hard to see what full social inclusion would look like for these women, and without some reassessment of the sexual division of labour in society this will continue to be the case. The underclass debate evades these issues by marginalising the status of single mothers; thus single motherhood is presented as a moral issue, and as a departure from the norms and values of mainstream society. Yet the break-up of the nuclear family household is happening at the centre of society; changes to household structures and the decreasing viability of marriage as a life-time condition are more far-reaching, and more centrally placed in society than the underclass debate has ever suggested. So too is a dependent status for women.

Conflicting obligations

Recent developments in the conceptualisation of social citizenship have placed at least as much emphasis on obligations as on rights, the prime obligation being work as a means to self-reliance, and not ironically to care for the next generation of citizens (cf. Pateman, 1989). This places women in an ambiguous position; either they earn their 'public' citizenship rights by their own paid employment, or they perform their 'private' family obligations and remain dependent. This conflict can only be resolved by either a redistribution of the 'private' obligations of unpaid labour, by some acknowledgement of the 'public' service such labour performs, or by increasing state involvement in the 'private' obligation to care for children, alongside fundamental labour market reform. The current situation, however, leaves individual women in something of a dilemma, especially if the fathers of their children are unwilling or unable to perform *their* traditional role. These women become the new 'undeserving poor'.

Thus, the underclass debate stigmatises women's dependency in the context of a tradition which has constructed women as dependent. This tradition has been challenged but not overcome, and is still maintained by beliefs about appropriate gender roles, beliefs about the significance of motherhood and also by the disadvantaged position of most women in the labour market. For single mothers the dilemma is particularly clear; as benefit dependants they are stigmatised members of the 'underclass', and as such are failing in their distinctively female role of socialising the next generation. It is argued that the children in such households suffer from the absence of a breadwinning role model, and yet the weak position of the majority of sole mothers in the labour market prevents them from easily assuming this role themselves. Even were they to do so this would raise the problem of childcare, and more generally of whether they were meeting their traditional obligations as a mother. One response to this complex of problems has been strongly to reaffirm the strengths of traditional arrangements. More recently we have seen the withdrawal of 'special treatment' for single parents in the benefit system as part of the 'welfare to work' drive, and an ideological assertion of 'family values'. However, any more radical solution to the impasse over women's rights to social inclusion can only be achieved by a fundamental and far reaching review of many taken for granted aspects of social life.

What we are currently witnessing is a breakdown in the family–work–welfare nexus on a number of fronts: employment for men has declined, the nuclear family is under challenge, and the use of welfare to fill the breach is increasingly seen as politically unacceptable. Yet women with children have no easy route to independence, because of their principal role in childcare and their limited labour market opportunities. The public anxieties surrounding these issues have been captured by the rhetoric of the underclass, which by isolating and stigmatising single mothers seems to offer at least a containment of the problem. That problem, however, pervades the whole of society, which is undergoing some renegotiation of the organisation of work, family and welfare. The nature of that change cannot be understood through a focus on a residual group, argued to be inadequately socialised, and without whom it is believed the problems will go away.

Notes

1   Young adults on training schemes, for example, are not included in the unemployment count, and there have been numerous other changes since unemployment began to rise in the late seventies.
2   Figures on economic activity show higher rates for men, largely because of their over-representation in self-employment, though women's work in family firms will often be hidden.

References

Auletta, K. (1982) *The Underclass*, New York, Random House.
Beveridge, W. (1942) *Report on the Social Insurance and Allied Services*, Cmnd 6404, London: HMSO.
Brown, J. (1990) 'The Focus on Single Mothers', in C. Murray, *Losing Ground*, New York: Basic Books.
Buckingham, A. (1996) 'A Statistical Update', in R. Lister (ed.) *Charles Murray and the Underclass: the Developing Debate*, Choice in Welfare Series No. 33, London: Institute of Economic Affairs.
Dex, S. (1985) *The Sexual Division of Work*, Brighton: Wheatsheaf.
Dilnot, A. and Kell (1989) 'Men's Unemployment and Women's Work', A. Dilnot and A. Walker (eds), in *The Economics of Social Security*, Oxford: Oxford University Press, 153–68.

General Household Survey (Living in Britain), various, London: HMSO.

Harris, C. C. (1987) *Redundancy and Recession in South Wales*, Oxford: Blackwell.

Hills, J. (1995) *Income and Wealth: Report of the JRF Enquiry Group*, York: Joseph Rowntree Foundation.

Irwin, S. and Morris, L. D. (1993) 'Social Security or Economic Insecurity?', in *Journal of Social Policy*, 349–72.

Jordan, B., James, S., Kay, H. and Redley, M. (1992) *Trapped in Poverty*, London: Routledge.

Labour Force Survey (various).

McLaughlin, E., Millar, J. and Cooke, K. (1989) *Work Welfare and Benefits*, Aldershot: Avebury.

Marshall, T. H. (1950) *Citizenship and Social Class*, Cambridge: Cambridge University Press.

Micklewright, J. (1986) *Unemployment and Incentives to Work: Policy Evidence in the 1980's*, Discussion Paper 92, ESRC Programme on Taxation Incentives and the Distribution of Income, London: London School of Economics.

Morris, L. D. (1995) *Social Divisions*, London: UCL Press.

—— (1996) 'Income Maintenance and Household Living Standards', in *Journal of Social Policy*, 25, 459–83.

Pahl, R. E. (1984) *Divisions of Labour*, Oxford: Blackwell.

Pateman, C. (1989) *The Disorder of Women*, Cambridge: Polity Press.

Social Trends (1997).

Weale, A. et al. (1984) *Lone Mothers, Paid Work and Social Security*, London: Bedford Square Press/NCVO.

Women Avoiding being Working Class

12

Beverley Skeggs

Key words

Social class, working-class women, distinction, class position, class identity, respectability, cultural capital

---

Skeggs explores the experience of young working-class women. She asks how their socialization affects them in the transition to adulthood, how they deal with a sense of powerlessness and potential lack of public esteem, and what consequences this has on their sense of class, femininity, sexuality and political identification. Starting in 1980 and using ethnographic techniques, she contacted 83 working-class young women with low levels of educational qualification who were enrolled at a further education college on care courses. She talked to them repeatedly over a twelve-year period, during which they joined the labour market and started families. She notes how they 'disidentify' with the working class. They don't talk about class, but they experience its effects. They refuse the label working class for themselves and try hard not to appear to be working class, pursuing strategies for 'improvement' and attempting to 'pass' as middle class. Skeggs observes that, despite their efforts, they always remain anxious and insecure, apologetic or resentful victims of a system of social classification in which working-class people are made to feel inferior in material and symbolic terms.*

[. . .]

Class was central to the young women's subjectivities. It was not spoken of in the traditional sense of recognition – I am working class – but rather, was displayed in their

* This study is described in more depth in N. Abercrombie and A. Warde et al., *Contemporary British Society* (2000), pp. 173–5.

multitudinous efforts *not to be* recognized as working class. They disidentified and they dissimulated. Theirs was a refusal of recognition rather than a claim for the right to be recognized. It was a denial of the representations of their positioning. This should not surprise us, for [. . .] the label working class when applied to women has been used to signify all that is dirty, dangerous and without value. In the women's claims for a caring/respectable/responsible personality class was rarely directly figured but was constantly present. It was the structuring absence. Yet whilst they made enormous efforts to distance themselves from the label of working class, their class position (alongside the other social positions of gender, race and sexuality), was the omnipresent underpinning which informed and circumscribed their ability *to be*. This is a chapter about that relationship between positioning and identity. It is about the experience of class. Class operated in a dialogic manner: in every judgement of themselves a measurement was made against others. In this process the designated 'other' (based on representations and imaginings of the respectable and judgemental middle class) was constructed as the standard to/from which they measured themselves. The classifying of themselves depended upon the classifying systems of others.

Class is experienced by the women as exclusion. Whereas working-class men can use class as a positive source of identity, a way of including themselves in a positively valorized social category (Willis, 1977), this does not apply for working-class women. Warde (1994) asks if class in general ought to be defined by exclusion and deprivation, rather than by trying to locate attributes such as occupation and education which are shared by all class members. It is deprivations that persist over time even when actual occupations change or household composition alters. The exclusions occur because the women do not have *access* to economic resources and cultural ways to be anything other than working class. Their structural positioning does not enable access to productive resources. As this chapter will demonstrate they do not have any of the requisite capitals [. . .] to be middle class. The recent retreat from the study of class has been enacted by those who do have the requisite access and are claiming that their privilege is not an issue. However, access to knowledge is a central feature of class reproduction and it is very clear that those who want to dismiss class as a redundant concept want to abdicate responsibility from the relations of inequality in which they and the women of this study are very differently positioned. Class is absolutely central to how these women live their lives, exemplified in this chapter by their constant refusal to be fixed or measured by it.

[. . .]

Disidentifications

To me if you are working class it basically means that you are poor. That you have nothing. You know, nothing.

[Sam, 1992]

The real working class are the ones you see hanging round the dole. They're dead scruffy and poor and they haven't a job but I guess they may be working if they are working class, they may be working. If they're working class they should be working so they work, I guess, in all the bad jobs.

[Sheenah, 1992]

They're rough. You can always tell. Rough, you know, the women are common as muck you know, always have a fag in their mouths, the men are dead rough. You know.

[Andrea, 1992]

Just poor, trying to get by on very little, it's not their fault there's no jobs anymore they're the ones who are struggling.

[Michelle, 1992]

The ones who batter their kids.

[Pam, 1992]

It used to be you were working class if you worked in the railways say and it didn't mean you had no money, but now it's changed. Now it means that you don't work, like it's not those with the good jobs now it's those without jobs, they're the real working-class.

[Lisa, 1992]

No doubt Thatcherism has informed this slippage from working to underclass and has influenced the construction of distinctions within the working class. The real working class for these women is something from which they are desperately trying to escape. It is why they are doing college courses. They want to be seen as different. Their dis-simulations are not unlike the historical and popular representations of the working class (especially working-class women). In their accounts the working class are poor, deprived, depriving, dangerous and degraded. They are well aware of the jokes about 'Sharons and Kevins', about 'tackiness', about white high heeled shoes. Other studies of class representation such as Hill (1986) suggest a normalization of the middle classes and a pathologizing of the working classes through representations. Historical studies such as Stedman Jones (1971), Kuhn (1988) and Nead (1988) chart a long history in Britain in which the working class have been (through representation) continually demonized, pathologized and held responsible for social problems.

[. . .]

This is why for the women directly speaking of class is rare. Frazer (1989) found a similar problem when she asked two different groups of working- and middle-class girls to discuss class and found startlingly different responses. The working-class girls displayed an unusual reluctance to speak. They found class ambiguous, vague and embarrassing. This contrasted with a group of public schoolgirls who were well prac-tised in discussing class. In the United States, Press (1990) notes how the women she interviewed for her research were groping for the proper words with which to con-ceptualize class differences. Similarly, McRobbie found a complete absence of class discourse from the general talk of the young women she studied, arguing: '[b]eing working-class meant little or nothing to these girls – but being a *girl* over-determined their every moment' (1982: 48).

[. . .]

Improving and passing

The first time I had heard such emphasis being put on improving was when I inter-viewed the mothers, many of whom were concerned that their daughters should improve upon their lives. Improvement is a means by which cultural capital comes to take on greater value outside of the local. It is when it can be traded in a wider context. Education was the means by which they could convert their caring capital into an economic resource in the labour market: the use of femininity was the means by which they could try and secure future resources through the marriage market. Improving narratives came to take on a greater significance through the course of the research. They related to many aspects of their lives and were always based on generating, accruing and/or displaying cultural capital. They wanted to and/or were involved in improving their appearance; their bodies; their mind; their flats/houses; their relationships; their future. Class was configured through the improvement discourse because in order to improve they had to differentiate themselves from those who did not or could not improve. They were continually making comparisons between themselves and others, creating distances and establishing distinctions and tastes in the process. As Bourdieu (1986) argues, distinctions constantly proliferate. The women had a strong sense of what they did not want to be, but were less sure of what they wanted to be. The knowledge available to them to enable them to resist being classified as working class was based on media and educational representations and limited contact with middle-class people. The middle-class people they met were usually in positions of authority (such as teachers, doctors and social workers). As Press (1991) notes from her research, the working-class women she interviewed learnt about middle-class lifestyles predominantly from television. Their desires not to be seen as working class are lived through their bodies, clothes and (if not living with parents) their homes.

[. . .]

Displays of distinction and sites of investment are not just produced through bodies, appearance, children and leisure. Every site becomes a marker. The home is a central site for creatively producing a sense of themselves (and sometimes their family) through the use and organization of consumer goods (see Carter, 1990). The home is an important site for displaying cultural investments. Homes also become the site for guilt as they cost so much more to put together. When the women showed me round their houses, wardrobes, kitchens, record collections, and so on, there was an almost constant apology for the things I was being shown:

> We would really like to have real antiques but they cost so much money and they're not as solid as this furniture. So this'll have to do until we can afford better. Personally, I prefer this to something that's probably full of insects.
>
> [Janet, 1986]

Here is expressed a knowledge that antiques should be preferred and are the 'real' thing, alongside an ambivalence about the age, stability and hygiene of old furniture. Janet is caught between two different discourses, that of hygiene and antique authenticity. The former is used to discount the latter. Janet knows what she prefers, but also knows what she should prefer:

> I know you're meant to have real paintings on your wall, but I love these prints [Athena's ballet dancers]. I just think the price for real paintings is ridiculous and frankly we've got other uses for our money.
>
> [Janet, 1986]

When we moved in the kitchen was all white melamine, straight from MFI so we ripped it out straight away. I put my foot down, I said we're not having that cheap stuff in here. The kitchen cost a fortune but I love it and I love spending time in here. But I'm afraid that to get it right in here means we've not been able to afford to do anything else, so I'm sorry the rest of the house dulls by comparison. I think I'd spend all my time in here if I could. It's my room. We would have done the rest but what with all the redundancies at ICI now you've just got to be careful.

[Darren, 1992]

A lot of the stuff in here is just rubbish that our family gave me. It's like I'd never be seen dead with that sofa. We had a real row about it at first. I said I'm not going to have it in here, in my house. Me mam, she said, who did I think I was, she said I should sit on bare floorboards. She said I couldn't have it after I didn't want it. But I had to have something to sit on, didn't I. So she agreed in the end. It's like the drawers upstairs, they're horrible, did you notice them? They shouldn't have house room really but I had nowhere to put things.

[Janice, 1989]

We wanted to buy all new when we moved in but what with the cost of the wedding we just couldn't. I was dead upset at first. I was ashamed to have people round with everybody else's castouts, but we're replacing it bit by bit. It looks odd though, don't you think?

[Sharon, 1986]

The comments included here are expressed as questions in need of approval or as statements which dare to be challenged. All display a knowledge that there is another more highly valued way of doing things which they have yet to achieve.[1] The pleasure they get from their homes and the time they spend on them is always disrupted by their knowledge of a judgemental external other who positions them as surveillant of themselves, what Bakhtin (1984) identifies as a hidden polemic – the 'policing' of the superior other. This is not dissimilar to the women of Ann Gray's (1992) study whose responses to television viewing were always mediated through the discourse of populism. They were aware of what was considered to be in either good or bad taste and monitored their responses accordingly.

This surveillance covers not just what the women consume but also the way their labour is used to convert these consumer goods into an aesthetic disposition. It is their buying and creative practices which they evaluate on the basis of the imagined judgements of others. They are positioned by their furniture and paint. When a visitor enters the house they see their most intimate environments through the eyes of the other and they apologize. They continually doubt their own judgements. This is the emotional politics of class. They can never have the certainty that they are doing it right which is one of the main signifiers of middle-class dispositions (Bourdieu, 1986). This lack of certainty means that they cannot make use of social space in the same way: they close off their access through their doubt and scrutiny of themselves. They care about how they are seen in the eyes of the other. They feel they have to prove themselves through every object, every aesthetic display, every appearance. Their taste in furniture and aesthetic organization becomes along with their clothes, body, caring practices and every other aspect of their lives a site of doubt. A site where they are never sure if they are getting it right. They assume that certainty exists elsewhere: that others have it. There is no counter-cultural valuation of their homes.[2] The working class are never free from the judgements of imaginary and real others that position them, not just as different, but as inferior, as inadequate. Homes and bodies are where respectability is displayed but where class is lived out as the most omnipresent form, engendering surveillance and constant assessment of themselves.

[. . .]

They know that they do not have that option. They also know that this is how differences are maintained and that they are positioned through it. They know that there are certain ways of being and doing to which they do not have access. This generates resentment. There was not a clear split between those who wanted to pass and those who resented. These two affects were held together. The desires to pass, or not to be recognized as working class are generated from experiences of being positioned by others:

> We'd all gone up to Manchester the other Saturday, you know for a day out, the three of us. It was alright, in fact we had a right laugh . . . but we were in Kendals during the day, you know where the really posh food is, and we were laughing about all the chocolates and how many we could eat – if we could afford them – and this woman she just looked at us. If looks could kill. Like we were only standing there. We weren't doing anything wrong. We weren't scruffy or anything. She just looked. It was like it was her place and we didn't belong there. And you know what we just all walked away. We should have punched her in the face. We didn't say anything until about half an hour later. Can you imagine? Well and truly put in our place . . . It's things like that that put you off going. You feel better staying around here.
>
> [Wendy, 1986]

> That's like when you're walking through the perfume bit of Owen and Owen and they're spraying perfume all over the posh ones and you know you're not going to get any. Me and Jane we used to stand there till she sprayed us.
>
> [Morag, 1986]

> When I first went to work as a nanny I couldn't stand it. They really think they're something else. They treat you like shit. What I've noticed is they never look at you. Well they do at first they look you all over and make you feel like a door rag, but then they just tell you what to do. One of them once asked me if I had any other clothes. Some of them want you to know you're shit in comparison to them. I jacked it in shit money, being made to feel like shit. Even the kids. They learn really early that you're not worth the ground they walk on. They're bastards.
>
> [Cynthia, 1992]

> They always assume they have a right to anything and everything. It's like whatever they are doing that's their right. They just think the world is made for them.
>
> [Angela, 1989]

> When we were at school we used to beat them all up. We'd wait for them coming down our way going home from school. They frighten dead easy. But it's like now they're the ones getting their own back. They have money and cars and we're still hanging around here.
>
> [Therese, 1989]

These comments, selected from many, show the fear, the desire, the resentment, hatred and humiliation. Class relations are felt as they are lived, and these feelings generate strong emotions, sometimes violence, degradation *and* resistance. Space and place are consistent themes in their narratives. The women know they are being positioned as contagious, not-belonging or dirty: that is their situated knowledge. They know they occupy space in different ways. This is articulated as rights-to. They do not believe they have the same entitlements, the access to the same rights, which is made especially apparent in Angela's commentary. It is also shown in Wendy's account where she, at first, holds herself and friends responsible for the look they engender, 'we weren't scruffy or anything' she insists, as if being scruffy would warrant such a look. They are made to feel invisible, as Mary notes with anger and as Cynthia feels. It is this double movement of being made to feel invisible and under scrutiny which generates resentment. They are either designated wrong or they feel they do not exist.

[...]

Conclusion

[...]

As the historical and contemporary analysis of class representations suggests, we should not be surprised that the women do not want to be recognized as such. However, the definitions of working-classness were by no means straightforward. When they did attempt to identify themselves they first had difficulties finding a discourse of class and, second, had problems with the methods of classification used to define it. This was paralleled in the academic accounts of class where no clear meaning is agreed upon and where classifications systems are strongly contested. The women tried to make sense of their class positioning through employment, background, housing and money. They had a strong sense that their social and cultural positioning was unjust. They did not adjust to their social positioning as Bourdieu (1986) would suggest. Rather they made strenuous efforts to deny, disidentify and dissimulate. These were affective responses; class was lived as a structure of feeling. Class is still a hidden injury (Sennett and Cobb, 1977). They attempted to display their distinction from being classified as working-class through a variety of methods. To do so they made investments in their bodies, clothes, consumption practices, leisure pursuits and homes. These investments indicated a strong desire to pass as middle class. But it was only an imaginary middle class that they wanted to be. They did not want to take on the whole package of dispositions. Their responses to classification were informed by fear, desire, resentment and humiliation. They were individualistic responses produced through their own bodies and influencing their movement through social space. In this sense they become implicated in a similar mechanism to that which enabled the construction of the caring self. Their class subjectivity monitors itself dialogically through the real and imaginary experiences, perceptions and judgements of others.

[...]

Notes

1   One of the hidden injuries of class may be that a sign of being middle class is an indifference to such material signifiers through the normalization of their 'taste'.
2   This may be why Ikea and Habitat are so successful. They market 'taste' and modernity (in Ikea's case through national identifications) and provide the security of knowing it is possible to 'get it right'.

References

Bakhtin, M. (1984) *Rabelais and His World*. trans. H. Iswolsky. Bloomington: Indiana University Press.
Bourdieu, P. (1986) *Distinction: A Social Critique of the Judgement of Taste*. London: Routledge.
Carter, E. (1990) 'Design, Class and Lifestyle: A West Berlin Perspective'. *Magazine of Cultural Studies*, 2, 8–11 October.
Frazer, E. (1989) 'Feminist Talk and Talking about Feminism: Teenage Girls' Discourses of Gender'. *Oxford Review of Education*, 15: 3: 281–90.
Gray, A. (1992) *Video Playtime: The Gendering of a Leisure Technology*. London: Routledge.
Hill, J. (1986) *Sex, Class and Realism: British Cinema 1956–1963*. London: British Film Institute.
Kuhn, A. (1988) *Cinema, Censorship and Sexuality, 1909–1925*. London: Routledge and Kegan Paul.
McRobbie, A. (1982) 'The Politics of Feminist Research: Between Talk, Text and Action'. *Feminist Review*, 12: 46–59.
Nead, L. (1988) *Myths of Sexuality: Representations of Women in Victorian Britain*. Oxford: Blackwell.
Press, A. (1990) 'Class, Gender and the Female Viewer: Women's Responses to *Dynasty*', in M. E. Brown (ed.) *Television and Women's Culture: The Politics of the Popular*. London: Sage, pp. 158–83.
—— (1991) *Women Watching Television: Gender, Class and Generation in the American Television Experience*. Philadelphia: University of Pennsylvania Press.
Sennett, R. and Cobb, J. (1977) *The Hidden Injuries of Class*. Cambridge: Cambridge University Press.
Stedman Jones, G. (1971) *Outcast London: A Study in the Relationship Between Classes in Victorian Society*. Oxford: Clarendon.
Warde, A. (1994) 'Employment Relations or Assets: An Alternative Basis of Class Analysis'. Paper presented to Lancaster Regionalism Group, 13.12.94. Lancaster University.
Willis, P. (1977) *Learning to Labour: How Working Class Kids get Working Class Jobs*. Farnbrough, Hants: Saxon House.

Racial Harassment

13

Satnam Virdee

Key words
Racial harassment, crime, racism, ethnicity, racial abuse, police

Following a number of well-publicized cases, the harassment of members of ethnic minorities has been much in the news in recent years. This extract explores the data on the extent, nature and consequences of such harassment. Police statistics do not give an accurate view of the extent of the problem because many people do not report incidents of racial harassment. The British Crime Survey (BCS), which is based on victims' own accounts, records a much higher rate of racially motivated crime. The BCS, however, does not include incidents of low-level harassment which the victims do not define as crime. Virdee's study is based on a survey which explored this non-criminal abuse, which is still deeply upsetting and may, indeed, provide the environment for future acts of violence. The extract deals with the perpetrators of such abuse, noting that they are typically young white men, often in groups. Virdee concludes that racial harassment of this kind is related to the prevalence of racist beliefs among the white population. In other parts of the chapter, not included in the extract, he notes the negative view of the police held by members of ethnic minority communities. Not only do the police fail to act in cases of harassment, sometimes they appear to be the perpetrators of them.

[. . .]

Apart from the findings of the 1988 and 1992 British Crime Surveys, there is little in the way of systematic national evidence on the type of person that perpetrates acts of racial violence and harassment. The Fourth National Survey will be useful in provid-

| Table 1 | The type pf perpetrator involved in the most serious incident of racial harassment |

column percentages

	Racial attacks	Racially motivated property damage	Racial insults
Perpetrator seen: Yes	98	75	99
No	2	25	I
Of those seen			
Neighbours	7	52	13
Acquaintances	7	5	6
People at work	8	1	16
People in shop	0	0	11
Place of entertainment	12	2	4
Police officers	6	1	3
Other officials	2	0	2
Complete strangers	67	36	62
Others	7	10	6
Weighted count	*57*	*78*	*600*
Unweighted count	*51*	*79*	*529*

It should be noted that because the victims, in some cases, identified more than one type of perpetrator for any single incident, the figures will not always total 100 per cent.

ing a detailed outline profile of the type of person that engages in this type of activity so that further research on perpetrators themselves can then begin to provide a clearer understanding of the motives of such people.

We asked those who had been racially harassed to describe the people who had been responsible for the most serious incident. It needs to be borne in mind that owing to the relatively small number of respondents who reported being racially attacked or having property damaged, the conclusions drawn about the perpetrators of these especially serious incidents should be treated with some caution and should be seen as being indicative rather than definitive. Moreover, as Table 1 shows, only three-quarters of the people who reported being subjected to racially motivated property damage saw the perpetrator; the others could not provide any kind of description.

Table 1 goes on to show that two-thirds of the people involved in racial attacks were complete strangers. One in eight were identified as either staff or customers in places of entertainment, while a further fifth were identified as people the victim knew before the attack such as neighbours, acquaintances or people at work. Table 1 also shows that almost three-fifths of the people engaged in racially motivated property damage were identified as neighbours and acquaintances. This reflects the fact that property damaged was normally the victim's home or car. However, in over a third of these cases of racially motivated property damage, the perpetrator was said to be a complete stranger. The types of people who engaged in racial insults and other types of insulting behaviour were more varied, reflecting a wider range of locations in which such incidents took place. Three-fifths of the people who had been racially abusive were complete strangers. One in five, however, were described as being neighbours or acquaintances and a further one in six were people who were abusive at work.

The combined data from the 1988 and 1992 BCS provides information on the characteristics of offenders in incidents of racially motivated violence and threats only. It found that in three-fifths of all incidents of racial violence and threats against Caribbeans the perpetrator was identified as a complete stranger, whereas for South Asians the comparable figure was two-thirds (Aye Maung and Mirrlees-Black 1994, 17).

Data from the 1988 and 1992 British Crime Surveys also found that three-quarters of South Asian victims were involved in racially motivated incidents of violence and threats where more than one offender was involved, and two-fifths were subject to incidents involving groups of four or more. For Caribbeans the equivalent figures were 50 and 10 per cent respectively (Aye Maung and Mirrlees-Black 1994, 18).

Table 2 shows the response of victims in this national survey when they were asked to state how many people were involved in what they believed to be the most serious incident. Racial violence and harassment were often undertaken by groups of individuals. Approximately half of the people who were victims of a racial attack said it had been carried out by more than one person; a fifth of them by groups of more than five people. Over four-fifths of people who said they had suffered from racially motivated property damage in the past year, said it had been carried out by more than one person, while nearly two-fifths said it had been undertaken by more than five people. Over three-fifths of the people who had been racially abused in the past year said there was more than one person involved; one in five by a group of more than five people.

Data from the 1988 and 1992 British Crime Surveys suggest that in more than a third of all cases of racially motivated violence and threats against Caribbeans and in more than half of the cases of racially motivated violence and threats against South Asians, the perpetrator was described by the victim as being aged between 16 and 25 (Aye Maung and Mirrlees-Black 1994, 17).

Table 2 also shows that half the perpetrators of racial attacks in our survey were thought to be aged between 20 and 29; a quarter were teenagers and, perhaps surprisingly, a third were identified as being aged over 30. Of those who carried out racially motivated property damage, three-quarters were identified as being teenagers or younger and a quarter were between 20 and 29. Two-fifths of the people who racially abused members of ethnic minorities were identified as being teenagers or younger; almost two-fifths as being aged between 20 and 29 and a further third as being aged over 30. The data strongly suggest that racial violence and harassment is not undertaken merely by a small proportion of 'anti-social' youth and young adults but also by a small but significant minority of adults over the age of 30.

The 1988 and 1992 BCS found that three-quarters of the racially motivated violence and threats against Caribbeans and nine out of ten incidents of racially motivated violence and threats against South Asians were carried out by males (Aye Maung and Mirrlees-Black 1994, 17). We also found that the overwhelming majority of people who were racially attacked in the previously 12 months identified the perpetrator as a male, although one in eight identified them as females or females acting with males (see Table 2). Of the people who were subjected to racially motivated property damage in the past year, four-fifths identified the offender as being a male. No-one identified

| Table 2 | Characteristics of perpetrators involved in the most serious incident of racial harassment |

column percentages

	Racial attacks	Racially motivated property damage	Racial insults
Number of perpetrators			
I	48	14	37
2–4	34	48	45
5 or more	18	38	19
Weighted count	*59*	*64*	*503*
Unweighted count	*54*	*65*	*442*
Age of perpetrators[1]			
Under 13	2	15	9
Teenage	25	60	30
20–29	49	25	37
30+	35	13	34
Weighted count	*59*	*71*	*528*
Unweighted count	*54*	*70*	*459*
Gender of perpetrators			
Male	87	79	66
Female	7	0	12
Both	6	21	22
Weighted count	*59*	*73*	*554*
Unweighted count	*54*	*73*	*486*

[1] In some cases of racially motivated property damage and racial abuse which were undertaken by more than one person, the victims have identified perpetrators in different age bands. Consequently, the figures will not always total 100 per cent.

solely women being involved in this type of racial harassment, although one in five did identify women acting together with men to damage property. Two-thirds of those people who had been racially abused were insulted by men acting alone. However, one third stated they had been racially abused by women, either acting alone or alongside men.

The 1988 and 1992 BCS showed that, in the case of Caribbeans being racially attacked or threatened, the perpetrator was normally white. However, in just under a sixth of cases of violence and threats against Caribbeans, the perpetrator was identified as being 'black'. In the case of South Asians, the perpetrator was almost always white (Aye Maung and Mirrlees-Black 1994, 17). Table 3 shows clearly that the perpetrators responsible for racial attacks, racially motivated damage to property and racial abuse were almost always white. However, in a small proportion of racial attacks and racial insults, the offender was described as being 'black'.[1]

Table 3	The ethnicity of perpetrators involved in the most serious incident of racial harassment

column percentages

	Racial attacks	Racially motivated property damage	Racial insults
Ethnicity of perpetrators			
White	93	92	90
Black	5	1	3
Asian	0	0	1
Chinese	0	0	1
Mixed:			
Mainly white	1	6	4
Mainly black	1	1	1
Mainly Asian	0	0	<1
Weighted count	*59*	*77*	*552*
Unweighted count	*54*	*75*	*485*

The white population and racial prejudice

The preceding section has demonstrated that the people most likely to subject ethnic minorities to racial harassment were young white men, often acting in groups. Attempts have been made to explore those factors that motivate such people to commit such acts of racial harassment. One explanation put forward is that acts of racial harassment represent the most extreme component and expression of the racism faced by Britain's ethnic minorities more generally. It is contended that it is from this much wider and deep-rooted racist culture, present among sections of the white population, that some draw the moral legitimacy they require to act upon these beliefs (Husband 1994a; 1994b; Virdee 1995).

This survey investigated to what degree the white population held such racist beliefs. It asked our sample of whites whether they were prejudiced against four non-white groups: the Chinese, South Asians, Caribbeans and Muslims. A measure of prejudice against Muslims was sought because the past 15 years have witnessed growing academic interest in the Muslim population (Modood 1992). Some of the more important factors which have served to place this important issue at the forefront of current debate have been the Honeyford Affair in Bradford, the Rushdie Affair and the Gulf War. Among some elements of society, these events (coupled with others external to Britain) have served to create an atmosphere where Islam has been demonised in the public consciousness and a wave of 'Islamophobia' launched.

The findings that are reported upon ought to be interpreted with some caution because of the limitations associated with the question asked: first, the question seeks to capture a measure of racial prejudice in a direct and somewhat crude manner and, second, past research has suggested that these types of questions are likely to provide

Table 4	White people who said they were racially prejudiced against ethnic minorities, by gender		
			cell percentages
	White men	*White women*	*All whites*
Asian	28	24	26
Caribbean	23	18	20
Muslim	28	23	25
Chinese	9	8	8
Weighted count	*1276*	*1591*	*2867*
Unweighted count	*1201*	*1666*	*2867*

an underestimate of the scale of racial prejudice among the white population (see Airey 1984).

As shown by Table 4, a quarter of whites admitted they were prejudiced against Asians and Muslims compared with 20 per cent who said they were prejudiced against Caribbeans. These findings are consistent with those of the annual British Social Attitudes Survey which, since the early 1980s, has regularly recorded that white people think there is more racial prejudice against South Asians than against Caribbeans. In 1991, 58 per cent of whites thought that there was considerable prejudice against Asians compared with 50 per cent against Caribbeans (Young 1992, 181). The ethnic group that whites were least likely to be prejudiced against were the Chinese (10 per cent). Additionally, the table clearly shows that white men are more likely to be prejudiced against the main ethnic minority groups than white women.

The data also showed that a smaller proportion of young white people aged between 16 and 34 were prejudiced against Caribbeans than older whites. However, this was not the case with South Asians and Muslims, against whom similar proportions of young whites and older whites were prejudiced. The lower level of reported racial prejudice against the Caribbean population (but not against South Asians) among the young white population may be explained in part by the increasing adoption of a hybrid Caribbean/white identity by sections of the young white population resident in urban areas and mediated through the cultural forms of popular music and sport (Modood et al. 1994). At the same time, there is research evidence to suggest that this process has been accompanied among parts of the white population by a hardening of racial prejudice against other ethnic minority groups (Back 1993).

The data suggest that a current of racist beliefs is clearly evident among a significant proportion of the white population. It may be that the small minority of mainly young white men who carry out acts of racial harassment have been informed and influenced by this current of opinion to act upon their beliefs. It is a certainly an aspect of the problem that requires further investigation.

[. . .]

Conclusions

Although racial violence and harassment is a phenomenon that has existed within Britain since at least the end of the First World War (Fryer 1984), the problem arrived on the public policy agenda only in the early 1980s. It led to a demand among policy makers for accurate statistics on the scale of the problem. It was argued that it needed to be reliably quantified to ensure that appropriate resources and measures could be introduced towards tackling it effectively. However, it was not until 1988 that reliable national statistics, in the form of the British Crime Survey, first emerged.

'Low-level' racial harassment has been an aspect of the problem that has been greatly neglected when attempting to understand the nature of the phenomenon. It is important to establish the scale of this form of racial harassment because it holds the key to a more informed understanding of the phenomenon more generally. The more we learn about racial violence and harassment, the clearer it becomes that the publicly reported police statistics represent the visible tip of the iceberg. Recent research suggests that there are other, and potentially much wider spread, forms of racially insulting and threatening behaviour which are not seen as criminal events in themselves (Virdee 1995; Beishon et al. 1995). This pyramid of violence and harassment is probably based on a continuing level of racism in sections of the white population of which harassment is only a symptom. For the first time in a national survey, PSI's Fourth Survey of Ethnic Minorities addressed this important gap in the research by providing a measure of the extent of 'low-level' racial harassment to which ethnic minorities have been subjected in one year.

Racial harassment has, however, to be seen in the context of the experience of crime more generally. This survey found that there was considerable diversity among the various ethnic groups and their experience of crime. Similar proportions of whites and South Asians reported being attacked, whereas a significantly higher proportion of Caribbeans and a significantly lower proportion of Chinese were subjected to physical attacks. When it came to reported property damage, the survey found that, apart from Bangladeshis, about one in seven of all ethnic groups (including whites) reported having had property damaged in the previous 12 months. The Bangladeshis were only half as likely as the rest of the sample to report property damage.

This survey showed clearly that within this experience of crime the prevalence of racial harassment was widespread. A total of 13 per cent of the total ethnic minority sample reported being subjected to some form of racial harassment in the past year. There was some variation in the overall extent of racial harassment to which the different ethnic minority groups were subjected. A significantly higher proportion of Caribbeans, African Asians, Pakistanis and Chinese reported being subjected to some form of racial harassment than Indians and Bangladeshis, but this difference refers only to the reports of racial abuse and insulting behaviour and not racial attacks and racially motivated property damage. One per cent of the total sample of ethnic minorities in the national survey said they had been racially attacked in the previous year and 2 per cent said they had had their property damaged for reasons to do with their 'race' or colour. Twelve per cent, however, reported they had been racially abused or insulted in the previous 12 months.

By extrapolating from the total adult ethnic minority population in England and Wales (nearly 2 million), it is possible to estimate the total number of people who have experienced any of these different forms of racial harassment. The results from the survey would suggest that, in a 12-month period, there were about 20,000 people who were racially attacked, 40,000 people who had been subjected to racially motivated damage to property and 230,000 people who were racially abused or insulted. Overall, the survey results would suggest that more than a quarter of a million people were subjected to some form of racial harassment in a 12-month period.

In addition to providing a quantification of the problem, the survey shed some light on the type of person that was most likely to report being subjected to racial harassment. Although the data suggest that it is not wise to construct a profile of a 'typical' victim, men under the age of 45 seem to be most vulnerable. Repeat victimisation was a problem for well over half of all people who were racially harassed in the previous 12 months. Indeed, nearly a quarter of those who had been racially harassed were victimised five or more times – 3 per cent of all members of the sample, representing about 60,000 people. These findings suggest that further work needs to be undertaken to understand why particular individuals from ethnic minorities are subjected to such harassment.

This national survey also provided valuable insights into another aspect of the problem, that is, those who undertake harassment. Most of the findings from this part of the survey confirmed what many have suspected from anecdotal evidence: about three-fifths of people that had been racially attacked or abused said the perpetrator was a complete stranger, whereas in those cases where people had been subjected to racially motivated property damage the perpetrator was most likely to be a neighbour or acquaintance. A disturbing finding to emerge was the degree of racial harassment that took place at work: one in six people who were racially abused said it had taken place at work. The data also strongly suggest that racial violence and harassment is not undertaken merely by a proportion of 'anti-social' young men, but also by a small but significant minority of adults over the age of 30.

South Asians were more likely to report racially motivated attacks and damage to property to the police than Caribbeans. On the other hand, similar proportions of Caribbeans and South Asians reported being racially abused to the police. About half of those respondents who had reported being subjected to some form of racial harassment were dissatisfied with the police response. After detailed investigation of the verbatim transcripts, two broad explanations emerged as to why these individuals felt dissatisfied with the police response. First, the police were perceived to have shown a lack of interest or indifference towards addressing the problem even though the incident constituted a criminal assault, and, secondly, the police response was interpreted as being racist or in implicit sympathy with the actions of the perpetrators.

No doubt in part informed by such negative contact with the police on this problem, this survey showed clearly that there has been a further strengthening of the historically antagonistic relationship between Caribbeans and the police. The study showed that three-quarters of Caribbean respondents believed they could not rely on the police to protect them from racial harassment. This lack of confidence in the police being able to protect ethnic minorities from racial harassment was also expressed by over two-fifths of South Asians.

On an important and related matter, this survey found that the police, rather than being one of the most important agencies responsible for tackling the problem of racial harassment, were sometimes responsible for actually engaging in it. Three of the 59 people who had been racially attacked and two of the 103 people that reported racially motivated property damage identified the offender as a police officer. A further 3 per cent of all people who had been racially abused in the previous year identified the perpetrators as police officers (21 out of 608). Few of the people who had been subjected to such racial abuse had actually complained to the police. Unlike racial abuse in general, reports of racial abuse from the police came mainly from Caribbeans.

A significant proportion of the ethnic minority population in the survey worried about being racially harassed. The actions taken by them to avoid some common everyday scenarios in order to lessen their chances of being racially harassed clearly demonstrate that the problem has a significant impact on the quality of life they are able to lead.

Note

1   In approximately half those cases where the perpetrator of racial harassment was identified as black, the victim was of Caribbean origin.

References

Airey, C. (1984) 'Social and moral values'. In R. Jowell and C. Airey (eds) *British Social Attitudes: the 1984 Report.* Gower
Aye Maung, N. and C. Mirrlees-Black (1994) *Racially Motivated Crime: a British Crime Survey analysis.* Home Office Research and Planning Unit
Back, L. (1993) 'Race, identity and nation within an adolescent community in South London', *New Community*, 19 (2), pp. 217–33
Beishon, S., S. Virdee and A. Hagell (1995) *Nursing in a Multi-Ethnic NHS.* Policy Studies Institute
Fryer, P. (1984) *Staying Power: The History of Black People in Britain.* Pluto Press
Husband, C. (1994a) 'General Introduction: Ethnicity and Media Democratization within the Nation-State'. In C. Husband (ed.) *A Richer Vision: the Development of Ethnic Minority Media in Western Democracies.* UNESCO: Libbey
—— (1994b) 'Following the "continental model"?: implications of the recent electoral performance of the British National Party (BNP)', *New Community*, 20 (4), July, pp. 563–79
Modood, T. (1992) *Not Easy Being British: Colour, Culture and Citizenship.* Runnymede Trust and Trentham Books
—— S. Beishon, and S. Virdee (1994) *Changing Ethnic Identities.* Policy Studies Institute
Virdee, S. (1995) *Racial Violence and Harassment.* Policy Studies Institute
Young, K. (1992) 'Class, race and opportunity'. In R. Jowell et al. (eds) *British Social Attitudes: the 9th report.* Dartmouth

Part III

Family and Household

Changing Families

14

Sarah Irwin

Key words

Family formation, marriage, fertility, family size, youth, demographic change

---

In the following extract, which is taken from a larger study on the transition from youth to adulthood, Irwin reviews changes in family formation over the twentieth century. She argues that a trend towards a 'modern life course' that reached its peak in the 1960s and 1970s has been, in certain respects, modified since the late 1970s. The most important characteristic of 'modern' family formation is that life course events occur within a shorter period. For example, most people married within an eight-year span between ages 17 and 25 in the 1970s while the corresponding span in the nineteenth century was 20 years. Furthermore, childbearing was clustered in the early years of marriage until the 1970s, together with a decline in ages at marriage and childbearing. The changes are clearly related to the overall fall in family size from the nineteenth on into the twentieth century.

In the early 1970s some of these trends towards a modern family form were reversed. The age at first marriage, for example, has started to rise again in the last three decades after a long period of decline, together with an increase in the proportion of those not marrying. At the same time, the numbers of couples living together before marriage has also increased. However, this is not simply a form of marriage which effectively reduces the age of marriage again. There is generally a delay in the attainment of independence and in the timing of family formation, combined with continued decrease in fertility and rise in age of the first birth, although there is also a growing diversity across the population in these elements.

[. . .]

Demographic change and rites of passage

The making of the 'modern' life course

Anderson, in his description of historical change in the individual and family life course, suggests that the 1960s and 1970s might be characterized as embodying 'the modern life cycle' (Anderson 1985). However, the reversal in the 1970s of the long-term trend to younger ages at family formation gives some aspects of this characterization an already dated prospect. Anderson proposes that the historical tendency towards a clustering of the ages at life course events across the population is the principal feature in the emergence of the modern life course. For example, in the 1970s most people married within an eight year span, between ages 17 and 25. This compares with a spread of 20 years in the mid-nineteenth century and of 17 years in 1917 (Anderson 1985). Further, there has been a marked reduction in the span over which certain life course transitions occur over the life course of individuals. Accompanying the sharp decline in fertility from the mid-nineteenth century to the 1920s there was a clustering of childbearing in the early years of marriage and a continued decline in ages at marriage and childbearing until the 1960s. As we shall see, the age span over which childbearing occurs across the population has subsequently widened. Through the eighteenth century until the mid-nineteenth century the median age of women at the birth of their last child is estimated by Anderson to have been 39, by the 1930s to have been 32 and by the 1970s to have been 28 (Anderson 1985; see also Modell et al. 1976, for a similar analysis of changes in life course event timing in the United States). Some of the changes in average ages at different life course events are illustrated in Table 1.

The ages at parenthood shown in Table 1 hint at, but do not fully reflect, the dramatic nature of changes in fertility rates from the end of the nineteenth century to the 1930s. A decline in family size occurred amongst the middle classes from the 1870s, a pattern explained in terms of parents' aspirations for their children, in particular for maintaining customary living standards and for enabling provision for their children's education (Banks 1954). Significant reductions in fertility rates became the general pattern through the first decades of the twentieth century as working-class families had fewer children. In 1860 approximately 20% of married couples had two children or fewer, compared to 67% by 1925 (Royal Commission on Population 1949, reported by Gittins 1982). Gittins, in her research into change in family size and structure between 1900 and 1939, explores declining fertility rates amongst the working classes and, in particular, the diversity of family size and birth control across couples in different regions and occupations. In general the improvement in infant mortality rates was significant in shaping decisions that reduced family size. The position of mothers and children was, Gittins argues, bound up with an increasingly elaborate 'ideology of childhood' and with policies that reinforced the centrality of the male wage to household resourcing (Gittins 1982; cf. Lewis 1980; Davin 1978). It is difficult to assess the contributions of different family members to household resourcing across the population, but there is a substantial amount of oral history evidence that points to the importance of the contributions of teenage children to working-class families, a development that Gillis associates with the removal of younger children from wage labour and the

| Table 1 | Estimates of the average ages at different life course events |

	Year of birth					
Life course event	1850	1870	1890	1910	1930	1950
First marriage						
Men	27	27	28	27	27	24
Women	26	26	26	25	24	22
Birth of first child						
Men	29	29	30	29	28	26
Women	28	28	28	27	26	24
Birth of last child						
Men	37	36	35	32	30	28
Women	36	35	33	30	28	26
Spouse's death						
Men	56	60	62	64	66	63
Women	55	58	61	63	65	67
Own death as widow/er						
Men	75	77	79	80	81	82
Women	75	79	81	81	82	83

Source: Halsey 1986.

reduced participation of women (Gillis 1981). The importance of the contributions of teenage children to household resourcing in working-class families continued beyond the time of Rowntree's survey at the turn of the century through the inter-war years (Jamieson 1987).[1]

At a rate of 10%, fewer married women were active in the labour force during the period 1900 to 1939 than had been in the latter half of the nineteenth century (Hewitt 1959, reported by Lewis 1980). Pahl describes the inter-war period as 'the high water mark of the privatized little domestic unit', a situation explained in part by the greater involvement of central government in family-related matters, including the introduction of the marriage bar, preventing women in some occupations working after marriage (Pahl 1984). In the context of a growing concern about the health of children and fears about population decline and national security, the child and maternal welfare movement and state policies reinforced a model of the family where 'good mothering' was a full-time home-centred affair (Lewis 1980). It is important to stress the diverse experience of the period, and that many married women did work, particularly amongst the poorest households (Gittins 1982; Roberts 1986). However, the rise of the family wage system in the latter part of the nineteenth century, while not fully realized in practice, labels a general set of developments in the structure of employment and of household resourcing from the turn of the twentieth century into its early decades. It is interesting to consider how new notions about motherhood seem to have corresponded with improvements in earnings and living standards (for those in employment) and the level of adequacy of a single wage for resourcing households.

Evidence suggests that the family wage was an ideal that was shared by the middle class and the skilled working class, where it was women's ability to remain out of wage labour, rather than their entry into it, which was seen as a sign of progress (cf. Lewis 1986; Roberts 1986).

It is worthy of note that high levels of abortion, estimated as terminating 16% to 20% of conceptions, were prevalent during the period (Inter-Departmental Committee on Abortion 1939, reported by Gittins 1982). Some commentators have pointed to the widespread availability of the Pill from the 1960s as a cause of recent patterns of delay in family formation but the dramatic changes in fertility in other periods must call into doubt this sort of technology-led explanation.

The Second World War is often seen as a convenient marker of change in life course patterns, in part because of the subsequent development of the modern Welfare State but, perhaps just as significantly, because it separates the Great Depression years from post-war prosperity and growth. Linked with the latter was a set of changes in the structure of the household as an economic unit, yet these changes have been understated in accounts of contemporary patterns of transition from youth to adulthood. This neglect has contributed to the incompleteness of accounts of the relationship between resource availability and orientations in shaping patterns of transition to adulthood. Anderson has suggested that prior to the Second World War the contours of the life course were shaped in relation to demographic and economic uncertainty. From the war to the 1970s, he argues, improved health and longevity, full employment and the Welfare State were essential in shaping the modern life course (Anderson 1985).

The historical tendency to an increasingly 'normal' pattern in the timing of life course events as well as in, for example, family size, identified by Anderson, has been equated with a rise in individualism and in the salience of social norms in determining patterns of leaving home, household and family formation by a number of, mostly American, commentators. Social and economic security, concomitants of post-war prosperity, full employment and a state welfare system are seen in these arguments to have enabled a greater degree of choice than previously possible in the timing of early life course transitions. In part, too, this choice is seen as a consequence of changes in family structure, freeing youth from obligations to their parental family. The context in Britain in the early decades of this century, was one where young adult children were likely to have many more obligations to their parental household, both financial and caring, than is typical of the post-war period. Many had several siblings, and still high levels of mortality amongst the working class often disrupted households, and entailed the loss of the main breadwinner's earnings (Jamieson 1986).

[...]

Patterns of family formation

The long-term trend to lower ages at family formation from the early part of the twentieth century, quite marked during the 1950s and 1960s, was reversed in the early 1970s with a significant decline in marriage and birth rates, especially amongst those under 25. These demographic patterns are aggregate level measures of change in

Table 2	Percentages of males and females who had ever married by certain ages, by birth cohort, 1900–65

	Age							
	Males				Females			
Birth year	20	25	30	50	20	25	30	50
1900	2	40	73	93	7	49	72	85
1905	1	31	68	91	6	44	69	85
1910	2	32	70	91	7	47	74	88
1915	2	36	69	90	8	54	76	89
1920	2	42	76	92	13	62	83	92
1925	4	47	77	91	15	67	84	92
1930	3	51	81	92	19	74	89	95
1935	3	57	83	93	21	79	91	96
1940	6	60	83		27	81	91	
1945	7	63	84		29	81	92	
1950	9	60	81		29	78	88	
1955	10	52	73		32	75	87	
1960	6	41			22	61		
1965	3					12		

Source: after Haskey 1987.

domestic life course events, central to the recent youth research agenda, yet they have received remarkably little attention amongst youth researchers. This section outlines the changes that have occurred over recent decades in ages at departure from the parental home, household and family formation.

Full details of age at marriage were not recorded before the beginning of the twentieth century. Estimates of the percentages of men and women married by certain ages are shown in Table 2. Deaths in the First World War resulted in an imbalanced sex ratio, reflected in the contrasting proportions of men and women, born in the early 1900s, who ever married. The twentieth-century low point in marriage rates occurred amongst the cohort born in 1905, and is explained by Haskey as a consequence of the Great Depression (Haskey 1987).

The average age at first marriage amongst men rose from 26 to 27 between the mid 1880s and the early 1900s. By the end of the First World War it rose by a further year to 28, fell to 27 by the Second World War, then to 25 by the mid 1960s and reached a minimum of 24.4 in 1970. Since then it rose to 26 by 1985. Ages of women at first marriage followed similar trends over the century with average ages two years below those cited for men (Haskey 1987). Increasing ages at marriage and falling marriage rates have continued throughout the 1980s. Of all women aged 15 to 44, 61% were married in 1980 compared with 54% in 1989. These changes were accompanied by a continued rise in average ages at first marriage that reached 24.8 years amongst women, a rise of 22 months over the period (Cooper 1991).[2] While first marriages

Table 3 | **Age-specific fertility rates**

	Birth year					
Age group	1961	1966	1971	1976	1981	1986
Under 20	37.3	47.7	50.6	32.2	28.1	30.1
20–24	172.6	176.0	152.9	109.3	105.3	92.7
25–29	176.9	174.0	153.2	118.7	129.1	78.1
30–34	103.1	97.3	77.1	57.2	68.6	78.1

Source: *Population trends* 1988, figures for England and Wales.

have been postponed and the proportion of women who have never married has increased, so pre-marital cohabitation has risen substantially over the last 20 years. More than half of the women marrying in 1987 had lived with their husband before marrying, compared with 36% of those marrying in 1980 and 8% of those marrying in 1970 (Haskey & Kiernan 1989). However, declines in marriage rates amongst younger age groups are not a simple consequence of increasing rates of unmarried cohabitation but part of a more general pattern of delay in the attainment of independence and in the timing of family formation. The decade from 1971 to 1981 saw an increase in the proportion of time spent by young people aged 16 to 30 living with their parental family, or living alone, and a decline in the amount of time spent living as part of a couple or with a child of their own. Using data from the OPCS Longitudinal Survey, a 1% sample linking individuals enumerated in the 1971 and 1981 censuses, Penhale estimates that over the decade the average period spent living with one or both parents increased from 35% to 38.6% of time amongst women, and from 48.8% to 51.5% of time amongst men aged 16 to 30.[3] More strikingly, the average time spent by members of the age group in a household of their own making (as a couple, with or without children, or as a lone parent) decreased from 55.8% to 49.4% amongst women, and from 39.4% to 32.8% amongst men (Penhale 1990). During the period the median age at leaving the parental home increased by six months to 22.8 for men and 20.9 for women (Penhale 1990; see also Wall & Penhale 1989).

As well as a pattern of delay in ages at marriage from the early 1970s onwards, there has been a decline in fertility rates amongst younger age groups and a rise in average ages at first childbirth. Table 3 shows the decline in fertility rates, from the late 1960s, amongst women over 20. The small decline in fertility rates between 1976 and 1981 shown in Table 3 reflects a recovery between 1977 and 1980 that has been followed by a steady fall in fertility rates amongst women in their early twenties and a growing divergence in age-specific rates with significant increases in births to women in their early thirties (Werner 1985; Jones 1992). Age-specific fertility rates refer to aggregate fertility within age groups and reveal less about the specific timing of births or birth order. Evidence on the timing of first births shows significant changes in patterns of family formation with women born from the mid 1950s onwards delaying the timing of their first birth, at ages over 20, relative to previous cohorts (Thompson 1980).[4] Birth rates continued to decline through the 1980s with the steepest decline over the decade occurring amongst women aged 20 to 24 amongst whom rates fell by 19% (Jones 1992). The mean female age at first birth within marriage was 26.6 years in 1988, the highest figure recorded since 1946 (Dollamore 1989). Mean ages of women at first birth within marriage rose from 24.2 in 1965 to 25.5 in 1982, and from 1971 to 1981 the percentages living with a child at age 29 fell from 79% to 69% amongst women and from 63% to 52% amongst men (Penhale 1990).

The median interval between marriage and first birth increased from 19 months in 1970 to 31 months by 1978, and declined to 27 months by 1988. The increase through the 1970s occurred alongside an increase in average ages at marriage (Shaw 1989). While there have been dramatic increases in the percentage of births outside marriage over recent years, this rise does not appear to explain the older ages at parenthood within marriage. In 1964, 7.2% of all births occurred outside marriage, rising to 10.2% in 1978, 15.8% in 1983 and reaching over 25% by 1988 (Population Trends 1989). The increase to the late 1970s was therefore quite gradual compared to the rapid increases over the last decade and does not coincide with the patterns of deferral of parenthood within marriage. Further, the upward trend in mean ages at childbirth has occurred both within and outside marriage (Dollamore 1989).[5]

Over the period 1970 to 1983 birth rates to women aged under 25 fell across all social classes. First-birth rates to women with husbands in skilled non-manual occupations were higher than to women with husbands in other social classes. In 1970 the lowest first-birth rates occurred to women with husbands in Registrar General social classes I and II, but by 1983 women married to men in skilled manual occupations had the lowest birth rates. In part this was due to middle-class women being increasingly likely to start childbearing in their thirties. It is amongst this age group that the most significant differences in class-related fertility trends emerged over the period. Amongst women aged 30 and over in 1970 the distribution of fertility rates across Registrar General social classes was within 4% of the average rate for all classes, yet by 1983 women married to men in social classes I and II had a fertility rate 29% above the national average and women married to men in skilled manual occupations had a fertility rate 21% below the national average (Werner 1985; figures for England and Wales). Class-related changes in first-birth rates to all married women aged 15 to 44 are shown in Table 4.

Werner suggests the possibility that childless married couples with husbands in skilled manual occupations may be more strongly committed to uninterrupted labour force participation than middle-class women married to men whose rising earnings through their thirties make it easier to forego, at least temporarily, wives' earnings (Werner 1985). The restructuring, through the 1980s especially, of skilled manual work, with increasing casualization and less security for workers in some sectors, may have contributed to a greater reliance on female income amongst affected couples. Evidence from the National Child Development Survey (NCDS) suggests that, in the late 1970s, the men most likely to become young fathers were in skilled manual occupations. Amongst men in such occupations at age 26, the probability that they had become fathers by 22 was 80% greater than amongst their contemporaries in non-manual occupations but also, surprisingly, 30% greater than amongst their contemporaries in semi- and un-skilled occupations (Kiernan & Diamond 1983). This is contradicted by other evidence that shows a straightforward correlation between social class and age at childbirth, with those in the most disadvantaged circumstances likely

| Table 4 | Legitimate first-birth rates per 1000 married women by social class of father |

| Year of birth | National average | Social class of father | | | |
		I/II	IIIN	IIIM	IV/V
1970	44	38	50	43	47
1973	39	38	43	38	39
1977	34	35	36	31	36
1980	38	36	43	37	42
1983	35	34	40	33	37

Source: Werner 1985. The rates are based on estimated populations of married women aged 15 to 44 in each social class. Birth rates up to 1977 are based on the 1970 OPCS classification of occupations; subsequent rates are based on the 1980 classification of occupations.

to have children at the youngest ages (Joshi 1985; Jones 1986; Werner 1985). The traditional expectation that the most disadvantaged will attain independence and families of their own at young ages has not been satisfactorily reconciled with hypotheses of delay in family formation as a consequence of 'new' forms of disadvantage in the labour force. [...] With respect to characterizations of general patterns of change in the latter part of the twentieth century, it is clear that, along with new class-related differences, there is a growing diversity in the timing of family formation across the population. The supposed tendency to an increasingly age-related, 'normal' pattern of life course transitions appears to reflect a temporary pattern specific to the 1950s and 1960s. However, the suggestion that national economic retrenchment and unemployment caused the subsequent patterns of delay in household and family formation is too narrow a model, embodying a static and deterministic notion of the relationship between economic processes and life course structure.

[...]

Notes

1 The minimum school-leaving age was raised to 14 in 1918, and to 15 in 1947.
2 These cross-sectional rates will underestimate the cohort average.
3 The percentages are based on estimations for each yearly cohort, in order to control for the consequences of any imbalance in the age distribution (Penhale 1990).
4 Thompson's data refer to births within marriage because details on birth order and mothers' ages were not available for births registered outside of marriage.
5 It seems likely that this late twentieth-century turning point in trends from lower to higher ages at family formation will not be superseded by a new demographic transition for some time. OPCS projections of fertility, made in the mid 1980s, assumed that falling rates for

women in their early twenties and rising rates for older women would level off. This had not happened by the end of the 1980s and OPCS now predicts that the overall mean female age at childbirth will rise from 27.3 years in 1989 and to 28.7 years by the end of the century and will fall back to 27.8 years by 2015. The mean female age at birth of the first child is predicted to continue to rise from 25.3 years in 1989 to 26.5 years by 2000 before beginning to fall (Shaw 1990).

References

Anderson, M. 1985. The emergence of the modern life cycle in Britain. *Social History* **10** (1), 69–87.

Banks, J. A. 1954. *Prosperity and parenthood*. London: Routledge & Kegan Paul.

Cooper, J. 1991. Births outside marriage: recent trends and associated demographic and social changes. *Population Trends* **63**, 8–18.

Davin, A. 1978. Imperialism and motherhood. *History Workshop Journal* **5**, 9–65.

Dollamore, G. 1989. Live births in 1988. *Population Trends* **58**, 20–6.

Gillis, J. 1981. *Youth and history. Tradition and change in European age relations, 1770–present*. New York/London: Academic Press.

Gittins, D. 1982. *Fair sex. Family size and structure, 1900–1939*. London: Hutchinson.

Haskey, J. 1987. Trends in marriage and divorce in England and Wales: 1837 to 1987. *Population Trends* **48**, 11–19.

—— & K. E. Kiernan 1989. Cohabitation in Great Britain – characteristics and estimated numbers of cohabiting partners. *Population Trends* **58**, 23–32.

Jamieson, L. 1986. Limited resources and limiting conventions: working class mothers and daughters in urban Scotland c. 1890–1925. In *Labour and love. Women's experience of home and family, 1850–1940*, J. Lewis (ed.). Oxford: Basil Blackwell.

—— 1987. Theories of family development and the experience of being brought up. *Sociology* **21** (4), 591–607.

Jones, C. 1992. Fertility of the over thirties. *Population Trends* **67**, 10–16.

Jones, G. 1986. *Youth in the social structure: transitions to adulthood and their stratification by class and gender*. PhD thesis, University of Surrey.

Joshi, H. 1985. *Motherhood and employment: change and continuity in post war Britain*, OPCS Occasional Paper 34, British Society for Population Studies.

Kiernan, K. E. & I. Diamond 1983. The age at which childbearing starts – a longitudinal study. *Population Studies* **37**, 363–80.

Lewis, J. 1980. *The politics of motherhood. Child and maternal welfare in England 1900–1939*. London: Croom Helm.

—— 1986. The working class wife and mother and State intervention 1870–1918. In *Labour and love. Women's experience of home and family, 1850–1940*, J. Lewis (ed.). Oxford: Basil Blackwell.

Modell, J., F. F. Furstenberg, T. Hershberg 1976. Social change and transitions to adulthood in historical perspective. *Journal of Family History* **1** (1), 7–32.

Office of Population Censuses and Surveys, Social Survey Division. *General household survey*. London: HMSO.

Office of Population Censuses and Surveys. *Population Trends*. London: HMSO.

Pahl, R. E. 1984. *Divisions of labour*. Oxford: Basil Blackwell.

Penhale, B. 1990. *Living arrangements of young adults in France and England and Wales*. SSRU, City University, LS Working Paper 68.

Roberts, E. 1986. Women's strategies 1890–1940. See Lewis (1986).

Shaw, C. 1989. Recent trends in family size and family building. *Population Trends* 58, 19–22.

Thompson, J. 1980. The age at which childbearing starts – a longitudinal study. *Population Trends* 21, 10–13.

Wall, R. & B. Penhale 1989. Relationships within households in 1981. *Population Trends* 55, 22–6.

Werner, B. 1985. Fertility trends in different social classes: 1970 to 1983. *Population Trends* 41, 5–13.

15 | Divorce and the New Family

Carol Smart

Key words

Divorce, fatherhood, motherhood, family and household, gender relations, marriage

---

There has clearly been a debate for some time about the impact on children of the rising rate of divorce. Recently, this debate has concentrated on the role of fathers after divorce. Children, it has been argued, may be particularly affected by the absence of fathers.

Smart argues that, during marriage, most fathers only relate to their children through their mother. Mothers actually take the major responsibility and the father's role is largely supportive. If fathers can only satisfactorily be fathers through the mother, the divorce will create serious difficulties for the continuation of a fatherhood role. Post-divorce, substantial re-negotiation of both motherhood and fatherhood roles will be required. Fathers can no longer depend on the mother to mediate and to interpret children's needs. On the other hand mothers may feel that they are unable fully to trust their ex-husband to take on responsibilities which previously he had neglected.

In her study of a group of divorced parents Smart considers these issues. She finds that mothers after divorce continue to feel responsible and this extends to making sure that their ex-husbands look after the children properly when they are in their care. At the same time, fathers often try to repudiate responsibility apparently attempting to preserve the balance between motherhood and fatherhood struck during marriage. However, some of the fathers in Smart's sample wanted to re-negotiate the relationship in the realization that they could not continue their pre-divorce practices, a move which makes new demands on both fathers and mothers.

Throughout the 1980s and 1990s in Britain there has been a growing debate over fatherhood, in particular the question of the role of fathers after divorce.[1] This has been conceived in terms of either a failure in fatherhood, in which it has been argued that men have not adjusted to a new role, or as a crisis in fatherhood,[2] in which it is argued that men no longer seem necessary to the family. This debate has coincided with another set of concerns which arose in the 1980s, namely a growing fear about the perceived harmful effects of divorce on children.[3] Although much of the research on which the concern about harm was based was originally North American, it was taken up in Britain and contributed to a growing alarm over a perceived increase in under-achieving and delinquent children. The link between these two sets of concerns lay in the argument that what caused this harm to children on divorce was, in fact, the lack of a 'proper' father. This argument signified a shift from previous concerns which saw the harm caused to children as arising from the poverty that so many divorced mothers and their children endured.[4] Thus we witnessed a shift from a basically socio-economic argument to a psychological argument in understanding the harms of divorce for children. Although the empirical basis of this shift is now being revised (Burghes, 1994, 1996; Kiernan, 1997), by the end of the 1980s there had become established a presumption that fatherhood was undergoing a change (or crisis) and that childhood was being irreparably damaged by a family policy which was perceived to encourage the separation of children from their fathers at the point of parental divorce. These concerns gave rise to a major change in policy on divorce in England and Wales in the shape of the Children Act 1989.

[. . .]

Mothering and fathering in 'intact' families

The thinking behind the Children Act presumed that a distinction could be made between adult/adult relationships and adult/child relationships within a marriage (or cohabitation). Thus part of the argument resided in the idea that while divorce would foreclose on the spousal relationship, it need not affect the parents' relationship with the child. Thus two sets of relationships are envisaged which appear to be autonomous of one another and which operate independently of one another. To this way of thinking, there is no reason to imagine that the parent/child relationship should be harmed or reduced because of adverse spousal relationships. This dualism is reflected in everyday thinking and speech where it is not unusual to hear it said (especially by mothers) that an individual might be a very good father but a poor husband, and so on. But I want to suggest that this is an oversimplification of parental relationships. Parents do not only relate to children, they relate to one another *as parents*, not simply as spouses (or partners). A mother's relationship to a father is not the same as a wife's relationship to a husband. Even more importantly, a father's relationship to his children may thrive simply because of his wife's mothering skills. This point is best illuminated by reference to the work of Kathryn Backett (1987).[5]

While there has been a burgeoning of studies which have looked at whether modern fathers 'do' more childcare than previously,[6] Backett's work brought to light a rather different dynamic in the relationship between mothering and fathering. Backett suggests that fatherhood is mediated through the behaviour of the mother and that it does not operate (in the main) as an independent relationship with the children. She suggests that because it is mothers who take the greatest share of the responsibility for children, fathers adopt largely a supportive role. Most significantly, to be regarded as a perfectly satisfactory father, the father did not have to participate in all aspects of childcare. It would be enough for him to deputize for the mother in her absence or to take over now and again if she was tired or stressed. Thus Backett points out that in ongoing relationships couples do not identify the good father as one who carries out 50 per cent of the childcare, or who necessarily relates in a direct and independent way with the children.

> In other words, for father involvement to be subjectively satisfactory it did not tend to be measured against some abstract set of behavioural ideals. It was negotiated and evaluated in terms of the paternal behaviour perceived as appropriate by the spouses within their own special situation at any one point in time.
>
> (Backett, 1987: 79)

In an ongoing relationship therefore, a satisfactory paternal relationship might be one in which the father has very little direct contact with the children. But Backett points out that, even where fathers have considerable contact with their children, how they relate to them is *mediated* through the mother. She explains that fathers were reliant on mothers to translate the children's moods or to interpret their needs in order that he could interact with them in a satisfactory way. Thus, in the intact family (at least in the middle-class families she studied) fatherhood could not be understood as a direct relationship with the children. Even where both parents proclaimed that they shared parenting between them, Backett argues that, in practice, fatherhood was negotiated with the mother rather than with the children.

In her study Backett found that fathers were not unhappy with this arrangement.[7] Few wanted to spend a lot more time with their children and, in the main, they recognized the limitations that a full-time caring role imposed on their wives. Thus in an ongoing marriage or cohabitation it is possible to argue that fatherhood depends upon motherhood for its satisfactory existence as a relationship (as opposed to as a biological fact). Although the extent to which a father's relationship with his children is negotiated through the mother may change as children get older, Backett suggests that it does not have an autonomous existence in the way that motherhood tends to.

This clearly has major implications for the way in which fatherhood can be enacted after divorce. If the father has relied on the mother in order to have a relationship with his children, he will find that when he no longer has a wife he no longer has the medium which provided a relationship with the children. Basically, he can no longer be a father unless he changes the nature of his relationship rather quickly. This realization was expressed very eloquently by one of the fathers in our study.[8]

Leon Holt: I hadn't really thought about it. We were still living in the house together for about a year when we were going through really difficult times, moved into separate rooms. It was a case of I'd always worked really hard, I'd come home, gone up to the study and the children were there. My role as a father was to go out to work, to bring the money in, to try and look careerwise and the children were young and it was a case of just saying 'Hello, sit on my knee, then off to bed'. And I was just there and I probably didn't pay them much attention at all. *It was only when I realized that they might not be part of my life that gave me a real shock and it made me more aware and during that year I made more effort to spend time with the children.* (Emphasis added.)

Not only does he need to alter the basis of his relationship with his children, but also with the mother of the children. He can no longer rely on her to do much of the emotional work for him because once she stops being his wife she no longer owes him that emotional labour (although she may feel that she owes it to the children). We might therefore argue that pre-divorce fatherhood is usually a poor training for post-divorce parenthood. We might further argue that post-divorce fatherhood is not simply about taking on more of the practical tasks of caring for children (although this is important) but it is about forging a new relationship with the mother, not simply ending a relationship with a wife.

If pre-divorce fatherhood ill-equips a father for post-divorce fatherhood, the question that needs to be asked is whether pre-divorce motherhood is also in some way a problematic preparation for the post-divorce situation. I want to suggest that there are significant discontinuities. It is clear, for example, that mothers find it hard to 'trust' fathers to care adequately for the children because in an intact relationship they have usually felt themselves to be the most responsible parent and also the main provider of care. In such a situation the fact that a father might only do half a job or might only participate in a restricted range of activities with children is not problematic. But as soon as the father has to be fully responsible a post-divorce mother may find it hard not to become extremely anxious and worried about his capabilities. She may also find it hard to act as mediator for the father/child relationship too. This means she might be less willing to 'cover-up' for a father who always arrives late or who fails to relate to a child in a direct fashion. This in turn might mean that the father/child relationship becomes difficult, not because she undermines it but simply because she is no longer prepared to shore it up.

The problem of the extent to which mothering in an intact relationship ill-prepares women for post-divorce family life is not simply linked to the quality of parent/child relationships however. In many respects the mother's situation is the reverse image of the father's. During the relationship or marriage he might have had an indirect relationship with his children because he maintained his status as a citizen in paid employment with access to resources and benefits which go with this status. The price that he pays for this is (often) a less close relationship to his children. For the mother the opposite is true. She has a close, direct relationship with her children but the price she pays is a diminished citizenship status. As Young argues,

> The male head of household exhibits the virtue of independence, supporting dependent mothers and children. The citizen virtue of mothers does not entail independence but, rather, the virtues of caring and sacrifice necessary for nurturing children to be good citizens.
>
> (Young, 1995: 544)

The citizen status of the mother is diminished because, as Young argues, liberal democratic societies celebrate and reward independence, while denigrating those who make themselves [*sic*] or become dependent on others. Laying claim to the citizen virtues of independence gives the head of household personal autonomy and a sense of self-confidence, both of which are denied to the dependants in a family unit. Of course, as

Young points out, the independence of the head of household depends on the invisible support of a wife (see also Finch, 1983), but he still accrues the benefits of apparent self-sufficiency and self-reliance in the public sphere. He is also likely to regard himself as a citizen with rights. The mother, on the other hand, is, by virtue of her position as carer, unlikely readily to avail herself of the cultural capital embedded in this notion of the good citizen. She is unlikely to have a well-paid, secure job; indeed, she may not be in the labour market at all. The organization of the benefits system, in combination with low pay for women, may mean that she cannot hope to become a self-sufficient, independent citizen for several years. She will therefore not enjoy the self-confidence which comes from being regarded as a full citizen nor is she likely to see herself as the holder of rights. She is clearly far from powerless in terms of interpersonal relationships. Indeed, as Backett argues, her relationship to the children makes her quite powerful in relation to the father. But she remains extremely economically vulnerable and also vulnerable to a loss of self-identity and self-esteem.

It is now apparent that we need to have a much more complex picture of how relationships which are formed during a marriage or cohabitation can be reshaped or transformed after divorce or separation. It is inappropriate to imagine that parenthood simply continues as it might in an intact relationship as the Law Commission seemed to hope. Not only do we need to understand some of the material consequences of these transformed relationships, but also the gendered power dynamics and the significance of the concept of citizenship for parenthood. (Here I am using citizenship as a short-hand way of referring to a sense of legitimate selfhood which is, in turn, accorded respect and rights in contemporary society.) It is too simplistic to imagine that the difficulties facing divorced parents simply arise from personal antagonisms which can be overcome by focusing on the needs of children. Parents need to change in relation to each other as well as in relation to their children, but at the same time it is important to recognize that there are structural obstacles to change as well as emotional and cognitive ones.

I want, therefore, to pursue these ideas through the findings of our[9] empirical study of 60 parents who negotiated arrangements for their children under the new ethos of the Children Act. This study interviewed 31 mothers and 29 fathers twice over a period of two years. We were therefore able to gather a picture of the process of divorce and of making arrangements for children which spanned a time-scale from the original separation or decision to part (which was gathered retrospectively), to the point of finalizing legal matters and again some 18 months later. We were therefore able to see how the situation of the parents changed and how they adjusted to changing circumstances. We were also able to ask them to reflect upon their decisions and feelings at different moments in the whole process rather than simply establishing their reactions at one specific time. This time element was vital in establishing a more complex picture of the process of post-divorce parenting because we were able to see how parents gradually adjusted to situations which, at first, they would not tolerate or, conversely, how acceptable arrangements became unacceptable as the consequences of early decisions became clearer or as circumstances changed.

I propose to explore the issues raised above in the context of how these parents negotiated post-divorce parenthood. I will look at three interlocking issues. First, the issue raised in Backett's work about the central role of the mother and the extent to which mothers mediate fatherhood even after divorce. The key issue here is the extent to which mothers feel responsible for the children. Secondly, I will explore the question of how parents can adjust to sharing the care of children and a change in their understanding of their identity as mothers or fathers. Finally, I shall turn to the issue of citizenship and the problem of the ongoing, unresolved consequences of gender inequality in marriage and parental relationships.

Responsibility

In our sample of 60 parents, only in one family did we find a situation in which the responsibility for the children was fully shared before the divorce or separation. Although some fathers had been involved in their children's lives to a considerable extent, the overwhelmingly dominant pattern was one where the mothers had given up work or had worked part-time in order to provide the main care for the children. This gave rise to the situation that Backett describes where the father's relationship tended to be an indirect one and where the mother never felt free of a sense of responsibility for the children.

Linda Hewitt: It is quite nice to wake up on a morning and think, 'Oh, I don't have to get up and go to school at half-eight' but the thing is that my life still functions around that kind of time-scale. Even if I don't have him, I'll still wake up and think 'Agh!' and even if I'm not picking him up I'll still think 'My god, it's three o'clock, I ought to be outside school!' I'm programmed to that.

This mother was sharing the care of her son on an equal basis with her former partner, but she had not been able to relinquish an overriding sense of responsibility for the child which she felt acutely while the child was away. It is worth quoting her at length because she typifies the comments of so many of the mothers we interviewed.

Linda Hewitt: Yes, I worry about if he's ill whether Ivan would pick up on it because he's not very good at that. And I also discovered . . . a few months ago that he was letting David go round to some shops and cross a very busy road, which I was amazed at and said so and Ivan then said 'OK, I won't let him do it'. But he had done it in the first place.

Linda also reflected upon the way in which she was much more in tune with things which were important for her son to which his father seemed oblivious.

Linda Hewitt: I mean to children it's very important that they have the right things for school or whatever and sometimes that goes sort of haywire. Like I know that he hasn't washed his football kit and I'm the one that's saying 'Don't forget to do it' even though it's not my day and it's nothing to do with me because I know that David will get upset if it isn't done.

Not only is Linda extending her 'care work' into the time where she need not feel responsible, but she is ensuring that Ivan remains – in her son's eyes – a caring father. It is Ivan who would get the 'credit' from David for looking after his needs even though it is Linda who ensures that he does not fall short. When Linda remarks that 'to children it is very important' she is acknowledging that children and adults have different priorities and needs and that she is in tune with these. She is capable of seeing the world through her son's eyes and anticipates his emotions but she is doubtful that her former partner can do this.

The issue of responsibility would often focus on things like illness, food and clothing as these are tangible signs of caring activities. Often mothers would remark that fathers did not notice that a child was ill or that they would return them to their mothers rather than doing anything about the illness themselves.

Stella Drew: Ralph was ill and he was with Nick the day and the night, and I said to him 'If he's ill tomorrow are you going to sort something out?' and he just went mad with me on the phone. 'I am not prepared to accept that level of responsibility, it is up to you to sort that out, that is not my responsibility.' And I burst out laughing, I couldn't help it. I was annoyed at the time but it was a point I was making that I was just sick of having all the responsibility, it gets too much sometimes. I think, 'I can't take another day off work I really need the money'. I'm self-employed. But it's always me that has to do it and I just felt that was such a classic.

It is clear that this father did not want to alter the type of relationship he had had with the children during his marriage in the post-divorce situation. His relationship stayed one based on 'quality time' which is to say it embraced only fun things at weekends and holidays. Moreover, he did not even want 'children's things' to eat into his time with them.

Stella Drew: . . . it's me who does the swimming lessons, does the beavers, does the cubs, and he does complain about it if he has to do any of the children's activities when he's got them if it's too much because he feels it eats into his time.

If fathers refused to take on more responsibility after divorce, while still insisting on maintaining contact with their children, it led to real strains in the parental relationship. While mothers would often shoulder the responsibility during a marriage, they would become increasingly resentful of it once the marriage was over. This was particularly so when they found themselves living alone with the children while trying to work for a living. Former husbands often seem incapable of recognizing how much harder their wives' lives had become and how much responsibility they had to take on as lone working mothers.

Erica Dawson: The first week I started on shifts he didn't want the children that day. He didn't want them early in the day. He didn't want them on Saturday, he just wanted them on Sunday. Sometimes he only wanted them on Friday night and not the weekend. I said, 'What are you doing here? I'm trying to earn a living!' and it was very difficult. It caused a great deal of upset and bad feeling and made a tremendous amount of pressure and stress. Anyway, I worked through it and shifted my hours around a little bit more and just did the best I could.

A particular bone of contention was often money and the extent to which fathers would spend money on 'frivolous' activities with the children when they were in need of new shoes, clothes or large items of expenditure.

Samantha Abdul: He took them down to the arcade and he were just putting pound after pound into the machines. I said, 'It just makes me sick to see you throwing money into the machines'. They needed clothes, they needed trainers but he could spend over £30 on stupid arcade machines. I said, 'I know you don't understand but I'm on £75 a week.'

Where a father's irresponsible behaviour became damaging mothers often ceased to 'mediate' for them any more. So when a father was late or failed to turn up to collect a child, the mother might stop making excuses for him. Alternatively, she might stop 'prompting' the father to do the right thing and gradually allow the children to appreciate for themselves their father's limitations. But this was not always easy to do because the mother often wanted to protect the child.

If a post-divorce father would not, or could not, take on more responsibility for his relationship with his children, the mother was often obliged to remain his 'spouse' in the sense that one of her key roles, that of mediating, remained unchanged. In these cases divorce did not seem to bring about a new set of relationships so much as perpetuating an old relationship across different households. It seemed to produce a situation in which, to be a good mother, a woman had to remain a wife.

Sally Burton: I think he thought that he could leave, have this new lover and I would still be at home to come back to, and he could come, have meals, spend time with the children and it's only very recently he's begun to realize that that isn't going to happen.

Meg Johnson: I didn't feel that I had my independence or my space. While David could be away from our home and be on his own, doing his own thing, I went to live with my mother and that wasn't enough. . . . Yes, I did consider [the children's] needs, but I was thinking about myself too. That I couldn't carry on being just mother and 'spouse' because I wasn't being a spouse and that's when I wanted to do something about it.

As these two quotations show, although some mothers were prepared to carry on as 'spouses' for a while, it was impossible for them to sustain this position for long – even for the sake of their children.

While many (although not all) of the mothers we interviewed wanted the fathers to take on more responsibility, many of the fathers were seriously annoyed that their former wives exercised this responsibility. They did not want to be 'told' to be punctual, to wash clothes, to take the children to the dentist or to be advised on what to feed the children. They saw the exercise of this responsibility as an exercise of power and they frequently became aggressive or hostile in response. Thus they were willing to allow their wives to exercise responsibility for the children during the marriage (none, for example, complained that their wives had done *too much* in relation to caring for the children), but at the point of divorce the mother's special position was interpreted as an unfair advantage (see Simpson et al., 1995).

Jack Hood: They hold all the cards and you're the one who's got to crawl back. I wanted to give her a good hiding or shake her. I couldn't even upset her. You've got no choice, you've got to go by what they say.

George Daley: I can't go up and see him any time I want to, it's got to be done through an appointment, so where does your parental rights come into it?

The fact that so many fathers at the point of divorce or separation were extremely angry with their wives/partners for having a special relationship with the children indicates the extent to which motherhood is taken for granted in most heterosexual relationships. Mothering is, in effect, invisible. It only becomes apparent when it no longer fits smoothly into space that fathering typically leaves vacant. But this anger also suggests that fatherhood is changing too. Although there may be little evidence that fathers are yet willing to take on the structural disadvantages of motherhood, it may be the case that we are witnessing a symbolic shift in fathering which means that more men want to retain an emotional relationship with their children (Beck and Beck-Gernsheim, 1995). It is in this domain that mothers become problematic, at least if they are perceived as already doing all the necessary emotional labour required to nurture children. In this scenario the mother has to be dislodged.

Adjusting to change

Not all of the fathers in our sample wanted simply to retain the benefits of married fatherhood while being divorced. Some recognized that if they were really to remain (or become) real post-divorce fathers, they were going to have to change both in relation to the children and in relation to their former wives or partners.

Leon Holt: I think at the time I felt, and probably still do, that it's still up to the father to prove that he can be a major part of the children's lives. . . . You have to prove that you are a responsible parent and you have a right of access and what you can do for them on an equal footing, then I think that will change the whole situation and actually make it more amicable in a sense that both parents realize you can talk to the other to make it work.

Leon had been a typical father during his marriage and acknowledged that he had no real relationship with his two daughters. But because he wanted to form a relationship at the point of divorce he did not seek to 'dislodge' the children's mother but to supplement her mothering as much as he could until she came to trust him and to trust her daughters in his care. He did not demand to have them half of the time as if it was his automatic right. Rather, the amount of contact he had grew over a period of months in a rate commensurate with the accumulation of trust. He knew that his wife was in a very strong position in relation to the children when they separated, but he saw this as ethically justified even though he wanted to change the *status quo*. The difference between Leon and the fathers who became aggressive and hostile at this realization is that he acknowledged his own part in the creation of the typical gendered division of labour that had been a feature of his marriage. He did not assume that it was his right to benefit from such an arrangement and that it was equally his right unilaterally to overturn it on divorce. As a consequence he was able to become a 'real' father for the first time after his marriage ended. A number of other fathers in our sample managed to achieve this also.

Ann Black:	Yeah [he's changed]. Obviously he doesn't see her the amount of time as when he was here, but I think he makes an effort for when they are there.
Colin Hanks:	I feel more of a father now. I think the most important thing for me, anyway, is to show a healthy interest in the children and a respect for the children.
Felicity Lessing:	They are the most important thing in his life and he has blossomed with them since we split up.
Jim Walters:	That's a good question! I think probably I take more responsibility as a father now than I did when I lived there, in a sense.

The question is, however, whether when the father becomes more of a father, the mother has to become less of a mother. Some mothers felt relieved that the fathers were lifting some of the burden from them and were also glad to be able to share worries and problems with the other parent. Some were also glad to have 'free' time to pursue other interests, other relationships, or simply to be alone. But it was difficult for mothers sometimes to relinquish an identity which went with being a primary carer. The case of Felicity Lessing expresses this problem with immense clarity. Felicity had given up a professional position to become a virtual full-time mother to two sons. She had taken on occasional work when the opportunity arose, but she had forgone her career prospects. Her husband Simon had continued in his career and was being very successful, but he formed a relationship with another woman at his workplace and decided to leave his wife. At the point at which they separated Simon did not have a direct relationship with his young sons. Indeed, Felicity felt that he had withdrawn from them and that he was not particularly concerned to see them after he left. But he did maintain contact with them and, at the point at which he bought a new house and moved in with his new wife, he was wanting to have the children 50 per cent of the time. This was very hard for Felicity to accept at first.

Felicity Lessing:	The basic attitude was that I felt the children should have a home that was their base and that it was with me. Not just because he had left me for another woman but because that is how our roles had mapped out. That was my attitude about it and this is where we were at loggerheads because his attitude was that it was totally irrelevant who had left who from the children's point of view and that their home should be as much with him as it was with me and that my having left my career was irrelevant now since the situation was different. That was where the two of us could not see eye to eye at all.

It is clear that Felicity assumed that they had entered into an agreement when she gave up work and that her job was to be to raise the children while his was to have a career. She felt that she had made a sacrifice which should not simply be seen as irrelevant. But Simon's argument was that it was irrelevant from the point of view of the children. Ultimately, Felicity came to agree with this. She could see that from the children's point of view none of this mattered at all.

Felicity Lessing:	I could have fought about things but the arguments on the other side are too strong for me. If he says, 'Well, the children need their father', then I quite agree. Why should the children see less of their father because I feel it's not fair on me?

The problem for Felicity, however, is that being a full-time mother was also her identity and not just a job. Although she gets work when she can, she cannot accept offers which clash with the time when she has the children and she can no longer travel. Simon, on the other hand, has a wife who now supports him in his childcare and who collects the children from school and deputizes for him when he cannot be there. Yet, as Felicity herself acknowledges, she cannot really mount a case that she should have the children more of the time once it is accepted that it is in the children's best interests to spend time equally with both parents. Moreover, it is precisely because Felicity has invested so much in the welfare of her children that she cannot really pursue an argument which she feels might be the slightest bit harmful to them – even at great cost to herself.

But the case of Felicity and Simon raises some very wide questions for motherhood and fatherhood in the late twentieth century. Is it really completely irrelevant that Felicity gave up a career, pension and financial security? If so, what does this mean for women who continue to make this 'choice'?

[. . .]

Notes

I wish to acknowledge the contribution of Dr Bren Neale who worked with me on this project and with whom I have co-authored several papers and a book. I also wish to acknowledge the role of the Economic and Social Research Council in funding the research on which this chapter is based (reference no.: R000234582). Finally, I would like to express my gratitude to Elizabeth Silva for her comments on this chapter.

1   See Burgess and Ruxton (1996), Burghes, Clarke and Cronin (1997), Dennis and Erdos (1993), Ferri and Smith (1996), French (1993), Lewis (1986), Lewis and O'Brien (1987), Moss (1995), Simpson et al. (1995), Smart and Sevenhuijsen (1989).

2   The headline in *The Observer* on 21 April 1996 is typical. It read 'Fatherhood at crisis point'. See also 'Death of the Dad' by Melanie Phillips in *The Observer*, 2.11.97.

3   See Burghes (1994), Maclean and Wadsworth (1988).

4   The work of Kiernan (1997) has reintroduced the significance of poverty into the debate about the harms of divorce. Her research suggests that poor 'outcomes' for children are related to poverty before family breakdown rather than to the breakdown alone.

5   The significance of Backett's work is also appreciated by Simpson et al. (1995).

6   See Lewis and O'Brien (1987), Moss (1995), Burgess and Ruxton (1996), Burghes, Clarke and Cronin (1997).

7   The interesting question for the 1990s is, of course, whether more fathers do now wish to have a greater involvement with children while a marriage/relationship is ongoing. The study by Ferri and Smith (1996) is not promising in this regard.

8   This study was called 'The legal and moral ordering of households in transition' although we came to call it 'Negotiating parenthood' for convenience.

9   As I worked on the project jointly with Dr Bren Neale, I shall refer to 'we' or 'our' when I discuss the finding of the research.

References

Backett, K. (1987) 'The negotiation of fatherhood', in C. Lewis and M. O'Brien (eds), *Reassessing Fatherhood*. London: Sage.

Beck, U. and Beck-Gernsheim, E. (1995) *The Normal Chaos of Love*. Cambridge: Polity.

Burgess, A. and Ruxton, S. (1996) *Men and Their Children*. London: Institute for Public Policy Research.

Burghes, L. (1994) *Lone Parenthood and Family Disruption: The Outcomes for Children*. London: Family Policy Studies Centre.

—— (1996) 'Debates on disruption: what happens to the children of lone parents', in Elizabeth B. Silva (ed.) *Good Enough Mothering? Feminist Perspectives on Lone Motherhood*. London: Routledge.

—— Clarke, L. and Cronin, N. (1997) *Fathers and Fatherhood in Britain*. London: Family Policy Studies Centre.

Dennis, N. and Erdos, G. (1993) *Families Without Fatherhood*. London: Institute for Economic Affairs Health and Welfare Unit.

Ferri, E. and Smith, K. (1996) *Parenting in the 1990s*. London: Family Policy Studies Centre.

Finch, J. (1983) *Married to the Job*. London: George Allen & Unwin.

French, S. (ed.) (1993) *Fatherhood*. London: Virago.

Kiernan, K. (1997) *The Legacy of Parental Divorce*. CASE Paper 1. London: London School of Economics.

Law Commission (1988) *Family Law Review of Child Law: Guardianship and Custody*. Law Commission No. 172. London: HMSO.

Lewis, C. (1986) *Becoming a Father*. Milton Keynes: Open University Press.

—— and O'Brien, M. (eds) (1987) *Reassessing Fatherhood: New Observations on Fathers and the Modern Family*. London: Sage.

Maclean M. and Wadsworth, M.E. (1988) 'The interests of children after parental divorce: a long-term perspective', *International Journal of Law and the Family*, 2: 155–66.

Moss, P. (ed.) (1995) *Father Figures: Fathers in the Families of the 1990s*. Edinburgh: HMSO.

Simpson, B., McCarthy, P. and Walker, J. (1995) *Being There: Fathers after Divorce*. Newcastle upon Tyne: Relate Centre for Family Studies.

Smart, C. and Sevenhuijsen, S. (eds) (1989) *Child Custody and the Politics of Gender*. London: Routledge.

Young, I.M. (1995) 'Mothers, citizenship, and independence: a critique of pure family values', *Ethics*, 105 (April): 535–56.

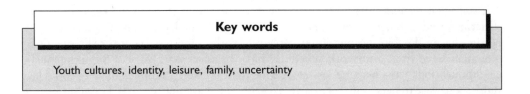

British Youth Cultures in the 1990s

16

Ken Roberts

Key words

Youth cultures, identity, leisure, family, uncertainty

Roberts's article is a contribution to a debate about the character of postmodern societies. Some accounts suggest that social life is much more fluid, uncertain and unstable than it was, say, fifty years ago. The social structures of social class, ethnicity, age, gender or locality no longer provide fixed points of reference or identities. Instead, it is argued, people, and young people in particular, take their identities from lifestyles formed by consumption and leisure.

Certainly the life situations of young people are changing and are becoming more diverse. Youth has been prolonged, as young people delay the point at which they live independently; young people's biographies have been individualized; the future prospects facing any young person are uncertain and risky, whether this be in work or personal life.

Roberts argues that youth cultures certainly have altered their character in response to the changes described above. A wider age group is involved; gender differences are not so clear-cut with youth cultures no longer so male dominated; class divisions are more blurred and do not determine taste in the way that they used to; youth culture is more fragmented; groupings that form around particular leisure and consumption tastes may indeed produce a sense of belonging. Although it might therefore seem that leisure and consumption are the bases for the construction of identity by young people, Roberts suggests that this is not the case. Actually, social class, gender and ethnicity continue to be central organizing principles of young people's lives.

[. . .]

Introduction

Debates about postmodernity have penetrated most areas of social research, not least leisure studies. The present-day leisure of some social groups, with young people being a frequently cited example, is said to be pervaded by symptoms of a postmodern condition, or, at any rate, illuminated by postmodern thought. Applying these perspectives, it is claimed, enables us to see that although there are some continuities, today's youth cultures have a different significance than those of earlier years and/or that interpretations of youth cultures which passed as knowledge in the 1960s and 1970s are now in need of revision. The following passages consider these claims, and the relevant evidence, but argue that although there have certainly been changes these have not made a fundamental difference to the role of youth cultures.

Lifestyles and identities

A feature of postmodernity is said, in some interpretations, to be a weakening of former structures and a blurring of older divisions. It is argued that labour markets have become more flexible, occupational careers have become less secure, risks of unemployment have risen and work schedules have become more varied. Simultaneously, neighbourhoods have become less close-knit than formerly, families have become less stable, and researchers now recognize a variety of masculinities and femininities (see for example Karsten, 1995; Mort, 1996). The globalization of economic relationships and cultural flows, and the spread of information technology, are usually held to be deeply implicated in these trends (see Featherstone, 1988, 1991). Former solid fixtures in the social and economic landscapes are said to have become fragile. As former structures have loosened, everyday life is said to have lost its 'solidity', and, it is claimed, old social markers such as age, sex and occupation have ceased to supply 'given' identities (Giddens, 1991; Laermans, 1994). The old social structures created deep divisions, advantages and disadvantages, but, it is argued, at least people knew their places and with whom they shared interests. Individuals may have been discontent, but they knew what they were discontent about and who their allies were. Nowadays it is claimed that these older certainties have disintegrated and 'givens' such as age, sex and occupation no longer provide secure positions, clear interests and identities.

However, writers on leisure and consumption have noted that, compared with the earlier industrial or modern era, many people today have more money, some have more time at their disposal, and they are surrounded by a plethora of consumer industries supplying goods and services rich in symbolic meanings as well as material uses. This, it is claimed, presents possibilities for individuals to create identities according to what, when and how they consume (Featherstone, 1991). According to Bocock (1993, p. x), 'Consumption now affects the ways in which people build up, and maintain, a sense of who they are, and who they wish to be. It has become entwined with the processes surrounding the development of an identity.'

This account of how leisure has grown in qualitative importance certainly looks more plausible today than earlier forecasts of a society of leisure which was to appear as people's leisure values and interests provoked a flight from work, demands for more leisure-like work environments, as leisure became increasingly central in family life, and as people's leisure commitments dictated where they were willing to live, and where and when they were prepared to work (Dumazedier, 1967, 1974).

Some of the best-known British studies highlighting the contributions of leisure to lifestyles, which create social identities for the actors, have focused upon sections of the upper middle classes (see Butler and Savage, 1995; Savage et al. 1992; Thrift, 1989; Wynne, 1990). It has been argued that, within these strata, class formation no longer occurs primarily at workplaces or within work-based social relationships, but increasingly through consumption. Such claims are, of course, controversial as are arguments that in developing lifestyle-based identities the upper middle classes are acting as a social vanguard, and that, in time, other groups will follow (Lash, 1990). Only time will tell decisively. At present it is possible to counter-argue that the examples of upper middle class lifestyles have all developed within, and have not obliterated any older social divisions, and moreover that lifestyle distinctions within social classes have a very long history.

Young people are the other group commonly cited, and from which evidence is drawn, about the rise of lifestyle-based identities. It is certainly the case that young people have felt the full force of all the broader trends which are said to have been rendering older structures fragile, and they are also the section of the population with the highest levels, and most diverse patterns of cultural consumption. Youth cultures may therefore be regarded as test cases. If there is a trend towards people 'placing' each other, and defining themselves according to their lifestyles rather than using the older social markers, then, it can be argued, there should be clear evidence of this among young people.

Youth's new condition

There have undoubtedly been major changes in young people's situations. Some of these changes have contributed to, or been an aspect of a general destandardization of the life course. Major life events are no longer as closely linked to specific ages as in the past. People today often retire from their main occupations when, in other respects, they are at the peak of adulthood. Other people in mid-life have been restarting careers, sometimes by returning to full-time education or training. More people in their 30s and 40s are now experiencing the dissolution of domestic partnerships and rejoining the singles scenes. An upshot is greater variety within all age groups. It has become hazardous to generalize about the circumstances and behaviour of people of any given age. Among women aged 25–40, for example, there are still many traditional housewives, but more are now in dual career partnerships, while simultaneously there are also more single parents, and more are also single and childless. This is just one example how, in social science and everyday life, age has become less useful as a social predictor. This applies equally earlier in the life course. Many 25 year olds are established in good jobs but nowadays there are also many with most of their labour market experience in poor jobs, various types of training schemes and unemployment. Nowadays there are also many 25 year olds who are still full-time students. There is no longer a normal situation for a person aged 18, 21 or 25, and this is a symptom of youth's new condition which has been created by a series of inter-related trends.

Firstly, youth has been prolonged, or perhaps it is more accurate to state that the life stage has become more varied in length. There are still some young people in Britain who enter full-time employment at age 16, and there are still teenagers who marry and become parents. But the typical ages at which these thresholds are crossed have risen. This is partly because jobs are more difficult to obtain, but it is also because young people have become more willing to remain in education in order to become as well-qualified as possible. There has been no upward movement in the (always imprecise) chronological age at which youth commences. Sixteen has been the statutory school-leaving age in Britain since 1972. By age 16 the majority of young people have adopted some adult leisure practices. For example, the majority are drinking regularly, usually with at least the tacit consent of their parents (Sharp et al., 1988). The age of first full sexual intercourse is probably as good as any single indicator or how slowly or quickly young people are establishing independent lifestyles, and this age, typically 16 in Britain nowadays, has not risen. Nor has there been an all round upward movement in the ages at which young people first leave their parents' homes to live independently. The mean age has actually fallen as more young people have entered higher education (Jones, 1995). Most young people nowadays experience an intermediate stage between leaving their parents' homes and marrying. Cohabitation has been normalized. Travelling is another way in which some young people fill some of the life space created by the prolonging of their transitions.

Secondly, young people's biographies have been individualized. This is partly due to the variety of courses in post-compulsory education, training schemes, part-time and temporary jobs, and periods of unemployment that young people now experience. It is also due to the contraction of the major firms and industries that once dominated many local labour markets, and the break up of neighbourhoods that were once knit by the residents' life long acquaintance. These trends have made it difficult to conduct youth ethnography in the traditional ways. It was once possible for fieldworkers to make contact with (usually male) peer groups in given localities and emerge with portraits of their typical backgrounds, attitudes, ways of life and futures. Such groups are no longer present in most districts.

Thirdly, young people's futures have become uncertain. It is now more difficult than formerly for young people to know the kinds of adults they will become. This is partly a straightforward consequence of individualization. When large numbers from a cohort travelled into adulthood together, sharing common experiences in their neighbourhoods, primary and secondary schools, then in the labour market, it was relatively easy for them to look ahead at what had happened to earlier cohorts of young people like themselves, and thereby glimpse their own most likely futures. Uncertainty is also a consequence of the substantial numbers of young people who enter recently introduced educational courses and training programmes with no established track records. Equally, it arises from the larger numbers on long established routes, in higher education for example. Nowadays there are so many university students that their qualifications cannot unlock as attractive career prospects for them all as rewarded earlier generations of graduates. Perhaps most basically, uncertainty is a consequence of the sheer pace of economic and social change which means that the adult roles that many of today's children will play are still unknown. For today's young people, basing self-concepts on what they hope and expect to become has become more hazardous than in the past. Rebelling and dropping out from otherwise predictable futures have not become unfashionable so much as impossible.

Fourth, a corollary of their uncertain futures is that most of the steps that young people can take have become risky. They cannot avoid risk taking. Higher education may still lead to an excellent career but a university entrant today would be unwise to rely on this. Employer-based training may lead to a skilled job. If so, the occupation may last for many years. But there is simply no way for anyone to be sure. Personal relationships have become equally risky. Marriage may lead to lifetime domestic security or despair. Individuals have to take risks and the stakes are their own future lives. They have to travel into adulthood without reliable maps, as if in private motor cars, albeit with differently powered engines since some have already accumulated advantages, rather than the public transport vehicles in which entire cohorts once embarked along clearly signposted routes (see Berger et al., 1993).

Post-war youth cultures

It would be amazing if the above changes in young people's situations had not affected their leisure and we shall see that there have indeed been changes which become comprehensible with reference to the broader trends outlined above. However, the changes have occurred within major continuities. Leisure performs some standard functions for all age groups such as allowing individuals to express their selves (to 'let off steam' if they feel the need), to acquire skills that may subsequently prove useful in other domains, and bonding the participants into groups. Then there are additional functions that young people's leisure has performed in all modern (and some pre-modern) societies (see Roberts, 1983). Specifically, it is normally through leisure that young people first assert independence from adults, typically with the blessing of their elders, and learn to associate with equals without external supervision. Another age specific function of leisure is acting as a milieu in which young people learn to play sexualized roles and express the associated feelings. These age specific functions give young people's leisure a special significance even when they take part in the same activities as adults such as going out for a drink or staying in to watch television or listen to music.

The continuities in young people's leisure across the decades can easily beguile all age groups into believing that nothing of importance has changed. However, in the past, alongside the continuities, there have been major transformations in youth cultures. One such transformation occurred after the Second World War and the late-twentieth century could be witnessing a comparable shift. However, just as it is possible to under-estimate, it is also possible to exaggerate the significance of the periodic upheavals that have occurred, and this could be happening in the 1990s within the discourse on lifestyles, identities and postmodernism.

Youth cultures pre-date 1945. Throughout the nineteenth and early twentieth centuries young people in urban Britain found space for themselves, usually on the streets, where they established their independence and sexual reputations. But at that time youth cultures were typically local phenomena which occasionally earned wider reputations, usually for their exceptional criminality (see Davies, 1992). There was little commercial leisure targeted specifically at young people. Between the World Wars the dance halls catered for the young but the cinema, radio, spectator sports, commercial music, pubs and cafes had mainly adult customers. Young people were dependent on their families. Teenagers in employment were usually paid boy or girl wages which, until they were aged 21 or became engaged, were normally handed over to their mothers in exchange for pocket money. Young people 'on the streets' were generally considered 'at risk'. The boys were said to be at risk of criminality while the girls risked pregnancy or, almost as disastrous, blighted reputations. Middle class families protected their teenage children by keeping them at home, in schools and universities. Youth movements and clubs were intended for working class youth. Those not 'in contact', especially the so-called 'unclubbables', were regarded as the high risk group. They tended to be from the most disadvantaged, often 'rough' rather than 'respectable' working class backgrounds.

After the Second World War new kinds of youth cultures appeared. In Britain there were Teddy Boys and, later on, mods and rockers. These youth cultures were unexpected and unprecedented. Their appearance was associated, in 1950s' media discourse, with the rising rates of juvenile delinquency and teenage pregnancies. With hindsight, in practice from the 1960s onwards, it has been easy to see that the new youth cultures were products of full employment, narrower differentials between teenagers' and adults' earnings, teenagers going 'on board' at home from the beginning of their working lives, and the 'affluent teenager' becoming a market segment which was targeted by the suppliers of a range of leisure goods and services, especially clothing and music. When more commercial options became available young people began to vacate the traditional youth clubs and movements. Young people's new ways of life, or at least their styles, gained unprecedented visibility. By virtue of how they dressed and their musical tastes, young people could identify, and be identified with, flamboyant national and even international youth scenes.

By the 1960s it was possible to see that the young people who became involved in these new cultural scenes were not, despite all the fears and warnings, threatening civilization as formerly known. Sociological studies began to interpret the post-youth cultures as contributing to 'continuous socialisation'. The young people were not really dropping out. Actually they were making accelerated transitions to adulthood. Progress into adult employment accelerated and the mean age of marriages fell. Young people's new situations and their new youth cultures were enabling them to establish adult identities and play adult sexual roles at younger ages than their pre-war counterparts. The 'teenage rebels' of the 1950s and 60s grew into the next generations of respectable parents, often retaining their initially 'rebellious' teenage idols – Elvis, Cliff Richard and the Beatles for example.

Another feature that became apparent as soon as researchers were able to 'stand back' and identify the main patterns in the post-war youth cultures was that they incorporated conventional social class and gender divisions. The central actors in most of the new youth scenes were males. Girls had peripheral roles. Their 'lives of their own' were most likely to be based around 'bedroom cultures' (see Griffin, 1985; Sharpe, 1977). Participation in the new youth cultures was also found to be class related. A generation war was not replacing earlier class struggles. This was emphasized by researchers based at Birmingham University's Centre for Contemporary Cultural

Studies. The new youth cultures of the 1950s and 60s were shown to be mainly working class phenomena. Young people on working class trajectories were making the most rapid transitions to adulthood and earning the 'good money' that enabled them to participate in the new commercial scenes at the youngest ages. It was not just that the youngest and most active participants in the new youth cultures tended to be working class. It also became apparent that their youth styles incorporated specifically working class values – about masculinity, the importance of solidarity among mates, being able to enjoy a good time and display disrespect towards authorities, for example (see Hall and Jefferson, 1976; Hebdige, 1979; Mungham and Pearson, 1976; Willis, 1977). Far from challenging, the new youth cultures were reflecting and helping to reproduce established gender and social class divisions. Through the styles that they adopted or developed, young people were expressing, and sometimes addressing problems and contradictions arising from their gender and social class locations. Some of the studies that emphasized these features of post-war youth cultures could be accused of ignoring the extent to which the participants were also addressing problems rooted in the processes of growing up, and overlooking the fact that the committed participants were not statistically representative of their sex or social classes (see Smith, 1981). The crucial point remained that rather than being a revolutionary threat the postwar youth cultures were socially and culturally conservative.

Another transformation?

The following passages argue that since the 1960s there has been another transformation in young people's leisure comparable with what occurred after 1945. There are in fact two direct parallels. Firstly, youth cultural forms have changed in response to wider changes in young people's circumstances. Secondly, once again the underlying functions of young people's leisure have remained unaltered. [. . .]

There are instantly visible, as well as underlying continuities in the 1990s, including young people remaining more susceptible than other age groups to the latest fashions, their higher levels of participation in most forms of out-of-home recreation, and the instability of their leisure interests, relationships and activities. Even so, it ignores swathes of relevant evidence to suggest that youth cultures in the 1990s are basically just the same as in the 1960s and before. First, a wider age group is involved in today's youth scenes. This is a result of the prolongation of transitions and the wider destandardization of the life course. Today's 30-somethings are often still mingling with the young singles while some of their age group are parents of teenage children. Nowadays the main age shift in musical tastes occurs not between teenagers and adults but after 40 (see Longhurst, 1996). When he interviewed a sample of young adults who were part of Newcastle-upon-Tyne's city centre nightlife, Hollands (1995) found that his respondents were aged up to 31.

There has been some speculation about whether youth cultures are disappearing altogether. The main threats to the distinctiveness of youth cultures do not arise from youth unemployment and poverty. Most students, youth trainees and many of the young unemployed manage to participate in a wide range of leisure activities with the cash that they raise from parents, welfare benefits, grants, loans, part-time jobs and casual work in the informal economy (see Roberts and Parsell, 1991). There are huge inequalities in young people's income and spending levels but their spending patterns prove that it is possible to participate in most youth scenes at different levels of expense. Nights out, holidays and new outfits can cost a lot or be managed more cheaply. The distinctiveness of youth cultures is under greater threat from pre-teen children being introduced to youth fashions and becoming an important market for popular music, individuals staying young into their 30s, adults reverting to adolescent lifestyles and the spread of consumer cultures into all age groups. Unlike in the 1950s, it is no longer only, or even mainly, young people who purchase leisure wear and recorded music.

A second post-1960s trend is that gender and social class differences have become less clear cut. This is not to say that either kind of difference has disappeared. Despite unisex fashions and the gay villages in some cities, most young (and older) people succeed in looking unmistakably male or female, and heterosexual masculinity and femininity are still expected if not demanded in most informal social settings. Nevertheless, youth cultures are no longer as male dominated as in the 1950s and 60s. Young women have broken out from the bedroom culture. The recent changes in their leisure behaviour are certain to be related in some way or another to young women making more headway in education and the labour market, and gaining control over their own fertility. Nowadays young women in Britain are just as likely as young men to use indoor sports facilities (Department for Education, 1995). They have been claiming space in other public places also – city centres, wine bars and throughout the club scenes. Young women no longer need male escorts in order to go out.

There has been a similar blurring of social class divisions. Since the 1960s popular culture has been adopted by young people on middle class trajectories, in higher education for example. This has not driven out high culture. It is more a case of some, generally well-educated young (and older) people now feeling able to enjoy both classics and rock. There is now more intermingling of the social classes in secondary and post-compulsory education. This, along with young people's less certain futures, has made them harder to 'classify' by researchers, and by one another. An outcome is that there are no longer any clear social class differences in the kinds of music that young people listen to, what they wear, or the leisure places to which they go. Club scenes divide young people according to their tastes in music but less obviously by their social class backgrounds or destinations (see Thornton, 1995). Hollands (1995) found that Newcastle city centre nightlife was equally popular among university students and local (mainly working class) young people. Those from middle class backgrounds, who are educationally successful, still tend to do more leisure activities, but the 'more' is of the same kinds of things in which working class youth are also involved (see Roberts and Parsell, 1994).

A third trend has been a splintering of youth cultures. Needless to say, there are still many things that most young people do. The majority go on nights out and consume alcohol, listen to popular music and play sport. However, there are no longer any specific musical genres or fashions that can claim to be dominant. There is a rapid turnover of hit parade numbers and artists. None seem able to exert the appeal of Elvis and the Beatles. New technology is part of the explanation. The music production and distribution industries have more players. There are more radio stations all trying to appeal to specific taste publics. But technology is not the reason why it is now equally fashionable for both males and females to have short cropped or long hair, or why there is no longer a 'uniform' worn as widely as blue denim in the 1960s and 70s. Young peoples' various tastes do not map neatly onto gender, social class or geographical divisions (see Roberts and Parsell, 1994). There is simply more variety within all groups which is likely to be related to the broader processes of individualization. Young people nowadays use leisure to develop and express their individuality. They can do this only via their sub-cultural affiliations but they do not need to adopt complete packages. They are able to pick and mix from the 'modules' that are offered by the various consumer industries.

A fourth trend has been towards young people's sub-cultures acting as bases for proto-communities (Willis, 1990) or 'new tribes' (Maffesoli, 1994) rather than expressing membership of pre-existent groups. The groups of young people (and adults) who become players in, or fans of spectator sports teams, and who attend 'raves' and similar scenes where their drugs of choice are available and their preferred types of music are played, can experience intense camaraderie (see Thornton, 1995). Much of the appeal of these occasions is that they are 'incredibly social'. Individuals find that they are accepted and experience a sense of belonging. None of this is completely new. The change over time has been that the young people who play together nowadays have rarely grown up together and attended the same local schools. Their sole bond is likely to be the leisure taste or activity. Yet being part of these scenes can be extremely important to those involved. Those studied by Hollands (1995) were going to Newcastle's downtown 2.7 times a week, and spending £16–18 per occasion on average, which amounted to 38% of their total incomes. They nearly all said that they would feel unacceptably restricted if they were unable to experience these nights out.

It is certainly plausible to argue that through their sub-cultural affiliations today's young people do not so much express as acquire group memberships and identities. It is claimed that young women are able to construct identities for themselves through their consumption of cultural products, especially clothing (see McRobbie, 1991, 1994). In a similar vein it has been argued that ethnic minority youth in Britain have adopted or developed uses of sport and musical genres which create alternatives to the subordinate roles into which they would otherwise be typecast (see Cashmore, 1982; Fleming, 1995; Gilroy, 1987; Hebdige, 1987). If education, occupations and gender no longer offer the clear identities that they conferred in the past, if today's young people cannot be sure about the kinds of adults that they will become, if they cannot know what their social class and occupational destinations will be, they may need to use their leisure and sub-cultural affiliations to establish who they are. It is not difficult to cite examples of young people who appear to be using their leisure in just these ways. And they could be the vanguard age group in this respect. They might carry their identity conferring strategies into their own later life stages. All this is plausible but this is different from being proven, and there is other evidence which shows that, in this case, the plausibility is misleading.

Basically still just fun

Up to now there has been no unambiguous evidence, only a mixture of anecdote, assertion and conjecture, that leisure activities act as a principal base for identity formation within any section of the population. If such evidence can be found anywhere, then, as argued earlier, one would expect to find it among young people. In practice, however, the researchers who have looked most thoroughly have not confirmed the theory.

Bynner and Ashford (1992) investigated this possibility in the evidence from the Economic and Social Research Council's 16–19 Initiative, a set of longitudinal investigations among representative samples of young people in four parts of Britain – Kirkcaldy, Liverpool, Sheffield and Swindon. This research found that the samples' social and political attitudes did not cohere neatly into a limited number of clearly defined life orientations. From the scores of attitude questions that were addressed it was possible to identify a number of 'factors' such as support for, versus opposition to, sex equality, fatalism, self-esteem, employment commitment, attitudes towards the police, anti-racism, political awareness, and concern for the environment. There was considerable fuzziness along all the scales and everything could not be condensed into a limited number of ideal typical world views. Overall, however, the young people's socio-political attitudes were more strongly related to their sex and career trajectories defined by their family backgrounds, educational attainments, and experiences in the labour market than to their uses of leisure. Most of the relationships were weak, but there were hardly any connections at all between the young people's attitudes and their leisure practices. In fact many of the correlations were near zero. 'Sexual values' was among the few exceptions. Class trajectories, in contrast, were consistently related to most socio-political orientations across all three sweeps of the research when the respondents were typically aged from 15–20. There was much greater stability over time in the young people's career trajectories, and the relationships between these and their attitudes, than in either their leisure activities themselves, or these activities' links with their attitudes. This suggests that their leisure styles were not acting as bases for the young people's core identities in which stable attitudes and values were becoming rooted. Class trajectories and gender were continuing to play this role even if they were unable to supply as well defined and powerful collective identities as in the past.

[. . .]

References

Berger, P. A., Steinmuller, P. and Sopp, P. (1993) Differentiation of life courses? Changing patterns of labour market sequences in West Germany, *European Sociological Review*, 9, 43–61.

Bocock, R. (1993) *Consumption*, Routledge, London.

Butler, T. and Savage, M. (eds) (1995) *Social Change and the Middle Classes*, UCL Press, London.

Bynner, J. and Ashford, S. (1992) Teenage careers and leisure lives: an analysis of lifestyles, *Society and Leisure*, 15, 499–519.

Cashmore, E. (1982) *Black Sportsmen*, Routledge, London.

Davies, A. (1992) *Leisure, Gender and Poverty*, Open University Press, Buckingham.

Department for Education (1995) *Young People's Participation in the Youth Service*, Statistical Bulletin, 1/95, London.

Dumazedier, J. (1967) *Towards a Society of Leisure*, Free Press, New York.
—— (1974) *Sociology of Leisure*, Elsevier, Amsterdam.
Featherstone, M. (ed.) (1988) *Postmodernism: Theory, Culture and Society*, Sage, London.
—— (1991) *Consumer Culture and Postmodernism*, Sage, London.
Fleming, S. (1995) *Home and Away: Sport and South Asian Male Youth*, Avebury, Aldershot.
Giddens, A. (1991) *Modernity and Self-identity*, Polity Press, Cambridge.
Gilroy, P. (1987) *There Ain't No Black in the Union Jack*, Unwin Hyman, London.
Griffin, C. (1985) *Typical Girls?* Routledge, London.
Hall, S. and Jefferson, T. (eds) (1976) *Resistance Through Rituals*, Hutchinson, London.
Hebdige, D. (1979) *Sub-Culture: the Meaning of Style*, Methuen, London.
—— (1987) *Cut 'n' Mix*, Comedia, London.
Hollands, R. G. (1995) *Friday Night, Saturday Night*, Department of Social Policy, University of Newcastle.
Jones, G. (1995) *Leaving Home*, Open University Press, Buckingham.
Karsten, L. (1995) Women's leisure: divergence, reconceptualisation and change, *Leisure Studies*, **14**, 186–201.
Laermans, R. (1994) Leisure as making time: some sociological reflections on the paradoxical consequences of individualisation, in Actas do Congreso Mundial do Lazer, *New Routes for Leisure*, Instituto do Ciencias, University of Lisbon.
Lash, S. (1990) *Sociology of Postmodernism*, Routledge, London.
Longhurst, B. (1996) *Popular Music and Society*, Polity, Cambridge.
McRobbie, A. (1991) *Feminism and Youth Culture*, Macmillan, London.
—— (1994) *Postmodernism and Popular Culture*, Routledge, London.
Maffesoli, M. (1994) *The Time of the Tribes*, Sage, London.
Mort, F. (1996) *Culture of Consumption: Masculinities and Social Space in Late-Twentieth Century Britain*, Routledge, London.
Mungham, G. and Pearson, G. (eds) (1976) *Working Class Youth Culture*, Routledge, London.
Roberts, K. (1983) *Youth and Leisure*, Allen and Unwin, London.
—— and Parsell, G. (1991) Young people's sources and levels of income, and patterns of consumption in Britain in the late-1980s, *Youth and Policy*, **35**, December, 20–5.
—— (1994) Youth cultures in Britain: the middle class take-over, *Leisure Studies*, **13**, 33–48.
Savage, M., Barlow, J., Dickens, P. and Fielding, T. (1992) *Property, Bureaucracy and Culture*, Routledge, London.
Sharpe, D. J., Greer, J. M. and Lowe, G. (1988) The normalisation of under-age drinking, paper presented to the *British Psychological Society*, Leeds.
Sharpe, S. (1977) *Just Like a Girl*, Penguin, Harmondsworth.
Smith, D. M. (1981) New movements in the sociology of youth: a critique, *British Journal of Sociology*, **323**, 230–51.
Thornton, S. (1995) *Club Cultures: Music, Media and Subcultural Capital*, Polity Press, Cambridge.
Thrift, N. (1989) Images of social change, in *The Changing Social Structure* (edited by C. Hamnett, L. McDowell and P. Sarre), Sage, London.
Willis, P. (1977) *Learning to Labour*, Saxon House, Farnborough.
—— (1990) *Common Culture*, Open University Press, Milton Keynes.
—— Bekem, A., Ellis, T. and Whitt, D. (1988) *The Youth Review: Social Conditions of Young People in Wolverhampton*, Avebury, Aldershot.
Wynne, D. (1990) Leisure, lifestyle and the construction of social position, *Leisure Studies*, **9**, 21–34.

17 Family Relationships and Family Responsibilities

Janet Finch and Jennifer Mason

Key words

Family, extended family, gender, ethnicity, family obligations, parents and children

There has been much public debate about the care and support given by individuals to the members of their wider family. In particular, it is often felt that families should care for their elderly relatives. In this extract, Finch and Mason describe the conclusions of their study, based on qualitative and quantitative data, of the flows of support between family members.

Finch and Mason show that flows of support – gifts of money, assistance in kind, e.g. babysitting or shopping, or emotional help – were common in the families they interviewed. Furthermore, these forms of support are treated as unremarkable; they are simply part of family life, a safety net. However, there are no patterns to be discerned. For example, it is not possible to predict what support might be given, or received, between two family members simply from knowing what their genealogical relationship is. Similarly, there are no simple ethnic, social class or gender differences.

What is the sense of family responsibility or obligation that underpins flows of support? Finch and Mason reject the idea that there are fixed rights and duties associated with being a member of a family; responsibilities do not flow automatically from a particular relationship. Rather, the sense of obligation and responsibility develops over time as the result of the relationship between two family members, an adult daughter and her mother, for instance. A pattern of reciprocal support is built-up over time which generates a sense of responsibility.

To use a phrase like 'sense of responsibility' suggests that there is a moral dimension to the exchanges of support between members of the family. Indeed, Finch

and Mason argue that the moral and material are intimately interwoven. In family exchanges the moral identities of individuals are being created and sustained – as a caring sister, for example. Of special importance is the way in which individuals are defined as independent or dependent. Most individuals in Finch and Mason's sample went out of their way to avoid being characterized as too dependent; they were keen to protect their moral identity as an independent person.

The reader should note that, since this extract is taken from the conclusion to an entire book, the references to other chapters within it are to that book.

[. . .]

We began by posing questions about the nature of kin relationships and responsibilities: how significant are kin as sources of practical and financial assistance? Do people accept that they have a responsibility to provide such assistance for relatives, or at least for certain relatives? Does the concept of 'family responsibilities' have any real contemporary meaning? Should all these questions be answered differently for women and men? We are now in a position to give some answers to these questions, and we want to highlight three elements of our analysis: (a) the significance of kin relationships as social support; (b) the nature of kin responsibilities; (c) material and moral dimensions. We follow this section with some brief comments about the broader implications of our analysis.

The significance of kin relationships as social support

The empirical evidence from our qualitative study shows kin relationships to be a significant source of assistance for many people. Most people have experience of money being lent or given, even if this involves quite small amounts in most cases. Many people have experience of living in a household which was shared with an adult relative (who was not part of a core nuclear family), at some point in their lives. Many have helped to look after someone who was ill or incapacitated, or been on the receiving end of such assistance. Some have also looked after a relative's children, given practical help with the house, the garden or the car, or given emotional support to a relative who was feeling fragile. [. . .] At the simplest level, our study updates the work of researchers who looked at family and kinship in Britain in the 1950s and 1960s (Young and Willmott, 1957; Bell, 1968; Rosser and Harris, 1968; Firth, Hubert and Forge, 1970). They concluded that, despite widespread beliefs to the contrary, the extended family was alive and well, and had a tangible reality in most people's lives. We are saying that, thirty years later, it still does.

However, our main point is not so much that these experiences of giving and receiving help within families were *common* experiences (though many of them were), but that they were treated as *unremarkable* experiences by many people who talked to us. They were seen as a characteristic part of family life. They form part of people's image of what constitutes 'a family' and most people in our study wanted to claim that they were part of 'a family' of this type. They were keen to show us that their family did actually work as a support system for its members, at least at a minimal level. We have suggested (in Chapter 2) that the minimal level is defined as everyone rallying round in a crisis to give practical and moral support. We have just one or two exceptions to this in our study population but for the most part our interviewees said that their own families worked at least at this level. Of course there were plenty of examples of conflict, or of people not actually receiving help when they felt they needed it. And our interviewees were very aware that some families appear to work better than others as support systems. But almost all of them presented their own family as 'working' at the minimal level at least, even if they also had indicated that they saw their own family as 'less close' than some others.

To put the point slightly differently, we are arguing that the kin group *is* seen as something which you can fall back on if things go wrong in your life, especially if there are unexpected traumas or disasters. But it is a safety-net which should be used as a last resort, not as a first resort. People expect that, for most of their adult lives, they will *not* be drawing on the support of kin apart from their spouses. [. . .]

So we are arguing that, while most people value a kin group which 'works' as a support system for its members, most can only be actually relied upon to do so in sudden crises and in situations of 'last resort'. In other circumstances our data suggest that the kin group is much more unreliable as a support system, at least when looked at from the outside. By this we mean that it is not possible to predict, simply from knowing the genealogical relationships, what kind of support is likely to be given to any individual. Knowing that Mr X has a brother, or five sisters, or two sons, does not enable me to say if he is likely to be looked after when he is ill, lent money if he needs to replace his car, or given a temporary home if his own household is split up by separation or divorce. Some brothers, or sisters, or sons would offer any of these forms of help; others would not. The offers of help do not flow straightforwardly from the genealogical relationship. Certainly it is more likely that parents and children will help each other – particularly down the generations, from parents to adult children – than will other relatives. [. . .]

Are these variations accounted for by other social characteristics of the individuals involved – their gender, their occupations, their ethnicity, their incomes? In previous chapters we have firmly rejected the idea that these kinds of 'structural factors' explain the help which passes in families in any straightforward way. Of course people who are in comfortable financial circumstances have more options about helping their relatives than do families where everyone is on the breadline. In that very simple sense, some of our variations are accounted for by people's economic and social circumstances. But the idea, for example, that working-class people in general are more inclined to value family support than are the middle classes – or indeed the other way round – simply does not square with our data, either the survey data or those based on qualitative interviews. One reason why 'structural factors' do not straightforwardly explain people's experience of giving and receiving help, is that they are in part a *product* of help given and received in the past. For example, parents' assistance to their children in getting them through higher education, in helping them to set up businesses or to buy houses, or to migrate to another country, all have an effect upon the occupational class position that the children occupy in adult life. Thus factors such as occupational class or housing tenure cannot be regarded as 'independent variables' in this context.

Two exceptions to this argument are ethnicity and gender because, except in very unusual circumstances, these are fixed at birth. In this study, we wanted to explore ethnic variations but were unable to do so effectively in the survey data [. . .]. In our qualitative data we have eleven interviewees out of eighty-eight who were of Asian or Caribbean descent – a number large enough to give us some indication of where the similarities and differences might lie, but obviously not the basis for making detailed and generalisable comparisons. In fact we are struck more by the similarities in the experience of our white interviewees and those of Asian or Caribbean descent, than by the differences between them. Certainly we can identify some obvious differences. For example, in kin groups of Asian descent, we found evidence of a continuing expectation that a son, rather than a daughter, will take responsibility for giving a home to elderly parents – though the labour of caring for infirm elderly people will largely fall on women in the household, as in the white community. But other than this kind of difference, built on specific or cultural norms about the responsibilities of kin, the ways in which our black and Asian interviewees (all of whom were young adults who had been brought up in the UK) approached family responsibilities had many similarities with those of the white people we talked to.

In relation to gender, there certainly are some differences but not of a simple kind. At the level of publicly expressed beliefs, women and men say essentially similar things about the value which they place upon assistance between kin and the circumstances in which it should operate. Therefore any differences in women's and men's involvement with their kin cannot be explained by the idea that they hold different beliefs about the family or adhere straightforwardly to different value systems. When it comes to looking at what happens in practice, women in general do seem to be more firmly locked into sets of responsibilities to relatives, and men are more peripheral. However, here, as with all our data, we find considerable variations between individuals and exceptions in both directions.

In this section we have sketched out the basic pattern which shows that kin relationships *are* significant as structures of social support, but in a variable way. In subsequent sections we refer to these patterns and attempt to develop our understanding of them.

The nature of kin responsibilities: rules, rights and commitments

The concept of responsibilities lay at the heart of our research agenda in this study. Where we find examples of people giving assistance to their kin, does it make sense to talk in terms of responsibility or obligation or duty, associated with family relationships specifically? [. . .] In essence, our answer is that the patterns of assistance which we have identified *are* underscored by a sense of 'family responsibility', but that we have to look carefully at what this means.

We need to clear away first of all what it does *not* mean. We found very little evidence to support the view that people see specific duties attached to family relationships. Our main purpose in the survey element of our study was to see if it is possible to identify anything approaching rules of obligation which are widely acknowledged at the level of publicly expressed norms. We found that there are not. The variations which we observed in practice, in the assistance which relatives give to each other, also suggest that responsibilities do not operate on the basis of fixed rules. The interviewees who came closest to talking about rules of obligation on the whole were people of Asian descent but even here, as we have noted, there were variations in how that worked out in practice. For most people responsibilities towards relatives were not fixed. They are far more fluid that the notion of 'rules of obligation' implies. To return to the distinction which we made in the introductory chapter, the concept of 'guidelines' seems to fit our data much better than 'rules'. Further, the guidelines which people recognise are procedural rather than substantive – they indicate how to work out whether it is appropriate to offer assistance to a particular relative, rather than ones which point to what you should do in concrete terms. It is for these reasons that we have chosen to use the word 'responsibilities', which perhaps has less of a sense of fixed rules than does 'obligations' or 'duties'.

So we would argue that the idea of 'duty' is an inappropriate way of thinking about family life. We would reject even more strongly its corollary, 'rights'. If there were fixed rules of obligation or duty in families, then we might expect that one person felt a duty to give assistance and the other felt a right to claim it. But our data show a particularly strong resistance to the idea that anyone has a right to claim assistance from a relative [. . .]. This is one of the strongest messages in our data and is supported, in different ways, by evidence from the survey and from the qualitative study. Claiming rights is definitely not seen as a legitimate part of family life. Even where one person accepts a responsibility to help, the other does not have the right to claim, or even to expect, assistance. We have argued that this is because the right to offer help must always remain with the donor – particularly important in a situation where there are no fixed rules of obligation. The fact that responsibilities are not mirrored by rights reinforces our basic point that they are fluid and not fixed.

So in what sense *can* we identify responsibilities within kin groups? Our most important point here is that a sense of responsibility for helping someone else *develops* over time, through interaction between the individuals involved. It is a two- (or more) way process of negotiation in which people are giving and receiving, balancing out one kind of assistance against another, maintaining an appropriate independence from each other as well as mutual interdependence [. . .]. As a product of these processes, one individual becomes committed to giving assistance to another. Responsibilities thus are *created*, rather than flowing automatically from specific relationships. [. . .]

We have found the concept of *developing commitments* particularly valuable in expressing the processes which we are uncovering. It is a conceptual framework which both helps us to understand the processes involved in negotiating responsibilities, and also helps to explain why we find the kind of variations which our data display. We are using the concept of commitments as developed originally by Howard Becker (1960) [. . .]. The essence of this idea is that people develop commitments *over time* and in ways which are possibly half-recognised but often not consciously planned. One person helps another out in a crisis and the other then wants to return the favour. Opportunities for doing this may occur easily or they may not. Where a pattern of reciprocal assistance builds up over time, each person invests something of themselves in *this* relationship and becomes committed to it as a relationship through which mutual aid flows. The essence of becoming committed, in Becker's terms, is that it becomes 'too expensive' to withdraw from the situation which is developing. The 'expense' is not necessarily calculated in material terms, though it can be. This was certainly the case in one or two instances in our data set where, for example, someone got locked into a set of commitments to an older generation because they were to inherit property and money when that person died. But more usually, it seems, the expense is calculated in terms of people's personal identities and their moral standing in their kin group and in the eyes of the world at large.

Thus the concept of developing commitments encapsulates much of what we have said about the ways in which family responsibilities are created between specific individuals over a period of time. It also helps us to understand why we have such a pattern of variation in people's experiences of assistance in kin groups, and in the pattern of responsibilities which they acknowledge. Such variations occur because responsibilities are a product of interactions between individuals over time. The course which such interactions take can be very variable even for members of the same family, including people in the same genealogical position (as sons, sisters, grandmothers or whatever). At the same time, the genealogical relationship of individuals does play some part in shaping the course which such interactions are likely to take. For example, we have argued that parent–child relationships – particularly 'down' the generations – come closest to being in a category of their own. However, we see the explanation for this as located within the framework of 'developing commitments', rather than the idea that fixed rules of obligation cover parent–child relationships. What we are saying is that the conditions under which people live their lives make it more likely that parents and children will develop commitments to each other, but that the underlying processes of developing commitments are the same for all categories of kin.

[. . .]

Material and moral dimensions of family responsibilities

One distinctive feature of the argument which we are developing is to emphasise the interweaving of what we are calling the material and the moral dimensions of family life. Though this is perhaps implicit in earlier research, in analysing our own data we have come to see the importance of bringing this into the foreground.

Essentially our argument is that it is not possible to understand the nature of family responsibilities, or how they operate in practice, if you concentrate only on their material dimensions and look at exchanges of goods and services solely in terms of their material value. Certainly such exchanges *are* 'reckoned' in material terms, but only up to a point. In order to see their full significance, and to understand the dynamic which such exchanges create and recreate, we have to also see the moral dimensions. By 'moral dimensions' we do not mean moral rules. We have already indicated that the evidence of our study leads us to reject the idea of following moral rules, as an inappropriate way of describing how family responsibilities operate. When we talk about seeing the moral dimensions of family responsibilities, we mean that people's identities as moral beings are bound up in these exchanges of support, and the processes through which they get negotiated.

Much more is at stake therefore, than simply the material value of the goods and services which are exchanged. People's identities are being constructed, confirmed and reconstructed – identities as a reliable son, a generous mother, a caring sister or whatever it might be. The concept of commitments links in here too. If the image of 'a caring sister' is valued as part of someone's personal identity then it eventually becomes too expensive to withdraw from those commitments through which that identity is expressed and confirmed. It appears that a particularly important aspect of identities constructed in relation to family responsibilities is the dependence–independence dimension. It has been a strong theme in our data [. . .] that most people strive to ensure that they do not become 'too dependent' upon assistance from relatives. A certain degree of interdependence is allowed, indeed is highly valued. But any situation where one person receives more than they can return to the other is definitely to be avoided.

Thus our argument is that, through negotiations about giving and receiving assistance, people are being constructed and reconstructed as moral beings. In thinking about the ways in which people's identities form part of these interactions, we have found it useful to talk abut 'reputations'. [. . .] Reputations, we have argued, are not simply the image which one individual has of another, but they have a more public and a more enduring character. Reputations are images of each individual which are *shared* by members of their kin group (and possibly by other people too) and they have an influence upon the course of future relationships. By stressing that reputations are shared rather than individual images we do not mean to imply that there is always total agreement. [. . .] We have shown earlier that there are cases where a person's reputation within their family is a matter of some dispute. But in a sense this reinforces our point that a person's reputation is public not private property. It is moulded and remoulded as that person's actions are observed and talked about by other members of their kin group.

In focusing on these moral dimensions of family life we also see very clearly the potential for conflict and for outcomes which do not suit one or more of the parties. This is an important counterbalance to our evidence that, on the whole, people do want to see themselves as part of a family that 'works' at least at a minimal level, and make some effort to ensure that it does. But when we see how closely people's identities and reputations are bound in with kin exchanges, it seems very unlikely that families are going to 'work' equally for all people all of the time. The ways in which they 'don't work' can vary. We have noted that there certainly are some examples of people in our study who have received little from their kin and have given little (see Chapter 2 and Appendix C). Family responsibilities seem to have a marginal place in the lives of these people and the family may not 'work' as a support system, even of last resort.

There are also ways in which the family 'doesn't work' for individuals on a moral level, even when it does seem to be working at the level of material assistance. The clearest of these examples arise when an ongoing process of exchanges between kin leaves one person 'beholden to' another. This can happen in a whole range of circumstances – where a young person has to rely on their parents' financial assistance after they feel they should be fully independent; in old age when a person may become physically dependent; at the end of a marriage when an adult child returns to the parental home, in need of moral support and assistance with child care. In such circumstances, it is possible in principle for the person in the position of donor to extract forms of repayment which might otherwise not have been given. 'Moral blackmail' is a phrase commonly used to describe such situations, and indeed it was used by some of our interviewees. In earlier chapters we have quoted a few examples which do seem to amount to a fairly naked exercise of such power. More commonly people do not actually take advantage of these situations in this way – indeed they may be careful to avoid opportunities to exercise the power which potentially they have. But this does not really change the situation fundamentally for the person who has become the net recipient in an unbalanced pattern of exchanges. Their identity and their position within the kin group has changed, and they *are* beholden to someone else, even if this is not openly acknowledged. The strenuous efforts which people make to try to avoid getting into such situations demonstrates how unwelcome this is.

We have emphasised the importance of the moral dimensions in understanding how family responsibilities operate but we do not mean to imply that the material dimensions are of no importance. In terms of the practical consequences of kin group exchanges, they are exceedingly important. The quality and standard of living of individuals can be enhanced or eroded in very significant ways through exchanges between kin of money, goods, labour and time. Also the material value of assistance is taken into account in 'reckoning' the moral dimensions of exchanges. We see this very clearly when we look at how people try to keep a balance between dependence and independence in relationships with their kin. Some very fine calculations (which of course may not be successful) take place to try to ensure that no one becomes a net giver or net receiver, or is beholden to someone else. The way such calculations are reckoned centrally concerns the material value of the exchanges.

In summary, our purpose is not to argue that the moral dimensions of exchanges are more important than the material, or vice versa. Our central theme is that the two are finely interwoven. To see either without the other is to miss the main point.

[. . .]

References

Becker, H.S. (1960) 'Notes on the concept of commitment', *American Journal of Sociology* 66: 32–40.

Bell, C. (1968) *Middle-class Families*, London, Routledge & Kegan Paul.

Firth, R., Hubert, J. and Forge, A. (1970) *Families and their Relatives*, London, Routledge & Kegan Paul.

Rosser, C. and Harris, C.C. (1968) *The Family and Social Change*, London, Routledge & Kegan Paul.

Young, M. and Willmott, P. (1957) *Family and Kinship in East London*, London, Routledge & Kegan Paul.

18 | The Local Networks of the Elderly

*Chris Phillipson,
Miriam Bernard, Judith Phillips,
and Jim Ogg*

Key words

The elderly, community, neighbours, the city

Britain is an ageing society. This fact has prompted a public debate about the care of the elderly and particularly the role of the family in that care. This article explores another side to the support of the elderly: the social network of the local community. It investigates the community lives of older people in three urban areas of Britain – Bethnal Green, Wolverhampton and Woodford, and makes comparisons with the results of studies of those three areas carried out in the 1940s and 1950s.

The social network of the community, comprising friends, neighbours and family, may be particularly important to older people; they cannot rely on the social relationships of work but may, on the other hand, have long experience of particular locality. The older people in the Phillipson et al.'s sample had been at their current address for more than twenty-five years. Their experience suggested that neighbours play a significant role in the support of older people. The authors found that there were high levels of contact with neighbours although it is important to note the depth of the relationship. Neighbours are important in offering short-term or emergency help; they are much less likely to be defined as 'friends'.

Introduction

Postwar research has confirmed the importance of family and community relationships in the lives of older people. However, the nature of such ties remains under-researched. Since the community studies of the 1950s and early 1960s, there has been little research focusing on older people's experiences viewed from a locality perspective.[1] The study reported here provides a contribution to this issue, examining changes to the social and family networks of elderly people in three urban areas of England: Bethnal Green, Wolverhampton and Woodford. These were the locations for work in the 1940s and 1950s which provided extensive material about the lives of elderly people (Sheldon, 1948; Townsend, 1957; Young and Willmott, 1957; Willmott and Young, 1960). Using these studies as a baseline, the paper examines patterns of neighbouring in the three localities.

To investigate these issues, the research was carried out in two main phases. The first comprised a questionnaire survey of 627 older people, in the three urban locations.[2] This was designed to explore general issues about social change since the baseline studies, including questions concerning neighbourhood ties; the personal networks of older people; attitudes towards neighbours, and experiences of support and help from neighbours. The main part of the second phase comprised a series of qualitative interviews with 62 white older people over the age of 75, these drawn from phase one. An additional group of interviews was also undertaken with Asian respondents in Bethnal Green and Wolverhampton. The purpose of both sets of interviews was to examine the issue of social change from the standpoint of a more vulnerable group of older people.[3]

The paper is divided into three parts: first, we examine the background to the research, highlighting current issues in the field of community studies, as well as research on neighbouring. Second, the paper reviews our research findings about the role and place of neighbours, this drawing upon quantitative as well as qualitative data. Finally, we discuss the implications of the research for understanding changes to the experience of community life in old age.

Urban communities, localities and neighbourhoods

A major focus of the research is on the ties which people have to their immediate locality. The issue of defining 'locality' and 'community' has been the subject of much controversy within sociology (Bell and Newby, 1971; Crow and Allan, 1994). However, there may be considerable value in applying issues falling under the heading of 'community' to the lives of older people, since as Crow and Allan (1994: 1) observe, the idea of community figures in many aspects of our daily lives:

> Much of what we do is engaged in through the interlocking social networks of neighbourhood, kinship and friendship, networks which together make up 'community life' as it is conventionally understood. 'Community' stands as a convenient shorthand term for the broad realm of local social arrangements beyond the private sphere of home and family but more familiar . . . than the impersonal institutions of the wider society.
>
> (Crow and Allan, 1994: 1)

This 'interlocking social network' may be especially important for older people, given their separation from relationships such as those associated with paid employment (Phillipson, 1993). Moreover, given older people's often long association with particular areas, they may view and experience social change rather differently to other age groups (Taylor et al., 1996). Both these points underline the case for developing a 'community' perspective in the study of old age.

The localities in the research in this study have developed in different ways since the baseline studies. In the case of Bethnal Green, re-development in the 1950s and 1960s amounted to a re-building of the community, with a scattering of at least some of the population to outlying suburbs and beyond (Porter, 1994). In Wolverhampton, there was also substantial re-development and slum clearance, but with the population affected moving relatively small distances (at least in geographical terms) to newly-built estates. For the suburbanites of Woodford, the process was one of consolidation rather than change, with a slowing down in the rate of development from the inter-war years.

Each area experienced a decline in population in the period between 1951 and 1981: in Wolverhampton and Woodford these were relatively small percentage decreases, compared with a decline of almost 50% in Bethnal Green. Damage to housing in inner city London before 1950, and subsequent demolition and clearance over the succeeding decades, accounts for part of the differences between the study areas. However, Wolverhampton's decline has been comparatively recent, compared with the other two areas. Indeed, Bethnal Green and Woodford have shown population growth since the early 1980s (Inwood, 1998).

Against this, we need also to look at what has happened to the older population. In 1951, Woodford was the 'oldest' of our three areas: with 15% of its population being of pensionable age, compared with 13.6% in Bethnal Green and 11.7% in Wolverhampton. In the intervening 40 years, all three study areas have experienced a marked ageing such that they now (1991 census figures) have figures of 20%, 17.5% and 18.6% respectively. This compares with a national figure for the UK of 18.2% of the population over pensionable age, and shows that while Woodford is still our 'oldest' study area, Wolverhampton has in fact 'aged' most markedly. Bethnal Green on the other hand, whilst ageing, has also experienced growing ethnic diversity and associated increasing proportions of children, in common with a number of other East London boroughs (Rix, 1996).

Following this review of the background to the research, we now consider other work on neighbouring and, in particular, some of the findings and conclusions from the baseline studies.

Neighbourhoods and neighbours

The importance of neighbours for older people has been a consistent theme in the gerontology literature. Wenger's (1984) research reported a high degree of friendliness and neighbourliness towards older people in rural areas. Her data showed that where an immediate response was critical, neighbours play an essential role and that crisis help and intervention are among the expectations of neighbourliness (Wenger, 1992). Urban environments, on the other hand, may illustrate a different experience to that described by Wenger. This may be especially the case with more mixed populations (in contrast with Wenger's predominantly middle-class rural setting). Here, theorists of neighbouring (such as Irving Rosow, 1967) would point to the problem of older people being dispersed among younger families, with contacts being reduced by the gradual movement of population, and the death of friends and neighbours their own age. These developments may be reinforced by more general changes to local attachments, these promoted by the spread of car ownership, longer journeys to work, and different patterns of shopping and recreation (Bulmer, 1987).

The findings on neighbouring reported in the baseline studies were somewhat mixed. Townsend summarised older people's views on the characteristics of a good neighbour as follows:

> He, or rather she, was someone who did not expect to spend time in your home or pry into your life, who exchanged a civil word in the street or over the backyard fence, who did not make a great deal of noise, who could supply a drop of vinegar or a pinch of salt if you ran short and who fetched your relatives or the doctor in emergencies. The good neighbour's role was that of an **intermediary**, in the direct as well as indirect sense . . . She was the go-between, passing news from one family to another, one household to another. Her role was a communicative but not an intimate one.
>
> (Townsend, 1957: 121)

In Wolverhampton, Sheldon found neighbours playing an active role in supporting older people, with more than one-third of the help available to old people in illness supplied by a neighbour (although often one who was related in some way to the older person). Willmott and Young (1960: 107) found that in Woodford there were '. . . plenty of examples of help given to old people by friends and neighbours', and an important finding of their study was the significant role of friends in a predominantly middle-class community. Given these findings, what kind of change can be identified since the original studies? What were the nature of people's attachments to Bethnal Green, Wolverhampton and Woodford, as expressed in their feelings about and contact with neighbours?

Residential attachment

Length of residence in an area has often been cited as an important element in the development of neighbouring. Young and Willmott (1957: 105) in their Bethnal Green study noted that: 'Long residence by itself does something to create a sense of community with other people in the district'. Our study found that in Bethnal Green, 31% of the white respondents had been born in the borough (the equivalent figure in Townsend's sample was 54%). Many had subsequently moved around the area following marriage or re-location as a result of housing re-development. A high proportion of Wolverhampton respondents had also been born in the borough or had moved to the town early in their married life; and 8% had lived in the same district in Wolverhampton all their life (the comparable figure for Woodford was 4%).

The older people in our study had lived, on average, for nearly 25 years at their current address. White respondents had lived significantly longer at their present address than those from minority ethnic groups. In the case of Bethnal Green, for example, white respondents had lived in their house or flat (mainly the latter) for an average of 22.3 years. This figure is in fact fairly close to that reported by Townsend in the early 1950s (24 years). By contrast, the figure for the Asian respondents was

8.5 years. Townsend also found a high proportion (27 per cent) of people who had been living in the same home for 40 or more years. In the 1990s, however, there has been a considerable change in this regard: just 6% of our sample in Bethnal Green had lived in the same home for this length of time. In Wolverhampton, however, this experience was more common, with nearly one in four of those interviewed (23%) having been in their home for 40 or more years (the figure for Woodford was 18%). Long-term residence at the same address is more common in Wolverhampton now than it was in the 1940s. Then, around 20% of older people were reported to have been at their present address for 30 years or more; and a similar figure for five years or less (Rowntree, 1948). In 1995, the comparable figures were 42% and 11%. 8% of older people in Wolverhampton had actually been at the same address for 50 or more years (compared with 6% in Woodford, and less than 1% in Bethnal Green).

Although directly comparable data for Woodford is unavailable, Willmott and Young (1960) found that amongst couples in their general sample with parents still alive, nearly half had been in Woodford less than 10 years, and another quarter between ten and twenty: Willmott and Young observe that 'They had moved *into* Woodford and away from parents'. Amongst our sample, couples or surviving partners reflect the 'ageing in place' since the time of the earlier study: 42% had been at their current address for 30 years or more; 10% five years or less.

Defining neighbours

How do older people define neighbours? Bulmer (1987) points out that all studies agree that **proximity** is an essential attribute; neighbours, in fact, are rarely regarded as living further afield than the street, block or apartment building (Willmott, 1986). Our respondents were evenly spread in identifying three main categories of neighbour: someone who lived next door; in the nearest five or six houses; or in the same street (Table 1). Older people in Wolverhampton, however, were more likely to

Table 1 Definitions of a neighbour

	Wolverhampton		Bethnal Green		Woodford	
	n	%	n	%	n	%
People who live next door	90	39	48	25	37	18
Nearest 5–6 houses	71	31	54	28	76	37
Same street	47	21	66	34	68	33
Larger area	13	6	18	9	16	8
Other	4	2	4	2	2	1
Non-response	3	1	5	3	5	3
Totals	**228**	**100**	**195**	**100**	**204**	**100**

$p < 0.01$.
Source: Keele ESRC Project.

Table 2 | **Households in street known by name**

	Wolverhampton		Bethnal Green		Woodford	
	n	%	n	%	n	%
None	8	4	19	10	5	3
One or two	39	17	28	14	15	7
Three or four	28	12	25	13	29	14
Five to nine	61	27	54	28	68	33
Ten or more	90	40	63	32	85	42
Refused	0	0	1	1	0	0
Can't say	2	0.9	5	3	2	1
Totals	**228**	**100**	**195**	**100**	**204**	**100**

$p < 0.01$.
Source: Keele ESRC Project.

identify with the first of these categories than was the case in Bethnal Green and Woodford, a finding which may reflect lower levels of migration and residential moves in the area.

Despite these differences, the majority of people agreed that neighbours are people who live within a relatively short distance, and certainly within the same street. Given this finding, how many neighbours did our respondents know by name? To standardise this, we asked about those who lived in the same street (block of flats/building) as our respondents (Table 2). There were, in fact, relatively few differences between the areas, with two-thirds saying that they knew five or more households in their street; 38% of respondents overall knew 10 or more neighbours. A minority claimed not to know anyone by name. This was slightly more the case in Bethnal Green, where 1 in 10 of those interviewed knew nobody by name, and a further 14% just one or two people. Overall, white respondents knew substantially more neighbours than those from minority ethnic groups, this almost certainly reflecting differences in factors such as length of residence and general experiences of the area.

Contact with neighbours

National surveys such as the General Household Survey (OPCS, 1996) indicate high levels of contact between older people and their neighbours. Findings from our study reinforce this picture. Our question asked whether respondents had talked to anyone in their street in the past month. The highest proportion was in Woodford where 96% had done so; the lowest in Bethnal Green at 84% (the figure for Wolverhampton was 89%). We also asked if people could say how many neighbours they had talked to in the last month (Table 3). More people in Bethnal Green and Wolverhampton (around one-fifth) said they had just talked to one or two people. For around two-thirds in

Table 3 How many neighbours have you talked to in the last month?

	Wolverhampton		Bethnal Green		Woodford	
	n	%	n	%	n	%
None	26	11	31	16	9	4
One or two	41	18	35	18	16	8
Three or four	37	16	26	13	41	20
Five to nine	54	24	46	24	73	36
Ten to fourteen	35	15	23	12	40	20
Fifteen to nineteen	15	7	7	4	10	5
Twenty +	19	8	25	13	14	7
Can't say	1	4	2	1	1	1
Totals	**228**	**100**	**195**	**100**	**204**	**100**

$p < 0.01$.
Source: Keele ESRC Project.

each of the areas it was nine or less. Bethnal Green, on the other hand, had respondents at both extremes, with a higher proportion (13%) reporting contact with 20 or more people.

A more revealing question in terms of contacts with neighbours concerns whether they actually came into the respondent's home. Regular contact with people on the street is one thing; inviting people into your home perhaps indicates a closer relationship, one which may involve reciprocal ties in some form or another. In fact, contact between neighbours may always have been subject to fairly strict limitations. In Bethnal Green, in the early 1950s, Townsend found nearly two-thirds of his respondents saying that they did not go regularly into the home of a neighbour, and nor did a neighbour visit them. And some of Willmott and Young's (1960) working-class respondents in Woodford expressed fairly strong views against allowing non-relatives into their home.

Our study asked whether anybody in the street had come into the respondent's home in the past six months. Overall, 70% had neighbours into their home, with the Woodford sample the highest (75%), followed by Wolverhampton (72%), and Bethnal Green (61%). There were some social class differences on this issue. Overall, non-manual respondents were more likely to have had neighbours into their home. This relationship held for Woodford and Wolverhampton but not for Bethnal Green, where there were no social class differences. There were no significant gender, age or ethnic differences on this issue.

We also asked respondents whether they thought of anyone living in their street as a 'friend'. This seeme to be an interesting issue in the light of evidence about the importance of neighbours in terms of offering short-term/emergency help to older people (Wenger, 1994), assistance which is perhaps more likely where there is evidence of a friendship of some kind. It is perhaps a reflection of some of the changes affecting Bethnal Green (discussed below), that over one-third (38%) of those interviewed were unable to identify anyone in their street as a friend (the equivalent figures for Wolverhampton and Woodford were 26% and 32% respectively). There were no significant differences on this question when controlling for age, gender, social class and ethnicity.

Experiences of the neighbourhood

So far this paper has focused on questions about the extent of contacts with neighbours. However, we also asked some questions about people's feelings about their environment: what did they like or dislike about living in the area? How would people feel if they had to move from the area? These questions were asked partly to contrast with some of the descriptions from the earlier studies: partly, as well, to provide a context for the information about the social networks gleaned from the survey (Phillipson et al., 1998).

The first question we asked was whether there was anything people particularly liked about living in their area. Overall, 79% of people could find something to like, with the highest proportion in Woodford (87%), and the lowest in Bethnal Green (65%). Many respondents felt they lived in a friendly area and that there was a 'community feeling' to where they lived:

> [. . .] everybody is fairly friendly, look after each other's interests. We have a Neighbourhood Watch going.
>
> (Wolverhampton, 70 year old married man)

> It's the East End and I like the East End. I've loved Bethnal Green ever since I've lived here. I've got so many friends here. It's a real community.
>
> (Bethnal Green, 70 year old man, widowed)

> More like a village. Everybody knows everyone else. It is very friendly.
>
> (Woodford, 60 year old woman, married)

Bethnal Green respondents were rather more likely than respondents in the other localities to stress their sense of having 'roots' in the area. The following comments are typical of this feeling:

> It's my home, my roots are here now. It's what I'm used to . . . living here and working here for so many years.
>
> (76 year old woman, widowed)

> It's where I was brought up. I wouldn't want to live anywhere else. All my friends are here and I wouldn't know anyone anywhere else.
>
> (67 year old man, widowed)

If a sense of identity with the East End was important for many of those in Bethnal Green, in Woodford advantages were often put in terms of the 'selectivity' of the area. The earlier Woodford study was carried out in the late 1950s, and issues relating to social class were a prominent feature of the research. In particular, it highlighted the importance which the middle-class in Woodford attached to differentiating themselves from those in the East End. As Willmott and Young (1960) put it:

If social class has an edge in Woodford, it is partly because so many people come from the East End. 'We don't tell people we come from Bethnal Green', said one woman. 'You get the scum of the earth there'. Mr Barber said, 'The East End is a different class altogether – people there call you Dad or Uncle or Auntie. We don't get any of that here.'

These attitudes were certainly replayed by some of our respondents, albeit with a contemporary gloss:

> It's always been considered a 'number one' spot. It's full of people who are quite well off. We don't have many one parent families here.
>
> (74 year old man, married)

> I've always liked it but I'm a private person and I think this area has a bit of class.
>
> (78 year old woman, married)

> I like living in Woodford Green as I came from East London and this is a very quiet area as opposed to the noise of London.

If most people could find something to like about their area, our respondents were rather more divided about whether there was anything to dislike. Overall, 52% highlighted some aspect which concerned them, although this was much more the case in Bethnal Green (64%), than in Woodford (46%) or Wolverhampton (48%). The issues that people raised showed some variation, although there were overlapping concerns. Some of these reflected developments which Roberts (1995: 201) identified in her study of three Lancashire communities. She found . . . 'a new development, still only observable in a small minority of areas: neighbours' property was abused and rights ignored. Neighbours were regarded with neither "distant cordiality" nor effortless "sociability" but with outright hostility. The neighbour was now the enemy'.

This observation is important given the traditional role allocated to neighbours of older people: neighbours are (or should be) friendly (indeed the terms 'friend' and 'neighbour' are treated as synonymous in many studies). Neighbours help in 'emergencies'; are the people to whom older people turn when relatives are unavailable. In reality, however, for a number of people in our survey, the experience of the neighbourhood was rather different. They did not seem to be surrounded by people with whom 'they had friendly contacts'. Neighbours now seemed potentially hostile: a view expressed with particular vigour by some of the older women in our survey:

> Neighbours . . . noisy, language terrible, possibly vermin from next door because of the rubbish.
>
> (Wolverhampton, 60 year old woman, married)

> People don't like doing for you . . . people don't bother they don't. Now everybody's got cars and you don't see people to talk to. I'm 81 now. I've just booked into a home but I don't want to go yet.
>
> (Wolverhampton, 81 year old woman, widowed)

> The neighbour used my washing lines. I told her not to. She ignored. Got my home help to cut my lines down. If I can't use them she is not going to use them. Kids come into my garden – one said 'I'll play wherever I want to'. It was a lot quieter where I was before.
>
> (Wolverhampton, 60 year old woman, married)

Terrible with the neighbours...they've broke my windows. They are on the rough side.

(Bethnal Green, 72 year old woman, single)

For a number of respondents, the problems they faced reflected the death or moving away of old neighbours, those replacing them viewed as bringing different values and attitudes:

It has 'gone down'. There were elderly people about our age but they are all young now.
(Wolverhampton, 83 year old man, married)

Got no friends here now [...] most of them have died. It's not very friendly here.
(Wolverhampton, 70 year old woman, widowed)

Some of the new tenants I am not keen on...the younger ones.
(Wolverhampton, 80 year old woman, widowed)

The neighbours – they let their children run riot. They kick balls around and slam doors.
(Bethnal Green, 70 year old man, married)

For older people, problems with neighbours merged with more general dislikes about the environment in which they lived. People had a sense of being 'shut in'; or that the area had 'gone down'; or that they felt 'threatened' on the streets; or that the place was just 'filthy':

One thing is the kids make the lifts dirty. The water doesn't run away in the balcony. There are a lot of pigeons and muck from them. We have cockroaches and rats and mice. I had a nervous breakdown because of it. And broken pavements [...] I have fallen down 6 or 7 times. It's disgusting.

(Bethnal Green, 74 year old woman, divorced)

It's gradually gone down. When we first came it was nice but not now. You can't seem to get anything done. My windows are falling apart and my roof leaks. It seems to be just pieces of paper flying around.

(Bethnal Green, 64 year old married woman)

The locality has gone down. You're in the heart of the slums...You can't do the shopping you used to locally. When we walk through the gate at the end we are faced with lots of rubbish put outside. My grandchildren don't even like coming to visit us.

(Bethnal Green, 65 year old married woman)

For some white elderly respondents such changes were linked with issues of race and ethnicity. Drawing on Cohen's work in social anthropology, Cornwell (1984) has argued that communities tend to be constructed through the drawing of boundaries between 'insiders' and 'outsiders', with ethnic origin central to the development of processes of 'in-clusion and ex-clusion'. In our study, it is clear that such distinctions remain important, but have been sharpened by the growth of inequalities since the early 1980s. Overall, when asked what they disliked about the area, 48 of the white respondents in Bethnal Green, made explicit reference to minority ethnic groups, with the following comments representative:

Since the war it's all changed . . . we're getting too many coloured people, blacks, Asians, Turks, Cypriots. It's getting out of hand. They want the law to suit themselves – there aren't any in Ireland where my son lives. In the old days no one feared of being mugged or broken into.

(81 year old man, widowed)

I don't like the way it's changed [. . .] it used to be typically Jewish when I moved here. Now there is Bangladeshis I think they are . . . they spit on the stairs and don't teach their children properly.

(72 year old woman, married)

The areas varied, however, in the extent to which older people reported problems with those living around them. Reflecting this, although only a minority of those surveyed said they would be happy to move (19%), there were clear differences between the localities: one in three respondents in Bethnal Green reported that they would be happy to move, compared with 15% in Wolverhampton and 7% in Woodford. In all areas, younger elderly people (60–74) had a greater wish to move than very elderly respondents. In Bethnal Green, 40% of those aged 60–74 said they would be happy to move: a remarkably high figure given the length of time most of the respondents had lived in or around the area.

Having examined likes and dislikes about the localities, we turn finally to consider each area in more detail, highlighting the ways in which experiences of neighbourhoods, neighbours and neighbouring have changed over the years.

[. . .]

Conclusion

What do our findings tell us about the value of studying ideas about community, neighbouring and locality amongst older people? What changes might be identified in making a contrast between the 1950s and 1990s? Three sets of issues might be identified in response to these questions. First, the relationship between people and places is perhaps even more important at the end of the 20th century than it was at the beginning, and perhaps even in the middle of the century. White elderly respondents had a sustained pattern of long-term residence, for many the first in their families to achieve such a state. Certainly, it would have been a rare experience in places such as London in the late-19th and early 20th centuries. Anna Davin (1996: 31), writing of this period, emphasises the regularity of moves in working class households, citing Charles Booth's observation that: 'the people are always on the move; they shift from one part of it [London] to another "like fish in a sea"'. The testimony of an elderly woman to the Royal Commission on the Housing of the Working Classes in 1885 reflects this sense of upheaval: 'I came to London 25 years ago, and I have never lived in any room for more than two years; they always pull down the houses to build dwellings for poor people, but I've never got into one yet' (cited in Inwood, 1998: 534). For many of our respondents, by contrast, the presence of the home as a site of memories and a feeling of achievement was substantial. There was a sense of 'belonging to a place' which should perhaps not be underestimated in wider discussions about displacement and loss of attachment to particular locations.

Second, this sense of attachment to place or 'investment' as Massey (1984) would call it, has different layers of complexity. Gender is one, and is an important issue for future research on neighbouring. Gerontologists have defined older women as often playing the role of 'kin-keepers', sustaining the family not only through care-work, but activities such as letter-writing, telephoning, and remembering birthdays. Our data suggests they may, in some instances, be 'neighbourhood keepers' as well, vigilant about the changing fortunes of the localities in which they have 'invested' much of their lives. This may perhaps explain why women expressed most concern about what they saw as a deterioration in the community, the replacement of physical capital apparently coinciding with what Putnam (1995) would view as a decline in social capital. But the issues here may be more accurately defined in respect of what Campbell (1993) and others define as the 'crisis in public space', and the conflict between women and men for the control of local areas. Here, and especially in inner city areas, what was viewed as a more threatening environment on the street, was matched by a decline in women's physical capacity to deal with the hurdles generated in urban space, notably, for our respondents, broken lifts, litter, cracked pavements, the threat of violence, and (for elderly Bangladeshis) racist abuse.

Third, studying older people from a community perspective provides both a sense of how localities change, and how elderly people manage this change. On the former, Wellman (1998) has argued that densely-knit solidarities no longer feature in contemporary communities. People now find themselves manoeuvring in sparsely-knit, loosely-bounded, frequently-changing networks. Wellman (1998) further argues that: 'The complex and specialized nature of personal communities means that these are fragmented networks. People must actively maintain each supportive relationship rather than relying on solidary communities to do their maintenance work'. But a fruitful area for further research is on variations in the management of more dispersed networks. For a working-class group, handling the greater distance between close kin poses difficulties in the context of reliance on public transport (less than one-fifth of respondents in Bethnal Green had access to a car). Even though dispersal of kin had also affected respondents in Woodford, they were themselves more mobile (around two-thirds owned or had use of a car) and were generally better placed to cope with changes to their personal network. Such findings remind us that although community is important to older people, they are acutely aware of changes over time in its meaning and impact on their lives. Studying and interpreting this issue remains a valuable and significant issue for sociologists to address.

Notes

1 Crow and Allan (1994) provide a valuable survey of issues relating to community studies.
2 The survey was based on the selection of a random sample of people of pensionable age, drawn from the age–sex registers of General Practitioners in the three areas following approval of the project by the respective District Research Ethics Committees. The size of the achieved samples in the original studies was 203 individuals in Bethnal Green, 210 in Woodford and Wanstead (older people only), and 477 in Wolverhampton. The Keele survey

aimed for around 200 interviews in each area, achieving 195 in Bethnal Green, 228 in Wolverhampton, and 204 in Woodford.
3   The material from the qualitative interviews in this paper is drawn from the white respondents. Later papers from the research will discuss findings from the interviews with Bangladeshi and Indian respondents.

References

Bell, C. and Newby, H., (1971), *Community Studies: An introduction to the sociology of the local community*, London: George Allen and Unwin.

Bulmer, M., (1987), *The Social Basis of Community Care*, London: Allen and Unwin.

Campbell, B., (1993), *Goliath*, London: Methuen.

Cohen, A., (1987), *Whalsay: Symbol, segment and boundary in a Shetland Island Community*, Manchester: Manchester University Press.

Cornwell, J., (1984), *Hard-Earned Lives: Accounts of Health and Illness*, London: Tavistock Books.

Crow, G. and Allan, G., (1994), *Community Life: An Introduction to Local Social Relations*, London: Harvester Wheatsheaf.

Davin. A., (1996), *Growing Up Poor*, London: River Oram Press.

Inwood, S., (1998), *A History of London*, London: Macmillan.

Massey, D., (1984), *Spatial Divisions of Labour: Social Structures and the Geography of Production*, London: Macmillan.

Office of Population Censuses and Surveys, (1996), *1995 General Household Survey*, London: OPCS.

Phillipson, C., (1993), 'The Sociology of Retirement', in J. Bond, P. Coleman and S. Peace, *Ageing in Society*, London: Sage Publications.

Phillipson, C., Bernard, M., Phillips, J. and Ogg. J., (1998), 'The Family and Community Life of Older People: Household Composition and Social Networks in Three Urban Areas', *Ageing and Society*, 18 (3), 259–89.

Porter, R., (1994), *London: A Social History*, London: Hamish Hamilton.

Putnam, R., (1995), 'Bowling Alone: America's disintegrating social capital', *Journal of Democracy*, 6 (1), 65–78.

Rix, V., (1996), 'Social and Demographic Change in East London', in *Rising in the East: The Regeneration of East London*, London: Lawrence and Wishart.

Roberts, E., (1995), *Women and Families: An Oral History: 1940–1970*, Oxford: Blackwell.

Rosow, I., (1967), *Social Integration of the Aged*, New York: The Free Press.

Rowntree, B.S., (1948), *Old People: Report of a Survey Committee on the problems of ageing and the care of old people*, published for the Trustees of the Nuffield Foundation, London: Oxford University Press.

Sheldon, S., (1948), *The Social Medicine of Old Age*, Oxford: Oxford University Press.

Taylor, I., Evans, K. and Fraser, P., (1996), *A Tale of Two Cities: A Study in Manchester and Sheffield*, London: Routledge.

Townsend, P., (1957), *The Family Life of Old People*, London: Routledge and Kegan Paul.

Wellman, B., (1998), 'The Network Community', in B. Wellman (ed.), *Networks in the Global Village*, Boulder, CO: Westview Press.

Wenger, G.C., (1984), *The Supportive Network*, London: George Allen and Unwin.

—— (1992), *Help in Old Age*, Liverpool: Liverpool University Press.

Willmott, P., (1986), *Social Networks, Informal Care and Public Policy*, London: Policy Studies Institute.

—— (1963), *The Evolution of a Community*, London: Routledge and Kegan Paul.

—— and Young, M., (1960), *Family and Class in a London Suburb*, London: Routledge and Kegan Paul.

Young, M. and Willmott, P., (1957), *Family and Kinship in East London*, London: Routledge and Kegan Paul.

Part IV

Fragmentary Cultures

The Dance Music Industry

David Hesmondhalgh

Key words

Popular music industry, economic organization, dance music, independent music companies

There is often a tension between commercial popular culture and forms of the popular arts that claim authenticity or radicalism. This is particularly true of popular music. Whole new styles, or particular bands, have emerged which reject the values of commercial pop and invent new musical styles. A recent example of this is dance. In the article from which this extract is taken, Hesmondhalgh explores this example, concentrating on the relationship between the independent dance sector and very large popular music record companies.

Hesmondhalgh argues that dance music has been the basis of a significant decentralization of musical production out of the major cities. A variety of factors are responsible for this. Relatively inexpensive digital production technology has lowered the costs of entry to the industry; many towns now have dance clubs; specialist record shops have grown up; promotion and marketing costs are low because the subcultural quality of dance means that audiences are intensely interested and seek out new music for themselves; and the audiences' focus on musical style rather than on the personality, or identity, of the performers.

In this extract, Hesmondhalgh further argues that it is difficult for small record companies to sustain themselves in the long term. They can try to get the music into the mainstream, but they then risk the loss of the specialist audience. Or, they can focus on compilations which are relatively cheap to produce and are most likely to be stocked by big record shops. But in the long term, independents are often forced into relationships with the major record companies. For these larger companies (and

*they may set up their own semi-independent labels) relationships with the inde-
pendent sector are valuable because the independents have credibility with artists
and audiences. The difficulties for small companies are compounded by the pressure from dance audiences to create new dance styles. Dance audiences, while they
reject the mainstream, paradoxically also want to see their music more widely
recognized. One solution to this is the creation of a star system but such a system
is very expensive in promotional budgets and only large companies can afford that.*

[. . .]

Recording and promotion costs are low in dance music [. . .]. The 12-inch singles at
the centre of dance music are cheap to press because the rise of the CD has left spare
vinyl-pressing capacity. 'Micro-companies', very small record companies formed by
individuals or small groups of friends, who wish to put out one or two records under
their own label name, can break even with relative ease. Hundreds of such companies
have appeared and disappeared in Britain over the last ten years, beyond the reach of
trade-body industry statistics. But to sustain companies over a number of years is more
difficult. Inevitably, some records will achieve less success than others, and even though
the break-even point may be as low, in some cases, as 1,000 sales, many releases will
not achieve this level. These less successful records need to be cross-subsidized by
records which make more money. There are two main ways in which such 'serious
money' can be made. The first is to have a 'crossover' hit. A record might be picked up
by the dance press, by an influential club DJ, or by a big radio show. The small record
company might then enter into a distribution and marketing deal with a bigger company
to ensure that the demand is capitalized upon. However, such crossovers, and the organizational strategies needed to achieve them, raise a key issue within the production
politics of dance music culture (and indeed, one common to all contemporary western
popular music cultures widely constructed by their audiences as subversive). This is the
presence of contradictory attitudes towards *popularity* itself.[1] While some sections of
a 'subcultural' music believe that they should be heard in the mainstream, others argue
that the music's force comes from its resistance to co-optation. But many audiences and
producers believe both at the same time. There is evidence of such splits, between and
within dance music afficionadoes, in dance music, and I want to explore it here via a
look at the relationships between economic and cultural capital. Dance music culture,
as Sarah Thornton (1995) has shown in her study of dance audiences, values the underground over the mainstream, and can be dismissive of any perceived attempt to appeal
to the masses by being 'commercial'. Thornton draws on Bourdieu's work on consumption and taste in *Distinction* (Bourdieu 1984) but more significant for my analysis here is Bourdieu's work on fields of cultural production, and especially his analysis
of the complex interplay between economics and aesthetics.

> Producers and vendors of cultural goods who 'go commercial' condemn themselves, and
> not only from an ethical or aesthetic point of view, because they deprive themselves of the
> opportunities open to those who can *recognize* the specific demands of this universe and
> who, by concealing from themselves and others the interests at stake in their practice,
> obtain the means of deriving profits from disinterestedness.
>
> (Bourdieu 1993: 75)

The danger for an independent in 'crossing over' is, in the terms of dance music culture itself, the loss of 'credibility': gaining economic capital in the short-term by having a hit in the national pop singles chart (or even having exposure in the mainstream or rock press) can lead to a disastrous loss of cultural capital for an independent record company (or an artist), affecting long-term sales drastically.

The second main way of making the level of profits which would allow the independents to subsidize risks elsewhere involves a more complex relationship between economic and cultural capital. At the heart of dance music economics are *compilation albums*. These consist either of tracks originally issued by the company as 12-inch vinyl singles, or of a series of tracks licensed from other companies and grouped together under some unifying theme. Compiling and packaging compilation albums sees the record company moving away from its traditional function as an originator and developer of sounds and musical talent, and taking on a different set of 'editorial' functions (Miège 1987): monitoring trends, co-ordinating licensing deals, and developing 'concepts' which would make a compilation attractive to buyers. The 'concept' is vital, and represents the company's chief creative input. Such multi-sourced compilations are usually sold on the basis of genre. The title might be a standard term, such as 'Best of Techno', but in the very competitive dance compilation market, the ideal is to develop a new name for a sub-genre, or to invent a clever variant on an existing style. The job of developing the concept might be subcontracted to a company which specializes in 'underground' styles and scenes less known to the independent company developing the album. React Recordings, for example, one of the most successful dance music labels specializing in compilations, had substantial success in 1995 with an album called *Artcore*, which consisted of jungle tracks with a sophisticated flavour, a sub-style which some journalists had called 'ambient jungle'. The term 'artcore' is a pun on the sub-genre of techno referred to above, hardcore. It was developed for React by a company called Stage One (who also serve as distributors within the 'happy hard-core' sub-genre). What Stage One were selling was their knowledge of the particular nuances of a contemporary subcultural language.[2] Other methods of uniting the tracks on an album include linking it to the name of a well-known DJ (with the suggestion that the compilation represents a typical set by that DJ). This has the added advantage that, as with a conventional album by an artist, someone is available for publicity interviews and appearances. Some dance commentators have suggested that DJs blur traditional processes of production and consumption in music-making. In fact, as such cases show, they have become the basis of a new star system, in recording as well as in the clubs.

There are a number of commercial reasons why such collections of material are profitable. Firstly, the costs of recording the tracks have already been undertaken when the tracks were released as singles. Secondly, the cost of a 12-inch single is usually between £4 and £5 at the time of writing, but the consumer can get 10 or 12 tracks on a CD compilation album for about £13. Thirdly, while many of the retail chains do not stock vinyl singles, they are much more likely to take such compilation CDs for a less specialist audience. Most of these compilations consist of tracks licensed from other independents. One reason is that major labels command a much higher royalty rate than independents.

> Their [the majors'] terms are very draconian, strong contracts heavily weighted in their
> favour, and they're also very careful who they give their material to (James Foley, of React
> Recordings, interview with author).

Foley argues that the independents are more flexible and responsive in becoming
involved in such licensing deals.

> When we want to license a track from Deconstruction, we will apply to the central licens-
> ing person at BMG, who then goes through to Deconstruction, who may then have to go
> to the artist, depending on a contract. With an independent, that tends not to happen.
> You can send a fax in the morning, and get it back signed in the afternoon. Major labels
> also tend to work on the basis that they don't like doing small deals, they have high over-
> heads, they have people on £40–50,000 salaries plus company BMWs . . . these people are
> not paid that kind of money to make $500 deals.

The willingness of the independents to become involved in such licensing deals means
that the compilation market acts as the commercial lifeblood of the independent dance
sector, and sustains a network of labels which are separate from the ever-increasing
ties between large and small companies.

The irony is that the compilation album is a commodity which is looked down upon
in the dance world, because of the high prestige attached to obscurity within such sub-
cultures (Straw 1993). Such compilations have the least credibility amongst dance
crowds, whereas 'white labels' have in the past had the highest (Thornton 1994: 179).[3]
This is because compilation albums release carefully-accrued, subcultural knowledge
into the mass market. The most important way in which small dance music labels have
sustained themselves is felt by many 'underground' insiders to be a debased form –
and this reveals the contradictions about popularity faced by entrepreneurs within
dance music culture.

Yet increasingly there are signs of the acceptance of compilation albums as a form.
Some have come to be considered as key moments in the development of the genre,
such as the compilations based on the North Midlands club Renaissance, issued by
Birmingham's Network label. While a hardcore of highly committed fans may see
such compilations as a betrayal, there is now a huge and relatively stable audience
for dance music which would have little truck with such accusations, even though
the opposition of 'commercial' and 'underground' still works to validate certain styles
and sounds. The relationships between economic and cultural capital are by no means
static in subcultural production and consumption, and are becoming increasingly
complex in the dance music world, as the culture fragments and multiplies. Nevertheless, there are clearly contradictions at work here: the very form which sustains the
independent sector at the heart of dance music's institutional challenge is widely felt
to be a *problematic* one. And while it would be strange to expect consistency from
any subculture, such problems point to the difficulties which dance music production
has had in living up to the inflated claims of commentators as to its democratizing
force. For the very process by which the dance music sector seeks to establish itself as
a rival to the 'mainstream' corporations is widely felt, often by the very same entrepreneurs themselves, in certain moods, to erode the basis of dance music's subcultural
opposition.

Major/independent partnership and the 'credibility' problem

Dance independents have inherited the anti-corporate rhetoric of the rock counterculture and of punk. Small record labels generally claim to be more responsive to subcultural trends than major companies, and to offer their artists greater artistic autonomy. Yet dance music has served as the most prestigious indigenous form of subcultural music in Britain and Europe in the 1980s and 1990s during a time of unprecedented collaboration between majors and independents. So how 'independent' is the dance music sector? Many recent commentators have suggested that the independent/major division needs to be dissolved altogether (e.g. Negus 1992: 16–18). Other writers have pointed out the similarity between such views, and the emphasis in 'post-Fordist' writing on new, supposedly consensual relationships between small and large firms (Longhurst 1995: 36–9, Hesmondhalgh 1996). Countercultural discourse clearly overstated the opposition between the two ideal-types, majors and independents. Nevertheless, it is perhaps premature to dissolve the difference altogether. The most important task in an era of unprecedented collaboration between small and large firms in the cultural industries, is to specify the relationships carefully, and to analyse their implications. The varieties of 'partnership' between corporations and 'independents' include a range of licensing, distribution, ownership and financing deals. Many small companies are distributed through a multinational corporation, although there are many independent distribution companies, offering alternative routes. Some distribution deals involve financing, whereby the major company will put money up for development costs, such as touring and recording. The small company can also license its recordings to a particular company for release overseas, and going with a major means that such releases might be better co-ordinated. Increasingly, the majors have been keen to base their financing deals on buying a stake in a smaller company, with the option for either party to withdraw from the deal after a specified period (see Hesmondhalgh 1996: 474–7 for a more detailed discussion of these relationships). Here I want to examine major-independent interaction in dance music, and to analyse the ramifications of such 'post-Fordist' links for understanding the intervention of dance music in the industry as a whole.

It is clearly beneficial for the majors to be able to attract musicians and staff with the kind of high-'credibility' subcultural knowledge at large within dance music culture. During any period, a particular genre will tend to attract many of the most talented young musicians. Such genres are often imbued with an anti-corporate attitude, for a mix of romantic, bohemian and political reasons. From the point of view of the majors, the main problem is how to attract such talented musicians and staff to the corporation, but allow them to retain their subcultural reputation, or 'credibility'. During the disco boom of the late 1970s, the job of dance specialists working within major corporations was to decide which of the parent company's US-originated records would be suitable for British release (Harrigan 1980). In order to compete with the dance specialist labels formed out of shops in the late 1970s (such as Groove, Elite, Record Shack and Bluebird), the majors formed specialist dance divisions. EMI set up Sidewalk, Pye/PRT had Calibre, and Polydor had Steppin' Out, for example (Lazell

1987). Disco insiders (e.g. Waterman 1978) complained that the British divisions were
putting insufficient effort into boosting the style, and that separate divisions should be
set up to nurture dance product until it 'crossed over' into chart success. But as its
stock rose, dance music could no longer be treated as a fad by the majors. Increasingly, dance music was being made successfully not only by American acts, but by
British musicians too, and the UK divisions of major companies became aware of the
need to make A&R signings. From the early 1980s on, the majors began to enlist
leading club DJs to help them with this process. One notable early case was the Kent-
based DJ Pete Tong, who was brought in by PolyGram to revive the London imprint
(formerly part of Decca in the 1960s) as a dance label in 1983. It was Tong who co-
ordinated the *House Sound of Chicago* compilation which popularized house music
in the UK.

Since rave culture intensified the commitment to an underground ideology in dance
music (and therefore led to a much stronger questioning of the intervention of the
multinationals in dance music), the corporations have adopted various means of
making it look as though dance specialists are autonomous of their parent companies.
EMI brought in respected dance specialists from an independent label (XL, part of the
Beggars Banquet network) in order to set up a company which has separate offices,
and a separate name (Positiva), but which is effectively part of the major company.
PolyGram's holding company structure has been effective in creating the illusion that
acquired, large independent companies such as Island are fully separate from the
parent. In cases where these large subsidiaries have usually dealt in rock or other forms,
they have tended to set up their own dance/black music offshoots, such as 4th and
Broadway at Island, and Go!-Beat at Go! Discs. This is also the case at EMI's two
main acquired subsidiaries, Virgin (10 and Circa) and Chrysalis (Cooltempo).

The European branch of Sony has taken a distinctive approach, having set up a
Licensed Repertoire Division (LRD) to carry out a series of ownership, financing and
licensing deals with small labels, including Creation, Network, Nation and others.
This creates an extra level of separation between 'independent' and major: the Licensed
Repertoire Division can present itself as a rogue element within corporate culture.
As Neil Rushton of Network puts it, 'Jeremy Pearce [then head of the LRD] is a real
maverick down at Sony' (interview with author).[4] The German-owned multinational
BMG, meanwhile, signs funding and distribution deals with smaller companies on an
ad hoc basis. Some (such as Deconstruction, the UK's most successful dance music
label in the early 1990s) move into BMG's corporate headquarters, while others such
as Dedicated (an indie rock/pop label set up by Doug D'Arcy, formerly of Chrysalis)
stay in their own premises. PolyGram and EMI too have sometimes set up this
kind of short-term deal with specialist companies. Of the majors, only Warner Music
has taken the approach of setting up a specialist dance division under the name of
one of its fully-owned corporate companies (the East-West Dance Division), but it
also has the Perfecto label, run by leading DJ and mixer Paul Oakenfold within its
headquarters.

It is vital for the corporations and their connected 'independents' to present the relationship between them as one which allows relative autonomy for the small company.
Some popular music researchers have accepted this version of events. Keith Negus,
for example, has argued that under the new 'tight-loose' regimes operated by major
companies,

staff within major entertainment companies and the labels connected to them experience a large degree of autonomy in carrying out their daily work.

(Negus 1992: 19)

But it is no more true to say that the small labels work autonomously of their parent companies, than to say that musicians work autonomously of the firms they are signed to. There is 'creative freedom' if the creative decisions of the contracted parties prove to be compatible with the long-term aims of the parent company, and result in commercially successful products. Power particularly resides in the parent company's right to hire and fire senior staff. Like any artist, an independent record company, attracted to a major by a good relationship with a senior manager there, will often find this figure has moved on to another job, in another company, another country, another sector.[5] While contractual obligations can limit the intervention of parent companies, the very fact of take-over can change the culture of a record company by making it off-limits to those who would lose credibility by working for a corporation. Thus the ideology of independence, dismissed by recent commentators such as Negus (1992: 18) as the romanticization of 'entrepreneurial capitalism', can serve to limit the power of the major entertainment corporations. Of course, some sub-divisions of majors are given considerable autonomy to make prestigious signings, and develop careers for musicians. But this is very much a licensed autonomy, granted only to sub-divisions which are targeted towards niche audiences who will be attracted to 'quality' acts. This, it could be argued, is the case with PolyGram's acquired subsidiary, Island, or EMI/Virgin's Circa, both of which have prestigious acts who are granted a good deal of 'artistic control'.

The risk for the independent operator of losing credibility through their association with a major is compensated for by a number of factors, amongst them the greater financing available for studio budgets and artist advances, and by the distribution power that the majors can wield. Although, for the majors, control might be diminished, or refracted through, the label managers, such joint ventures mean not having to deal with 'difficult' artists, who may well be suspicious of the culture of corporate life. Such strategies should not be conceived of as examples of corporate 'flexibility' (Hesmondhalgh 1996), with its connotations of a relinquishing of control. Rather, they can be seen as a pragmatic response by multinational firms to the anti-corporatism inherited from rock and soul mythology which runs through various forms of 'alternative culture' in the late 1980s and early 1990s. They provide the majors with what are effectively specialist dance sub-divisions, but with a separate identity so that credibility can be maintained amongst subcultural audiences and producers. Besides the fact that such vanguard subcultural scenes are often the source of key musicians and record company staff for years to come, it is also important for the majors to appear munificently responsive to new trends. Not that such tactics have gone unnoticed. The term 'pseudo-independence' has been widely used to describe these new relationships (see True 1993). One member of staff at a company which has recently been the object of approaches from majors interested in the company's fashionable underground jungle/drum and bass sound, describes the larger companies' motivations succinctly: 'They'd be buying cred from us' (Caroline Jones, Moving Shadow, interview with the author). In spite of the knowing scepticism of some insiders, the process of pseudo-indification has limited the extent to which dance music has been able to offer channels of production and distribution which are genuinely 'alternative' to the entertainment corporations. The majors have worked to assimilate as rapidly as possible the symbolic resonances attached to independent record companies.

The tentative interventions of dance

There are other factors which are limiting the ability and inclination of dance independents to act as an 'alternative' to the music divisions of multinational entertainment corporations. One is the gradual undermining of the politics of anonymity which, I argued above, has sustained low promotional costs in the dance sector. The more established sections of the dance music industry are very keen to see the development of name artists, and the rise of a star system in the dance world which would run in parallel to that of the popular music industry as a whole. In part, this is simply because, as we have seen, the logic of capital accumulation is in favour of the star system: groups and artists act as brand names for music, and the fruits of promotional work can be transferred beyond one record to a series, as audiences carry certain expectations about sounds and messages from one record to the next. In addition, albums by established stars can be sold as 'back catalogue', a source of income which has become much more significant as the multi-media environment of the late twentieth century offers more and more opportunities for copyright owners. The atmospheric, wordless aesthetics of dance music make it particularly suitable for use on film and TV soundtracks, and the corporations' media cross-ownership can provide their associated independents with access to these opportunities for exploiting secondary rights. So the impulse towards a greater concern with authorship represents a recognition on the part of label owners, promoters and so on of their own economic interests.

But the drive to develop recognizable dance acts also comes from the desire on the part of dance audiences to see the music they like have an effect within the mainstream, to take its place alongside the indie, rap and pop acts on MTV, for example. We return here to the issue, introduced above, of discursive splits over the value of mass popularity and clashing definitions of success. The 1990s have seen the growth of an audience for dance music which rejects the values of obscurity and anonymity discussed earlier. Instead, a new crossover dance audience accepts the authorship politics previously associated with rock culture. The hugely successful dance act, The Prodigy, exemplify this: they tour, they make videos, they release singles in order to promote albums. They are a dance act, with the industrial features of a rock act. But there are many other such acts emerging. In addition, a number of musicians inspired by dance music culture and its relatives, hip-hop and dub reggae, have become 'serious' album artists, nominated for industry prizes, the object of critical attention in the 'quality' daily newspapers.

While the development of a star dance act will, of course, benefit a particular independent company greatly, the independent dance music sector as a whole can only be disadvantaged by such a move towards a rock-style star system. As the promotional costs associated with such a shift rise, majors and the pseudo-independents linked to them will dominate the market, because they are best able to absorb the great risks associated with increased promotional budgets. This risk is especially great in a genre which has such a fast turnover of styles and fashions. So a complicated logic emerges.

Dance fans call for recognition for the music they love, but recognition is only granted via the star system. And the star system itself destroys the conditions which allow an independent music sector to thrive, and which I outlined above: a committed audience which is prepared to seek out information about new sounds; and the consequent low promotional costs which such an audience helps to bring about.

[. . .]

Notes

1 See Born (1993: 236–8) for a valuable discussion of the subjectivities of cultural producers, with regard to popularity. I return to these issues later.
2 See Lash and Urry (1994: chapter 4) on the increasing tendency for cultural industries to market such knowledge.
3 Though this has changed in recent years – see Lanaway 1993. There have been many changes in dance music culture over the last ten years, and I can only present a snapshot of what I consider to be the dominant features. In particular, the rise of jungle/drum and bass has drastically altered its cultural politics. Nevertheless, given the lack of attention paid to dance music culture as a whole, it is vital to talk on a general level, before debates can move on to a more exact specification of changing dynamics.
4 Since this interview, conducted in December 1994, the relationship between Sony and Network has dissolved acrimoniously, Jeremy Pearce has left LRD for another label, and Network has gone out of business.
5 Some label-to-label contracts have a 'key man' provision, as do artist contracts. This makes the contract null and void if a certain executive leaves.

References

Born, G. 1993 'Against Negation, For a Politics of Cultural Production', in *Screen* 34(3): 223–42.
Bourdieu, P. 1984 *Distinction*, London: Routledge.
—— 1993 'The Production of Belief: Contribution to an Economy of Symbolic Goods', in *The Field of Cultural Production*, Cambridge: Polity.
Harrigan, B. 1980 'Do Ya *Still* Like Soul Music? Yeah Yeah! Yeah Yeah!', *Record Business* 12 May: 11.
Hesmondhalgh, D. 1996 'Flexibility, Post-Fordism and the Music Industries', *Media, Culture and Society* 15(3): 469–88.
Lanaway, M. 1993 'Setting Up Your Own Label', *DJ Supplement* 11–24 February: 2–3.
Lash, S. and Urry, J. 1994 *Economies of Signs and Spaces*, London: Sage.
Lazell, B. 1987 'Dancing to a New Label', *Music Week*, Disco/Dance Special 19 September: 6–9.
Longhurst, B. 1995 *Popular Music and Society*, Cambridge: Polity.
Miège, B. 1987 'The Logics at Work in the New Cultural Industries', *Media, Culture and Society* 9(3): 273–89.

Negus, K. 1992 *Producing Pop*, London: Edward Arnold.

Straw, W. 1993 'The Booth, the Floor and the Wall: Dance Music and the Fear of Falling', *Public* 8: 169–83.

Thornton, S. 1994 'Moral Panic, the Media and British Rave Culture', in A. Ross and T. Rose (eds) *Microphone Fiends*, New York: Routledge.

—— 1995 *Club Cultures*, Cambridge: Polity.

True, E. 1993 'Majors v. Independents', *Melody Maker* 17 April: 35–8.

Waterman, P. 1978 '1978: the Year of the Disco?', *Record Business*, 25 December: 17.

20 | The Transformation in the British Press

Brian McNair

> **Key words**
>
> Newspapers, trades unions, industrial relations, political economy, newspaper production, industrial conflict

This piece is about a radical change in newspaper production. Until the early 1980s in Britain, newspapers had been produced by methods largely unchanged for the previous fifty years. The papers were typeset and usually printed on the premises and were then distributed by rail. The trades unions were extremely powerful and able to command high wages for their members partly because of their ability to stop production at will. By the 1970s, costs in the industry were seriously affecting the profitability of newspapers and several of them were losing money.

In the early 1980s, newspaper proprietors, led by Rupert Murdoch, began to investigate new production technologies which lowered costs and broke the power of the unions. McNair describes the process by giving an account of the move by The Times *newspaper out of Fleet Street. Once one newspaper had adopted new production methods, others followed. It has been argued that the greatly decreased costs of newspaper production mean that a greater range of titles can be produced which more accurately reflect the political views of the population. Others respond that the start-up costs of newspapers are still so high that anybody contemplating it will have to have substantial financial backing which is unlikely to be available to newspapers espousing left-wing views.*

[. . .]

Fleet Street, it has been argued – the historic centre, physically and figuratively, of the British newspaper industry – ceased to exist on January 26, 1986, 'the day on which

Rupert Murdoch proved that it was possible to produce two mass circulation newspapers without a single member of his existing print force, without using the railways and with roughly one-fifth of the numbers that he had been employing before'.[1] The flight of News International's newspaper production from buildings in the City of London to a custom-built, high-technology 'fortress' at Wapping in London's Docklands was, on one level, the entirely rational and, as it turned out, highly profitable act of a ruthless and hard-headed publisher. But it also, in combination with the actions of another media entrepreneur, Eddie Shah, set in motion processes which, according to one viewpoint, revitalised a moribund, loss-making industry and created the conditions for its profitable expansion. An opposing view asserts that the 'Wapping revolution' has in fact done nothing to address the longstanding problems of the British press, particularly those of concentration of ownership, right-wing political bias, and deteriorating editorial standards.

[. . .]

The 'newspaper revolution', which began in 1983 and climaxed in the Wapping dispute of 1986 was, as in the case of the restructuring of broadcast journalism, closely related to the ascendancy of radical right-wing principles in the British government. Just as the Conservative Government in 1979 had begun a sustained attack on the public services, so too had it identified the trade unions as a major obstacle to the implementation of the Thatcherite economic project. Having come to power on an anti-union ticket, exploiting popular anger caused by the 'winter of discontent' which saw the unions locked in bitter industrial disputes with James Callaghan's Labour Government, Margaret Thatcher quickly moved to neuter the union's power by introducing a series of employment laws. The cumulative effect of legislation introduced in 1980 and 1982 was to make it extremely difficult, if not impossible, for unions to organise meaningful industrial action against determined employers. The most important measure in this respect was the outlawing of 'secondary action' – action taken by unions in support of other unions – and the tight restrictions placed on the numbers of those allowed to picket places of work. These measures made illegal the effective expression of solidarity between different groups of workers while, of course, employers could still cooperate to defeat industrial action.

This legislation established the conditions in which employers could, if they dared, engage their employees in disputes over hitherto sacrosanct staffing levels and working practices. Within the trade union movement as a whole, few groups enjoyed terms of employment which were more advantageous than the printworkers of Fleet Street. In the traditional manner of labour aristocracies, the print unions – primarily the National Graphical Association (NGA) and the Society of Graphical and Allied Trades (Sogat) – had secured relatively high wages for their skilled members, high levels of employment, tight closed shop agreements, complete control over entry to the printing trade (women were excluded from the lucrative typesetting positions, for example), and 'Spanish' working practices such as claiming payment for shifts not worked. Such terms were of course extremely expensive, and contributed substantially to the poor economic health of the industry identified by the McGregor Commission when it noted that in 1975 four of eight national dailies were in loss, and six of seven national Sundays. McGregor noted that labour was the main component of the newspaper industry's costs, since staffing levels were exceptionally high, as were wages (1977, p. 31).

The ability of the printers to extract such terms from their employers was a reflection of their pivotal position in the newspaper production process, combined with the short shelf-life of news as a commodity. The 'hot metal' process, employed in Fleet Street since the nineteenth century, was heavily dependent on printers' labour which could easily be withdrawn, with damaging loss of output. In the late 1970s the printers used this power to resist the introduction of new technologies, which could have made newspapers more profitable, but at the cost of fewer print jobs. These included the techniques of photocomposition, and direct input of editorial copy by journalists into pagesetting computers.

In 1978–9 the *Times* newspapers closed for almost a year, at a cost in lost production to their owners, Thomson, of £40 million. Between 1976 and 1985 industrial action by *Times* and *Sunday Times* printworkers led to the loss of six million copies. These losses played a key part, according to Harold Evans, in persuading the Thomson Group in 1981 to sell *The Times* and *Sunday Times* to Rupert Murdoch (Evans, 1983). In 1984, with Rupert Murdoch now in control, the papers lost 11.4 million copies to industrial action.

For some on the left, such militancy on the part of the unions represented the wholly legitimate defence of their members' interests in the face of big business. Others, however, by no means unsympathetic to the goals of the Labour movement in general, argued that 'Luddism' on the part of the print unions would be counter-productive to the long-term survival of the industry, and the jobs which it provided. As Tom Baistow noted before the Wapping dispute, 'in Fleet Street the corrupting cynicism that can come with unfettered power is not the monopoly of the press barons: the erosion of journalistic standards and ethics by self-interested proprietors and their house-trained editors . . . has been paralleled down the years by an equally self-interested distortion of the economics of production by a workforce that has played its part in creating the conditions for that decline' (1985, p. 77). After Wapping, Baistow again referred to a 'Fleet Street workforce that played its part in creating the conditions of decline which paved the way to Wapping . . . the whole tragic affair was much of the chapels' own making, the bitter fruits of greed and arrogance and a sectarian selfishness that betrayed the collective principles of honest trade unionism' (1989, p. 65). Former industrialist and Labour peer Lord Goodman writes that 'there can have been no period in industrial history where a greater demonstration of reckless irresponsibility has been displayed by a section of organised labour . . . the behaviour of the unions prior to the Murdoch revolution can only be described as suicidal.'[2]

The print unions, like others in the Labour movement, had grown used to the status and influence bestowed upon them by the post-war social democratic consensus, and failed to recognise the extent to which Thatcherism had undermined their position. With the Employment Acts of 1980 and 1982 the legal framework was in place – backed up by political will at the highest level – to allow proprietors to begin to erode the unions' power.

The struggle began, not in Fleet Street itself, but in Warrington in the north-east of England, where from 1980 local freesheet publisher Eddie Shah had been striving to loosen the grip of the NGA on the production of his *Stockport Messenger*. The NGA resisted Shah's attempts to introduce electronic publishing technologies and thereby reduce staffing levels, leading to a dispute which culminated in November 1983 in illegal mass picketing outside Shah's Warrington plant. Shah successfully took the NGA to court, and became the first employer to 'sequestrate' – i.e. have seized by the court – a union's assets. The dispute and its outcome were enthusiastically covered by Rupert Murdoch's *Sunday Times*, whose editor Andrew Neil correctly recognised it to be a watershed in industrial relations within the British press. Shah's success in destroying the NGA's power in Warrington thus became the catalyst for News International to attempt an analogous feat – though on a much bigger scale – in Fleet Street.

Since buying into the British newspaper industry in the 1960s Rupert Murdoch had been forced, like other Fleet Street proprietors, to accept the print unions' reluctance to countenance new technologies, and absorb the consequent losses. Shah, however, showed that with the help of Conservative employment legislation the unions could be taken on and defeated. In March 1984, a stoppage at the News International plant in London's Bouverie Street cost Murdoch the loss of 23.5 million copies of the *Sun*, and three million copies of the *News of the World*. This dispute, Sogat's General Secretary was later to concede, probably convinced Murdoch that radical measures had to be taken if his newspapers were to be made profitable in the long term. And achieving such profitability was crucial to the expansion of what was, by the mid-1980s, a global media empire spanning Europe, the United States, and Australia – an empire, moreover, in some financial difficulty.

By 1985, Murdoch's new printing plant at Wapping had been constructed. He had a plant in Glasgow intended for printing Scottish and northern editions of his titles, but this lay idle because the unions would not permit the facsimile transmission of copy from London. By February of that year, Murdoch had apparently lost patience with trying to win agreement from the printers to bring these new facilities into production, and announced to his senior managers that he was making a 'dash for freedom' (Melvern, 1988, p. 122).

For the rest of 1985 News International management planned and prepared for the transfer of all newspaper production from the plants at Gray's Inn Road and Bouverie Street to the new Docklands site, secretly installing an Atex computer, and putting in place a system which would enable the company to dispense with thousands of print-workers. Negotiations continued with the unions, but without success, each party blaming the other for their failure. In the unions' view, Murdoch had already decided on a course of action and had no intention of negotiating a compromise agreement. According to this view his final, unproductive meeting with the unions before the move to Wapping on January 23, 1986, was calculated to provoke a strike which, under Tory employment law, would mean that he could dismiss the printworkers without being legally required to offer expensive compensation. Murdoch, for his part, insisted that he and his managers had made every effort at conciliation over a long period of time, but that union obstinacy prevented a negotiated solution.

On January 24, 1986, following the meeting with Murdoch, the Fleet Street printers announced strike action to close down the News International titles. That evening, journalists and support staff at the two City plants were invited to turn up for work the next day at Wapping. Failure to do so would be treated as resignation. At about 8.00 p.m. on Saturday, January 25, with only one day's edition of the *Sun* lost, the production lines at Wapping began to run and, as Linda Melvern puts it in her account of the dispute, 'two hundred years of Fleet Street history were over' (ibid., p. 155).

News International's ensuing dispute with Sogat and the NGA was one of the most bitter and violent in Britain's industrial relations history, but with the full weight of the government and the state behind him, Murdoch was never in danger of losing. He used the services of Australian haulage company Thomas Nationwide Transport (TNT) to establish a union-proof distribution network for his titles, all of which would now be printed in Wapping and Glasgow. Attempts at a settlement were made, but never came to anything, and by the end of 1986 the printers had conceded defeat. Soon thereafter, other newspapers joined the exodus out of Fleet Street.

With the unions thus emasculated, Murdoch and the other proprietors could begin to transform their cost structures and increase profitability. While the treatment of the unions was presented by Murdoch as a regrettable necessity for which the workers themselves were to blame, the proponents of change held out the promise that lower labour costs and the introduction of new technologies would lead to a more diverse, pluralistic, and financially sound print media. In the words of Cento Veljanovski (in a book, it might be noted, published by News International itself), 'improved industrial relations [*sic*] combined with advances in print technology have significantly lowered barriers to entry, enabled the introduction of new enhanced graphics and colours, and stimulated the proliferation of magazine titles and other publications' (1990, p. 11). If concentration of ownership and political bias were indeed valid concerns, the argument went, the Wapping revolution would ease the problem by extending access to new groups, hitherto excluded because of prohibitive start-up and running costs.

[. . .]

Notes

1 Wintour, P., 'Life at the longest funeral', *Guardian*, June 26, 1987.
2 Goodman, A., 'Tradition and talent in an age of transition', *UK Press Gazette*, June 13, 1988.

References

Baistow, T. (1985) *Fourth-rate Estate: An Anatomy of Fleet Street*, London: Comedia.
Evans, H. (1983) *Good Times, Bad Times*, London: Weidenfeld & Nicolson.
McGregor, O.R. (1977) *Royal Commission on the Press*, Final Report, Cmnd. 6810, London: HMSO.
Melvern, L. (1988) *The End of the Street*, London: Methuen.
Veljanovski, C. (1990) *The Media in Britain Today*, London: News International.

Food and Class

21

Alan Warde

Key words

Middle classes, working class, social class, cultural capital, taste, distinction, consumption, food habits

Drawn from a general study of changing food habits in Britain, this extract explores class differences in food tastes. Using data from the Family Expenditure Surveys of 1968 and 1988, the patterns of spending on food items by individuals and households are subjected to statistical analyses to examine whether class differences have altered. The chapter analyses differences between middle- and working-class households, and differences within the middle classes. The argument relies on applying to the data a common statistical technique, discriminant analysis. In this instance, the procedure involves identifying distinctive patterns of consumption, measured as the proportion of per capita spending of households on dozens of different food items, and then examining how strongly those patterns were associated with household social class position. In each example in the chapter, attempts were made to predict into which of four class groupings a household might fit on the basis of its expenditure pattern. If there was no association with class position, households would be allocated at random, and therefore 25 per cent of cases would appear in each class group. The actual results reported in the chapter show that the association was not at all random, and from that the strength, character and persistence of class differences is estimated. The chapter interprets tastes in food as a specific example of the way in which social distinctions, emanating from the unequal distribution of 'cultural capital', are manifest in consumption behaviour.

[. . .]

1   Class differences over time

Sociology has always been more interested in the group differentiation arising from social norms and relationships than that arising simply from money income. The best-established sociological accounts of consumption began from the premise that consumption practices were themselves, in advanced capitalist societies, a clear reflection of class position. Class position always provides some basis for different patterns of consumption behaviour because it is ineluctably associated with the unequal distribution of income and wealth. But in the past it was always seen as more than that. While Veblen was impressed by a simple effect of opulence, Bourdieu maintained that consumption reflected complicated class distinctions and the transmission of cultural capital. To a significant extent, poor workers came to like those things that they could afford while the more affluent middle class developed extravagant tastes. Social hierarchies were expressed through display of commodities and engagement in activities which were attributed different degrees of honour. It has been widely accepted that in the United Kingdom class cultures existed as a result not only of financial power, but of learned tastes that were deeply ingrained in, and consistent with, other aspects of daily life. Accounts depicting patterns of class differentiation in modern British history are numerous, and have involved descriptions of coherent and mutually exclusive class cultures (e.g. Benson, 1994; Burnett, 1989; Cronin, 1984).

Few deny that some class differences still exist, and for analysts of nutrition and health this remains a basic datum (e.g. Townsend et al., 1988; Calnan, 1990). But the currently popular belief is that class differences have been declining, at a particularly fast rate since the 1970s. However, the evidence for this thesis, at least in the field of food, is not strong. Even though my evidence is unable to offer a highly refined indication of symbolic significance, the data exhibits considerable continuity over time. This is apparent to some extent in terms of the kinds of foodstuffs purchased and also, more significantly, in the persistence of social distance between classes.

Expenditure differences between socio-economic groups

The existence of class variation in food consumption is demonstrated by Table 1, which describes simply some differences in household expenditure on strategic items in 1988. The table distinguishes households headed by small industrial and commercial employers, the more affluent self-employed professionals, routine white-collar workers, the *petite bourgeoisie* and skilled manual workers.

Households headed by a self-employed professional (group 5) spent the largest amounts of money on food, the routine white-collar workers the least. This partly reflects household size. Examining the percentage of food expenditure on particular items shows strong similarities between skilled manual and *petit bourgeois* households and the strongest contrast between them and professionals. The professionals spent proportionately most on beef, fish, fresh vegetables and fresh fruit; and proportionately least on sausages, cooked meats, fish and chips, fresh milk, canned vegetables, potatoes and tea. Of all groups, the professional had the diet that would be most strongly endorsed by nutritionists, avoiding fresh milk, sugar, potato products,

| Table I | Expenditure (£s) per week and percentage of food expenditure, by socio-economic group of heads of household, for selected food items, 1988 |

	Socio-economic group*									
	3		5		9		15		12	
	£	%	£	%	£	%	£	%	£	%
Bread, rolls	2.11	3.7	1.58	2.6	1.59	4.0	1.89	4.0	2.05	4.5
Cereals	0.99	1.7	1.25	2.0	0.86	2.2	0.79	1.6	0.83	1.8
Beef & veal	3.62	6.3	4.02	6.6	1.58	4.0	2.16	4.5	2.35	5.2
Bacon & ham	0.79	1.4	0.78	1.3	0.62	1.6	0.84	1.8	0.84	1.8
Sausages	0.39	0.7	0.35	0.6	0.28	0.7	0.37	0.8	0.45	1.0
Cooked & canned meat	1.10	1.9	1.01	1.6	0.88	2.2	1.18	2.5	1.35	3.0
Poultry & game	2.27	4.0	2.37	3.9	1.50	3.8	1.65	3.4	1.57	3.5
Fish	1.39	2.4	1.50	2.5	0.93	2.4	1.00	2.1	0.90	2.0
Fish & chips	0.65	1.1	0.38	0.6	0.42	1.1	0.58	1.2	0.53	1.2
Milk – fresh	3.10	5.4	2.74	4.5	2.02	5.1	2.68	5.6	2.62	5.8
Fresh veg.	2.16	3.8	2.85	4.6	1.50	3.8	1.66	3.5	1.37	3.0
Canned veg.	0.51	0.9	0.39	0.6	0.44	1.1	0.56	1.2	0.60	1.3
Potato products	0.90	1.6	0.53	0.9	0.70	1.8	0.86	1.8	0.94	2.1
Potatoes	0.76	1.3	0.51	0.8	0.52	1.3	0.67	1.4	0.71	1.6
Fruit – fresh	1.95	3.4	2.56	4.2	1.44	3.6	1.40	2.9	1.29	2.9
Tea	0.60	1.0	0.32	0.5	0.38	1.0	0.53	1.1	0.47	1.0
Coffee	0.68	1.2	0.87	1.4	0.49	1.5	0.61	1.3	0.61	1.4
Sugar	0.32	0.6	0.26	0.4	0.20	0.5	0.30	0.6	0.32	0.7
Eating out	12.70	22.1	17.87	29.1	8.95	22.6	11.04	23.1	9.03	20.0
All food expenditure (£)		57.47		61.42		39.58		47.80		45.17
Total expenditure (£)		297.00		370.05		233.44		244.93		
Food as % all expenditure		19.4		16.6		17.7		19.5		
N households		152		81		395		349		733

* Socio-economic groups: 3. Small industrial and commercial employers; 5. Professionals, self-employed; 15. *Petite bourgeoisie*; 9. Routine white-collar workers; 12. Skilled manual workers.

sausages and the like. The professionals spent the highest proportion, and much the largest absolute amount, on eating out.

Perhaps the most interesting feature of this table is precisely the distinctiveness of the eating habits of independent professionals. This is probably the class with the highest cultural capital and with income sufficiently substantial to express its cultural knowledge and judgment. Eating out in stylish restaurants, experimenting with domestic cuisine and eating more healthily probably are features of the food experiences of this class. But they constitute a small proportion of the British population and their experience is probably not widely shared.

The household expenditure of the small employers and the routine white-collar workers were less distinctive. Socio-economic group 3, small employers, spends a much larger proportion of its food budget on eating at home and spends more absolutely on some items than any other of these groups – bread, fresh milk, potatoes and potato products, fish and chips, tea and sugar. These are some of the staples of recent British working-class diet and make their culinary habits appear generally conservative. This suggests that it is professionals rather than the bourgeoisie that are the cultural innovators, at least in the sphere of food. The foodways of the *petite bourgeoisie* (self-employed without employees) bear more similarities to those of the skilled working class than to the professional classes.

There are, then, differences in spending patterns between socio-economic groups, but it is not clear whether these are properly class differences. To be meaningfully described as class differences entails that socio-economic groups can be amalgamated into some kind of meaningful larger entities (classes) and that there is some homogeneity within, and differences between, classes in food purchasing patterns. The purpose of the discriminant analysis exercise was to see whether such patterns exist.

The working class and the middle class

There was a considerable degree of difference between working-class and middle-class patterns of food consumption and this persisted from 1968 through to 1988. Using a model that contained only households whose head was an employee currently in employment, and distinguishing professionals, managers, routine white-collar workers and blue-collar workers, it was possible to classify successfully 55 per cent of households in 1968 and 47 per cent in 1988. In 1968 (see Table 2b), there was a very clear division at the manual/white-collar boundary and the successful identification of the large number of manual workers (63 per cent) is the main reason for the power of the model. The inaccurate allocation of working-class households was 9 per cent to each of the professional and managerial groups and 18 per cent to the routine white-collar workers, indicating a considerable social distance from the two higher social class groupings.

The equivalent model for 1988 (see Table 2a) had a lower, though still fair, success rate of 47 per cent. A declining capacity to predict membership of white-collar groups, which constituted a much larger proportion of households, resulted in a poorer model overall. However, an even higher proportion of working-class households (65 per cent) were correctly identified in 1988. This strongly suggests the maintenance and consolidation of a distinctive working-class diet but with the weakening of patterns, based on occupational divisions, within the middle class.

The food items which distinguished working-class people were very similar in both years: expenditure was comparatively high on bread, sausages, cooked meats, beer, fish and chips, sugar, tea and canned vegetables, and relatively low on fresh vegetables, processed fruit, wine, meals out and fresh fruit. The only item that was typically middle class in 1968 that became common in all household budgets twenty years later was coffee. That differences are not just due to income is confirmed by a comparison of spending on different categories of food by professional and manual households with similar levels of income. Table 3 shows that there are statistically significant variations,

| Table 2 | Class differences in household food expenditure, per capita (households with head in employment), 1968 and 1988 (discriminant analysis) |

(a) Classification results: 1988

		Predicted group membership			
Actual group*	No. of cases	1	2	3	4
Group 1:	808	307	167	165	169
professional & auxiliary		38.0%	20.7%	20.4%	20.9%
Group 2:	771	191	213	176	191
managerial		24.8%	27.6%	22.8%	24.8%
Group 3:	530	121	77	166	166
routine white collar		22.8%	14.5%	31.3%	31.3%
Group 4:	1,713	173	119	308	1,113
working class		10.1%	6.9%	18.0%	65.0%

Percentage of 'grouped' cases correctly classified: 47.07.

* Classes: 1. Professional and auxiliary workers (socio-economic groups 5, 6, 7); 2. Managerial (socio-economic groups 2, 4); 3. Routine white collar (socio-economic groups 8, 9); 4. manual working class (socio-economic groups 10, 11, 12, 13, 14, 18).

(b) Classification results: 1968

		Predicted group membership			
Actual group*	No. of cases	1	2	3	4
Group 1:	628	229	120	168	111
professional & auxiliary		36.5%	19.1%	26.8%	17.7%
Group 2:	353	72	127	73	81
managerial		20.4%	36.0%	20.7%	22.9%
Group 3:	501	94	83	189	135
clerical		18.8%	16.6%	37.7%	26.9%
Group 4:	3,296	314	299	599	2,084.0
manual		9.5%	9.1%	18.2%	63.2%

Percentage of 'grouped' cases correctly classified: 55.02.

* Classes: 1. Professional and auxiliary (socio-economic groups 2, 4); 2. Managerial (socio-economic group 3); 3. Clerical (socio-economic group 5); 4. Manual (socio-economic groups 8, 9, 10).

irrespective of income and household composition, with manual working-class households spending more on take-away meals, beer, cooked meats and sugar, and less on wine, fish, fresh fruit, vegetables and cereal. The implications for present purposes are that the manual working class, though smaller now than in the 1960s, retains distinctive dietary practices, suggesting the persistence of class taste, class culture and a firm class boundary with higher classes.[1] However, at first glance, the expanding middle class appears to be becoming more heterogeneous, raising the question of whether it is possible to identify its component parts.

| Table 3 | Expenditure per capita (£s per week) on selected food items by households with a disposable income of £125–175 per capita, headed by manual and professional workers, 1988 |

	Manual	Professional
Food expenditure per capita	20.74	21.12
Meals out	2.99	3.44
Takeaway meals	0.75	0.41**
Beer drunk away from home	4.63	2.50**
Wine taken home	0.47	1.28**
Coffee	0.29	0.37
Cooked meats	0.6	0.38**
Poultry	0.76	0.84
Fish	0.43	0.62*
Milk products	0.26	0.37*
Fruit juice	0.18	0.37**
Bread	0.70	0.70
Cereal	0.29	0.47**
Fresh vegetables	0.61	0.93**
Fresh fruit	0.61	0.90**
Sugar	0.11	0.07*
Total household disposable income	305.94	375.44
Per capita disposable income	142.50	150.30
N	187	108

Significant differences (t-test): * >0.05, ** >0.01.
Source: calculated from Family Expenditure Survey for 1988.

2   The middle class and distinction

The greatest sense of refinement of taste might be expected among the middle and upper classes. Historically, the social prestige of these strata has been associated not just with their greater financial power, but with their claims to be cultured. Education, the cultivation of aesthetic sensibilities and the promotion of civilized modes of conduct have been elements of the self-image of the higher classes of western societies. This is the basis of Bourdieu's notion of cultural capital, the process whereby those with other bases of power have attempted to legitimize their own taste as good taste, and thereby further justify their own superiority by proclaiming themselves deserving and worthy of respect. From the 16th century the struggle over good taste was perceived as, essentially, between the aristocracy and the bourgeoisie, because extravagance, expensive tastes, and the jockeying for status were available most obviously to that minority section of the population whose incomes were far above subsistence level. However, such behaviour had spread to the urban working class by, at latest, the Victorian era, causing lower white-collar households to struggle to exhibit a respectable distance from manual worker households. Consumption practices have, then, long been symbolically significant among the middle class in Britain.

Divisions within the middle class, 1968–88

Mere difference from the working class does not entail the existence of a middle class which is internally coherent in its consumption practices. Indeed, the sharp growth of the white-collar workforce, the different levels of remuneration for those with authority compared to those doing routine jobs, and the difference between the conditions of men and women, might imply rather the opposite. Whether the upper echelons of the British middle class are becoming more homogeneous in their values and aspirations is subject to debate (see Butler & Savage, 1995). Goldthorpe (1982, 1995), for instance, anticipates that the 'service class' of professional and managerial workers, who fill higher positions in the bureaucratic organizations and who deploy similar strategies to transmit their privileges to their offspring, will become more coherent and more conservative over time. Savage et al. (1992), by contrast, argue that there are three quite distinct 'fractions' of the middle class. Based on their possession of different kinds of 'assets' – property, organizational position and cultural capital – owners, managers and professionals adopt different strategies for economic security and for transmitting their privileges to their children. Savage et al. show some differences in the consumption habits of these different groups: managers are generally fairly undistinguished; there is an ascetic, often public sector, professional group with preferences for health and exercise, particularly individual pursuits like hiking, climbing, skating and yoga; and there is what they ironically describe as a 'champagne and jogging' group of younger, private sector, professionals, who have considerable incomes and who, *par excellence*, exhibit the antinomy between health and indulgence. Although there is an imperfect correspondence between consumption and asset-holding, cultural practices are central to the creation and reproduction of these fractions.

Within the middle class food expenditure provides some evidence of the fragmentation of taste. In those calculations designed to ensure strict comparability on categories of food items, a number of patterns emerged. Taken as a whole, the employed middle class, compared with other large groupings, became less easy to identify. Distinctions between the intermediate and the service classes remained quite stable. This did not, however, have the effect of creating a more homogeneous and distinguished service class, as was anticipated by Goldthorpe (1982). Most apparent was the increasing heterogeneity of managerial workers. As Table 2a showed, by 1988 managerial workers seemed to have almost nothing in common, being distributed almost evenly across all four classifying groups. This was the case throughout the discriminant analysis. It is just possible that this might indicate that they systematically exhibit a tendency to individual diversity and that the absence of a coherent collective pattern to their behaviour disguises high-level capacities for personal and individualized discrimination in food taste. But it seems much more likely that they are, as Savage et al. (1992) claimed, 'inconspicuous consumers'. Lack of shared taste can be explained by the varied jobs that come under the label of manager, the great variety of career trajectories involved, and the absence of channels for developing shared cultural capital that arise from common educational experiences. Overall, even though the contemporary middle classed might be thought structurally most susceptible to informalization and individualization (see Warde, 1991), patterns of shared cultural behaviour based in occupational position have not disappeared. With the exception of those in managerial occupations, the evidence does not suggest a rapid dilution of class-based consumption patterns, nor their replacement by unregulated individual choice.

Core middle-class groups

This chapter, so far, has used the 'collapsed' set of food items which was designed to make the comparison between 1968 and 1988 more exact [. . .]. However, when using the full range of categories for itemizing food expenditure in 1988, stronger evidence of well-developed, significant internal differentiation within the middle class appeared. Apart from managers, other middle-class fractions maintained their distinctiveness. The model that most successfully discriminated between middle-class groups was one that distinguished between 'employers', 'professionals', 'routine white-collar workers' and 'the *petite bourgeoisie*'. This model hence excluded from consideration the more heterogeneous middle-class socio-economic groups, including managers and supervisory workers. It was especially powerful when applied only to single person households, where it suggested considerable nuanced variation. One problem with the analysis of households containing more than one person is that it is never entirely clear whose tastes are reflected in food purchasing. There is little scope for ambiguity with single person households, where people buy what they themselves consume. Unsurprisingly, models for single person households give higher scores using the technique of discriminant analysis. The extent to which models are improved is very striking.

Table 4a shows that 67 per cent of middle-class single person households were classified correctly in 1988. (With multiply occupied houses the success rate for an equivalent model was only 46 per cent.) In Table 4a the significance levels of the F statistic are all 0.001 or better, indicating that the small number of cases in each group is not responsible for the findings. This offers strong evidence for the existence of formed and differentiated tastes within the contemporary middle class. The patterns of food preferences are similar to those in multiply occupied households, but are expressed more strongly. In 1988, the *petite bourgeoisie* shared working-class tastes for buying beef, bacon, margarine and potatoes, and for drinking beer away from home. Routine white-collar workers avoided eating in restaurants and drinking in pubs, but otherwise shared preferences with professionals for cereals, poultry, fish and fruit juice. Table 4a shows that it is possible to identify the occupational class category of two middle-class individuals out of every three by reading their weekly grocery bills. Given difficulties of measurement, the still high levels of aggregation of the food items used, and especially the fact the indicator of class position used is no more sophisticated than current occupation, the strength of this model is remarkable. There were some very coherent tastes among middle-class occupational groups in 1988.

Though comparison was inexact because of altered class categories, the closest model for 1968 was less accurate, explaining only 61 per cent of the variance (see Table 4b). Because the social characteristics of employed people who live alone changed significantly between 1968 and 1988, it would be hazardous to interpret the comparison in detail. But it is possible that the distinctive tastes of identifiable, 'core' fractions of the middle class have increased rather than diminished since the 1960s. Such a trend is perceived in the USA, for instance by Levenstein (1993: 222), who argued

Table 4	Differences in household food expenditure, single-person households, in the middle class (households with head in employment), 1968 and 1988 (discriminant analysis)

(a) Classification results: 1988

		Predicted group membership			
Actual group*	No. of cases	1	2	3	4
Group 1:	8	5	1	1	1
employers		62.5%	12.5%	12.5%	12.5%
Group 2:	64	0	43	9	12
professionals		0.0%	67.2%	14.1%	18.8%
Group 3:	28	1	5	18	4
petit bourgeois		3.6%	17.9%	64.3%	14.3%
Group 4:	139	4	29	12	94
routine white collar		2.9%	20.9%	8.6%	67.6%

Percentage of 'grouped' cases correctly classified: 66.95.

* Classes: 1. Industrial and commercial employers (socio-economic groups 1 & 3); 2. Professionals and auxiliaries (socio-economic groups 5 & 6); 3. *Petit bourgeois* (socio-economic groups 15 & 17); 4. Supervisory and routine white collar (socio-economic groups 8 & 9).

(b) Classification results: 1968

		Predicted group membership			
Actual group*	No. of cases	1	2	3	4
Group 1:	27	17	1	3	6
self-employed white collar		63.0%	3.7%	11.1%	22.2%
Group 2:	57	4	36	3	14
professional		7.0%	63.2%	5.3%	24.6%
Group 3:	18	1	2	11	4
self-employed, manual		5.6%	11.1%	61.1%	22.2%
Group 4:	75	6	11	14	44
clerical		8.0%	14.7%	18.7%	58.7%

Percentage of 'grouped' cases correctly classified: 61.02.

* Classes: 1. Employer and self-employed, white collar (socio-economic group 1); 2. Professional and auxiliary (socio-economic groups 2, 4); 3. Self-employed, manual (socio-economic group 7); 4. Clerical employees (socio-economic group 5).

that 'food again became an important sign of distinction' during the 1960s and that 'the widening of the class gap seemed to accelerate in the aftermath of the 1973–5 oil shock, the spread of the Rust Belt, and other industrial woes'.

Significantly, it was the incorporation in the discriminant models of detailed evidence, previously muffled by the collapsed spending categories, about expenditure on eating out and on alcohol, that disclosed strong internal striations within the middle class. As Table 1 showed, professional workers spend large sums, and a comparatively large part of their food expenditure, on eating out. In the discriminant analysis it was particularly their tendency to use restaurants, rather than take-aways, cafés and so forth, that make them easy to identify. They were also distinguished by their propensity to spend disproportionately on wine. If, then, eating out and a taste for wine are contemporary symbols of extravagance, then the professionals are deploying them most extensively. It is also significant that, in 1988, those items which are consumed visibly and in public were best able to discriminate between fractions. Hence, the discriminant analyses give some genuine support to Savage et al.'s view of internal differentiation within the service class by suggesting the existence of some 'core' styles of food consumption sported by different occupational fractions.

Gender differences among the middle class

Analysis of the middle class can be further developed by taking account of gender differences in behaviour. Gender operates partly independently of occupation. Men and women in the same occupational classes do not always have the same tastes. Moreover, the items which differentiate between classes are not the same for men and women separately, as was shown by examining models for middle-class men and women separately. Interestingly, the differences among middle-class men, which were as strong as for women in 1968, had much abated by 1988. Intra-class distinction among women living alone and employed in non-manual occupations, however, persisted. Perhaps most remarkable was the coherence of taste among professional women workers, who in 1988 were correctly allocated in no less than 80 per cent of cases ([. . .] for further details of this model and its implications see Warde & Tomlinson, 1995). It may be that, overall, it is women who principally inherit and reproduce the class taste which underpins class-based patterns of consumption. Speculatively, the persistently strong class differences among women in middle-class occupations is perhaps a function of their comparatively recent incorporation into these sections of the labour market and their having had fewer opportunities for social mobility than men, for improvement in access to higher education has been slow. It would be consistent with the limited available evidence (McRae, 1990; Goldthorpe, 1987) to imagine that women currently in professional positions are particularly likely to have originated from professional households. By comparison, the much larger group of female routine white-collar workers, whose tastes, while still very distinct, are less homogeneous, originate from more diverse class backgrounds.

Overall, the models indicate that the food expenditure of middle-class socio-economic groups shows quite considerable, yet still patterned, variance. This was the case in both 1968 and 1988. The idea that class, as a function of occupation, inheritance and education, is no longer significant, or is in precipitate decline, should be rejected. Change since the 1960s is fairly negligible. Indeed, given the escalation of market discipline in the UK in many areas of life under successive Conservative governments, sociologists might predict *increasing* class inequalities.

[. . .]

Note

1   In general, this parallels Heath et al.'s (1985) conclusions on the basis of studies of voting: that the working class itself has not changed much since the 1960s, except that it has decreased in size.

References

Benson, J. (1994) *The Rise of Consumer Society in Britain, 1880–1980*. London: Longman.

Bourdieu, P. (1984) *Distinction: a social critique of the judgment of taste*. London: Routledge & Kegan Paul.

Burnett, J. (1989) *Plenty and Want: a social history of food in England from 1815 to the present day*. London: Routledge.

Butler, T. & Savage, M. (eds) (1995) *Social Change and the Middle Classes*. London: UCL Press.

Calnan, M. (1990) 'Food and health: a comparison of beliefs and practices in middle-class and working-class households', in S. Cunningham-Burley & N.P. McKeganey (eds) *Readings in Medical Sociology*. London: Tavistock, pp. 9–36.

Cronin, J. (1984) *Labour and Society in Britain, 1918–1974*. London: Batsford.

GBDE (Great Britain Department of Employment) (1976) *Family Expenditure Survey 1968* [computer file]. Colchester: ESRC Data Archive.

GBDE (Great Britain Department of Employment) (1990) *Family Expenditure Survey 1988* [computer file]. Colchester: ESRC Data Archive.

Goldthorpe, J. (1982) 'On the service class, its formation and future', in A. Giddens & G. MacKenzie (eds) *Classes and the Division of Labour*. Cambridge: Cambridge University Press, pp. 162–85.

—— (1987) *Social Mobility and Class Structure in Britain*. 2nd edition. Oxford: Clarendon Press.

—— (1995) 'The service class revisited', in T. Butler & M. Savage (eds) *Social Change and the Middle Classes*. London: UCL Press, pp. 313–29.

Heath, A., Jowell, R. & Curtice J. (1985) *How Britain Votes*. Oxford: Pergamon.

Levenstein, H. (1993) *Paradox of Plenty: a social history of eating in modern America*. Oxford: Oxford University Press.

McRae, S. (1990) 'Women and class analysis', in J. Clark, C. Modgil & S. Modgil (eds) *John H. Goldthorpe: consensus and controversy*. Brighton: Falmer, pp. 117–34.

Savage, M., Barlow, J., Dickens, P. & Fielding, T. (1992) *Property, Bureaucracy and Culture: middle-class formation in contemporary Britain*. London: Routledge.

Townsend, P., Phillimore, P. & Beattie, A. (1988) *Health and Deprivation; inequality and the North*. London: Croom Helm.

Veblen, T. (1925) *The Theory of the Leisure Class: an economic study of institutions*. London: Allen & Unwin. First published 1899.

Warde, A. (1991) 'Gentrification as consumption: issues of class and gender', *Environment and Planning D: society and space*, 9(2): 223–32.

—— & Tomlinson, M. (1995) 'Taste among the middle classes, 1968–88', in T. Butler & M. Savage (eds) *Social Change and the Middle Classes*. London: UCL Press, pp. 241–56.

22 | The Relationship between Television and Real Life in a London Punjabi Community

Marie Gillespie

Key words

Ethnicity, television, gender, community, family, soap opera, kinship

Gillespie carried out a study of television use amongst young people in a Punjabi community in Southall, London. She argues that there is a homology – a similarity in structure and behaviour – between the Southall community and the fictional community depicted in the soap opera Neighbours. *On the face of it, this is an improbable similarity because the two communities are culturally so very different. Gillespie points out, however, that gossip and rumour play a central role in both communities and, in Southall particularly, represent a powerful form of social control often deeply resented by the young people whom Gillespie studied. They identified, or in their own words, 'associated' with characters in* Neighbours.

Although Gillespie's book ranges widely, the extract printed here discusses the use of the soap opera in talking about community and kinship. As far as the first is concerned, Neighbours *offers models of the relationships which obtain between families and their neighbours. The soap opera community is contrasted by Gillespie's respondents with the actual Southall community in which there is a tension between neighbourliness and a critical need for privacy, a tension generated by particular conceptions of family honour. Similarly, the characters and plots of* Neighbours *allow the Southall teenagers to talk about the tension between western and Indian values in kinship relations – and the necessary negotiation between the two sets of values in which they are involved.*

[. . .]

'Community'

Young people compare and contrast neighbourly relations in Southall with those in *Neighbours*. They do so by juxtaposing notions of 'how things are' and 'how they ought to be'. The theme song suggests an idealised mode of conduct, and when young people sing it, they do so with ironic inflexions:

> Neighbours, everybody needs good neighbours
> With a little understanding you can make a perfect plan
> Neighbours are there for one another
> That's why good neighbours become good friends
>
> Neighbours, everybody needs good neighbours
> Just a friendly word each morning makes a better day
> Neighbours should be there for one another
> That's why good neighbours become good friends.

In fact this ideal is constantly threatened by feuds between neighbours in the soap narrative which, merely in order to continue, actually depends on an interminable succession of misunderstandings and conflicts between neighbours. Rajesh and Kulbir are 16-year-old boys. They both watch *Neighbours* regularly. They compare what they see as a rosy state of affairs on Ramsay Street with their own experiences of neighbours. The following extract is taken from a taped conversation they had about soaps:

Rajesh: It's like living in a dream, innit? Because everyone gets on so well together.
Kulbir: Everything happens in Ramsay Street.
Rajesh: It's an ideal way of living innit? Cos all the neighbours get on and that, they get on really well and they're always there when you need them – take my neighbours for a start, I don't know when man, we ain't spoken to them since I don't know when man, them on the right-hand side, we spoke to them when we moved in but we ain't spoken to them since, they're stuck up and that innit?
Kulbir: It's like where I live innit?
Rajesh: In Ramsay Street that's how you wanna be innit?
Kulbir: Yeah but look at it, it's a closed street, it's a dead-end street innit?
Rajesh: Yeah.
Kulbir: Well I got cousins living in a dead end street and they don't get on with their neighbours the way they show it.
Rajesh: Yeah but it's just fiction innit? Who gets on with their neighbours that way, tell me?
Kulbir: Nobody.
Rajesh: Exactly!

They make a straight comparison between neighbourly relations in the soap and in their own lives and the ideal nature of neighbourly relations in the soap is dismissed as 'fiction'. They do not mention the conflict and misunderstandings which propel the narrative forward, although they must be aware of them. This might be due to the high incidence of short-term conflicts which get (more or less) speedily resolved compared to the relatively few long-term conflicts which remain unresolved for months or years. By contrast, in real life and in Southall, neighbours are not seen to get on well.

They may be 'stuck up' or just as likely, they may be deliberately excluded from domestic and family intimacies. (This is certainly not unique to Southall with its concerns regarding *izzat*. According to *Social Trends 1990*, 82 per cent of the British population claim they would not have moved into their home if they had known who their neighbours were.)

The contrast between how things are and how one would like them to be is evident when Rajesh comments that 'Ramsay Street is how you want to be'. But neighbourly intimacy and support in times of trouble could militate against the primary value of family honour. This is also apparent in an exchange between Camila and Sukhi, both 16-year-old girls. However here there is a reversal of the previous situation. In this case it is not the neighbours who are 'stuck up' but the speaker's family who need to protect themselves from gossip and interference. The exchange took place in an informal group discussion in a Media Studies lesson, while watching the title sequence of *Neighbours*. Camila's dislike of her own neighbours becomes apparent, though, like many exchanges, this begins in earnest only to end in farce. As the title sequence, showing all the neighbours gathered around the Ramsay's swimming pool, appears on screen, the girls are singing along to the theme song: 'Neighbours should be there for one another . . .':

Camila: But oh my god! [laughing] Neighbours gossip! My neighbours are horrible, they're always looking out the window watching what we're doing, they're Mangels.
Sukhi: Yeah, real neighbours don't always get on so well, I mean what do neighbours share?
Camila: Swimming pools! . . . even their knickers! [raucous laughter]

Whilst this last comment is an obvious send-up, a way of gaining attention and esteem among friends whose main preoccupation is 'having a laugh', the point is clear: real neighbours are more likely to gossip about you than share things, and thus hardly behave in the ideal way portrayed in the title sequence. This raises questions about 'neighbourliness' in a town which is often constructed by outsiders as a 'community', and within which the term 'community' is also frequently invoked in a variety of senses.

Neighbours offers models of, and opportunities for talking about, the tensions which exist between families and their neighbours. The delicate balance between privacy and sociability is a tension that requires working through by neighbours and friends in any local area, but this tension takes on culturally distinctive hues in Southall, where there is a very high premium on privacy and where gossip poses a particular threat. These factors are somewhat at odds with the notions typically implied by invocations of 'community'. In Southall, this term is often used to express a range of meanings: from a sense of 'belonging' and loyalty to a place, to the sharing of similar backgrounds and values; from the sense of a shared social and geographic boundary, to a distinctiveness from other local areas. However, notions of 'community' are highly ambiguous and largely mythical, for internal cleavages of status, gender, generation and, most crucially in Southall, religion, are more significant markers in daily life than is any supposedly unified 'community'. Indeed, the term is typically invoked when inhabitants feel some threat from the outside, or when a spokesperson elects him or herself to speak on behalf of the 'community'. In such cases the sense of 'community' is strengthened and for a short while differences are forgotten.

Whilst individuals may consider themselves to be part of a 'community', and many young people in Southall do, in the sense that they have a strong sense of shared local identity, they also consider themselves members, respectively, of several different 'communities' which coexist within Southall, 'communities' of religion and cultural heritage. And it is the networks of actual social relations, maintained both within and outside the local area, which count when it comes to questions of the control of information about family life, questions of *izzat*. The high density of kin living locally and the closely knit nature of the associated social networks form the basis of the communications networks that exist.

Social ties may be strong, as well as highly competitive, between families whose members attend the same place of worship or the same place of work; families of school friends; and families formerly from the same village in India, who are treated 'like kin', ostensibly, although relations are not subject to the same binding obligations of unrestricted reciprocity which apply to 'true kin':

Gurinder: We stay close to families who have come from the same village in India, if you can imagine these families lived together for hundreds and hundreds of years and often have the same ancestors going way back, they used to do the same jobs, they were the same caste, they shared their experiences over time and that makes you very close and that closeness usually continues in England, they are more like real neighbours but they don't live next door.

In the parental culture the ideals of community and neighbourly relations are crystallised in the word *baradari* (or 'brotherhood') and founded upon village life in India, where historical, regional, religious and caste similarities forge a very deep sense of solidarity and belonging. These relations have become idealised in 'exile', partly through the influence of the nostalgia propagated by Hindi films in which [. . .] traditional village life is represented as 'morally pure' in contrast to the corruption of modern city life. Such ideals are hardly to be realised in the urban context of Southall. Ballard, discussing second-generation South Asian-British youth, argues that:

> Although everyone accepts that family loyalties should be sustained, the value of participation in more far-flung social networks of extra-familial kinship is looked upon with increasing scepticism, especially since they tend to generate a suffocating traffic of gossip and scandal.
>
> (1982: 196)

There is nevertheless an attempt to maintain village ties where they exist, and close friends are certainly treated in many contexts as if they were kin.

In some ways the social networks of certain families in Southall bear some residual features of those in Punjab villages, where component families within the local group are so closely connected and related that they are clearly marked off from external relations. In such networks, privacy is at a premium: it is not something that has been valued or even experienced traditionally, but it has become an imperative as a result of the dislocations of migration and settlement. If one adds to this the general lack of individual privacy which is a feature of extended families, one can begin to appreciate how families encapsulated within activities known to so many cannot escape the informal sanctions of gossip and public opinion. In this sense, the 'community' of

Ramsay Street appears, to Southall youth, to represent an alternative ideal, even though this perception might not seem to do justice to the less than idyllic neighbourly relations which actually obtain in the narrative.

Kinship

Whilst young people's own families and those in their social networks provide their primary frame of reference about family life, soap families extend this frame of reference and offer alternative sets of families which young people use to compare and contrast, judge and evaluate and, in some cases, attempt to critique and transform aspects of their own family life. As we have seen, migration and settlement in Britain has meant that Punjabi families are undergoing significant changes in their economic, social and moral environments. Punjabi family life is recognised by young people to be based upon sets of norms and values, duties and responsibilities, roles and expectations, rules and regulations which differ in certain fundamental respects from those which apply in 'white' families. In some families these are being revised, whilst in others there is an attempt to maintain more or less strict adherence to traditional family norms and values. Thus parents differ markedly in the degree of conformity to traditional values they expect of, and attempt to impose upon, their children; young people too vary considerably in the degree and nature of the rebelliousness or conformity they express verbally and or in their behaviour.

Despite this variety, and change and adaptation, certain fundamental features of kinship organisation prevail, albeit in modified form, in conjunction with certain sets of norms and values. The very high density of kin living in Southall is a distinctive feature of local life. In the youth survey [. . .] 34 per cent of respondents reported more than ten cousins living in or near Southall; 36 per cent of Sikh respondents reported grandparents living in or near Southall [. . .]; over one third of households have between six and eight people eating together. These figures point to a prevalence of larger households and suggest that one in three is a three-generational household. The very high density of kin ensures that the principles of binding reciprocity, respect and co-operation (rather than self-interest) prevail, even though many families are now breaking into smaller household units.

The relative complexity of kinship ties (compared with white families) is evident in the extensive kinship terminology which young people have at their disposal and which they use to delineate, with precision, an individual's position in the family. Thus four kinds of uncle and five kinds of aunt are distinguished by terms which express, for example, the distinction between the father's elder and younger brothers. This has consequences for their perceptions of kinship relations in *Neighbours*, as competence and speed in defining kinship relations with precision assists them in understanding soap families. One group of 16-year-old girls constructed a kinship and household diagram for *Neighbours* with great ease, displaying an impressive depth of knowledge about the kinship ties. Their informal talk while they were working on this diagram is one of the main sources of the comments reported below.

In Punjabi families individual needs or desires are subordinated to the demands of *izzat*. Many young people find themselves in a position where, at home, parents claim the superiority of Punjabi cultural traditions and family values over English or 'western' ways. Experiences at school or when viewing *Neighbours*, they claim, encourage individual self-determination and personal freedom. Whilst most parents and children alike are sceptical of the wholesale adoption of western ways, it is clear that established norms and values, duties and responsibilities, roles and expectations, rules and regulations are up for negotiation as far as young people are concerned. 'Soap talk' is one of the means whereby such issues are negotiated.

Soap talk further allows young people and their parents to discuss changes in gender roles within the family. Approximately 70 per cent of mothers are now in paid employment outside the home, predominantly in manual work in local industries [. . .]. Only 28 per cent define themselves as 'housewives'. In theory, at least, this has allowed greater financial independence for women and in some families served to challenge traditional domestic roles. However, it is clear from both quantitative and qualitative data that conventional expectations prevail and that women and girls are burdened with an unequal share of domestic duties. Furthermore, women are over-represented in low-paid, part-time labour, often without the benefits of a contract. Those mothers who are in full-time employment often do gruelling amounts of overtime to supplement the household income and are, in some families, the main breadwinners.

All these factors, moral, economic and social, exert pressures on families. There are marked variations in the ways in which different families respond to and deal with challenges to traditional family norms and values. Yet at age sixteen the family and wider kin are the primary source of love and affection, as well as of control and constraint in one's life. Young people have to develop verbal bargaining skills if they are to assert their individual needs on the family stage and if they are to ensure some involvement in decision-making about their lives with regard to their future, especially in the spheres of education, work and marriage.

Many girls consider that the code of *izzat* restricts young people from asserting and expressing themselves openly, as this is held to militate against the primary virtues of respect and obedience to one's elders:

Lukbir: It drowns your own sense of identity, you can't do what you want, you always have to think of your family honour [. . .] you are supposed to be modest, simple, reserved [. . .] you're not supposed to wear make-up and you should cover your legs and above all you shouldn't talk back to older people.

In *Neighbours*, young people, especially girls, are seen to exercise considerably more freedom and control over their lives than do youngsters in Southall. Therefore one of the most attractive features of *Neighbours* to young people is watching how young people assert themselves, especially verbally, to their parents and elders. The favourite characters like Bronwyn and Henry, for example, are admired because they are good 'backchatters', or because they know how to stand up for themselves and what they believe in. Watching how young people negotiate their family relationships is a key attraction of *Neighbours*.

Gender roles within the family are of major concern to many girls and although families vary considerably in the restrictions they impose on girls, it is a widely held view that double standards exist:

Amrit: You can see that families in *Neighbours* are more flexible, they do things together as a family, they don't expect that girls should stay at home and do housework and cooking, boys and girls are allowed to mix much more freely [. . .]. Indian families do go out together to eat and that but most of us can only get out with the family, they can't go out with their mates like the boys do [. . .]. Boys live on the outside and girls on the inside.

In making judgements about soap families in their everyday interactions at home and at school young people are giving indirect expressions to norms associated with family life. For example, the Robinson family is seen as ideal in the sense that they are loyal and supportive yet offer their younger members independence, space and privacy:

Paramjit: They stick by each other as a family and always support each other through bad moments [. . .]. They trust each other and if they have a problem they don't try to avoid it, they sit down and talk about it logically and reasonably and try to sort it out together, they don't end up rowing [. . .]. There's a great family bond between them all.

Paramjit's view of the Robinson family is typical. Above all, effective communication in the family is valued and seen to ensure the bonds of love and loyalty. The soap's matriarch and grandmother character, Helen Robinson, is pivotal to the perceived success of this family's relationships. She is seen to have a unique ability to listen to and understand people, including teenagers, and their problems. She is everyone's ideal 'agony aunt'. She is caring and understanding and she offers realistic, sound advice. She is able to help young and old people sort out their problems.

Trust between parents and children is an area of key concern to many girls and poses a serious dilemma. Even a slight aberration in behaviour may, in some families, incur a breakdown of trust on the part of parents. Open and honest communication may also lead to a breakdown of trust or to parents becoming suspicious that their daughter or son is getting 'spoilt' (in the sense of 'tainted') and this may lead to even tighter control and regulation of their daughter's movements and communication with friends. But some girls claim that they, too, have reasons to lack trust in their parents. In some cases, the discovery of a romantic liaison may lead parents to quickly arrange a marriage without involving their daughter in the decision-making. The issue of open, truthful communication and trust between parents and children recurs frequently in talk about soaps and real life.

The Ramsay/Bishop household is admired for being a 'fun' family, mainly because of Henry, who is the key young comic character in the soap. He is seen to be given support and independence:

Kamaljit: They have a nice open atmosphere in their house, they're funny, I like the way Henry picks on Harold [his stepfather] and the way Madge and Harold argue, they always stand by each other but they let their kids stand up on their own two feet, like when Henry has problems they let him discover for himself how hard it is to do certain things like get a good job [. . .]. I like how they all get on.

The Mangels are seen as less successful:

Amar: It's a small family so it's not interesting, Joe is crafty and not that respectable, they're a rough-going family, they use a lot more slang, they don't have people round for dinner parties and that like the Robinsons, they treat each other as strangers, not as a family, they're not organised and they're hopeless with housework, they also interfere with others when no one wants them to get involved.

But Hilary's household is seen as the least successful of all, and she is also despised as the major gossip character:

Farzana: I hate Hilary because she's always bossing Matt and Sharon, she never lets them do what they want, she rules their lives and expects them to take orders [. . .] she makes everyone lives hell [. . .] she's a really bitchy gossip [. . .] she spoils teenagers' fun [. . .]. Her way of being a mother is no good! She never listens and you can't tell her anything, she's not to be trusted.

It is clear from these comments that young people are using these families to articulate their own emergent norms and values and are indirectly commenting upon their own families. But while they use the families in *Neighbours* to judge their own, the reverse case is also true. Given the limited access to 'white' families, the viewing of soaps enables young people some, albeit fictional, insight into them. It is frequently commented upon that the Robinson household is an extended family consisting of three generations. It is also seen to share some similarities with Southall families, in that they have kinship links with two other households in the same street:

Baljit: It's an extended family, they've got Helen living with them and then there's Paul who lives in the same road and Hilary, who's Jim's cousin's sister in the same road [. . .] it's a bit like our family.

However, this is as far as the perceived similarity goes.

Their sophisticated understanding of kinship ties draws their attention to what most regard as the highly unconventional constitution of many Ramsay Street households, which are 'reconstituted' families as a result either of death, divorce or remarriage.

Baljit: We have bigger families than they do and our households aren't shared like theirs, ours are strictly for family [. . .], there isn't as much divorce and single-parent families [. . .], there's no swapping around of households like Bronwyn does, she's lived in nearly every household in the street [. . .], there's no lodgers or people being adopted who come to live with you.

Sharing one's house with people other than kin by blood or by marriage is considered most unusual. Taking in lodgers, especially those who have lived in the same street, would be considered highly risky, especially as regards safeguarding family honour and protecting the family from revelations about their private internal affairs.

Neighbours is seen to be 'white' rather than Australian. As Diljit points out, 'All families in *Neighbours* are white, I don't really see them as Australian'. Young people readily admit that they know little or nothing about white families:

Anopama: We don't know nothing about white families [. . .] except the Robinsons [bursting into laughter] [. . .] they're not even real, they're only a soap family [. . .] we probably have very stereotyped ideas, it makes you realise what sheltered lives we lead.

Indeed many young people claim they get most of their ideas of 'white' family life from soaps like *Neighbours*:

Paramjit: We get more ideas about white families from TV than we do from our own experience, so it's helpful to see how they live and relate to one another because you get to know the characters in their family situation.

Viewing the private life of 'white' families is seen to serve a useful function:

Mohinderpal: If we didn't see white families on TV, like in *Neighbours*, we'd probably be even more suspicious of white people even more cos we don't know what they're really like and we don't chat to them [. . .] and we'd think they were all racist to us but when you see families like the Robinsons you think, oh my God! they're just like us, they love one another and they look after their children and they're not as bad as, er . . . um . . . some Indian people think they are.

But *Neighbours* also encourages slightly overinflated ideas about the 'freedom' that young 'whites' have:

Rashpal: They've got more freedom than us, they can go out and stay out until a reasonable time, families seem to care less about what others think of them [. . .] they don't have arranged marriages and it's like dating is the norm [. . .] it seems so strange to us that a girl could bring home her boyfriend and sit round the table and eat with her parents [. . .] and that her parents would approve!

Of course, these issues – of 'dating', or romance and courtship rituals, and marriage – are a prime area of young people's concern, consistently highlighted by their soap talk.

[. . .]

Reference

Ballard, R., 1982, 'South Asian Families in Britain', in R. Rappoport, ed., *Families in Britain*, London: Routledge & Kegan Paul, pp. 179–205.

23 | Shopping and the Work of Femininity

Celia Lury

Key words

Consumption, shopping, domestic divisions of labour, gender divisions, femininity, masquerade

---

The late twentieth century witnessed a rapid increase in the variety of goods and services offered through market exchange. More and more items came to be purchased. Shopping became an ever more important skill as an increasing proportion of the activities associated with material subsistence and cultural reproduction were delivered through commercial retail outlets. The increased salience of consumption in modern Britain is reflected in the frequent use of concepts like consumer culture and consumer society.

Celia Lury, in the process of examining the nature of consumer culture, explores women's role in consumption. She identifies the way that women both do most of the work of shopping and then are often domestically responsible for doing further work on the purchased commodities in order to make them useful for other members of the household. In the process, women effectively are encouraged to create some form of feminine self-identity for themselves. Whether this is to be considered an externally imposed imposition, or whether it might be welcomed precisely because women appreciate that the formation of their identity through consumption is subject to their own control – as in, for example, a masquerade – is debated. The extract demonstrates how mundane daily activities are implicated in sustaining gender differences.

[...]

Gender and the family economy

[. . .]

A number of writers have argued that it is important to acknowledge that housework typically includes not only practical, but also emotional, sexual, reproductive and symbolic work done by women for men within family relationships (Delphy and Leonard 1992). It is not only work done on the house that is important here – the cleaning of the house, the stylization and ordering of its furnishings, and the preparation and presentation of food – but also caring work in relationships such as mothering, and work done by women on themselves, what might be called the work of femininity (Winship 1987), the work that women do on their appearance, manner and personal identity.

Housework defined in this way does not fit the common preconception of work as paid employment, but it can be seen as such once it is situated in relation to the notion of a family economy (Oakley 1976; Delphy 1984). This economy exists alongside and is interlinked with the industrial or capitalist economy. The family economy is structured by conditions of inequality, in which women tend to be in a position of economic dependence upon men. This dependence is socially structured by relations of power within the household, the state and the labour market, and has meant that the amount of time a full-time housewife with children spends on housework has stayed relatively constant during the course of the twentieth century: it is still 60–70 hours a week (Anderson, Bechhofer and Gershuny 1994). The amount of time that most men spend on housework has gone up slightly over this period of time; but it is still 5–10 hours a week, even when the woman in the shared household is not only doing the housework, but also doing paid work of some kind. The man may offer to *help*, but housework is still typically assumed to be the woman's responsibility.

Delphy and Leonard (1992) argue that, within the family, there are three types of economic activity: production, consumption and the accumulation and circulation of property. They write that the inequalities generated by these activities will be missed if the family is taken as a natural unit, in which all members equally participate, and argue that

> the fact that the family can be treated as a unit of production or consumption or of property-holding for certain purposes does not mean that the family (in the sense of all its members) produce and consume and hold property together as a block, nor that all have the same economic status and identical interests.
>
> (Delphy and Leonard 1992: 107)

As they go on to note, however, while it is often recognized that much production and property-holding is carried out by members as separate individuals, this fact is far less commonly noted as regards consumption. It is usually far from clear when authors speak of the family household as a 'unit of consumption' whether they are referring to the total consumption of all the members wherever it takes place, or just to that part of consumption which takes place within the home. Delphy and Leonard argue that even if 'family production' and 'family consumption' are used to refer to what is done or used by family members actually within the home, these processes are not the same for all the members of the family.

This last point, the existence of differences in the extent and quality of consumption of family members, is explained by contrasting the industrial economy and the family economy. Delphy and Leonard write:

> In the labour market, workers are paid a wage by their employer, but in the family-based household, members are maintained by its head. This means dependents have less choice as to what they get than if they were given money. What is provided for them is what is favoured (or at least agreed to) by the head. In addition, since much of what family members produce is consumed within the family, this in itself prevents goods and services consumed in the family being the same for all members. For example, when the husband and children consume meals served by the wife, she provides the services, so she cannot consume them in the same way as they do: as work done by someone else. She cannot both wait and be waited on. Hence, there are real problems in treating the family as a 'unit of consumption' in any analysis.
>
> (1992: 108)

The point being made here is that the separate statuses of men and women are marked out by their different places in what only *appears* to be the same consumption space. While he is watching television, she is getting dinner. Even at the dinner-table, the woman is likely to be the one serving the food. She is required to be a facilitator of other people's consumption rather than (or as well as) an active participant.

In short, while it is often noted that it is women who make up the majority of consumers, in the sense that it is women who actually purchase goods on a routine basis, it is not so often recognized that they will generally go on to work on the goods bought. Women are typically the *producers* of goods and services of which men as husbands are the *consumers* or final users. Indeed, given the relations of inequality within which much shopping and other housework is done, some feminists argue that it is inappropriate and misleading to consider shopping as an example of consumption, and suggest that it is more accurate to see it as part of family production – the work of selecting, transporting and transforming the raw materials or resources of housework. But it is possible to suggest that both interpretations are correct. Shopping may be seen as an instance of consumption in relation to the cycle of commodity production (that is, production of goods for exchange on the market), but as a moment of production in relation to household or domestic production (for exchange in the family). What this dual location of shopping illustrates is the importance of looking at *cycles* or circuits of production and consumption within society as a whole. It also shows that it is necessary to think of consumption not simply in relation to the market and commodification but also in relation to other economic systems, notably the family.

The domestic revolution and consumption

[...]

It has sometimes been argued that the ever-increasing availability of finished goods for sale as commodities will lead to a decline in the amount of housework that is done by women; that is, as industrial production comes to provide more and more of the goods that used to be made in the home, women will be released from housework and increasingly enter the paid workforce, resulting in the end of the sexual division of labour both in the household and in paid work (see, for example, Braverman 1974). However, this kind of argument tends to ignore the continuing hold of power relations within the family. While more and more women have entered the labour market during the twentieth century, the broad patterns of the domestic division of labour have not changed very much. While there has been some change in the kinds of tasks that are done as part of housework – more and more tasks are associated with the transformation of commodities (shopping itself has become an increasingly important aspect of housework and now takes up one full day a week compared with two hours in the 1920s, as both more goods and a wider range of goods become available through the market) – it is still typically done by women for men on an individualized basis.

This is, in part, a consequence of the ways in which the process of suburbanization, while facilitating the entry of the market into the household, helped preserve hierarchical power relations between men and women. The unequal division of labour was fixed through the very architecture of the home and the geographical separation of home and work:

> Suburbia's socio-spatial patterns typically anchored in *place* the *market* arrangements of the postwar period. . . . Buying a house, at least one car, and domestic equipment integrated households into a national landscape of mass production and consumption.
>
> (Zukin 1991: 140)

Similarly, in relation to the introduction of so-called labour-saving devices, Game and Pringle write:

> New technology in the home has contradictory effects. While it has removed a lot of the heavy work it has done little to reduce work frequencies and in some cases has created new forms of drudgery. For instance, no aspect of housework has been lightened so much as laundry, yet time spent on it has actually increased. Women can now be expected to wash clothes daily instead of weekly.
>
> (1984: 125)

Gershuny (1978; 1983) has also argued that the introduction of new technologies has meant a shift towards what he calls the domestic provision of services, a shift which rearranges but does not fundamentally disturb gender relations within the home. In other words, while the increase in consumer goods has contributed to a change in the content of housework, it has not removed gender inequality within the family.

Nevertheless, simultaneous with the increasing dependence of housewives on goods provided by the market, there have been changes in the organization of housework. These also relate to what is sometimes described as its *emotionalization* and *aestheticization*. So, for example, while it might have been expected that as housework was 'modernized' through the introduction of new domestic technologies, it would have become less emotionally involving, the reverse appears to be true:

> Laundering became not just laundering but an expression of love; cooking and cleaning were regarded as 'homemaking', an outlet for artistic inclinations and a way of encouraging family loyalty; changing nappies was not just a shitty job but a time to build the

baby's sense of security and love for the mother; scrubbing the bathroom was not just cleaning but an exercise of maternal instincts, keeping the family safe from disease.
(Game and Pringle 1984: 127)

By the mid-twentieth century, housework had become not just a job, but an expression of love and warmth performed by each woman for her own family.

Significantly for the development of consumer culture, there has also been a process by which housework has been *aestheticized* in the sense that the standards by which housework is judged have come to include not only 'scientific' or 'technical' standards of hygiene and efficiency, but also those of style, harmony and 'atmosphere' (Forty 1986; Partington 1991). This aestheticization has been closely tied in with prevailing notions of masculinity and femininity. According to Forty, until the mid-nineteenth century, the choice of domestic furnishings seems to have been primarily a male activity. However, by the 1860s, the choice of domestic decoration and furnishing became an accepted and even expected activity for (first middle-class and then working-class) women. The principles women were encouraged to adopt by the many handbooks that began to appear were, first, that the home should be as unlike the husband's place of work as possible, and second, that the interior should express the personality of its occupants, especially that of the lady of the house. So close had the identification between woman and the house become in the late nineteenth century that a woman who failed to express her personality in this way was in danger of being thought lacking in femininity. In an essay published in 1869, for example, Frances Power Cobbe asserted:

A woman whose home does not bear this relation of nest to bird, calyx to flower, shell to mollusk, is in one or another imperfect condition. She is either not really mistress of her home; or being so, she is herself deficient in the womanly power of thoroughly imposing her personality upon her belongings.
(Quoted in Forty 1986: 106)

More specifically, the activity of buying has itself come to be increasingly defined as worthy and significant, creating a new role for women as administrators of the home, directing consumption by their selection of the goods and services. In this way, women have been drawn into the development of consumer culture. So, for example, department stores – 'palaces of consumption' – were constructed as welcoming and inviting places for women in particular. At the Bon Marché in Paris, for instance, diaries, calendars, bulletins and even transport to the store were provided to encourage women to shop and feel at ease once they got there (Bowlby 1985). However, while shopping was seen as peculiarly feminine, it was not positively valued, but, rather, was constructed as irrational, fanciful and frivolous. Women shoppers were encouraged to think of themselves as being prone to become out of control, having an insatiable desire to buy. Managers of department stores helped create this perception through the way shoppers were treated once in the store. So, for instance, floor walkers, men who escorted women around the store helping and controlling their purchases, were common until the 1920s (Benson 1986). There were also medical studies which purported to show sexual dysfunction as the cause of kleptomania or shoplifting in women. Perhaps not surprisingly, there were also attempts to rationalize housework in general and shopping in particular. So, for example, this period sees the introduction and growth of domestic science in schools, the proliferation of housework manuals, and a torrent of advice to housewives on how best to look after their home and family in, for example, women's magazines.

[. . .]

Winship (1987) emphasizes how definitions of gender have been linked to the development of consumer culture, illustrating how women's magazines in the twentieth century promoted particular kinds of femininity through the representation of consumption practices. In a study of British women's magazines, she identifies some broad shifts in the ways in which the role of the woman reader as housewife, mother, wife and consumer was constructed, most notably, a shift from the representation of women in terms of their roles as wife and mother in the early and middle years of the twentieth century – along similar lines to those identified by Dowling – to an increasing stress on feminine individuality through an emphasis on glamour, sexuality and appearance towards the end. This argument has important implications for the issue of how consumer culture may have helped shape contemporary ideals of personal identity as a possession, reflexively created in practices of self-fashioning.

This shift towards an invitation to women to understand themselves in terms of feminine individuality is analysed by Winship by reference to the magazine *Options*, launched in 1982. This magazine was described in the publicity surrounding its launch as 'a magazine about choice', a choice which was later presented in terms of 'Better food, Better homes, Better fashion, Better living'. It is addressed to a reader who is invited to see herself as 'an entirely new breed of consumer', defined exclusively in terms of what she buys:

> She sees herself as the kind of woman who should have a calculator in her handbag, a stereo in her car, a note recorder in her office. She is the generation for whom video and telecom were made. Busy women with open minds who will take advantage to make work more efficient and play more fun. The first generation of women for whom freezers, dishwashers and microwave ovens are not luxuries but essentials.
>
> (*Options* launch material, quoted in Winship 1983: 47)

This is the new woman who can be independent *and* feminine, who can look attractive *and* create a fulfilling family and home life even when carrying out a demanding job.

The representation of consumption dominates this and many other women's magazines. Not only is about half of the magazine taken up by advertisements, but almost all the colour photography, both in advertisements and features, illustrates commodities of some kind. In feature articles and advertisements, the modern woman is represented as a superwoman, enjoying the skills and pleasures of consumption, not in a passive way, but by actively appropriating and reworking commodities to construct a lifestyle which expresses her *individuality*. Winship writes that in *Options* 'the activities involved around consumption constitute a *creative skill* – the creation of a "look", whether with clothes, furnishings, food or make-up – which are both *pleasurable to do* and *to look at*' (1983: 48). The sphere of consumption is held up as the arena in which women can selectively choose 'options' to express their own unique sense of self by transforming commodities from their mass-produced forms into expressions of individuality and originality. The magazine provides optimistic encouragement to keep on trying, offering examples of women who have 'found themselves' through the adoption of an individualized lifestyle.

Winship argues that an important part of this latest stage in the representation of women in relation to consumption is the way in which women are invited to view their own lives as their *own creations*, and buy an identikit of different images of themselves created by different products. This latest stage in the constitution of women through consuming is linked by Winship to the growing importance of the *work of femininity*. Other writers too have argued that consumption practices have become an increasingly important source of the creation of the feminine self.

One instance of this is provided by the relation between the notions of beauty and femininity. Winship argues that, while beauty is not a new component of femininity, advertising in women's magazines has played an important part in redefining its meaning. She suggests that advertising has contributed to the idea that beauty is not a natural given – either absent or present – but instead is something that is achievable by any woman, though only through the application of the correct products. The way in which advertising has done this, according to Winship, is through its representation of women as 'the field of action for various products'. She points to the way in which in advertisements, women's bodies are broken down into different areas as sites for the actions of commodities.

Winship suggests that advertising builds on the creation of an anxiety to the effect that, unless women measure up, they will not be loved. They are set to work on their bodies labouring to perfect and eroticize an ever-increasing number of erotogenic zones. Every minute region of the body is now exposed to scrutiny. Mouth, hair, eyes, eyelashes, nails, fingers, hands, skin, teeth, lips, cheeks, shoulders, elbows, arms, legs, feet – all these and many more have become areas requiring work. Winship sees this in terms of the imposition of a cultural ideal of feminine beauty and the multiplication of areas of the body accessible to marketing. It is the introduction of this idea that beauty is something that can be achieved, that it is something to be worked on, that Winship identifies as the work of femininity, and she suggests that consumer culture has been able to feed on and extend this work through its promotion of a multiplicity of products.

Winship further suggests that through the representation of beauty as an achievable goal of self-transformation through the use of commodities, women are constructed as consumers of themselves *as possessions or commodities*. John Berger makes the same point when he writes that, 'the publicity image steals [a woman's] love of herself as she is and offers it back to her for the price of the product' (1972: 134). Kathy Myers (1986) catches this contradictory nature of consumption for women by describing it as a kind of cannibalism. The point that is being made here is that women are both the *objects* or *signs* of representation in advertising and the *market* for the majority of products advertised. They are thus simultaneously located at two moments of the cycle of commodity exchange – that of a privileged sign in advertising and commodity aesthetics and the principal target market. They are also, in one sense, the principal actors in the moment of use of commodities. From this point of view, the emotionalization and aestheticization of housework – including, most importantly, the intensification of the work of femininity – may be seen to have contributed to the emergence of the distinctively stylized nature of consumer culture in contemporary society and the ideal of a possessive individual. However, the extent to which women are active agents, in the sense of being in control of how to use commodities, whether they are self-possessed or possessed by others, is a much debated question.

[. . .]

The pleasures of femininity

It has recently been argued that much of the work discussed so far presents an overly pessimistic view of the role of women in the history of consumer culture, minimizes their role as active intermediaries in bringing about changes in consumption practices, and overlooks the ways in which access to consumer culture may have provided resources to help women challenge gender inequality and their own objectification (Nava 1992). From this point of view, the opening of department stores may indeed have contributed to the emancipation of women!

This line of argument points out that, with the advent of the department store, shopping lost its previous automatic association with purchase and further use. It was no longer simply the purchasing of predetermined requirements, but became an activity in its own right, and as such provided an opportunity for women to explore their own desires outside the confines of the family economy. Rachel Bowlby catches this moment in the title of one of her books: *Just Looking* (1985). This development took place in the period that saw a dramatic increase in the use of transparent display windows, improved lighting inside stores, and a sense of theatrical excess in the display of items. As a result of these developments, stores can be seen to have provided a focus for women's fantasies, a site of entertainment, and a possible escape from the confines of domestic femininity. They provided a space within which (first middle-class and then working-class) women could participate in public life, in which they could experience some of the shocks, speed and spectacle of modernity, in which they could have brief encounters, and make 'unwise' purchases for themselves.

One way in which this argument has been developed is to look at the ways in which women have adopted resistant or subversive modes of consuming. So, for example, Mica Nava claims:

> Consumption . . . has offered women new areas of authority and expertise, new sources of income, a new sense of consumer rights; and one of the consequences of these developments has been a heightened awareness of entitlement outside the sphere of consumption.
> (1992: 166)

It has also been suggested that the construction of the female consumer as irrational has provided the basis from which women could wilfully challenge their subordination in relation to men. From this point of view, women do not simply passively adopt the versions of femininity which they are encouraged to emulate, but actively seek to redefine the meaning of these femininities. For example, it is argued that women have subverted the idea that beauty is something that can be achieved, put on and taken off, and have developed ways of seeing femininity as a *masquerade*, a performance, in ways which enable them to play with their personal identity, and take pleasure in the adoption of roles and masks.

From this point of view, masquerade, or the simulation which is femininity, enables temporary resistances to impositions of power, including the operation of the male gaze, and is a strategic response, adopted by women in situations that are not necessarily beneficial to them. It thus suggests that self-possession is not the only possible basis from which to participate in consumer culture, and that the masquerade offers other possibilities. This more active understanding of women's participation in consumption practices can be used to explain the emergence of the dynamic, ironic and self-conscious manipulation of style which is said to be characteristic of contemporary consumer culture. In this view, women are not only central to the stylization of consumer culture, but may stand to benefit from it, and can thus be seen as key cultural intermediaries.

[. . .]

The implications of masquerade for women in consumer culture

However, it is important to point out that not all women have been able to take part in the pleasures associated with consumption in the same way. Black women, for example, have often been excluded from the relations of looking outlined above. So, for example, Jane Gaines (1988) points out that while some groups have historically had the licence to 'look' openly, other groups, such as black people, have only been able to look illicitly. Carolyn Steedman (1986) has also pointed out that only some women are able to buy new fashions and styles for themselves, while others – working-class women especially – know that their desires have to remain subordinated to the needs of others, usually men and children. These points indicate that different groups of women have participated unevenly in the development of consumer culture, both implicated and excluded from cycles of production and consumption in contradictory ways. They also suggest that the adoption of simulation, while it may offer a feminine mode of fashioning the self, is cross-cut by class and race (see Skeggs (forthcoming) and Tyler 1991 for further discussion of this issue; the latter also introduces questions of sexual difference).

Beverley Skeggs explores some of the complexities of the practices of imitation and masquerade in her study of young white working-class women. She suggests that while the women in her study had a clear knowledge about their 'place' they were always trying to leave it. To this end, they adopted the tactics of passing as middle-class through the display of certain kinds of femininity, in part developed in consumption practices. These tactics, she says, are those of denial, disidentification and dissimulation in relation to being working-class and simulation in relation to being middle-class. However, she argues that passing as middle-class did not and could not involve irony: the young women wanted to be taken seriously. She writes: 'In this sense their attempt to pass is not a form of insubordination; rather it is a dissimulation, a performance of a desire not to be, a desire not to be shamed but a desire to be legitimated.' What this suggests is that irony may be a strategy which is most useful in relation to the middle classes (both men and women), who can afford, and indeed may be able to profit from, the ability to make visible the playfulness of their passing.

Skeggs also points out that this non-ironic passing engenders anxiety and insecurity; so, for example, when the young women showed her round their homes, they apologized for the things she was shown:

> I know you're meant to have real paintings on your wall, but I love these prints [Athena's ballet dancers]. I just think the price for real paintings is ridiculous and frankly we've got other uses for our money.

> When we moved in the kitchen was all white melamine, straight from MFI so we ripped it out straight away. I put my foot down, I said we're not having that cheap stuff in here. The kitchen cost a fortune but I love it and I love spending time in here. But I'm afraid that to get it right in here means we've not been able to afford to do anything else, so I'm sorry the rest of the house dulls by comparison. I think I'd spend all my time in here if I could. It's my room. We would have done the rest but what with all the redundancies at ICI now you've just got to be careful.

Skeggs suggests that these comments indicate the ways in which the young women's judgement of themselves – in terms of their ability to pass as having middle-class tastes – is filled with self-doubt and anxiety about the possibility of being caught out. Skeggs thus describes her analysis of the narratives of improvement through which the young women spoke of their class positioning as 'a study of unease'.

References

Anderson, M., Bechhofer, F. and Gershuny, J. 1994 (eds): *The Social Economy of the Household.* Oxford: Oxford University Press.

Benson, S. P. 1986: *Counter Cultures: Saleswomen, Managers and Customers in American Department Stores.* Urbana and Chicago: University of Illinois Press.

Berger, J. 1972: *Ways of Seeing.* London: BBC Books.

Bowlby, R. 1985: *Just Looking: Consumer Culture in Dreiser, Gissing and Zola.* New York and London: Methuen.

—— 1993: *Shopping with Freud.* London: Routledge.

Braverman, H. 1974: *Labour and Monopoly Capital.* London: Monthly Review Press.

Delphy, C. 1984: *Close to Home.* Cambridge: Hutchinson.

—— and Leonard, D. 1992: *Familiar Exploitation: A New Analysis of Marriage in Contemporary Western Societies.* Cambridge: Polity.

Dowling, R. 1993: Femininity, place and commodities: a retail case study. *Antipode*, 25: 4, 295–319.

Forty, A. 1986: *Objects of Desire.* London: Thames and Hudson.

Gaines, J. 1988: White privilege and looking relations – race and gender in feminist film theory. *Screen*, 29: 4, 12–27.

Game, A. and Pringle, R. 1984: *Gender at Work.* London: Pluto Press.

Gershuny, J. 1978: *After Industrial Society.* London: Macmillan.

—— 1983: *Social Innovation and the Division of Labour.* Oxford: Oxford University Press.

Myers, K. 1986: *Understains: The Sense and Seduction of Advertising*. London: Pandora.

Nava, M. 1992: *Changing Cultures: Feminism, Youth and Consumerism*. London: Sage.

Oakley, A. 1976: *Housewife*. Harmondsworth: Penguin.

Partington, A. 1991: Melodrama's gendered audience. In S. Franklin, C. Lury and J. Stacey (eds), *Off-Centre: Feminism and Cultural Studies*. London: Harper Collins, 49–68.

Skeggs, B. (forthcoming): *Becoming Respectable: An Ethnography of White, Working-class Women*. London: Sage.

Steedman, C. 1986: *Landscape for a Good Woman: A Story of Two Lives*. London: Virago.

Tyler, C.-A. 1991: Boys will be girls: the politics of gay drag. In D. Fuss (ed.), *Inside/Out: Lesbian Theories, Gay Theories*. New York and London: Routledge, 32–70.

Winship, J. 1987: *Inside Women's Magazines*. London: Pandora.

Zukin, S. 1991: *Landscapes of Power*. Berkeley and Los Angeles: University of California Press.

24 Consumption, Tribes and Identity

Kevin Hetherington

> ### Key words
>
> Consumption, youth culture, moral panics, alternative life-styles, travellers, tribes

Travellers – *those who move about the country often living in their vehicles and taking what work they can find – have attracted much public attention. Hetherington writes about one group of travellers who have made a practice of holding a summer festival at Stonehenge and, having been prevented from doing that, looked for alternative sites. He investigated why the travellers are interested in Stonehenge, why there is so much hostility towards them, and what form the social relationships of the travellers take.*

Hetherington starts from the hypothesis that the gathering at Stonehenge was like a medieval market in which goods and services were sold and exchanged. It was also a festival in which the participants were distanced from the routines of ordinary life. For the rest of society, the travellers' festival at Stonehenge represents the intrusion of the chaotic and disorganized qualities of modern life. They are hated because their lifestyle is associated with sources of risk. It is not surprising that the travellers, in embracing a chaotic lifestyle, should adopt a timeless place like Stonehenge which is defined as outside normal everyday existence.

Hetherington further develops an account of the nature of the social relationships uniting groups of travellers. In his view, in contemporary societies, the traditional bases of identity – class, gender, locality, ethnicity, for example – are no longer as effective and, consequently, people look for alternative forms of sociation. These alternatives are organized around shared beliefs, styles of life and consumption practices. These tribe-like groupings, of which the Stonehenge travellers are an example, are relatively unstable and require considerable effort and maintenance from their members.

[. . .]

Stonehenge as a site of consumption

Festivals have always been associated with markets and the Stonehenge festival has been no exception. Almost anything could be bought at Stonehenge: drugs, New Age paraphernalia, health remedies, old bits of tat, scrap, vehicle parts, food, services; one person used to provide hot baths in an old tub in the middle of the field (surrounded by a screen), somebody even had the enterprising idea of selling people breakfast in bed, strawberries and Champagne if it was your birthday, otherwise fried-egg sandwiches! And yet the festival promoted the idea that it was free with no admission fees (except when some tried and succeeded in collecting entrance fees from the gullible and uninformed). The music was free, bands such as Hawkwind and many others would just turn up and play, often over ropy old public-address systems. There were also 'traditional' entertainers like the Tibetan Ukrainian Mountain Troupe, assorted jugglers, clowns, performers and festival-goers in various states of intoxication just having a go. The fact that such a festival should be associated with a solstice ceremony of sun worship, even if only by a minority of festival-goers, provides us with a good example of what Bakhtin describes as the carnivalesque, a heterogeneous, playful inversion of acceptable modes of behaviour, a world turned upside down, the mocking of authority, the exclusion of policing agencies from the site, the celebration of dirt, mess, abandon, intoxication, excess and waste (Bakhtin, 1984).

The festival was not only a place for large numbers of people to congregate for several weeks of festival but it was also a market for the New Age travellers, at which they could make some money, meet up with old friends and acquaintances, swap stories, reminisce and take part in the festival. Many of the goods and services were provided by the travellers to the others at the festival who led more sedentary lives but went to festivals like Stonehenge and Glastonbury during the summer months. The Stonehenge festival was itself part of a 'season' of summer free festivals. Like the periodic markets of medieval times, travellers would move on from one fair to another, earning money, selling goods, offering and exchanging services. The carnival element was present at the other festivals, even the more 'commercial' ones like Glastonbury, where admission fees were charged and the commercial and festival entertainments were more organized, licensed and regulated. But Stonehenge was special to those who went there; the ambience of the site, the myths and legends associated with it were stronger and it generated more hostility from its detractors.

The ambivalent nature of Stonehenge, a *topos* associated with carnival and markets, make it a good example of what has been described as a liminal zone, a margin or boundary, the crossing of which involves ritualized forms of transgression (Turner, 1969). The transformative potential of such a site is represented not simply in terms of carnivalesque rituals, pagan ceremonies and drug-induced states, but significantly by commercial activities whose meaning takes on transformed significance when associated with such liminal spaces. Consumption at Stonehenge when related to festival is highly ambivalent. It is both spontaneous and organized, monetary but with a strong emphasis placed on gift exchange; it is removed from all associations with rational consumption (licensed, taxed and regulated) but the sense of reciprocity is strong. Consumption in a liminal space reveals its archaic 'sacrificial' character: as an act of destruction, devouring, consuming, fetishizing, destroying, transforming the product of labour into waste. Consumption in such an unregulated manner led to the accumulation of filth and garbage. It is consumption primarily associated with satiating bodily desires, through food, alcohol, drugs and ritual adornment. There is a strong element of idealizing the transformative potential of consumption here; that which is 'devoured' gives the destroyer powers, whether they be associated with hallucinatory experiences, states of relaxation, beauty or sexiness. The outcome is waste and decay, the bad trip, the hangover and excrement.

Stonehenge as a festival of consumption was a destructive event that left the destroyer surrounded by the waste and decay: it represents a lifestyle of excess, liminally constituted and a deliberate challenge to the established order of things. The transient nature of social activities is revealed through festival, that things cannot last or that the consequences might be unpleasant. Festival after all has often been associated with death, as a release from the anxieties associated with one's ultimate demise.

The travellers and other festival-goers celebrate their marginal lifestyle not simply in terms of what they consume but through the inversions and rituals of festival. Consumption under these conditions becomes an *enactment of lifestyle* rather than simply the means to a lifestyle, with the site, or topos, in this case Stonehenge, providing the dramaturgical stage for these liminal practices. As such the performance has a dual role, as a practice through which identity and solidarity are held together and as a means of distanciating the proponents of such a lifestyle from the routine and mundane activities of everyday life. What is significant to both is the spatiality of this enactment. Such activities only have significance if they are visible, while at the same time being closed off from 'non-members'. It is this visible enactment of an alternative lifestyle that has been the source of much of the conflict surrounding the Stonehenge festival, a conflict that has its source in the problematic status of the visible transgression of the accepted conventions of what should be open to public view. While it is drug-taking, sexual licence and an appearance that seems strange that are often the source of concern, their visibility makes the space in which they occur the source of conflict as much as the practices themselves. This conflict over space and the types of lifestyle that exist therein *together* form the basis of this particular lifestyle. In order to understand that lifestyle more fully and therefore the significance that consumption plays, one first has to understand the significance of the context in which it arises.

Space and social order

Stonehenge is a prime example of a social spatialization. '[The] ongoing social construction of the spatial at the level of the social imaginary (collective mythologies, presuppositions) as well as interventions in the landscape . . .' (Shields, 1991a: 31). It is a site with many conflictually produced and contested meanings, but they centre around two fundamental social spatializations: that of *heritage* and that of *festival*. The creation of meaningful, competing contemporary social spatializations can be seen in the descriptions of Stonehenge as an important archaeological site, a temple, an ancient astronomical instrument, a tourist attraction, a symbol of ancient Britain as culturally and technologically skilled, a New Age site of worship, part of England's cultural heritage, a node in a system of powerful ley lines and the site of an annual rock festival (Chippindale, 1983; Chippindale et al., 1990). It is the latter and its connection with New Age religious meanings that provide us with the example of Stonehenge as a site of festival embodied in the celebration of the solstice and through forms of popular culture. The other examples, although diverse, provide us with the view of Stonehenge as a site of heritage.

As a site overburdened with meaning it has become policed, both literally in the form of thousands of police officers at the time of the now banned festival, with the use of perimeter fencing, admission fees, and symbolically through the way meanings are given to such a space. Despite its ancient origin, the host of meanings given to Stonehenge are all modern. Even the Druids who hold their own ceremony during the solstice are a modern phenomenon founded at the beginning of the eighteenth century, despite their claims to be able to trace an unbroken lineage to the ancients (Piggott, 1985). Stonehenge is more than just a contested space, it is a modern site at which some of the fundamental features of modernity come into conflict. This is not however a contest between modernity and tradition, between new and old interpretations of the significance of the stones, but *reflexively* the conflict between modern and counter-modern tendencies using an ancient site to legitimize different sets of practices and individualized lifestyles.

Both the concepts of heritage and festival are related to fundamentally opposing conceptions of time. Heritage implies continuity and a link with the past, while festival implies breaking the continuity of time and celebrating the present as if it were eternal. Heritage is about continuity and order while festival is about transgression and mocking in public the temporal authority of tradition. These conceptions of time are coupled with perceptions of space. For the archaeologist it is ancient, sedimented in the past, a static space to be meticulously picked over, catalogued and mapped in order that we might come to know more about a dead time. For the heritage tourist, the meaning of this space is also dead but this time as a dead space in living time (memory being the recreation of meaningful time); tourists can only visit spaces, but the nostalgia and the attempt to possess something different from the present leads to the re-temporalizing of heritage spaces. Stonehenge is what survives from another time, it resonates with pastness, but this is a past that can only be recaptured in memory. As such it is also for the tourist, like the archaeologist, and an institution like the National Trust, a space that is to be preserved rather than used, a space to be gazed upon (Urry, 1990) but not changed, used or touched.

For the New Age travellers Stonehenge represents not the archaeological sediment of historical memory but a renewal of the present in a world in which the continuity of time is disrupted. These visitors worship in effect the aura of the present, of what they see as the living ambience created by the stones. It is fitting that a prominent feature of their lifestyle should be a transient life on the roads. Shunning a sedentary way of life, these 'nomads of the present' (Melucci, 1989) live a different time, one that has seasonal continuity, but exists disjunctively with everyone else. Their calendar is a regulated one suited to stopping in winter and moving in summer. The travel from festival to festival, which often take place at ancient pagan sites such as stone circles, of which Stonehenge is only the most famous, forms a significant feature of their life on the road.

In order to interpret the significance of the competing meanings and identities attached to Stonehenge, I shall start by claiming that the contestation of the meaning of a site such as Stonehenge derives from the modern dislocation or 'disembedding' of our everyday lives in time and space (Giddens, 1990) and the subsequent attempt to resolve resulting uncertainties through the creation of 'place myths' that are one of the results of this process. Stonehenge as a contemporary site is significant as both a heritage space and a festival space as both are defined in relation to the disintegration in everyday life of communally created meaningful spaces, which represent continuity in time, and of place as a collective basis for identity and culture, by the fleeting, disjunctive experience of time within a capitalist society always disrupting the spatial stability of everyday life (Simmel, 1990; Harvey, 1989; Giddens, 1990). Stonehenge, as a modern site, provides us with a good example of a topos of insecurity that symbolically articulates the consequences of conflicts surrounding the ambiguity of lifeworld experiences of place as detached from the *durée* of everyday life.

The fear of 'chaos', disordered practices that are out of place, and its production by processes of modernization in which the temporal aspects of human relationships are both reified in particular practices and uncoupled from the spatially proximate aspects of those relationships, serve to make spatial rather than temporal relationships the basis of giving order to everyday life. But modern disembedded spaces remain aporial and a source of ontological insecurity. All forms of feeling, emotion and affective sociality can only be allowed to exist in public if those spaces are clearly defined and regulated, as in the sporting arena. But this sociality is a persistent part of the underlying basis to everyday life, normally repressed and confined to the private lives of individuals; however, it continually emerges from that realm as the basis for new lifestyles offering a challenge to the mundane and routine that have become the common experience in the private lives of many. Public space becomes for some the space in which to transgress the routinized and emotionless character of public life and to create new meaningful identities and lifestyles out of a disordered existence.

We also witness the counter-measures to this process. Any space where the appropriate activity for the setting is in any doubt is subjected to policing and surveillance. As a consequence Stonehenge, as a mysterious space, becomes the site of conflict between modern and counter-modern perspectives. Not only does it offer the possibility through the various interpretations of heritage of a sense of continuity and order, it also offers the possibility of mystery and disordered uses expunged from the modern consciousness. Pagan, expressive, emotive, magical, carnival, ritualized and full of uncertainty, the un-appropriated uses of Stonehenge threaten to spill out into the outside world. The source of anxiety and the strength of the reaction by the 'locals' is due not to any physical danger (although it may be articulated as such), but is related to uncertainties surrounding new visible lifestyles which are associated by default as the source of the modern characteristic to disrupt the indexicality of place.

Subsequently those who celebrate festival at this space are treated as *Other* because they adopt a lifestyle that, given its self-produced form, represents the chaotic, disorganized and transient features of modern life that transgress the routines and familiarities of everyday life. Collectively, they constitute and identify with the stranger that inhabits the modern world who, in Simmel's words, 'comes today and stays tomorrow – the potential wanderer so to speak, who, although he has gone no further, has not quite got over the freedom of coming and going' (Simmel, 1971: 143).

Just as has been the case with Jews and gypsies down the centuries, the 'New Age travellers' are hated not because they are always on the move but because they might stay and 'contaminate' through their ambivalence and bring down all manner of horrors upon the 'locals' (Bauman, 1990). They are out of place not because they belong somewhere else, as in the case of an enemy, but because they belong nowhere and are thus not simply unplaceable, but in their celebration of festival and mobility are outside of time itself; they inhabit the disjuncture between experiences of time and place in human relationships; 'unclean', 'slimey' (Douglas, 1984), their status is as uncertain as their origins. Above all as strangers who are harbingers of uncertainty and discontinuity, their lifestyle is associated with sources of *risk*. It is notable that 'the horrified', when commenting on the travellers, saw them not only as dirty, scrounging thieves and peddlers in drugs, but also as a source of pollution (Rojek, 1988).

While these anxieties may be clothed in expressions of horror in relation to dirt, disease and drug-taking, an attempt is made to make visible unseen anxieties, by defining those with a visibly different lifestyle in terms of the source of risk. It is something of an irony, not to say a self-fulfilling prophecy, that those who construct their lifestyles differently should do so latterly around the very risks that they have become associated with. They end up putting themselves in danger from the things others fear so much: transientness, eviction, ostracism, placeless identities, poverty, harassment and uncertainty in one's life.

It is not surprising therefore that those who deliberately assume 'risk identities', who celebrate chaotic and expressive lifestyles, should adopt a 'timeless' space like Stonehenge as their spiritual 'home'. This lifestyle strikes directly at the opposing world-view that is associated with heritage. Those attending the festival would see this as an outlook running counter to the original sacred significance of the stones, yet while their festival is meant to be an enactment of renewal it is also a deliberate political challenge to those they know will be offended by their activities.

The festivals of the past were intimately related to the continuity of the calendar in world where the succession of time was ordered in terms of seasons and the *durée* of human life and therefore had a natural meaning. In the past natural disasters and disruptions were hazards expected with fatalism and celebrated through the carnivalesque practices of grotesque imagery and of death (Bakhtin, 1984). The contemporary festival lifestyle reintroduces this into the modern life-world, with all its disorder, drug-taking and the fact of uncertainty in our lives through processes of consumption. Through their hedonistic, anti-authoritarian stance, their dress, drugs, visible expressions of release from imposed social constraints, the festival-goers mock, through carnival, all those who hold ideals of progress and satisfaction through effort.

Consumption and sociality

To bring all these elements together – time-space relations, festival, risk and consumption – what is required is a theory of sociality and sociation, that is, an understanding of the social preconditions, the emotional bases to the collective experience of the activities involved and the forms this takes as distinct lifestyles (Maffesoli, 1989; Amirou, 1989; Hetherington, 1990; Shields, 1991b). In order to understand the significance of the combination of features that I have suggested are associated with Stonehenge, one needs to consider two processes that are involved, the deregulation through modernization and individualization of the modern forms of solidarity and identity based on class occupation, locality and gender (Beck, 1992) and the recomposition into 'tribal' identities and forms of sociation (Maffesoli, 1988). Such processes that stem from changes within capitalist economies produce a heightened, more reflexive form of individualism, which is no longer able to base itself in class cultures, regional identities or established gender roles, leading to a process of de-individualization as people seek to recombine in new forms of sociation based on political, cultural, sexual, religious and therapeutic identities. These non-ascriptive 'neo-Tribes' as Maffesoli calls them, are inherently unstable and not fixed by any of the established parameters of modern society; instead they are maintained through shared beliefs, styles of life, an expressive body-centredness, new moral beliefs and senses of injustice, and significantly through consumption practices. The participants are drawn primarily from the disaffected and disempowered, notably young middle-class people, whose former cultural identity was neither bourgeois nor proletarian, but centred around a culture of displacement so to speak, based on social, educational and spatial mobility, and on gender role and occupational displacement (Beck, 1992). All of which undermine a shared and meaningful social existence.

It would be wrong to see these 'tribes' as the creators of a new sense of *community*. As Schmalenbach argued over sixty years ago, drawing on not that dissimilar observations of the German Youth Movement in the early part of this century, the concept *Bund* or *communion* better captures the reality of these unstable affectual forms of sociation than that of community (*Gemeinschaft*) (Schmalenbach, 1977). A *Bund* is an intense form of affectual solidarity, that is inherently unstable and liable to break down very rapidly unless it is consciously maintained through the symbolically mediated interactions of its members.[1]

As well as small-scale, achieved rather than ascribed, unstable and affectual forms of sociation (Schmalenbach, 1977), *Bünde* are also maintained symbolically and through active, reflexive monitoring of group solidarity by those involved, in other words they are highly self-referential and involve creating a medium of symbolic practices through which a particular lifestyle emerges. The social bonding involved is very weak, requiring considerable effort in maintenance (Gurvitch, 1941). As marginalized risk identities are involved, these *Bünde* are self-enclosed and very tribal or autotelic – that is, as social forms they rapidly become their own goal; styles of dress, political or religious beliefs, adherence to musical styles or modes of living are often deliberately accentuated and defended. Associated with sites of transition or liminality (Turner, 1969), these *Bünde* are innovative, transgressive and often involve a re-skilling or empowering of the life-worlds of their 'members'. They are a sociation that combines aesthetic, ethical and expressive styles of life into impassioned group identities often centred around charismatic leaders or strongly held beliefs. As forms of sociation they most clearly encapsulate the seemingly contradictory modern processes of individualization and de-individualization. They are places where individuals, burdened with their sense of displaced individuality, go to lose themselves, only to rediscover the fact that strong group identities of this sort require personal skills and a reflexive sense of self. The intensity of interpersonal relations, and of a re-emergent individualism can only lead to the fragmentation of a *Bund* and its re-combination and transition into more stable forms of sociation. This is a form of sociation whose sociality is at once intense and fragile, strongly empowering but the source of possible bitter recrimination.

Amongst the travellers, we find many *Bünde*; some have names (both real and imagined): the Tibetan Ukrainian Mountain Troupe, the Rainbow Warriors, the Rainbow People, the Brew Crew and before them the Yellow Tipi as well as a whole host whose names are lost or unknown! Many of the named groups could be divided into subgroups often hostile to one another, and 'membership' need not be exclusive to one group. However, it is consumption, notably at festivals, that plays a strong part in holding this lifestyle together. They often have a rugged, dirty appearance, some with bright clothes, others in dark greens. Ethnic jewellery, multicoloured blankets, lovingly cared-for tools and hand-made objects of various sorts all provide some of the symbolic cement that goes into holding together an otherwise fragile form of sociation. Drugs of course are important, significantly cannabis and acid, although speed and heroin are not unheard of (cocaine though tends to be too expensive). Alcohol is also significant, notably Special Brew. The type of vehicle often provides status; they have tended to get bigger over the years, and double-decker buses are now favoured, especially ones with diesel engines (some even have microwaves and cell phones), although horse-drawn caravans and canal boats look set to become significant.

Travellers have a variety of sources of income, festivals and fairs being the most significant but also seasonal work, selling bits of scrap, car-boot sales, selling the products of learned craft skills, entertainment, music, drug-dealing and social-security payments. This is one of the reasons why the festivals are so important; they are the place to make lots of money, to get one's vehicle roadworthy, to buy furniture and clothing. Skills and resources are shared amongst travellers (the festival at Stonehenge was perhaps the finest example of intricate networks of relationships that go to make up the black economy). But also these consumption practices play a significant part in maintaining a lifestyle derived from a *Bund*. Partly this is symbolic, but significantly it is social, ties of reciprocity, gift (in Mauss's sense of honour, status and debt) (Mauss, 1969). The festival also acts as a social gathering and meeting place at which to make collective decisions just as at the markets of old.

Areas of the festival field 'spontaneously' found themselves organized into pitches from which 'tribes' sold their goods, sometimes through the money economy, sometimes through barter, sometimes through gift-exchange. The whole ethos of gift underlay these *free* festivals, yet at the same time some real cut-throat business was conducted with consequences for anyone who didn't follow the rules! The symbolic relations of gift with their association with honour and debt are well suited to the *Bund* form that requires self-conscious, ritualized and symbolic practices of group maintenance that counterpose with more contractual relationships.

As well as being invested with the symbolism of gift, these *Bünde* are also the sites of re-skilling, what Giddens, in another context called the 're-skilling of everyday life' (Giddens, 1990). While the activities, notably the commercial activities of these *Bünde*, may appear disorganized, ill-conceived, they have spawned both directly and indirectly a whole host of subsequent commercial practices. Magazines, pamphlets, craft skills, musical and other entertainment skills, skills derived from living on the road – vehicle maintenance, skills in seasonal labour. Although not directly related to the travellers, holistic medicine, therapies, New Age and occult shops it can be argued are all in some way related to such one-time counter-cultural, *Bund*-like activities, of which the travellers are just one of the more visible examples.

[. . .]

Note

1 As well as Schmalenbach's concept *Bund*, which was developed in response to the group surrounding Stefan Georg and also the German Youth Movement, Gurvitch (1941) and Turner (1969) have also developed similar concepts of 'Communion'. I intend here to produce a synthesis of the three.

References

Amirou, R. (1989) 'Sociability/"Sociality"', *Current Sociology* 37 (1): 115–20.
Bakhtin, M. (1984) *Rabelais and His World*, Bloomington: Indiana University Press.
Bauman, Z. (1990) *Modernity and Ambivalence*, Cambridge: Polity Press.
Beck, U. (1992) *Risk Society: On the Way to an Another Modernity*, London: Sage.
Chippindale, C. (1983) *Stonehenge Complete*, London: Thames & Hudson.
—— et al. (1990) *Who Owns Stonehenge?*, London: Batsford.
Douglas, M. (1984) *Purity and Danger: an Analysis of the Concepts of Pollution and Taboo*, London: Ark.
Giddens, A. (1990) *The Consequences of Modernity*, Cambridge: Polity Press.
Gurvitch, G. (1941) 'Mass Community and Communion', *Journal of Philosophy* 28: 485–96.
Harvey, D. (1989) *The Condition of Postmodernity*, Oxford: Basil Blackwell.
Hetherington, K. (1990) *On the Homecoming of the Stranger: New Social Movements or New Sociations*, Lancaster Regionalism Group Working Paper 39, Lancaster: University of Lancaster.
Maffesoli, M. (1988) *Les Temps des Tribus*, Paris: Meridians Klincksieck.
—— (1989) 'The Sociology of Everyday Life (Epistemological Elements)', *Current Sociology* 37 (1): 1 –16.
Mauss, M. (1969) *The Gift*, London: Cohen & West.
Melucci, A. (1989) *Nomads of the Present*, London: Radius.
Piggott, S. (1985) *The Druids*, London: Thames & Hudson.
Rojek, G. (1988) 'The Convoy of Pollution', *Leisure Studies* 7: 21 –31.
Schmalenbach, H. (1977) 'Communion – a Sociological Category', *Herman Schmalenbach: On Society and Experience*, Chicago: University of Chicago Press.
Shields, R. (1991a) *Places on the Margin: Alternative Geographies of Modernity*, London: Routledge.

—— (1991b) 'The Individual, Consumption Cultures and the Fate of Community', *BSA 1991 Conference Paper. Consumption and the Politics of Identity Stream.*

Simmel, G. (1971) 'The Stranger', in Simmel, G. *On Individuality and Social Forms*, Chicago: University of Chicago Press.

—— (1990) *The Philosophy of Money* (Second Edition), London: Routledge.

Turner, V. (1969) *The Ritual Process: Structure and AntiStructure*, London: Routledge & Kegan Paul.

Urry, J. (1990) *The Tourist Gaze*, London: Sage.

Part V

Old and New Politics

25 | The Political Implications of the 1997 General Election

David Sanders

> **Key words**

> Voting, party system, political parties, partisanship, electoral volatility, class dealignment, 1997 general election

The 1997 general election brought eighteen years of Conservative government to a close as the Labour Party, led by Blair, achieved a massive parliamentary majority. David Sanders offers an interpretation of the implications of that victory for our understanding of electoral behaviour in Britain. The election result was all the more remarkable because until a year or two beforehand many had predicted that the Conservative Party had an almost unremovable grip on government office, because opposition parties were divided and unpopular.

Sanders uses the opportunity furnished by preliminary analysis of the election results to reflect on the nature of the British party system and to reassess some of the main arguments about voting behaviour including volatility, partisanship and class dealignment. He argues that the Labour victory signals a return to competitive party politics, greater individual volatility in the voting decision because class and established party preferences have reduced in influence, and a change in the nature of judgements about the economic competence of the major parties. Confirmation of his conjectures awaits full analysis of more detailed evidence about the election, but Sanders offers a provisional account of an unexpected outcome which indicates both continuities and change in party politics.

[. . .]

Labour's response after its fourth successive general election defeat in 1992 was, quite simply, to cease to be a socialist party. Labour's residual commitment to socialism had been a major factor preventing an electoral breakthrough. In these circumstances, socialism and any belief in challenging the interests of the capitalist class had to be comprehensively abandoned, and the new (i.e., old) principles of sound money, private enterprise, and tightly controlled state spending had to be warmly embraced. The transformation of socialist old Labour into social democratic New Labour under Tony Blair was not lost on large swathes of the British electorate. The voters showed by the way they cast their votes in May 1997 that they were indeed convinced that Labour had undergone a fundamental change. [. . .]

The 'one-party system' that appeared to be emerging after the 1992 election collapsed under the weight of its own contradictions. After the 1992 general election, in the wake of four successive Conservative victories, a number of commentators wondered whether Britain might not be moving in the direction of a one-party state.[1] They were not implying that Britain was becoming totalitarian but that it might be becoming a country in which the electorate continually votes the same party into office over a protracted period – as occurred in Sweden between 1930 and 1985 and in Japan between 1948 and 1993. The outcome in 1997 laid to rest such fears (or hopes). Three characteristics of the incipient one-party system contributed to the Conservatives' downfall – evidence, perhaps, that in a mature democracy self-correcting mechanisms are likely to ensure the maintenance of party competition over time.

One feature of the emergent one-party system was that the Opposition's arguments were increasingly ignored by a government that seemed to view itself as having a monopoly of truth and a unique ability to identify and defend British interests. It became common practice for Conservative party spokespeople, both in public and in private, to dismiss Labour as both unelectable and absurd. Conservative ministers increasingly gave the impression that it was some years since they had last talked to a living human being. More and more they enveloped harsh realities in clouds of official statistics. Asked about the length of hospital waiting lists, they recited meaningless statistics about the total numbers of people being treated by the NHS. Asked about falling educational standards, they cited statistics, which might or might not mean anything, about the numbers of pupils passing A-levels each year. The government's numbers were clearly meant to impress, but all they did was persuade more and more voters that Tory ministers were either incorrigibly evasive or never set foot outside their offices. There can be no doubt that this 'arrogance of power' caused considerable resentment among voters in Scotland and Wales, who had voted in very small numbers for the Conservatives in 1987 and 1992 and felt increasingly marginalised by the policies emanating from Westminster. By the same token, voters throughout the country, who feared that the NHS and state schools were being systematically weakened by Conservative policies, believed their concerns were being ignored – no matter what messages they sent to the government via local elections, by-elections, and opinion polls. It was hardly a surprise in the end that the Tories lost all their seats in Scotland and Wales and the votes of almost everyone who put education and the NHS at the top of their list of personal concerns.

The second feature of the one-party system after 1992 was that, with Labour and the Liberal Democrats seemingly in permanent opposition, lobby groups increasingly used contacts with Conservative backbenchers as a means of influencing government decisions. There was little point in lobbying Opposition parties since their views were invariably discounted by the government, and there appeared to be little prospect of their achieving power. This pattern of lobbying led in turn to the development of a virtual 'market' in backbench influence, with Conservative MPs, among other things, accepting cash for asking parliamentary questions. The activities of the lobbyist Ian Greer, and his association with MPs such as Tim Smith and Neil Hamilton, led to allegations of widespread sleaze in Conservative ranks and eventually to the establishment of the Nolan Committee. Neil Hamilton's determination to resist pressures on him to give up his Tatton seat, in the face of a considerable amount of published and unpublished evidence against him, ensured that 'sleaze' remained high on the political agenda through the election campaign. [. . .] Sleaze in the end may not have been crucial in bringing about the Conservatives' defeat. To the extent that it did play a role, however, the abuse of office and other forms of malpractice in the Tories' ranks had undoubtedly been fostered by the Conservatives' mounting conviction, developed over much of the previous decade, that they were electorally invulnerable, that they did not merely control the institutions of government but actually owned them.

The third feature was that, however long the Conservatives remained in power, regardless of the diminishing size of their Commons majority, the main opposition was the government's own backbenchers. Conservative ministers learned anew, if they had ever forgotten, that their *opponents* sat on the opposite side of the House of Commons; their *enemies* sat on their own. After 1992 this phenomenon increasingly produced what Anthony King called 'over the shoulder' politics, with ministers apparently more concerned to debate policy points with their own backbenchers than with the Opposition.[2] The ironic twist to this development was that it was constant backbench Conservative sniping over Britain's relations with the EU that fatally weakened Conservative unity. And this damage to what had hitherto been one of the Conservatives' greatest electoral assets also figured significantly in the Conservatives' defeat. In short – and in an almost dialectical fashion – the nascent one-party system that had appeared to be emerging in 1992 was swept away under the weight of its own contradictions. The result was probably good for British politics. Heaven knows what might have happened if Labour, following its dramatic move to the centre and the Conservatives' massive display of inner turmoil, had failed to win.

It is worth noting, in addition, that Britain's newly revived competitive party system is just that: a competitive *party* system. Notwithstanding the increased prominence of single-issue groups such as the anti-abortion lobby, the animal rights movement, and the direct-action anti-roads activists, groups of this kind have not yet usurped the traditional political role of parties as the articulators and aggregators of the many and diverse groups in British society. The Labour Party in the early 1990s, like the Conservative Party in the late 1990s, may have had fewer members and less income than the environmental group Greenpeace.[3] But it was Labour that decisively won the 1997 general election while Greenpeace remained what it had always been: a peripherally influential lobby group. Left-to-right ideology may have declined as a focus for interparty politics since the end of the Cold War and may yet decline still further. But, as and when new lines of political cleavage emerge, it is likely that political parties will still remain the focus for groups intent on effecting major changes in British society and the British economy.

'Electoral tribalism' has continued to decline and 'consumer voting' has continued to grow. One of the trends evident in British politics over the past thirty years has been the decline of class-based voting. In the 1960s, British voters tended to support the party

| Table I | Occupational Class and Vote, 1964–97 |

	1964		1997	
	Nonmanual (%)	Manual (%)	Nonmanual (%)	Manual (%)
Conservative	62(a)	28(c)	38	29
Labour	22(b)	64(d)	40	58
Liberal Democrat	18	8	18	12

	Absolute class voting index[a]	Relative class voting index[b]
1964	76	6.4
1966	78	6.4
1970	64	4.5
1974 (Feb)	64	5.7
1974 (Oct)	59	4.8
1979	52	3.7
1983	45	3.9
1987	44	3.5
1992	47	3.3
1997	29	1.9

a $(a - b) + (d - c)$.
b $(a/b)/(c/d)$.

that they thought best represented their class interests.[4] The Conservatives' stance as the party of property and enterprise resonated with the middle class and the rich, while Labour's broadly redistributive position attracted disproportionate support from working-class voters and the less-well-off. In 1964 roughly three-quarters of middle-class voters supported the Conservative Party, while two-thirds of the working-class voted Labour.[5] These proportions declined gradually during the 1970s and 1980s, leading to the conclusion that a process of long-term 'class realignment' was taking place.[6] This process was presumed to be the consequence of changes in patterns of employment and lifestyle that had eroded traditional class communities and identities. In addition, the Wilson and Callaghan governments had both fought difficult battles with the trade unions, in the process undercutting their own distinctive appeal to working-class voters.

The pattern of voting in the 1997 general election put paid to any lingering doubts that class-based voting played anything like the role in the late 1990s that it had in previous decades. Table 1 compares the class–vote relationship in 1964 and 1997. The results are summarised in the changes in the two indices shown in the lower half of the table.[7] As these indices show, the class–vote relationship – whether measured in 'absolute' or 'relative' terms – progressively weakened from the 1960s to the 1990s. Indeed, the marked reductions in both indices between 1992 and 1997 suggest that the process may even be accelerating as Britain approaches the millennium.

The counterpart to the decline of class-based voting has been a decline in partisan identification. It has long been known that the proportion of British voters who 'strongly identify' with either of the two main parties declined from roughly three-quarters of the electorate in the mid-1960s to just over half in the late 1980s.[8] Recent evidence suggests that this figure has since fallen below 40 percent.[9] The proportion of the electorate that '*very* strongly' identifies with the main parties has shown a similar pattern of decline. In 1964, 20 percent of voters were very strong Conservative identifiers and 22 percent very strongly identified with Labour. By 1987 the corresponding figures had fallen to 10 and 9 percent respectively, and they have remained at similar levels since.[10]

But if the traditional influences on British voting preferences have largely lost their potency in recent years, what, if anything, has replaced them? One obvious candidate, though it is notoriously difficult to measure, is the growth of alternative sources of identity – apart from class – that have no obvious attachment to the established political parties. The sort of anecdotal evidence favoured by exponents of postmodernism suggests that ethnicity, region, gender, sexual preference, and even lifestyle are increasingly important for some people as ways of defining themselves. How far this is really the case is difficult to assess. One thing seems certain, however: important changes *are* taking place in the way in which voters think about party politics. These changes have significant implications for explanations of voting that focus on social cleavages as the main basis of partisan support. In terms of the Michigan school's 'funnel of causality,' it would appear that variables 'closer' to the vote may now have a greater impact on party preferences than the sort of deep-seated factors such as class and party identification that lie further back in the causal sequence.[11] On this account, voters are becoming more and more like discriminating consumers who evaluate competing products.[12] As a result, voting decisions are now more heavily influenced by voters' assessments of the main parties' relative managerial competence, by their issue preferences, and by their evaluations of the rival frontbench teams' leadership abilities.

Political commentators sometimes speak of particular elections as involving a major 'realignment' of the electorate. A realigning election is one in which a party attracts disproportionate support from 'new' groups of voters and then retains them, or most of them, in subsequent elections. Recent examples of realigning elections include Ronald Reagan's successful appeal, in 1980, to blue-collar workers and southern Democrats (who remained loyal to the Republicans in 1984 and 1988) and Margaret Thatcher's appeal to the manual working class (many of whom remained loyal to the Conservatives in 1983 and 1987). The idea of voters as consumers, however, suggests that 'alignment' and 'realignment' may be the wrong way of thinking about the sources of party support. It is entirely possible that in modern party politics there are no permanent or even semipermanent electoral coalitions. Freed from the constraints of their previous class and partisan identities, voters increasingly shift their allegiances towards whichever party is able to offer the most attractive policy or managerial package. If such a pattern is indeed emerging, it contains an important warning to New Labour. What was won so comprehensively in 1997 could be just as easily lost in 2001 or 2002 if Labour fails to please the huge numbers of floating voters who now exist.

There is certainly evidence to suggest that the British electorate has become more volatile in recent years. The so-called Pederson index of electoral volatility is constructed by summing the change in each party's percentage share of the vote between

| Table 2 | Pederson index of electoral volatility, average for 13 European party systems, 1948–94, and for Britain, 1948–97 (in percentages) |

	1948–59	1960–69	1970–79	1980–89	1990–94	1997
European average	7.8	7.3	8.2	8.5	13.8	
UK	4.4	5.2	8.3	3.4	5.1	13.0

Source: Jan-Erik Lane, David McKay, and Kenneth Newton, *European Political Data Handbook*, 2nd ed. (Oxford: Oxford University Press, 1997).

Notes: The index is constructed by summing the change in each party's percentage share of the vote between elections and then dividing by 2.

The reported figures for 1948–59, 1960–69, and so on, give the average volatility figures for election-on-election change during the specified period. The UK figure for 1980–89, for example, covers a period in which two elections occurred (in 1983 and 1987). The volatility score is calculated in this instance by adding the average change in each party's percentage share of the vote between 1979 and 1983 to the average change between 1983 and 1987, then dividing by 2. The figure for 1997 represents the average change that occurred between 1992 and 1997.

pairs of elections and then dividing by two.[13] Table 2 shows how Britain's volatility pattern compares with that of other European party systems over the postwar period. As the table shows, with the exception of a brief interlude in the 1970s (when support for the Liberals and Scottish Nationalists surged simultaneously), Britain's volatility score for much of the postwar period was well below the European average. Indeed, apart from the 1970s, British volatility remained both low and fairly constant from 1945 onwards: the 1990–94 score, for example, was not substantially different from those of the 1950s and 1960s.

In 1997, however, a marked change occurred. British volatility more than doubled, to approach the European average (an average that had itself increased since the 1980s), but without large changes in the vote shares of the Liberal Democrats and the SNP. Part of the explanation for this dramatic increase probably lies in the general impact on West European party systems of the end of the Cold War. With the collapse of Soviet-style communism, the right lost its rallying external threat and the left its prime example of socialist 'success.' These developments, in turn, reduced the potency of ideological brand imaging for parties right across the political spectrum. Amid the multiplicity of new appeals that parties were consequently obliged to make, voter volatility increased throughout Europe (though it remains to be seen whether the increased volatility of the immediate post-Cold War period represents a long-term step-shift, the beginning of new upward trend, or a temporary adjustment to an external shock). As table 2 shows, however, the increase in volatility in Britain in 1997 was even greater than that experienced elsewhere in Europe. It seems likely that this extra volatility represents the additional effects of the longer-term processes of class and partisan dealignment just described.

The credibility of the opinion polls has been restored. On the face of it, this topic might seem somewhat tangential to a subject of such importance as 'the character of British politics.' Yet, in a curious way, the failure of the opinion polls accurately to predict the outcome of the 1992 election had a significant effect on the course of party politics during the following five years. Given the Conservatives' strong showing in

1992, despite the pollsters' predictions of a hung Parliament or even a Labour victory, Conservative strategists were subsequently disinclined to believe the evidence of intense public disapproval revealed in poll after poll. It was firmly believed in Conservative circles, at least until the spring of 1997, that voters' opinion poll responses largely reflected the exigencies of 'political correctness' (it was unfashionable to admit publicly to supporting the Tories) rather than any deep-seated resentment towards them, that all would come right in 'the only poll that mattered,' that on election day. The idea that the Conservatives' policies and their leadership's failure to demonstrate any managerial competence were seriously prejudicing the Conservatives' chances of re-election was not seriously entertained. As a result, instead of either shifting its policy ground or taking radical action to restore its damaged leadership reputation, the party simply blundered on, offering more of the same to a wholly disillusioned electorate. That the 1997 outcome was broadly in line with opinion poll predictions came as a considerable relief both to the pollsters and to academics who base their research on sample survey evidence. It also provided an important warning to any future government that might be tempted to disregard such evidence. For all their real and imagined failings, opinion polls remain the least unsatisfactory way of gauging the state of public opinion, on both specific policy issues and the parties' overall images. One important aspect of the democratic process is that governments endeavour to respond to the wishes of the electorate. The restoration of the pollsters' credibility in 1997 meant that any evidence they provided about voters' views and preferences would have more attention paid to it – by both government and Opposition – than had been the case, on the government side at least, after 1992.

Economic voting was transmuted during the 1992 Parliament but did not disappear. The elections of 1992 and 1997 appeared to demonstrate the irrelevance of claims that 'it's the economy, stupid' that determines election outcomes. The Conservatives won the 1992 election in the teeth of the longest recession since the 1930s. They lost in 1997 when inflation, unemployment, and interest rates were at historically low levels and were predicted to remain so by most informed observers. QED: the economy does not matter. Such an account, however, fails to acknowledge the importance of voters' economic perceptions (as opposed to official economic statistics) as sources of their electoral preferences. In April 1992, notwithstanding objective economic conditions, most voters did not hold the Major government responsible for the length and depth of the recession, and many believed that their own economic circumstances were most likely to improve if the Conservatives continued in office. Within a matter of months, however, [. . .] these perceptions had been reversed. The ERM crisis of September 1992 produced a sea change in voters' perceptions of the Conservatives as competent economic managers. In the wake of the crisis, the Conservatives lost an electoral resource that they subsequently proved unable to recover. The loss of their reputation for competence, combined with the rival and newly moderated attractions of Blair's New Labour, meant that the Conservatives failed to convert the increased economic optimism of 1996–97 into greater electoral support. Pre-election moods of economic optimism undoubtedly helped the Conservatives to achieve their election victories in 1983, 1987, and 1992. The connection then between optimism and Conservative support, however, was predicated on the Conservatives' superior reputation for economic management. With that reputation destroyed by the ERM crisis, the recovery in expectations of 1996–97 failed to translate into a

Conservative political recovery.[14] Economic perceptions still mattered in 1997, but those perceptions focused on the managerial competencies of the major parties rather than on the 'feel-good factor' that had so ably assisted the Conservatives over the previous decade.[15]

[. . .]

Notes

1   Anthony King, 'The Implications of One-Party Government,' in *Britain at the Polls, 1992,* edited by Anthony King (Chatham, N.J.: Chatham House, 1992), 223–48.
2   Ibid, 228–31.
3   This somewhat disparaging comparison (for Labour) was drawn by Andrew Marr in his *Ruling Britannia: The Failure and Future of British Democracy* (London: Michael Joseph, 1995), 42.
4   David Butler and Donald E. Stokes, *Political Change in Britain: The Evolution of Political Choice*, 2nd ed. (London: Macmillan, 1974).
5   See table 1.
6   Bo Särlvik and Ivor Crewe, *Decade of Dealignment* (Cambridge: Cambridge University Press, 1983).
7   The two separate indices are provided to reflect the different interpretations of the class–vote relationship advocated by Crewe, on the one hand, and by Heath et al., on the other. Crewe favours the use of the absolute index on grounds of its simplicity and clarity. It shows that class location has become much less important as a determinant of vote since the 1960s and reflects the fact that the decision calculus of the typical voter has changed. Heath et al., in contrast, argue that changes in the political landscape, such as the increasing role played by the Liberal (Democrat) and nationalist parties and the disastrous performance of Labour in 1983 and 1987, have obfuscated rather than eroded the class–vote relationship; they suggest that the use of a relative index takes more account of these changing circumstances. Heath et al.'s conclusion is that the 'social psychology' of voting, as reflected in the class–vote relationship, has remained broadly constant over the last 35 years. Crewe's response is that the Heath et al.'s analysis confuses cause and effect. Crewe contends that the emergence of the Liberals in the 1970s and Labour's failure in the 1980s were results of class dealignment, not factors that need to be controlled for when a suitable measure of class voting is being devised. See Ivor Crewe, 'On the Death and Resurrection of Class Voting: Some Comments on *How Britain Votes*,' *Political Studies* 35 (1986): 620–38; Ivor Crewe, 'Changing Votes and Unchanging Voters,' *Electoral Studies* 11 (1992): 335–45; Anthony Heath et al., *How Britain Votes* (London: Pergamon, 1985); Anthony Heath et al., *Understanding Political Change* (London: Pergamon, 1991).
8   Ivor Crewe, Neil Day, and Anthony Fox, *The British Electorate, 1963–1987* (Cambridge: Cambridge University Press, 1991), 47.
9   Malcolm Brynin and David Sanders, 'Party Identification, Political Preferences and Material Conditions: Evidence from the British Household Panel Survey, 1991–92,' *Party Politics* 3 (1997): 53–77.
10   Ivor Crewe et al., *The British Electorate, 1963–1987*; *Gallup Political and Economic Index.*
11   Angus Campbell et al., *The American Voter* (New York: Wiley, 1960).

12   This notion was first advanced in the British context in Hilde T. Himmelweit et al., *How Voters Decide: A Longitudinal Study of Political Attitudes and Voting Extending over Fifteen Years* (London: Academic Press, 1981).

13   Mogens N. Pederson, 'The Dynamic of European Party Systems: Changing Patterns of Electoral Volatility,' *European Journal of Political Research* 7 (1979): 1–26.

14   David Sanders, 'Economic Performance, Management Competence and the Outcome of the Next General Election,' *Political Studies* 44 (1996): 203–31.

15   David Sanders, 'Why the Conservatives Won – Again,' in King, *Britain at the Polls 1992*, 171–222.

26 The Social Backgrounds of MPs

Pippa Norris and
Joni Lovenduski

Key words

Political representation, electoral bias, political elites, party organizations, gender, social class, ethnicity, members of parliament

---

It is a matter of public concern that a far larger proportion of middle-aged, middle-class white men sit in Parliament than would be expected on the basis of their statistical distribution in the population as a whole. This extract comes from a study of the recruitment of candidates for office by political parties. It explores the 'social bias' in the composition of the House of Commons. Norris and Lovenduski try to explain why and also to ask whether it matters. Their book examines who selects candidates and for what reasons, and analyses the social characteristics of those who are selected. The research was conducted in the three years leading up to the 1992 general election. Data collected included a survey, in twenty-six constituencies, of all party members who attended meetings. Norris and Lovenduski compare the social characteristics of the electorate with four levels of activist – party members, those who apply to be selected as parliamentary candidates, the candidates actually selected, and those subsequently elected to parliament in 1992. The data are interpreted through a supply-and-demand model, distinguishing between the attributes of those who put themselves forward as candidates for office (supply) and those sought in potential candidates by committees responsible for making a selection (demand).

The extract reproduced here analyses the effects of supply and demand on the bias in social group representation among candidates in respect of class, gender and race. Norris and Lovenduski show 'that parliament includes social bias towards the younger, better educated and those in brokerage occupations, in large rt because this reflects the pool of applicants' (p.122). That, however, raises estions, addressed in other parts of their book, about why other types of people ? discouraged from applying, and whether this can be explained by lack of ources, lack of motivation or expectations of discrimination.

[. . .]

Supply-and-demand explanations of social bias

w do we explain the social bias? The 'supply-and-demand' analytical framework inguishes between the factors influencing the 'supply' of candidates willing to come ward and the factors influencing the 'demand' of party selectors in making their decisions. On the *demand-side* the model assumes selectors choose candidates depending upon judgements about applicants. There are a wide range of factors which may enter these evaluations, including assessment of personal character, formal qualifications, and political experience. Is the person an articulate speaker, who can win the audience? Does the applicant seem confident, persuasive, clear? Does he or she appear trustworthy, honest, competent? Is he going to work hard, and campaign enthusiastically, for the local party? If elected, will she stay in touch with her constituents? All these judgements may be given different weight by different party members.

Since applicants are usually not well known by most selectors, perceptions of their abilities may be influenced by direct and imputed discrimination. The term 'discrimination' is used here in a neutral sense, to mean the evaluation of individuals by their group characteristics. Discrimination can be for or against certain groups, whether barristers, miners, trade unionists, Londoners, women or blacks.

[. . .]

Demand-side explanations suggest the social bias in parliament reflects the direct and imputed discrimination of party selectors, the key gate-keepers in gaining access to good seats. These explanations are pervasive in popular thinking, and often reflected in the academic literature, although rarely subject to systematic evidence, in part because of the problems of establishing convincing proof of 'discrimination'.

But discrimination by selectors is not necessarily the most significant cause of the outcome. Party members frequently claim they would like to select more women, ethnic minorities, or manual workers, but few come forward. *Supply-side* explanations suggest the outcome reflects the supply of applicants wishing to pursue a political career. Constraints on resources (such as time, money and experience) and motivational factors (such as drive, ambition and interest) determine who aspires to Westminster. Most citizens are legally qualified to stand, but few do so given the risks and demands of life at Westminster. Supply-side explanations of the social bias in parliament suggest that outcome reflects the pool of applicants seeking a political career.

[. . .]

To operationalise this model, we can compare party strata at different levels on the ladder of recruitment. As outlined in the first chapter, we can identify five distinct groups on the ladder: voters, party members, List Applicants, candidates and MPs. Each group has progressed at different stages up the ladder.

VOTERS > MEMBERS > APPLICANTS > CANDIDATES > MPs

If supply factors are important we would expect to find significant differences between those eligible who might consider a parliamentary career (the party members) and the pool of those who come forward (the applicants on national lists). On the other hand, if demand factors are important, we would expect the main contrast to be between applicants on party lists and candidates adopted by constituencies.

[. . .]

Explaining the social bias

Occupational class

The most important and complex of the background factors is occupation. As we have seen, over time parliament has become more socially homogeneous on both sides of the aisle, with a decline in Conservative landed gentry and Labour's manual workers. Today, in common with other legislatures, the House of Commons contains a disproportionate number of those drawn from the 'talking professions', notably law, journalism, and teaching.[1] Why? Previous research provides various demand-side explanations: Ranney suggests that party members, even in the Labour party, fail to choose working class candidates because of social deference.[2] Bochel and Denver found that manual workers were seen by party members as less able and articulate.[3] Greenwood argues that attempts by Conservative Central Office to increase the number of working-class trade union candidates failed because of local party resistance.[4]

On the supply-side, previous research by Ranney explained the class bias in parliament by the resources that middle-class professional occupations provide for a political career: flexible working hours, useful political skills, social status and political contacts.[5] The most illuminating supply-side explanation, by Jacob, uses the concept of 'brokerage occupations'.[6] This suggests that parliamentary careers are facilitated by jobs which combine flexibility over time, generous vacations, interrupted career-paths, professional independence, financial security, public networks, social status, policy experience and technical skills useful in political life. Brokerage jobs – barristers, teachers, trade union officials, journalists, political researchers – are complementary to politics. They minimise the costs and risks of horizontal mobility from the economic to political marketplace, and vice versa, since being a Member of Parliament is an uncertain life.

Interview evidence tended to confirm the perceived importance of brokerage occupations. Some applicants with early political ambitions consciously chose a brokerage career which they knew could be combined with pursuit of a seat. Some faced hostile employers, even the sack,[7] while others worked for companies who encouraged employees with parliamentary ambitions, since they recognised the political advantages of contacts in Westminster. The importance of flexible brokerage jobs and sympathetic employers was stressed by many applicants. Some referred to the need for suitable 'jumping off' points into politics:

[. . .]

What I thought, rightly or wrongly, was that as a solicitor in London I could earn my living there and be an MP, because my work is basically in court in the morning, whereas if you're a barrister you have all-day cases – so it would've fitted in.[8]

The brokerage explanation helps illuminate not just the class disparity, but also why women and ethnic minorities are under-represented in parliament, since they are often concentrated in low-paying skilled and semi-skilled occupations, or in family small businesses, with inflexible schedules and long-hours, in sectors which do not provide traditional routes to political life. In order to examine the importance of *occupational class* on a systematic basis party strata are compared using the respondents' occupational socioeconomic group, summarised into manual/non-manual categories. *Work status* is included, distinguishing those in paid work from others, and *trade union* membership since it was anticipated this might prove significant in the Labour party.

The analysis in table 1 confirms the familiar observation that MPs are drawn overwhelmingly from professional and managerial occupations. The parliamentary Labour party is dominated by public sector employees: lecturers, teachers, local government managers, and welfare officers. Another significant category draws on political career jobs: political researchers, trade union officials and journalists. This category has grown substantially over time, with the rise of 'career politicians'.[9] In the Conservative ranks, there are more private sector managers, company directors, financial advisers, and barristers.

But, more importantly, the results indicate the explanation for this phenomenon: *the class bias of parliament is the product of supply rather than demand.* Within each party, the socio-economic status of MPs, candidates and applicants is almost identical. If, for argument's sake, all incumbents resigned and all applicants took their place, the social composition of the Commons would be largely unaffected. Within each party the elite has higher social status than members, while members have higher status than voters. Parliament is dominated by the professional 'chattering classes' because journalists, lawyers, self-employed businessmen, financial consultants and university lecturers have sufficient security, flexibility and income to gamble on a political career.

[. . .]

Gender

[. . .]

A comparison of the characteristics of party strata by gender indicates that supply is more important for Conservative women while demand plays a greater role in the Labour party (see Table 2). Parliament includes 20 Conservative and 37 Labour women MPs. Given this situation, some believe that Conservative party selectors, with

Table 1 | Social class, work status and union membership

		Conservative					Labour				
		MPs	PPCs	List	Members	Voters	MPs	PPCs	List	Members	Voters
Class	Professional/tech.	44	46	41	33	20	61	66	56	46	13
	Managerial/admin.	54	46	56	39	16	24	24	23	19	4
	Clerical/sales	1	6	1	22	30	1	5	11	14	19
	Skilled manual	0	1	1	4	15	11	5	6	12	19
	Semi-skill manual	0	1	1	2	19	3	1	3	9	45
Class summary	Non-manual	99	98	98	94	66	87	94	90	79	36
	Manual	1	2	2	6	34	14	6	10	21	64
Work status	In paid work	100	98	92	39	59	100	94	95	65	52
	Retired	0	0	1	30	20	0	1	2	20	14
	Employed in the home	0	1	3	22	16	0	1	2	6	15
	Other	0	1	3	10	6	0	4	1	8	19
Union member	TU/SA member	8	14	17	14	19	99	97	91	78	34
	Not TU member	91	86	83	87	81	1	3	9	22	65
Housing tenure	Owner occupier	99	93	96	92	83	98	91	86	82	52
	Not owner	1	7	4	8	17	2	9	14	18	48
N.		142	222	225	601	1,405	97	318	127	885	1,000

Note: PPC = Prospective Parliamentary Candidate; List = Applicant on the National List.
Source: BCS, 1992; BES, 1987.

Table 2 Gender, family and race

		Conservative					Labour				
		MPs	PPCs	List	Members	Voters	MPs	PPCs	List	Members	Voters
Gender	Male	94	85	87	48	48	91	74	63	60	48
	Female	6	15	13	52	52	9	26	37	40	52
Marital status	Married	88	68	73	71	69	78	64	70	77	63
	Not married	12	32	27	29	31	22	36	30	23	37
Family	Children under 16	37	30	46	15	31	35	48	42	34	35
	None	63	70	54	85	69	65	52	58	66	65
Ethnicity	White	100	99	98		99	98	99	96	96	93
	Non-white	0	1	2		1	2	1	4	4	7
N.		142	222	225	601	1,405	97	318	127	885	1,000

Source: BCS, 1992; BES, 1987.

traditional family values, must be prejudiced against women. But the proportion of women Conservative candidates and applicants is about the same, which suggests that women party members are reluctant to pursue a Westminster career. Conservative women form the majority of the grassroots party, the backbone of the organisation in terms of constituency officeholders, the participants at party conference, but they are not coming forward in equal numbers to stand for parliament. The most plausible explanation is that many women members are middle-aged with traditional roles in the home, or elderly pensioners, with few formal educational qualifications. This generational difference was well expressed by a Conservative woman MP:

> There was an older generation than us, who didn't approve of us being political. They thought we should do the coffee mornings and the committees and all that sort of thing. And I think we, and I would say most of us in our forties and thirties, when we came along and were stridently political, this was a shock to them.

In the Labour party women have made considerable progress in parliament, almost doubling their numbers in the last general election, to comprise 13.6 per cent of Labour MPs. Yet, contrary to popular assumptions, women seem to face greater problems from Labour than Conservative party selectors. In the Labour party, women numbered 40 per cent of individual members, and about the same proportion (37 per cent) of applicants, but only 26 per cent of candidates. Thus more Labour women are coming forward than are being selected. The main reason for this, our interviewees suggested, was that more men had trade union connections which helped in terms of sponsorship and informal constituency contacts, an explanation which needs to be explored further.

Race

[...]

Our comparison of the characteristics of party strata confirms that in the Conservative party the main problem is probably supply-side: very few non-whites are active within the party at any level. Among those who do come forward, non-whites are relatively successful at getting on the approved list of applicants, and becoming candidates. In the Labour party the problems of supply and demand are combined. In absolute terms there are more non-white candidates and MPs in the Labour party. In relative terms, a lower proportion of black Labour applicants succeeds in becoming candidates.[10]

[...]

Notes

1   See Mellors, *The British MP*, Burch and Moran, 'The Changing Political Elite'.
2   Austin Ranney, *Pathways to Parliament*, p. 119; W. L. Guttsman, *The British Political Elite*, p. 27.

3 John Bochel and David Denver, 'Candidate Selection in the Labour Party: What the Selectors Seek', *British Journal of Political Science*, 13 (1983), p. 56.
4 John Greenwood, 'Promoting Working-class Candidature in the Conservative Party'.
5 Ranney, *Pathways to Parliament*, p. 4.
6 H. Jacob, 'The Initial Recruitment of Elected Officials in the US – A Model', *Journal of Politics*, 24 (1962).
7 One Conservative candidate reported being fired by an unsympathetic employer for requesting leave of absence to fight the campaign: 'They said to me they wanted me gone as soon as the election was called. So I had to face that election with absolutely nothing. It was terrible when you've got that at the back of your mind. You've got all the excitement of the campaign but I knew there was no job at the end of that.'
8 Interview No. 7.
9 See Peter Riddell, *Honest Opportunism: The Rise of the Career Politician* (London, Hamish Hamilton, 1993).
10 See Norris, Geddes and Lovenduski, 'Race and Parliamentary Representation' for more details.

References

Bochel, John and Denver, David. 'Candidate Selection in the Labour Party: What the Selectors Seek', *British Journal of Political Science*, 13, pp. 45–69.
Burch, M. and Moran, M. 'The Changing Political Elite', *Parliamentary Affairs*, 38 (1985), pp. 1–15.
Greenwood, John. 'Promoting Working-Class Candidatures in the Conservative Party: The Limits of Central Office Power', *Parliamentary Affairs*, 41, 4 (October 1988), pp. 456–68.
Guttsman, W. L. *The British Political Elite* (London, MacGibbon and Kee, 1968).
Mellors, Colin. *The British MP: A Socio-Economic Study of the House of Commons* (Farnborough, Hants, Saxon House, 1978).
Norris, Pippa, Geddes, Andrew and Lovenduski, Joni. 'Race and Parliamentary Representation', in Pippa Norris, et al. (eds), *British Parties and Elections Yearbook 1992* (Hemel Hempstead, Harvester Wheatsheaf, 1992).
Ranney, Austin. *Pathways to Parliament: Candidate Selection in Britain* (London, Macmillan, 1965).
Riddell, Peter. *Honest Opportunism: The Rise of the Career Politician* (London, Hamish Hamilton, 1993).

27 | Citizenship and Sexuality

Diane Richardson

Key words

Citizenship, politics, gender, sexuality, heterosexuality, gay, lesbian

To be a citizen is to be accepted as a full member of a political entity, most usually today a nation state. This is normally expressed as commonly shared, equal rights and obligations among all members of the political community. There has recently been much reflection on the concept of citizenship, with consideration of which rights are relevant to full membership of the community, and whether in fact all groups in the population are treated equally.

Diane Richardson's article begins by outlining several different definitions of citizenship, before examining whether gays and lesbians can be said to be treated equally as citizens. She identifies four different definitions. The classic definition, deriving from T.H. Marshall, argues that there are three sets of citizenship rights, civil, political and social. These refer to equality before the law, equal right to a political voice, most notably the right to vote, and the right to a certain level of welfare and economic security. This view ignores several other attributes of social membership, however. One might have formal rights without actually being rec- ognized as belonging to the national community, being identified as in some way a second-class citizen. Or one might be denied full membership of the community because one lacks some cultural attributes defined as appropriate for membership, a matter of importance in a multicultural society. And finally, it has been argued that because mass consumption is so central to social life, equal social participa- tion requires protection of certain consumer rights.

Richardson takes each of these definitions of citizenship and examines how well they are met with respect to people who are not heterosexual. She considers the

various ways in which gays and lesbians are granted fewer rights or are excluded in certain respects from full membership of the political community. Her analysis also considers some of the ways in which gender and ethnicity intersect with sexuality as bases of unequal treatment within the UK.

[. . .]

Within discourses of citizen's rights and the principle of universal citizenship the normal citizen has largely been constructed as male and, albeit much less discussed or acknowledged in the literature, as heterosexual (Warner 1993; Phelan 1995). This latter point is evidenced when the association of heterosexuality with citizenship status, as national identity say, is challenged or threatened. To illustrate this I will give an example under each of the definitions of citizenship [. . .] already outlined.

Within the traditional and dominant model of citizenship as a set of *civil, political and social rights* it can be argued that lesbians and gay men are only partial citizens, in so far as they are excluded from certain of these rights. This is evidenced by attempts to get equal rights such as, for example, formal marriages and similar legal status within the armed forces, with heterosexuals. A further aspect of civil citizenship, which relates to Marshall's conception of the right to justice, is the lack of protection in law from discrimination or harassment on the grounds of sexuality.

Turning to political citizenship, although lesbians and gay men are not denied the vote and are a part of the electorate, their ability to exercise political power is limited. The knowledge that someone is lesbian or gay has long been seen as a positive disadvantage, if not a disqualifier, for political office (see Hemmings 1980), although the number of 'out' MPs successfully fighting seats in the 1997 election suggests there are signs that this may be changing. Similarly, the incorporation of lesbian and gay concerns within mainstream politics occurs very rarely at both local and national levels. (See Carabine 1995 for a discussion of some of the factors which influence the reluctance to include such issues at local government level.) On the contrary, political parties are often at pains to distance themselves from being seen to be connected with lesbian and gay causes. For example, speaking on the financial support given to lesbian and gay organisations by the National Lottery Charities Board, the then British prime minster, John Major, commented: 'A small number (of grant awards) do not in my judgement reflect the way Parliament and the public expected lottery money to be spent' (*The Guardian*, 12 June 1996). Similarly the Labour party has at times sought to rid itself of the 'loony left' image which, fuelled by the association of certain Labour councils with lesbian and gay rights, was used by the Conservatives to discredit them (Stacey 1991). In a political context when mention of advocacy for lesbians and gay men is perceived as an 'electoral liability', it is far from clear that lesbians and gay men 'can ever expect British parliamentarianism to recognise our demands for civil rights across a wide range of institutions' (Watney 1991:175). It is this kind of denial of membership that has led some writers to claim that one of the main issues for lesbian and gay politics is recognition as members of the political community (Phelan 1995).

Social citizenship tends to be interpreted in terms of the social rights of welfare, and once again lesbians and gay men have highlighted their disadvantaged position. For example, same-sex relationships are not officially recognised or sanctioned, affecting pension rights, inheritance rights, as well as denying same-sex couples the tax perks that married couples are entitled to. Other areas where access to full social citizenship is (hetero)sexualised include education, parenting, employment, and housing (Rosenbloom 1996a).

British law and social policy currently denies lesbians and gay men full citizenship, what Anya Palmer refers to as the 'sexual equivalent of apartheid' (Palmer 1995:33). Nevertheless, the dominant ideology of Western capitalist societies has been receptive to certain lesbian and gay rights claims, primarily through the construction of lesbians and gay men as a minority group, different and *less than* the norm, but who cannot help 'being that way' and therefore should not be discriminated against on that basis. A classic example of this rationale is the 1967 Sexual Offences Act, which decriminalised consensual sexual acts between men over the age of 21 in 'private'.[1] Legitimate claims to citizenship are here grounded in essentialist understandings of sexuality and a liberal human rights framework. Indeed, the term commonly used in anti-discrimination laws and equal opportunity policies is 'sexual orientation', itself an essentialist concept. (It is also a concept which erases the gendered nature of citizenship in collapsing lesbian and gay men's claim to equal rights under one category.)

Lesbians and gay men are, then, seen as deserving of certain rights and protections in many Western countries; however the terms on which these 'rights and protections' are 'granted' are the terms of partial citizenship (Richardson, 2000a). Lesbians and gay men are entitled to certain rights of existence, but these are extremely circumscribed, being constructed largely on the condition that they remain in the private sphere and do not seek public recognition or membership in the political community. In this sense lesbians and gay men, though granted certain rights of citizenship, are not a legitimate social constituency.

This is a model of citizenship based on a politics of tolerance and assimilation. Lesbians and gay men are granted the right to be tolerated as long as they stay within the boundaries of that tolerance, whose borders are maintained through a heterosexist public/private divide. Furthermore, the expectation is that lesbians and gay men should remain minority groups. As 'good citizens', they should not increase in numbers either through, in the words of Section 28 of the 1988 Local Government Act, 'promoting homosexuality' or by raising children whom, it is feared, might grow up to have lesbian or gay relationships themselves (Sedgwick 1993).

This construction of lesbian and gay relations as belonging to the private sphere does suggest a difficulty in addressing citizenship using conventional frameworks which focus almost exclusively on participation in the public. The role of the public/private structuring of social relations in the exclusion of women from full access to the rights of citizenship has been highlighted by feminist theory (Lister 1990, 1996; Walby 1994). Such analyses have critiqued traditional conceptions of citizenship which use the private/public divide to draw a boundary around what can usefully be discussed in relation to claims to citizenship. For most social and political theorists, as Sylvia Walby (1994:389) remarks, 'The concept of citizenship depends upon the public; the term has no significant meaning in the private'. Taken to its logical conclusion, this would mean that social relations in the private sphere are considered to be of little or no relevance to understanding citizenship.

There is an interesting tension in the use of the term 'private' to demarcate the boundaries of (homo)sexual citizenship. Whilst lesbians and gay men are banished from the public to the private realm they are, in many senses, simultaneously excluded from the private where this is conflated with 'the family'. As Alan Sinfield argues (1995), the state withholds various rights of citizenship, 'especially in familial and quasi-familial contexts (partnerships; childbearing, entertainment in the home)', which are facets of the private sphere where, in the ideology of the public/private divide, lesbians and gay men are supposedly 'licensed'. Thus, notions of privacy, as well as of public space, are exclusionary; the right to privacy being primarily a right of legally married heterosexuals. In this sense, both the public and the private need to be understood as sexualised concepts.

If we take citizenship to mean *social membership of a nation state*, it would appear that even though lesbians and gay men are legal citizens of different 'nations', they are normally excluded from the construction of 'nation' and nationality. According to Taylor (1996:162), citizenship carries with it,

> not just the formal membership of a nation state, but a whole set of socio-economic and ideological practices associated with nationalism. These amount to mechanisms of exclusion and inclusion of particular groups and categories of individual. These have included, most notably, those without property, women, racialised groups and the differently abled, children and lesbians and gay men.

In many if not most nation-states citizenship is associated with heterosexuality. As David Sibley (1995:108) suggests in relation to Britain, we can recognise a number of 'key sites of nationalistic sentiment, including the family, the suburb and the countryside, all of which implicitly exclude black people, gays and nomadic minorities from the nation.' That is, it is implicitly the heterosexual (as well as white and non-nomadic) citizen who symbolises an imagined national community and underlies the construction of a notion of a shared collective national identity.

This is evidenced in a variety of ways. For example, the term 'homosexual' has long been associated with the charge of treachery and treason (Edelman 1992), usually 'justified' with the claim that homosexuals are liable to blackmail (Ellis 1991). This image of 'the homosexual' as a potential traitor has been used to signal fear of a threat to national security. Hence, this particular historical construction of homosexuality, based upon a presumed risk of betrayal, undermines the position of 'homosexuals' as legitimate members of a particular nation-state.

In Britain homosexuality has been perceived as a threat to the nation-state in other respects. A common version of this is the claim that the heterosexual family, which is frequently conceptualised as both natural and necessary for the good of the nation, is being undermined and destroyed by the emergence of different sexualities and family networks. The traditional family therefore needs defending against lesbians and gay men and other groups, such as single mothers, who supposedly pose a threat to it (Stacey 1991; Thomson 1994; Donovan, Heaphy and Weeks 1999). Appealing to such arguments, some politicians and policy-makers have justified the introduction of laws which are hostile to lesbian and gay relationships. For example, David Wiltshire, the member of parliament responsible for introducing Section 28 of the 1988 Local Government Act which outlawed the 'promotion' of homosexuality in local authority schools, claimed that his actions were motivated by the principle of supporting normality: 'Homosexuality is being promoted at the ratepayers' expense, and the traditional family as we know it is under attack' (*The Guardian*, 12 December 1987). This not only implies that lesbians and gay men are not ratepayers but also, as a consequence, suggests that they are not deserving of social services from local authorities (Carabine 1996).

[...]

Finally, if we take citizenship as social membership to mean 'humanity', belonging to what is called the human 'race', even then it can be argued that citizenship is premised within heterosexuality. Historically, there is a long tradition of understanding what it is to be human in essentialist terms. The term human is commonly used to refer to group membership based on biological criteria; the belonging to a particular species. Although this way of thinking continues to exert influence, within social theory the view has emerged that humanity should be thought of as socially constructed. In other words, we become human, through the process of social interaction whereby the categorisations 'person' and 'human' are attributed to individuals (Shotter 1993).

This is significant in terms of understandings of citizenship as social membership, for it suggests that, even at the most fundamental levels of social inclusion, the boundaries of membership are a cultural construction. Thus it is possible for people to be constructed as 'other' through relegation to the borders of human existence. One example of this process of dehumanisation is through the claiming of animal attributes for certain groups, thereby legitimising exclusionary practices on the grounds that they are less than human. This has been particularly evident in relation to the representation of colonised people, especially Australian Aborigines and African slaves, as well as other groups such as Jews and Gypsy communities (Sibley 1995).

Such dehumanising processes of exclusion can also be observed in relation to gender and sexuality. In so far as women have often been identified as closer to 'nature', they have also been at risk of exclusion from 'civilised' society. The interaction of gender with 'race', ethnicity and class has been important in this respect; it is particular groups of women, for example Black and working-class women, who have traditionally been represented as closest to nature and therefore lower ranking in a 'hierarchy of being' (Sibley 1995). Interestingly, whereas in the example cited above the processes of dehumanisation operate through the exclusion of those deemed to be closest to nature, and more 'animal-like', in the case of sexuality it also operates to exclude those who are not a part of nature so defined (as heterosexual) who are constructed as un-natural (as homosexual). The naturalisation of heterosexuality not only serves to dehumanise lesbians and gay men, it also provides the context in which the right to existence of lesbians and gay men may be questioned (see War on Want 1996, Amnesty 1997; Richardson and May 1999).

At an institutional level, processes of de-personalisation and dehumanisation can have important implications for access to the rights of civil, political and social citizenship. For example, despite appeals to universalism in speaking of basic human rights, conventional human rights frameworks have been selective in their use of this term. The women's human rights movement has demonstrated a number of different ways in which the dominant human rights discourse fails to address human rights abuses against women (Peters and Wolper 1995; Rosenbloom 1996b). Despite this, there is growing acceptance of women's rights as human rights; where there has been less progress is in addressing human rights violations against lesbians and gay men (Rosenbloom 1996a). The struggle to get lesbian and gay rights recognised as human rights reveals the way in which the concept of 'human rights' has historically developed in ways that have failed to recognise many of the abuses perpetrated against certain social groups. It also raises the question of whether such discourses serve not only to authorise which human rights claims are recognised as basic to humanity, but also to actively shape the social meaning and construction of what it means to be a 'person' who is recognised, to greater or lesser extent, as 'human'. In this sense we can understand the demand for lesbian and gay rights as a struggle not only about rights *per se*, but also about what those rights signify; as 'a struggle for membership in the human community' (Herman 1994:19).

Definitions of citizenship in terms of *cultural citizenship* also raise questions about the sexualised, as well as gendered, nature of social inclusion and exclusion and access to 'rights and entitlements'. (I have discussed the relationship between cultural citizenship and sexuality in more detail elsewhere (Richardson 2000b).) Historically, lesbian and gay relationships have been systematically denied and ignored in popular culture; existing only in covert or disguised articulations or, in the rare cases where lesbian and gay themes are made explicit, in highly negative and unidimensional representations. For example, in a comprehensive survey of images of lesbians and gays in films, Vito Russo (1981) found only a handful of examples, 'all of which only figure momentarily in the films and some of which you could easily not see as representing gays or lesbians at all' (Dyer 1990:7). Critiques of such stereotyped and negative representations have been an important concern of both feminist and gay movements since the 1970s. Although rarely expressed in terms of rights to cultural citizenship, such resistance has led to the production of more positive images and texts in a range of cultural sites.

In recent years, there has been a gradual increase in the participation and representation of lesbians and gay men in the media and popular culture, perhaps most noticeably on television, for instance in primetime 'soaps' such as *Brookside* and *East-Enders*, in Britain, and *Friends* and *Ellen*, in the United States. The significance attached to such sociological shifts is that whereas previously the focus of lesbian and gay representation was largely subcultural, as a result of cultural efforts by and for lesbians and gay men themselves, it is now increasingly mainstream (Cottingham 1996). At one level, it is possible to regard the inclusion of lesbian and gay images and narratives in dominant culture as constituting an important form of social recognition and access to cultural citizenship. However, such an interpretation is questioned by those who argue that the greater visibility of lesbians and gay men in mainstream cultural life is less an acknowledgement of cultural rights than evidence of a process of commodification and asssimilation into dominant culture (see, for example, Clark 1993; Torres 1993; Cottingham 1996). That is, cultural space is still normatively constructed as heterosexual. This is evidenced in responses to greater coverage of lesbians and gay issues in the media. Thus, for example, one newspaper editorial complained: 'Radio Five is devoting a weekly programme to homosexuals and lesbians. Why should this minority get so much special attention?' (*Daily Star*, 15 March 1994, quoted in Sanderson 1995:34).

Paradoxically, it is when we come to define *citizenship as consumerism* that 'non-heterosexuals' seem to be most acceptable as citizens, as consumers with identities and lifestyles which are expressed through purchasing goods, communities and services. This has often been referred to as the power of the 'pink pound', although this commercialisation has been predominantly Western and male. However, in the last few years there have been signs of a new commercialism associated with lesbians as consumers (Woods 1995).

What are the links between rights as consumers and other citizenship rights? Some regard this new 'commercial power' of lesbians and gay men as productively linked to access to other forms of citizenship; such as the development of social rights and entitlements (Evans 1993). Others take a more critical view of the extent to which the growth of 'pink capital' can help promote lesbian and gay rights (Woods 1995). Thus, for example, Jon Johnson points out that 'you cannot "consume" yourself out of being sacked purely because of your sexuality, being demonised because you are a lesbian teacher or jailed for having sex at the age of 17' (Johnson 1994:14; quoted in Binnie 1995).

Also, as with the other aspects of citizenship that have been considered, access to the right to consume is both a gendered and sexualised experience. Lesbians and gay men may be free to consume but only within certain spatial and cultural boundaries. The boundaries of citizenship as consumerism are the limits to where, when and how we can consume lesbian and gay 'lifestyles'; the boundaries of (heterosexual) tolerance and of 'public spaces' in which consumer communities can exercise their right to consume. Jon Binnie (1995) illustrates this in his discussion of the development of gay commercial districts in London and Amsterdam. It is also important to recognise, in considering the role of the market in sexual cultures, that consumer citizenship is significantly structured by access to time and money; a point that has been made earlier in terms of the limitations on women's effective participation in various forms of citizenship (Lister 1990, 1996).

[. . .]

Note

1   At the time of writing the current (unequal) legal age of consent for sexual relations between two men stands at 18 years of age.

References

AMNESTY INTERNATIONAL UNITED KINGDOM 1997. *Breaking the Silence: Human Rights Violations Based on Sexual Orientation*. London: Amnesty International United Kingdom.

BINNIE, J. 1995. 'Trading Places: Consumption, Sexuality and the Production of Queer Space', in D. Bell and G. Valentine (eds.), *Mapping Desire: Geographies of Sexualities*. London: Routledge.

CARABINE, J. 1995. 'Invisible Sexualities: Sexuality, Politics and Influencing Policymaking', in A.R. Wilson (ed.), *A Simple Matter of Justice? Theorizing Lesbian and Gay Politics*. London: Cassell.

—— 1996. 'Heterosexuality and Social Policy', in D. Richardson (ed.), *Theorising Heterosexuality*. Buckingham: Open University Press.

CLARK, D. 1993. 'Commodity Lesbianism', in H. Abelove, M.A. Barale and D.M. Halperin (eds), *The Lesbian and Gay Studies Reader*. London: Routledge.

COTTINGHAM, L. 1996. *Lesbians Are So Chic . . . That We Are Not Really Lesbians at All*. London: Cassell.

DONOVAN, C., HEAPHY, B. and WEEKS, J. 1999. 'Citizenship and same sex relationships', *Journal of Social Policy* 28:4, 689–709.

DYER, R. 1990. *Now You See It: Studies on Lesbian and Gay Film*. London: Routledge.

EDELMAN, L. 1992. 'Tearooms and Sympathy, or, the Epistemology of the Water Closet', in A. Parker, M. Russo, D. Sommer and P. Yaeger (eds), *Nationalisms and Sexualities*. London: Routledge.

ELLIS, C. 1991. 'Sisters and Citizens', in G. Andrews (ed.), *Citizenship*. London: Lawrence & Wishart.

EVANS, D. 1993. *Sexual Citizenship. The Material Construction of Sexualities*. London: Routledge.

HEMMINGS, S. 1980. 'Horrific Practices: How Lesbians were presented in the Newspapers of 1978', in Gay Left Collective (eds), *Homosexuality: Power and Politics*. London: Allison and Busby.

HERMAN, D. 1994. *Rights of Passage: Struggles for Lesbian and Gay Equality*. Toronto: University of Toronto Press.

JOHNSON, J. 1994. 'Politics and Passion, or Pilsner and Porn?', *Rouge* 16:14.

LISTER, R. 1990. 'Women, Economic Dependency and Citizenship', *Journal of Social Policy*, 19:445–68.

—— 1996. 'Citizenship Engendered', in D. Taylor (ed.), *Critical Social Policy: A Reader*. London: Sage.

PALMER, A. 1995. 'Lesbian and Gay Rights Campaigning: A Report from the Coalface', in A.R. Wilson (ed.), *A Simple Matter of Justice? Theorizing Lesbian and Gay Politics*. London: Cassell.

PETERS, J.S. and WOLPER, A. 1995. *Women's Rights, Human Rights: International Feminist Perspectives*. London: Routledge.

PHELAN, S. 1995. 'The Space of Justice: Lesbians and Democratic Politics', in A.R. Wilson (ed.), *A Simple Matter of Justice? Theorizing Lesbran and Gay Politics*. London: Cassell.

RICHARDSON, D. 2000a. 'Constructing sexual citizenship: theorising sexual rights', *Critical Social Policy* 20:7:105–35.

—— 2000b. 'Extending Citizenship: Cultural Citizenship and Sexuality', in N. Stevenson (ed.), *Cultural Citizenship*. London: Sage.

—— and MAY, H. 1999. 'Deserving Victims?'; sexual status and the social construction of violence', *Sociological Review*, 47:2:308–31.

ROSENBLOOM, R. (ed.) 1996a. *Unspoken Rules: Sexual Orientation and Women's Human Rights*. London: Cassell.

—— 1996b. 'Introduction', in R. Rosenbloom (ed.), *Unspoken Rules: Sexual Orientation and Women's Human Rights*. London: Cassell.

RUSSO, V. 1981. *The Celluloid Closet: Homosexuality in the Movies*. New York: Harper & Row.

SANDERSON, T. 1995. *Mediawatch: The Treatment of Male and Female Homosexuality in the British Media*. London: Cassell.

SEDGWICK, E.K. 1993. 'How to Bring Your Kids Up Gay', in M. Warner (ed.), *Fear of a Queer Planet: Queer Politics and Social Theory*. Minneapolis: University of Minnesota Press.

SHOTTER, J. 1993. 'Psychology and Citizenship: Identity and Belonging', in B.S. Turner (ed.), *Citizenship and Social Theory*. London: Sage.

SIBLEY, D. 1995. *Geographies of Exclusion: Society and Difference in the West*. London: Routledge.

SINFIELD, A. 1995. 'Diaspora and Hybridity: Queer Identities and the Ethnicity Model', paper presented at the Changing Sexualities conference, Middlesex University, July.

STACEY, J. 1991. 'Promoting Normality: Section 28 and the Regulation of Sexuality', in Sarah Franklin, Celia Lury and Jackie Stacey (eds), *Off Centre: Feminism and Cultural Studies*. London: Unwin Hyman.

TAYLOR, D. 1996. 'Citizenship and Social Power', in D. Taylor (ed.), *Critical Social Policy: A Reader*. London: Sage.

THOMSON, R. 1994. *Feminist Review*, 48:40–61.

TORRES, S. 1993. 'Prime Time Lesbianism', in H. Abelove, M.A. Barale and D.M. Halperin (eds), *The Lesbian and Gay Studies Reader*. London: Routledge.

WALBY, S. 1994. 'Is Citizenship Gendered?', *Sociology*, 28:379–95.

WARNER, M. (ed.) 1993. *Fear of a Queer Planet: Queer Politics and Social Theory*. Minneapolis: University of Minnesota Press.

WAR ON WANT 1996. *Pride World-Wide: Sexuality, Development and Human Rights*. London: War on Want.

WATNEY, S. 1991. 'Citizenship in the Age of AIDS', in G. Andrews (ed.). *Citizenship*. London: Lawrence and Wishart.

WOOD, C. 1995. *State of the Queer Nation: A Critique of Gay and Lesbian Politics in 1990s Britain*. London: Cassell.

<table>
<tr><td>

28

</td><td>

Social Class and Choice of Secondary Schooling

Sharon Gewirtz, Stephen Ball and Richard Bowe

</td></tr>
</table>

Key words

Privatization of economic organizations, working class families, welfare provision, cultural captial, marketization, consumption, schooling

Markets, Choice and Equity in Education* *is a detailed study of the processes through which parents select a secondary school for their children. The Education Reform Act of 1988 set out to increase parental choice by introducing quasi-market mechanisms into the procedures for allocating secondary school places. Local catchment areas were abolished and parents could seek to enrol their children in any school of their choice. Gewirtz, Ball and Bowe interviewed parents in London to discover how the new system worked. They analyse their results using the categories of Pierre Bourdieu, who stressed that differences not only of economic, but also of cultural capital, reproduce class inequality. Cultural capital comes from family cultural background, educational experience and general familiarity with the nuances of dominant, legitimate cultural forms. The chapter from which the extract is drawn uses data from interviews to describe three different approaches to the search for a secondary school. We have used the illustration of the third approach, that of 'the disconnected', working-class families who were reluctant to engage with the opportunities to view and evaluate options, which was the intention of the new system. The authors argue that replacing the previous system of allocation to local schools with market mechanisms privileges pupils with parents who have the skills and resources to obtain information, compare schools and negotiate with head teachers. These arrangements effectively secure*

---

* This study is described in more depth in N. Abercrombie and A. Warde et al. (2000), *Contemporary British Society*, pp. 445–7.

better opportunities for children from families who have most cultural capital, those with middle-class parents.

[. . .]

In this chapter we [. . .] consider precisely how cultural resources are used in the processes of school choice, in particular social contexts and what their effects are. There are two substantive points of focus, although these are strongly interrelated. The first is on the processes of, and constraints upon, choice-making. The second is on the role of choice in the maintenance of social class-related distinctions and educational differentiations.

[. . .]

Our contextual analysis of choice and class goes to the heart of the ideology of the market and the claims of classlessness and neutrality. Choice emerges as a major new factor in maintaining and indeed reinforcing social-class divisions and inequalities. The point is not that choice and the market have moved us away from what was a smoothly functioning egalitarian system of schooling to one that is unfair. That is crude and unrealistic. There were significant processes of differentiation and choice prior to 1988 (within and between schools). Some skilful and resourceful parents were always able to 'work the system' or buy a private education or gain other forms of advantage for their children. But post-1988, the stratagems of competitive advantage are now ideologically endorsed and practically facilitated by open enrolment, the deregulation of recruitment and parental choice. Well-resourced choosers now have free rein to guarantee and reproduce, as best they can, their existing cultural, social and economic advantages in the new complex and blurred hierarchy of schools. Class selection is revalorized by the market.

The substance of this chapter draws heavily upon our interviews with parents of Year 6 children (10–11 years) who were in the process of 'choosing' a secondary school for their child. [. . .] Three sets of interviews were conducted, in the years 1991–2, 1992–3 and 1993–4. The interviews were spread across three 'clusters' of 'competing' secondary schools. However, the extracts from interviews quoted below are more than usually inadequate in what they can convey; they are very much ripped out of context and lose impact and effect as a result. Choice-making is typically accounted for by parents in terms of long narratives or a complex social calculus of contradictions, compromises and constraints. The quotations are representative examples only – to provide a sense of things (see Gewirtz et al., 1993). Both presences and absences in the data are important to our argument, what is said and what is not said by families in different class groups.

Class choosing

Our analysis is structured by the presentation of three types of chooser identified within the data set: the *privileged/skilled chooser*, the *semi-skilled chooser* and the *discon-*

nected chooser. The typology is strongly class-related: the disconnected choosers are overwhelming working class; the privileged/skilled choosers are overwhelmingly middle class; and the semi-skilled are a mixed-class group. Perhaps in Bourdieu's terms, the privileged may be seen as 'inheritors' and the semi-skilled as 'newcomers'. But there are exceptions to the general pattern: as we know, class is an indicator rather than a determinant of family traits. Further, significant social and economic changes over the past twenty years mean that social-class categorizations are increasingly slippery and difficult to apply. While the class references here, and the relationships between class and choice, are presented fairly simply and straightforwardly, as Bourdieu suggests they rest upon 'a network of secondary characteristics' like age, gender and race. However, our central point throughout is that choice is thoroughly social, it is a process powerfully informed by the lives people lead and their biographies – in short, their position within a social network. Differences in choice-making are not a matter of relative deficiencies or of social pathology in which certain parents are less responsible, or efficient or effective choosers. Our use of the term 'skill' is intended to denote particular cultural capacities which are unevenly distributed across the population but which are valorized by the operation of the education market. In Bourdieu's terms, the market constitutes a particular cultural arbitrary which presupposes 'possession of the cultural code required for the decoding of the objects displayed' (Bourdieu and Passeron, 1990: 51–2).

We want to underline the point that the categories generated by our analysis are ideal types rather than naturalistic categories. Nonetheless, they represent certain very clear trends, relationships and patterns in the data. Thus, the majority of families interviewed fit well within the ideal types, although a few families display contradictory or mixed qualities or dimensions in their choice-making. We nevertheless wish to argue that the types illustrate or allude to a 'singular configuration' of explanatory factors related to school choice.

[...]

The disconnected – 'choice as necessity'

This type of chooser approximates to those parents Vincent (1993) describes as 'detached'. They are disconnected from the market in the sense that they are not inclined to engage with it. It is not that these parents have no views about education, or no concerns about schools and their children's experiences and achievements. They do, but they do not see their children's enjoyment of school or their educational success as being facilitated in any way by a consumerist approach to school choice. For these parents, the idea of examining a wide range of schools is not something which enters their frame of thinking. Whereas skilled/privileged parents sometimes find the many differences between schools somewhat baffling, the disconnected parents typically see schools as much the same.

> I think they are much of a muchness really. Perhaps one may have a better library, another one may have better sports facilities, but we've decided we're going to look at the two schools, and as long as there's nothing academically vastly different or better with one school then David [son] can make the final choice. We feel he's got to be happy.
>
> (Mrs Sutcliffe, 28 September 1993)

While the skilled/privileged choosers often ended with two possible schools from their process of elimination and comparison, the disconnected almost always began with, and limited themselves to, two. These would be schools in close physical proximity and part of their social community. There is little or no attempt to collect information about other schools and little awareness of other schools apart from those within the locality. Choice here means something different from the process gone through by the privileged or the semi-skilled. Choice for these parents typically seems more or less predetermined, often a process of confirmation rather than comparison. The reasons articulated in interviews are normally the reasons for the choice that is made rather than an account of a process of choosing. Visits to schools were often for the purpose of seeing the school already selected – 'a look around' – rather than part of a choice-making process. There is even sometimes a degree of haphazardness or chance to 'the choice':

> We didn't know the area and we'd heard . . . all things . . . You hear some people say, 'This school is good, no that school's good'. So in the end we thought we'd wait and see what came and, as it was, the very first thing that happened was that Tania's [daughter] school organized a visit to the local school down here, Lymethorpe, and the whole class went off for the morning . . . She came back saying she . . . had a very good time.
>
> (Mr Tufnell, 30 January 1992)

That was how Tania came to choose Lymethorpe. There is a reactive response to events here rather than the proactive or demanding engagement typical of the skilled/privileged. In a few cases choice is abdicated altogether to the child. The Fairlops were a case in point:

> We didn't think it was worth going too far . . . so it was really, for closeness I suppose, it was a choice of two schools, Parsons and Flightpath. And most of her friends were going to Parsons, which surprised me why she chose Flightpath, but she chose Flightpath and that was it. I mean, we didn't go to look at any of them . . . We wasn't really that bothered as I say . . . because to me, all schools are the same. I mean I'd have liked her to have gone to the same school I went to, because I liked it there, but it's a bit further still than Flightpath school, so she'd have had to have caught a bus or something, every morning, messing about like that. As I say, we left it to her and she chose Flightpath, so we were quite happy with it.
>
> (Mr Fairlop, 16 December 1992)

The happiness of the child is of great importance to this type of chooser, but happiness is generally a matter of social adjustment, friendship and engagement with 'the local', rather than the achievement of long-term goals or the realization of specific talents,

> I think he's always just thought, well I'll go to Lymethorpe.
>
> (Mrs Dublin, 28 September 1993)

Again, as with the semi-skilled, this is sometimes related to a fatalism about schools and about achievement, the idea that achievement is about doing your best and waiting to see what will happen. This is also rooted in the idea that schools are all basically the same and is all part of what Bourdieu (1986: 380–1) describes as resignation, realism and closure:

> The second one is doing better than the eldest one, she's quite bright, the second one, but it's not the school.
>
> (Mrs Stockwell, 22 November 1992)

This kind of perspective may be grounded in a belief that the child's willingness or ability to learn is fixed and innate, regardless of the learning environment (Carspecken, 1990; Vincent, pers. comm.).

Disconnected parents want a 'good' education for their children in their local school and do not see the need (nor do they necessarily have the resources) to 'seek out' a 'good' education elsewhere. A 'good' education is not measured by the examination performances of schools: examination results were not used to discriminate between schools nor did an awareness of poor results lead to rejection. Indeed, examinations were rarely mentioned without prompting.

> *Researcher*: Did you look at things like exam results?
>
> *Mr Tufnell*: Not particularly, because they really didn't mean anything to me, because he goes to school, he does his best, if he doesn't pass then it won't be for the want of trying ... so he can only do his best and it really doesn't matter to me, how many – like Flightpath [school], even if it had a very poor record I would still send him there, because they've got the stuff there to do the job, and if the teachers are training the kids, you can't blame the teachers if the kids can't learn, do you see what I mean?
>
> (Interview, 30 November 1992)

Factors such as facilities, distance, safety, convenience and locality are of prime concern to the disconnected chooser. In contrast to the issues of child personality, grouping, school policy and teaching methods talked about by the skilled/privileged, this is a realm of material matters. This then is class-choosing of a different kind.

These parents might be described as working on the surface structure of choice, because their programmes of perception rest on a basic unfamiliarity with particular aspects of schools and schooling. Usually this type of chooser left school early themselves and has little confidence in their ability to understand or interpret the language of teachers. They are more confident with the material realities of plant and facilities. Thus, Mrs Debden clearly knew something about her local school and was impressed with the building and equipment but nevertheless felt herself 'bamboozled' by 'what they were saying to us'. As Mrs Perivale put it, 'what do I look for?'

> They had a lot more to offer, Flightpath [school], but when we went round there on the open evening, I thought ... what have I got to sort of look for, and we had no idea ... They were good, they showed us round all the labs, well everything they showed us round, what the children were doing, they had children there, doing things so we could see what they were doing, and what Billy [son] would be doing. But I'm walking round thinking, 'What do I look for, a good teacher?' and think, 'well are you a good teacher or not? ...' I didn't know, I really didn't know.
>
> (Mrs Perivale, 24 November 1992)

Disconnected parents do not speak the language of secondary educational meanings. Authoritative accounts are sought from within local social networks or from direct experience – rather than from sources of 'public' information. Mr Perivale attended a local school himself and has other local knowledge to draw upon. These things are important as positive bases for choosing, but so too are the 'impressive facilities':

> The choice is really practically between the two schools, Lymethorpe and Flightpath, and because of my miserable time at Flightpath . . . although it is a vastly different school, I still feel it's too big and our neighbours' eldest daughter goes to Lymethorpe and she's done very well . . . I think they've got eight science labs, something like that, computers, everything. He loves drawing, they've got . . . art workshops . . . the facilities are tremendous.
>
> (Mr Perivale, 14 November 1992)

The information networks of disconnected choosers are limited in scope but nonetheless rich and useful. These networks themselves are indicative of the relationship between local schools, families and community.

> Well, Parsons [school] . . . , My sister-in-law's children go to Flightpath [school] and each one has done very very well. I've known children to go to Parsons and they haven't done well . . . As I say, I've got two nephews and one niece at [Flightpath] . . . and they were always talking about the diaries and I just asked what it was for.
>
> (Mrs Harper, 7 November 1991)

There is a collectivity to choosing, in contrast to the individuality of the child-matching strategies of the privileged. Thus, there is frequent mention of friends, neighbours and relatives in framing choice. Furthermore, the choices of disconnected choosers are much more likely to be located within the specifics of other decisions and preferences within the same family:

> No, we was quite happy when we took the eldest one down the first time, she's in the third year now, we quite happy with the school, and we're quite happy with her work over the past two years, three years, whatever . . . so I can't see the point in going to other schools when I'm satisfied with one school.
>
> (Mrs Wooley, 18 October 1993)

In south Westway, other notions of community and familiarity underlay the rejection of some schools by some families. For many white, working-class parents, the racial composition of Gorse school excluded it from consideration and elicited a range of racist comments.

> Beause it's all nig nogs, isn't it? It's all Asians and it is a known fact that they hold ours back. And the last I heard actually, some of the kids, they were complaining as well, you see, because some of them, while they're at home they talk English, some if they want to go to school they're alright, but you get the others . . . the kiddies while they're at home speak in Punjabi or whatever it is, so that when they come to school they can't understand a bloody word, you see? And this is what's happening down there, and there's no

way that he's going there. I mean I know somebody that goes there, and in her class there's about 35 I think, five are white, the rest are . . . , so he's not going down there. He's definitely not going there.

(Mr Tufnell, 30 November 1992)

Mrs Perivale: It was a good school on the whole, the actual education was good, wasn't it? But I think in the back of your mind, I don't think you would have sent Ben [son] there, would you? Because of the race . . . ?

Mr Perivale: No, it's 90, no, probably 80 per cent Asian pupils there and it's geared that way, or it seemed to be, it probably isn't, but it seemed to be geared that way, as well, the main intake is going to be from Westway [LEA].

(Interview, 24 November 1992)

No, there's too many Indians there.

(Mrs Stockwell, 22 November 1992)

This 'racially-informed' choosing works in reverse for some South Asian parents. For them, Gorse school is attractive because it is regarded as safe, and it has a strong and very overt emphasis on educational traditionalism and academic achievement.

Yes, I did see the exam results and my [niece and nephew] have been in that school . . . and secondly . . . the education of that school and the principal – it's very strict, you know, like the kids, if they're not in uniform or they haven't done their homework, things like that, if they muck about, they'll be told off and at the end of the day they're not so – you know all the time misbehaving in the school, things like that.

(Mr Kahn, 17 January 1992)

In contrast, the predominantly white Flightpath school is regarded with some suspicion as, or as having been, 'a bit rough' – which is probably a euphemism here.

Yes, I did think a lot about this other school . . . Flightpath, but I've never seen . . . Flightpath school . . . I haven't been in there, but I've seen the kids, they go from building to building over the flyover up there . . . and in fact some time ago we did read in our local paper what sort of school it was . . . the kids were a bit rough up there sometimes, things like that . . . I think some action has been taken by the education department . . . But it had a really bad name.

(Mr Kahn, 17 January 1992)

And for a few white parents the presence of South Asian children at Gorse school is seen as a positive attractor in their choice of school.

Gorse has a very high Asian count of children and it seemed that the Asian children, they are very much on education and discipline, and I think that rubs off on everybody else.

(Mrs Cole, 13 October 1993)

These racialized choices are related to communal interests and are based around social and family networks and informal sources of information, even if negatively and antagonistically constructed.

Choice of school, despite the way it is written about by many researchers and commentators, cannot be made separate from the interpersonal relationships, patterns of parenting and material environments which constitute and constrain the lives and opportunities of families. For the disconnected and some semi-skilled choosers, choice of school enters into a complex terrain of other concerns and necessities. School has to be 'fitted' into a set of constraints and expectations related to work roles, family roles, the sexual division of labour and the demands of household organization. The material and cultural aspects of this are difficult to separate. For the privileged/skilled and some of the semi-skilled, it was much more common to find family roles and household organization being accommodated to school. For the disconnected choosers, social reproduction is, as we have seen, more closely tied to a sense of locale and community, of which the family is a co-extensive part. The local school is in Cremin's (1979) terms part of a 'functional community' and is chosen positively for this reason. That is, reproduction is defined and constrained and achieved within a spatial framework. Family life, and things such as school choice, are played out within, and over and against, a space and time budget. For the disconnected choosers, space and family organization were very often the key elements in choice-making.

> Too far . . . I mean, supposing something was to happen, God forbid, that means I would have to go miles to get her . . . or get any of the children. I'd rather have a quick way of getting there.
>
> (Mrs Harper, 7 November 1991)

> Really only because her brother goes there and it's local as well, because she'll have to pick up her sister as well, so she's got to have something local . . . Because my husband really wanted him to go to Crawford Park [school], because he'd come from there, but we thought it was too far for him to go . . . that we wanted something really local and by having Trumpton [school], like my husband said, they can all go there, because it's a mixed school, which is good.
>
> (Mrs Nevin, 18 July 1991)

In transport studies, activity analysis 'examines inter-dependencies within the household in respect of the scheduling and time–space constraints placed upon individual household members' (Grieco et al., 1991: 1) and suggests that 'household organisation lies at the heart of the understanding of travel behaviour' (1991: 4). Among low-income households on time-constrained budgets, the limitations of private and public transport play a key role in a whole range of decision-making. These constraints and the forms of household organization which develop as a result are particularly associated 'with the gender roles of women' (Grieco, 1991: 4).

> Women in many such households are able to meet their daily domestic responsibilities and to respond to crises only by 'borrowing' time and other resources from other houses (principally kin) in their social network.
>
> (Grieco and Pearson, 1991: 4)

Access to a car, the pattern of bus, tube and train routes, the local transport timetables, the pattern of busy roads and open spaces and the physical location of schools all affect the possibility and the perception of choice. 'Spatial and temporal practices, in any society, abound in subtleties and complexities' (Harvey, 1989: 218). In part, these horizons (and the complex relationship of space to distance) relate what Harvey calls the 'representations of space' to 'spaces of representation' or imagination; particularly in the latter, 'unfamiliarity' and 'spaces of fear' are important.

Mrs Harper: She'd go across the crossing.
Researcher: Through the park?
Mrs Harper: Oh no, she won't go through the park, definitely not! There's a pathway, it goes all the way round, past the library and then under that footway bridge and then round the corner. She's been taught she don't go in parks, no way!
(Interview, 7 November 1991)

Where transport deprivation leads to the social isolation and segregation of particular social groups in particular localities, *social enclaves* are created. The existence of such enclaves reinforces the importance of *the local* and the need for complex intra- and interhousehold dependencies. The existence of enclaves can also be related to informational dynamics and local information structures (Weimann, 1982). These patterns and processes of time and space management and the existence of social enclaves and social networks are of prime importance in understanding school choice-making for certain class groups. Such an analysis begins to highlight the important interrelationships between market schooling and the other deregulation policies of the current Government, such as transport, housing, health, social welfare and employment training (see Carlen et al., 1992). Differences in the perception of time and space are related to differences in 'finite time resources and the "friction of distance" (measured in time or cost taken to overcome it) [which] constrain daily movement' (Harvey, 1989: 211). The distribution of 'time–space biographies' is class-related – and in this way 'the organisation of space can indeed define relationships between people, activities, things, and concepts' (Harvey, 1989: 216).

The complexities of choice for the disconnected parents reported here are created by the intersection of the values and constraints of locality. There are vestiges apparent here of the 'localism' which Clarke (1979: 240) refers to as 'a pervasive mode of working class culture'. But there are also a set of frictions and limitations and fears and concerns which tie disconnected choosers to their local schools. The sense of locality in disconnected choice and the more cosmopolitan activities of the privileged/skilled parents suggest that parents are orientated to different circuits of schooling [. . .].

[. . .]

Conclusion

We began this chapter by indicating the complexity of parental choice of school but we can end it by pointing to at least two very simple and straightforward conclusions. First, choice is very directly and powerfully related to social-class differences. Second, choice emerges as a major new factor in maintaining and indeed reinforcing social-class divisions and inequalities. Again, in stating that, we do not seek to celebrate or romanticize the *past* here. There is a degree of significant continuity in the crucial role played by social class in educational opportunity. The point is that one set of class-related processes is replaced by another set. The 'balance sheet of the class struggle' over educational goods is changed. Choosing is a multifaceted process and there are clear indications here of class, 'race' and gender dimensions to choice. That is, despite some commonalities, the meanings (and implications) of choice vary distinctively between classes: 'different classes have different ways of life and views of the nature of social relationships which form a matrix within which consumption takes place' (Featherstone, 1992: 86). Where most recent analyses of class differentiation in education have stressed the work of selection and allocation done by schools and teachers, here selection and differentiation is produced by the actions of families. (Not that selection of the first sort has disappeared from the system [. . .].) The onus is now more on the 'classified and classifying practices' of the proactive consumer. Education is subtly repositioned as a private good. The previous interrupters of class schooling (ineffective as they often were), like comprehensives with balanced intakes and mixed-ability grouping, are now being displaced. The ground rules of the class struggle over educational opportunity have been significantly changed.

The use of cultural capital in the decoding of schools and interpretation of information and in the 'matching' of child to school is a crucial component of choosing and then getting a school place, although economic capital is also important, most obviously in relation to the independent sector. Here we can see the actual realization of social advantage through effective activation of cultural resources (Lareau, 1989: 178). By linking biography to social structure, the analysis of school choice in relation to class and capital also illuminates the reproduction of class position and class divisions and points up the changing form and processes of class struggle in and over the social field of school choice.

References

Bourdieu, P. (1986). *Distinction: A Social Critique of the Judgement of Taste*. London: Routledge.
—— and Passeron, J.-C. (1990). *Reproduction*. London: Sage.
Carlen, P., Gleeson, D. and Wardhaugh, J. (1992). *Truancy: the Politics of Contemporary Schooling*. Buckingham: Open University Press.
Carspecken, P. (1990). *Community Schooling and the Nature of Power: The Battle for Croxteth Comprehensive*. London: Routledge.
Clarke, J. (1979). Capital and Culture. In Clarke, J., Critcher, C. and Johnson, R. (eds) *Working Class Culture*. London: Hutchinson.
Cremin, L. A. (1979). *Public Education*. New York: Basic Books.
Featherstone, M. (1992). *Consumer Culture and Postmodernism*. London: Sage.
Gewirtz, S., Ball, S. and Bowe, R. (1993). Parents, privilege and the education market. *Research Papers in Education* 9(1):3–29.
Gray, L. (1991). *Marketing Education*. Buckingham: Open University Press.
Grieco, M. (1991). *Low Income Families and Inter-Household Dependency: The Implications for Policy and Planning*. Oxford: University of Oxford, Transport Studies Unit.
—— and Pearson, M. (1991). *Spatial Mobility Begins at Home? Re-Thinking Inter-Household Organisation*. Oxford: University of Oxford, Transport Studies Unit.

Harvey, D. (1989). *The Condition of Postmodernity*. Oxford: Basil Blackwell.

Lareau, A. (1989). *Home Advantage: Social Class and Parental Intervention in Elementary Education*. Lewes: Falmer Press.

Vincent, C. (1993). *Parental Participation in Primary Education*. Coventry: Centre for Research in Ethnic Relations, University of Warwick.

Weimann, G. (1982). On the importance of marginality: one more step in the two-way flow of information. *American Sociological Review* 47:764–73.

29 | Student Peer Groups and Masculinity

Máirtín Mac an Ghaill

Key words

Masculinity, peer group subcultures, youth, educational organizations, schooling, ethnic divisions, middle-class rebels, sexuality, national identity

Mac an Ghaill's book is a study of the formation of masculinities among different groups of students at a co-educational inner-city 11–18 comprehensive school in the English Midlands, 'Parnell', where he conducted ethnographic research. Mac an Ghaill identified four peer groupings of white and black heterosexual males in the year eleven cohort of 1990–1, 'macho lads', 'academic achievers', the 'new enterprisers' and the new middle-class 'real Englishmen'. The extract concerns the experiences of masculinity of two of these groups, the first and the last. Thus are illustrated the ways in which young males learn to become heterosexual in the context of different types of peer groups.

Mac an Ghaill observes (1994: 52), 'Contemporary modes of masculinity are highly complex, displaying power, violence, competition, a sense of identity and social support.' He describes some aspects of this complexity with reference to earlier studies of school sub-cultures and with particular attention to attitudes to school. In parts of the chapter not reproduced here, Mac an Ghaill relates the experiences of the four groups to developments in the nature of training for work, deteriorating job opportunities for young men and changes in family forms. He sensitively explores the complicated effects of class, race and ethnicity on sex and gender identities.

[. . .]

One of the main weaknesses of earlier male ethnographic research on young males was the failure to note how intra-class variations, among an internally divided working-class, helps to shape school masculinities (Cohen 1983). I found the interplay of masculinities, intra-class variations and ethnicities highly generative of diverse gender/sexual identities. This is critically important with the recomposition of the working-class in the late 1980s and early 1990s. A crucial element of this recomposition is the current crisis in schooling, and the state response in terms of a new vocationalist curriculum and training regimes that have served to disrupt working-class students' transitions into work (Finn 1987; Hollands 1990).

[. . .]

Cockburn (1987: 44) makes clear the complexity of gender resistance, with some young men ridiculed for refusing a macho-style masculinity, while 'others resist the class domination of school precisely by means of masculine codes'. It may be added that for black students the adoption of specific masculine codes of contestation and resistance are also developed in response to schools' racist social and discursive practices. At Parnell School, black students were aware of the historical and current contradictions of black masculinity, with the denial of the patriarchal privileges of power, control and authority that is ascribed to the white male role (Mercer and Julien 1988: 112).

The links between the male students' differing relations to schooling and their developing masculine identities were highlighted in their contrasting narratives. I have summarized these in the following terms: that of the Macho Lads' 'survival against authoritarianism', the Academic Achievers' 'ladders of social mobility', the New Enterprisers' 'making something of your life' and the Real Englishmen's 'looking for real experiences'. These links were further displayed by the students' differential participation in and celebration of formal and informal school rituals, through which masculine subjectivities are constructed and lived out, such as attendance at prize-giving and involvement in the playground smoking gang (Griffin 1993).

The Macho Lads: the three Fs – fighting, fucking and football

At Parnell School, a system of setting was in place. All of the Macho Lads were in the bottom two sets for all subjects. For some, this was a result of demotion, while others were placed there on their arrival at the school. Orientations towards school began to crystallize during year nine. The Macho Lads came together as they found other male students with similar negative responses. Their shared view of the school was of a system of hostile authority and meaningless work demands (see Mac an Ghaill 1988). They were seen by teachers and students as the most visible anti-school male subculture. 'Looking after your mates', 'acting tough', 'having a laugh', 'looking smart' and 'having a good time' were key social practices. As is indicated below, it was 'your [male] mates' who were the significant others in relation to evaluating what school is 'really about' and 'where you are going in the future'. Their vocabulary of masculinity stressed the physical ('sticking up for yourselves'), solidarity ('sticking together') and territorial control ('teachers think they own this place') (see Corrigan 1979; Cockburn 1983; Jenkins 1983).

John: The main way that we protect ourselves is by sticking together [as a gang]. From about the end of the third year a group of us got together and we now have a reputation. A lot of the teachers and the kids won't mess with us and we protect other kids.

Darren: I suppose a lot of kids here are able to defend themselves but it's the teachers that make the rules. It's them that decide that it's either them or us. So you are often put into a situation with teachers where you have to defend yourself. Sometimes it's direct in the classroom. But it's mainly the headcases that would hit a teacher. Most of the time it's all the little things in the place really.

M.M.: Like what?

Gilroy: Acting tough by truanting, coming late to lessons, not doing homework, acting cool by not answering teachers, pretending you didn't hear them; that gets them mad. Lots of different things.

Peer-group masculine identities were developed in response to the school's differentiated forms of authority. This was highly visible in relation to the Macho Lads' experience of the school's social relations of domination, alienation and infantilism that were mediated through their location in the lowest sets. These social relations were of central importance in the construction of their masculinity through 'conflict with the institutional authority of the school' (Connell 1989: 291; Johnson 1991).

[...] In relation to the Macho Lads, the primary function [of teachers] was that of policing, which tended to make explicit the construction and moral regulation of teacher and student subjectivities (Walkerdine 1990). The school disciplinary regime operated in more overt authoritarian modes of interaction with this sector of students. The school's moral imperatives, which included a wide range of disciplinary instruments, were translated into the surveillance of the Macho Lads' symbolic display of working-class masculinity. The senior management, who were becoming experts at decoding the semiotic communication of contestation and resistance, legislated new control and surveillance mechanisms for these 'non-academic' students. At this time there was a vigilant policing, and subsequent banning, of the anti-school male students' clothes, footwear, hairstyles and earrings. This was accompanied by a high-profile surveillance of the students' bodies, with the constant demands of such teacher comments as: 'Look at me when I'm talking to you', 'sit up straight' and 'walk properly down the corridor' (Bourdieu 1986).

As Westwood (1990: 59) notes: 'Discourses as registers of masculinity are worked through a variety of spaces.' Spatially, Parnell School was geared to a set pattern of movement, which systematically discriminated against low-set students, who were viewed with suspicion if during breaks they were found in certain academic locations, such as the science laboratories or computer centre. These students frequently complained about the prefects' arbitrary power as they patrolled corridors and restricted their movement around the school.

Paul: We have different names for the teachers: big ears, big nose, big eyes and that sort of thing.

M.M.: What does it mean?

Jim: It's obvious. Teachers are always trying to catch you out. They're always trying to rule you. They use different means, some are really nosey, others try to catch you smoking and then others are always trying to get you to tell on your mates.

As Mayes (1986: 29) makes clear, in writing of the culture of school masculinities:

A masculine ideal which allows competition and aggressive individualism may take its toll. The alternative status sought by the boys who fail in the system may result in an aggressively 'macho' stance, dangerous to themselves and others.

The Macho Lads rejected the official three Rs (reading, writing and arithmetic), and the unofficial three Rs (rules, routines and regulations). They explained why they opted for the three Fs – fighting, fucking and football (Jackson 1968). They interpreted their secondary school biographies as masculine apprenticeships in learning to be 'tough'. Like the 'anti-school' Asian male students, the 'Warriors', in *Young, Gifted and Black* (Mac an Ghaill 1988), the Macho Lads objected to the *function* not the *style* of teachers, which they saw as primarily causal of school conflict. They refused to affirm the teachers' authority, claiming that it was illegitimate authoritarianism. Spending more time 'on the streets' than other students increased their visibility to the police. Hence, they linked teacher and police authoritarianism, seeing themselves as vulnerable to both state agencies of social control. In response to institutionalized surveillance and interrogation, they developed a specific version of masculinity, around collective strategies of counter-interrogation, contestation and survival (Mac an Ghaill 1988: 136). Their accounts reminded me of the under-reported experiences of young people in Northern Ireland, who have a longer history of dealing with the 'harder face' of the state, in the context of the British military occupation.

Kevin: I'll tell you something, when we came to this dump we believed in the three Rs, we were right little piss artists, real plonkers. Well we learnt what schools were for, for keeping you down and bossing you about. Over the last couple of years we've been doing the three Fs.

Arshad: When kids come here in the first year, you can see that they're not tough. It's the main thing that you have to learn.

M.M.: Is it very important?

Arshad: In some ways, real ways, you know what I mean, you won't survive. You see the whole place is planned to boss you around. That's the main difference between here and posher schools. Somehow the kids in the posh schools accept it more.

Leon: The teachers think, I'm going to put this little sod down because he thinks he can rule the place. The kid isn't thinking that but the teachers think that he is.

M.M.: Why do the teachers think that?

Leon: I don't know. Teachers have to win all the time, don't they? So, I don't know, maybe they think, I'll get him before he gets me, you know what I mean?

Noel: Teachers are always suspicious of us [the Macho Lads]. Just like the cops, trying to set you up.

Like Willis's Lads, the Macho Lads at Parnell School made a similar association of academic work with an inferior effeminacy, referring to those who conformed as 'dickhead achievers'. Consequently, they overtly rejected much school work as inappropriate for them as men. They were also a pivotal group within the school in creating a general ethos in which the academic/non-academic couplet was associated with a feminine/masculine division for a wider group of 'ordinary' male students, who were not overtly anti-school (Jenkins 1983).

Leon: The work you do here is girls' work. It's not real work. It's just for kids. They [the teachers] try to make you write down things about how you feel. It's none of their fucking business.

Kevin: We live in the real world. The world where we are going to end up in – no work, no money with the stupid, slave training schemes. We've gotta sort this out for ourselves, not teachers. They live in their little soft world. They wouldn't survive in our world for five minutes. Now I'm leaving I feel sorry for them. Well, for some of them, some were wicked bastards to the kids.

Arshad: They [the teachers] just look down on us. They think we're nothing because they say, 'you're like your brothers, they never got on to good training' [youth training schemes]. Some of them will do the caring bit. 'I come from Yorkshire lad, my dad was down the pit and I know what the real world is like.' Do they fuck. I wouldn't even ask them, what do you know about being a black man looking for work, when even the white kids round here haven't got work.

[. . .]

The Real Englishmen: 'the arbiters of culture'

A main aim of this research is to deconstruct earlier male academic representations of white and black working-class school masculinities, highlighting the student heterogeneity in terms of the range of masculine identities that are inhabited. It is hoped that a comparative case-study of middle-class young men may make clear the class-specific dynamics of the interplay between schooling and masculinity. In the process, this may make visible a mode of masculinity that tends to be absent from academic and teacher accounts of gender relations. About ten per cent of the student population at Parnell School were from a non-commercial, middle-class background. Their parents' occupations included lecturing, teaching, public relations and work in the media and the arts. As with the working-class students, there was a range of middle-class masculinities, including an emerging group of Politicos, who were involved with environmental and animal rights issues (see Hollands 1990: 119). I chose a small group of male students who displayed an ambivalent response to the academic curriculum and who consequently were the most problematic middle-class peer group for many of the teachers. A similar group has been identified by Peter Aggleton (1987) in *Rebels Without a Cause?* He was interested in broader issues around patterns of cultural affirmation and 'resistance' and the relationship of these to students' home lives and leisure activities. My findings have much in common with his work, and I am indebted to him in providing a framework within which to explore how a sector of the white English middle-class are negotiating a masculine identity within a school arena.

A central contradiction for the Real Englishmen was that unlike the Macho Lads' overt rejection of formal school knowledge and the potential exchange value it has in the labour market, the Real Englishmen had a more ambiguous relationship to it. They envisaged a future of higher education and a professional career. Like Aggleton's (1987) 'Spatown Rebels', they defined themselves as a younger generation of the cultural elite, who like modern-day high-priests positioned themselves as the arbiters of culture. From this self-appointed location, they evaluated both teachers and students in terms of their possession of high-status cultural capital (Bourdieu 1986). They were in the process of building a publicly confident school masculinity in which cultural capital was over-valorized.

Thomas: We're different to most of the people here. That's why we don't fit in. They're mostly boring people, no style, very conventional. I mean you couldn't have a real discussion with any of them.

Daniel: The teachers give you all the crap about having the right attitude to work and we shouldn't be going out at night and we shouldn't talk back to them. They have no idea there's some really interesting people out there that they'll never meet. I mean, who needs teachers' advice? What do they know about life?

Like the Macho Lads, the Real Englishmen, albeit on different grounds, refused to affirm the legitimacy of the teachers' authority, though their rebellion tended to take a more individualist and varied form. They brought with them into the school values that emphasized personal autonomy and gave high evaluation to communication strategies. They expected to be able to negotiate with teachers, particularly about compulsory aspects of the curriculum. Teacher–student interaction with this sub-group produced specific conflictual masculine social practices. Many of the teachers found these middle-class students' capacity for elaborated verbal self-justification much more difficult to respond to, than what appeared to them as the Macho Lads' more open contestation of their authority. The teachers were often confused by the Real Englishmen's highly competent communication skills, with their appeal to rationality and fairness, that enabled the latter discursively to invert classroom power relations, with teachers positioned as culturally subordinate.

Edward: Mark's the best when he starts arguing with the teachers. They never learn. They start off talking down to him and then realize that he can defend himself. They get wickedly mad with him when he quotes some European philosopher they've never heard of. Then they're really shown up in front of everyone. And they hate that because that's their tactic with the kids.

The middle-class young men's name, the Real Englishmen, served as a triple signifier with reference to gender, sexuality and ethnicity, which were highly problematic inter-generational issues for them. Here I wish to concentrate on the development of their peer-group masculine identity in relation to working-class male peer groups. The Real Englishmen's own masculine values emphasized honesty, being different, individuality and autonomy, which they claimed were absent from middle-class culture. Against this background, the Real Englishmen were more ambivalent than the Academic Achievers towards the Macho Lads. At one level, this involved a fantasy of 'proletarian authenticity'. The Macho Lads were viewed as 'noble savages' for being unpretentious and unconscious of themselves. At another level, the Real Englishmen articulated excessive hostility towards the Macho Lads, who they referred to as 'trash', for their vulgarity and aggression, which was directed towards them. They were particularly resentful as they recalled how in earlier years the working-class lads had bullied them.

Adam: You see it if you go down the arts centre, all the middle-class are totally aware of themselves, thinking that people are watching them all the time, as if they're always on show. And you see it in the kids, in their humour and everything, it's just not real. But the working-class are not so aware of their bodies. They are more straightforward, act more spontaneous.

Andy: The Macho kids in this place are just wankers. When we first came here, they terrorized us. We hadn't mixed with them before. They're just very crude and loud. They'd beat you up for looking at them. It's their idea of being real men. The girls find them ugly.

The Real Englishmen were also critical of 'hard-working' students, including their middle-class peers and such groups as the working-class Academic Achievers and the New Enterprisers. The Real Englishmen's dismissive evaluation of these students as 'sloggers' had implications for their relationship to the academic curriculum. From their own self-appointed culturally superior position, they inverted the taken-for-granted relationship between academic success and a positive response to mental labour. Teachers working within discourses of individual under-achievement failed to acknowledge in the young men's response, their collective masculine investment and the links to family social practices. A key element of the students' peer group identity was a highly public display of a contradictory 'effortless achievement' to each other and outsiders (Aggleton 1987: 73). As members of a cultural elite, they rejected the school's dominant work ethic, assuming that intellectual talent was 'naturally' inscribed within their peer group.

Daniel: Teaching is a low-skill job. They're mostly technicists, not into ideas. They've no idea how patronizing they are to us. They don't like us because we're cleverer than them.
Robert: They're [the teachers] just guardians of mediocrity. They've this idea that you have to work all the time, slog, slog, slog to pass exams.
M.M.:   Why do you think they feel that?
Robert: Because that's how they got through. When Ben asked Williams [science teacher], why do we have to do homework, you could see he had never thought of it. And we joined in. He just couldn't argue his case. So, it came down to the usual crap, because I'm telling you boy. And this is supposed to be funny, teacher humour!

[. . .]

References

Aggleton, P. (1987) *Rebels Without a Cause? Middle Class Youth and the Transition from School to Work.* Lewes, Falmer Press.
Bourdieu, P. (1986) *Distinction: A Social Critique of Judgement and Taste.* London, Routledge and Kegan Paul.
Cockburn, C.K. (1983) *Brothers: Male Dominance and Technological Change.* London, Pluto Press.
—— (1987) *Two-track Training: Sex Inequalities and the YTS.* London, Macmillan.
Cohen, P. (1983) Losing the generation game, *New Socialist,* 14, 5.
Connell, R.W. (1989) Cool guys, swots and wimps: The inter-play of masculinity and education, *Oxford Review of Education,* 15(3), 291–303.
Corrigan, P. (1979) *Schooling the Smash Street Kids.* London, Macmillan.
Finn, D. (1987) *Training Without Jobs.* London, Macmillan.
Griffin, C. (1993) *Representations of Youth: The Study of Youth and Adolescence in Britain and America.* Cambridge, Polity Press.
Hollands, R. G. (1990) *The Long Transition: Class, Culture and Youth Training.* London, Macmillan.

Jackson, P.W. (1968) *Life in Classrooms*. New York, Holt, Rinehart and Winson.

Jenkins, R. (1983) *Lads, Citizens and Ordinary Kids: Working-class Youth Life Styles in Belfast*. London, Routledge and Kegan Paul.

Johnson, R. (1991) My New Right education. In Cultural Studies (ed.) *Education Limited: Schooling, Training and the New Right Since 1979*. London, Unwin Hyman/University of Birmingham.

Mac an Ghaill, M. (1988) *Young, Gifted and Black: Student–Teacher Relations in the Schooling of Black Youth*. Milton Keynes, Open University Press.

—— (1994) Local student cultures of masculinity and sexuality. In *The Making of Men: masculinities, sexualities and schooling*. Buckingham, Open University Press.

Mayes, P. (1986) *Gender*. London, Longman.

Mercer, K. and Julien, I. (1988) Race, sexual politics and black masculinity: A dossier. In R. Chapman and J. Rutherford (eds) *Male Order: Unwrapping Masculinities*. London, Lawrence and Wishart.

Walkerdine, V. (1990) *Schoolgirl Fictions*. London, Verso.

Westwood, S. (1990) Racism, black masculinity and the politics of space. In J. Headen and D. Morgan (eds) *Men, Masculinities and Social Theory*. London, Unwin Hyman.

30 | Women's Careers in Teaching

Sandra Acker

Key words

Professional occupations, gender divisions, labour market segregation, equal opportunities, careers

Despite the increased participation of women in the labour market, their much-enhanced credentials and the passing of legislation to promote equal opportunities, gender inequalities in the field of employment remain resistant to change. This issue has inspired much sociological research, with attention being increasingly paid to the development of professional and managerial careers for women. Explanation of why women who are as highly qualified as men continue to fail to get appropriate promotions is still required. Case studies of different occupations in varied contexts promise to contribute to our understanding.

Based on a study of the staff of two primary schools, Acker explores the ways in which teachers perceive and organize careers. She shows that career plans are provisional and changeable, but more so for women than men. The evidence shows that men achieve more promotion than women and she seeks to explain this. The original article provides qualitative evidence about gender differences in career planning, domestic commitments and support from head teachers, but this excerpt concentrates on why teachers thought that women were disadvantaged. Acker concludes that the reality of the career is 'individuals making tentative plans and judgments, in the context not only of their family situations and wider social constraints, but guided by experiences and observations in the school' (p. 160).

A fuller account of this study was subsequently published as Sandra Acker, *The Realities of Teachers' Work: never a dull moment* (Cassell, 1999).

'Career' as a concept seems to fascinate certain sociologists, myself included. We grope for a way of understanding its shades of meaning. Distinctions are made, for example, between objective and subjective careers (Hughes 1958; Evetts 1990), or personal and structural career contingencies (Carlson and Schmuck 1981).

In one sense, a career clearly is an individual construction. Individuals have work histories, perspectives on the past and desired future, the capacity to make choices. Yet at the same time there is inevitably a structural dimension. Structures are social arrangements largely outside our control, such as the size of steps on the pay scales, the number of teaching vacancies in a locale, the probability women will be appointed to senior posts even the configurations of national political and economic systems.

[. . .]

Teacher career structures

Table 1 shows that women are 47.1 percent of primary head teachers in England and Wales, and 17.8 percent of secondary head teachers. These figures look high by North American standards,[1] but it is important to note, first, that they still mean significant underrepresentation of women at senior levels compared to their presence in the occupation, and second, that they come about in part because of the many schools for younger primary pupils counted in the figures. These 'infant schools', which include

Table 1 Representation of women teachers and women heads, by type of school, England and Wales, 1987–88

School type	Numbers of teachers in each school type	Percentage of teachers who are women	Numbers of heads in each school type	Percentage of heads who are women
Nursery	1,643	98.7	589	99.3
Infant	24,588	98.3	3,057	97.6
First	19,152	89.4	2,573	70.5
Junior with infants	87,449	77.1	11,373	33.9
First and middle	4,465	79.1	368	32.9
Junior without infants	28,952	68.1	3,004	22.6
Middle deemed primary	6,812	66.0	597	20.8
Unattached and visiting	2,858	75.3	214	44.9
All nursery and primary	175,919	79.7	21,775	47.1
All secondary	218,776	46.9	5,009	17.8
All teachers*	397,167	61.5	26,869	41.6

* This category includes 2,472 teachers categorized as divided service (primary and secondary) and miscellaneous who are not included in the separate primary and secondary figures above.
Source: Calculated from Department of Education and Science, 1991.

children from ages 4 or 5 to age 7, are almost entirely staffed and headed by women, as table 1 shows. Women are less likely to head all-through (5 to 11) primary schools or the junior schools, which contain older primary pupils only (7 to 11).

One more table gives some idea what the probability is for each sex to move into senior positions (table 2). These 1987–88 figures have only just become available in 1991 and are the first to show the new system of main scale plus incentive allowances. The teachers with incentive allowances would in many cases have received them in exchange for their former scale posts (Department of Education and Science 1991). Some changes would be expected after 1988, as numbers of available allowances have increased.

Table 2 (like earlier ones based on the old system) shows women concentrated in the lower categories. Nearly three-quarters of women teachers in primary schools are on the standard scale without an incentive allowance, compared to just under a third of the men. In secondary schools, 58.5 percent of the women, but only 34.4 percent of the men, have no incentive allowance. Note, too, that over half of all the men in primary schools occupy headships or deputy headships. This will be significant for some of my observations later on. Also, the figures in tables 1–2 are for full-time teachers only. Part-time teachers are usually female and rarely hold an allowance (Department of Education and Science 1991).

Table 2 **Distribution of each sex across the grades, England and Wales, 1987–88**

PERCENTAGES

	Nursery and Primary		Secondary	
	Men	Women	Men	Women
Heads	32.3	7.3	3.6	0.9
Deputy Heads	20.1	8.3	5.8	3.4
Main Scale with Incentive Allowance				
E	0.1	0.0	5.1	1.6
D	0.4	0.1	19.5	7.5
C	0.2	0.1	0.4	0.4
B	12.2	8.3	28.8	24.1
A	2.5	4.3	2.4	3.6
Main Scale without Incentive Allowance*	32.3	71.5	34.4	58.5
TOTAL %	100.1	99.9	100.0	100.0
TOTAL N	(35,692)	(140,227)	(117,094)	(104,154)

* Includes a small number listed as paid on any other scale, e.g., those for unqualified teachers.
Source: Calculated from Department of Education and Science, 1991.

Careers in the workplace: two English primary schools

[. . .]

I believe that teachers arrive at perceptions about careers through their daily experiences in families, communities, and workplaces, experiences that reflect gender
divisions in society. Workplace experience is largely a missing level of analysis in the
literature on teacher careers. My own study involves observations in two primary
schools over several years, using an ethnographic approach that allows depiction of
the everyday lives of teachers in and, to some extent, out of school.

My main school I call 'Hillview.' I began observations there in April 1987. Hillview
is an inner-city school, with a mixed social class and ethnic intake. It has about two
hundred children, from ages 4 to 11, in seven classes. In 1987–89 the teaching staff
consisted of the head teacher, who is female, a deputy, five full-time and three part-
time teachers. All but one of the teachers were female and white. There were two
general assistants, one working mostly as school secretary.

A year later, in April 1988, I began observations in a second, contrasting, school.
'Rosemont' is larger, in a middle-class area, with about three hundred and sixty children in twelve classes. It caters exclusively to juniors (ages 7 to 11). Of the thirteen
teachers in 1988–89 (one part-time), four were men, as was the head teacher, and all
were white. There were two general assistants as well as a secretary.

[. . .]

My analysis suggests that career plans are provisional and changeable, especially
but not exclusively for the women. Most teachers in my study believe men in primary
schools have a career advantage, but it is taken more as a fact of life than a call to
feminist protest. The career structure for women is actually more complicated than the
outline I gave earlier, for there is a shadowy world of part-time posts and temporary
contracts, most of which are held by women. People often look back and feel that they
have made mistakes in career decisions, but most of those 'mistakes' seemed sensible
at the time. Careers are influenced by family stage and work needs of teachers' spouses,
as well as by unexpected life events. They are also strongly shaped by the school experience itself, and in this process the head teacher is a key figure. I now turn to the
results of my study [regarding] women's place in teaching.

[. . .]

Women's place in teaching

Disadvantage

Teachers were asked in interviews if they thought there were any particular advantages
in being male or female teachers in primary schools. Most stated that men had a career
advantage. Several had concluded that the crux of the problem was the scarcity of men

and the surfeit of women. Every school wanted some men, so men got preferential treatment in hiring and promotion.

Teachers thought that appointing committees, especially the parents and school governors on them, were working from stereotyped ideas such as women inevitably leaving to have children or not having the strength or strictness to keep the school in order. Some teachers had been to look at schools or attended interviews where 'it was quite clear they wanted a man' (Sheila Jones, Hillview teacher). They, or their friends, were asked questions such as how they would manage when their own children were ill.

A few teachers broadened the definition of disadvantage. George Middleton (Rosemont School) thought a man might be at a disadvantage if 'for promotion reasons' he ended up isolated in a staff room composed of older women teachers. Alison pointed out that a woman in a mixed-sex staff room finds it difficult to protest about sexist banter without being labeled aggressive and becoming disliked (cf. Cunnison 1989). Both Alison Holly (Rosemont's deputy head) and Helen Davies at Hillview believed that women had to work harder than men for equivalent rewards.

Marginality

Women who had children were thought to experience further disadvantages. Either they carried on, like Hillview's Debbie Stevens, with only a short break for maternity leave, or they were faced with returning to a lower-status, often marginal, position. Grant's (1989) review of studies of women teachers' careers identified the 'career break' as particularly deleterious to women's chances of career advancement in a system where 'promotion is tied to age-related norms' (p. 44). Alison, who herself had not had a career break, offered her observations on the fate of women who dropped out to look after children:

> They come back into teaching having been deputy heads, having even been heads, scale postholders, and they have to go back to the beginning and they're often derided. And feared, because they used to be something high up, and in fact they often don't get jobs for a long time and have to go through supply and fixed term contracts, and it's hell for them.

Nias (1989) discusses sources of satisfaction and dissatisfaction for primary teachers she interviewed. Those who were temporary, supply, or part-time were particularly likely to express 'disappointment, resentment or frustration' (p. 127). Chessum's (1989) interviewees voiced similar sentiments, one terming herself a 'part-time nobody.'

Certainly, such teachers provide flexibility for the *schools*. For the teachers there could also be advantages. Marjorie Howard from Hillview said, looking back, 'It suited me beautifully, doing part-time, with two children and a home to run.' Yet frustration and insecurity were evident, too. Helen Davies explained how difficult supply teaching is when you don't know where the staff room, the lavatory, and the office are. The children are hard to control and you have nowhere to keep your resources and records. Fixed-term contract teachers were by definition only temporary. Part-time teachers were subject to sudden changes in routine.

Marjorie commented, 'Mrs. Temple would send me anywhere at the drop of a hat.' She added that other teachers would get resentful if you didn't turn up to take their

groups, but '. . . it isn't easy for a part-time teacher to say "no" . . . you don't actually make up the timetable, do you, you just do what you're told.' Rosalind Phillips
explained that a part-time teacher needs to be diplomatic: 'In my role, I don't offend
anyone. I tread very carefully. If I'm asked my opinion I give it.'

Delegation of (what were often inadequate) budgets to individual schools, one of
the features of the 1988 legislation, was beginning to threaten all the 'marginal' teachers. It is important to realize these teachers are nearly always *women*.

The problem is not only lack of job security. These teachers, like the others, had
high standards. It was not unusual to hear a remark that a part-time teacher was trying
to do a full job in half the time. It is not surprising if they feel, as Nias (1989) suggests, that there is a discrepancy between their desired self-images as teachers who
should work hard and make a difference, and the reality of limited relationships and
smaller accomplishments imposed by their position.

Fatalism or feminism?

Interview questions and staff room conversations suggested that teachers believe men
have an advantage in promotions, and the statistics presented earlier also point toward
this conclusion. Moreover, it is mostly women who inhabit the world of temporary
and part-time positions. What was the response to such evident inequity? Although
I have quoted from interviews that showed an awareness of sex discrimination, the
topic came up only rarely in staff room discussions and any anger was fairly muted.
The stance was more fatalistic than feminist. 'Discrimination' and very occasionally
'sexism' were part of the explanatory framework, but never 'patriarchy' or 'oppression'. People did not self-identify as feminists in any informal conversations recorded
in my field notes.

There were even a few examples in my research where teachers (tacitly) supported
the sexual status quo. No one, except perhaps Helen Davies, who was trying hard
to secure a deputy headship herself at the time, seemed to object to the understanding that the new deputy at Hillview should be male, as the rest of the staff was
female. The appointment of a new head at Rosemont brought out certain contradictions. One woman and three men were being interviewed for the post. The teachers
by and large reacted very negatively, almost on sight, to 'The Woman,' as she was
termed, objecting to her demeanor. 'We've all crossed her off our lists,' Rosemary
Walker said.

It was unlikely that the teachers would adopt an overtly feminist perspective to
explain their own career patterns, for several reasons. One is probably the fringe status
of feminism in Britain, which means teachers may lack access to ideas that would give
them an alternative framework for their experiences (Middleton 1989).

Another reason is the reality of their competing domestic commitments. Several
teachers said in interviews that women were less likely than men to seek promotion
because of their dual role:

Question: Why do you think there are relatively few women primary heads?

Helen Davies: Well, either because they've opted for their families, and think that they
                     shouldn't have a career, either they think or they've been told that it doesn't

go hand in hand, and the pressures of life are so much that you can only do one or the other.

Debbie Stevens: I don't know – it's probably the same sort of reason that most of the cabinet ministers are men and most of the everything else . . . it's the same thing, isn't it. I think a lot of women probably take time out to have families, people like Sheila, who were very ambitious before they had children, and have taken the time out and now feel that they've jumped back so many years.

Rosalind Phillips: Often they are trying to do two things, aren't they, they are trying to hold down family responsibilities and do their work on a par with their male colleagues.

It was difficult to feel discriminated against, as Cogger (1985) also found in a study of Welsh teachers, when the *choice* to have a family was believed to be the cause of career blockage.

Moreover, as table 1 showed earlier, there *are* significant numbers of women in primary headships, even if they are underrepresented. People tended to look at their schools and their own experience (the 'middle ground') for guides, not to national statistics or feminist literature.

Question: Do you think there's any particular advantage or disadvantage in being a woman in primary teaching?

Rosemary Walker: I used to think it was easier for a male to get a promotion but I don't think that's so now. I'd have said it was fair, at the moment, it's become that way . . . I was expecting a man to be appointed here for science, because I thought, well, we're losing a man, but in fact he's been replaced by a female, and Alison replaced a male, so my experience is that it's fair at the moment.

'Mistakes'

This tendency to look at one's own experience rather than analyse structural constraints led teachers, especially women, to highlight 'mistakes' they had made in the past. 'Staying too long' in a school was a typical 'mistake.' Alison felt she had done this, as we saw, as did Helen, who had great difficulty securing a deputy headship elsewhere because she had spent her whole career, nineteen years, at Hillview. During that time, she had worked under five different head teachers and seen many other changes at the school. She had become strong and influential, becoming the head's deputy in all but name: 'Helen is the school,' Liz Clarke, Hillview's head teacher, told me. But her repeated efforts to move into a deputy headship were thwarted by the convention that one's experience had to be gained in more than one school.

Helen's career-mindedness had come relatively late when it appeared that she would not after all have children of her own. When she became seriously ambitious she found opportunities blocked:

I felt very frustrated. I had got as far as I could and I couldn't do anything, because I hadn't moved in my career at all. And they were saying well that's it, you've had it. And I felt very depressed.

She was rescued from this low ebb by the then-new head, Mrs. Clarke, who found ways of encouraging her, got her on a term's sabbatical to study at the university, and asked her to reorganize the infant department. Eventually she set in motion a train of events that was at last to lead to a move for Helen. Liz's own secondment was taken on the condition that Dennis, the deputy head, be made acting head and Helen acting deputy. This extra experience helped her case, and an advisor from the county subsequently suggested that she take over an acting deputy headship in another (difficult) school where the incumbent had a serious long-term illness.

Rosemary Walker provides a final example. She was terribly frustrated at not getting an incentive allowance or a major curriculum responsibility at Rosemont, although she worked extremely hard. She organized all the educational visits for the school. She attended many in-service courses. She was active and visible in extra-curricular activities with the children. Her teaching was relatively traditional in style but extremely creative. One half-term her room became a ship, for example, in both decor and linked educational activities. A parent said to me that she was the best teacher her child had had.

But when the incentive allowances were made available by someone leaving or an extra allocation to the school, they were often used to attract new, well-qualified staff, rather than rewarding more of the teachers already there. Although Rosemary recognized certain decisions taken by the head teacher had not been helpful to her, she also looked back with regret at some of her own actions. She had moved schools and counties several times, shifted from secondary to primary teaching, taught abroad and had periods doing work outside teaching. She told me:

> I would like to have done things in a different way. I haven't exactly tried to plan it; I should have started a long time ago. I left it too late. No, I'd like to go back to college again, I'd do far more courses at a younger age . . . be a head.

Rosemary's story illustrates the tension between individual and structural explanations, as well as the importance of workplace experiences for teachers' careers. We all want to be active shapers of our destiny, and this requires acceptance of our wrong as well as our right decisions. What is difficult is to hold onto that strength and sense of possibility without engaging in self-blame for conditions beyond our control.

[. . .]

Note

1   In the United States, women held 28.8% of elementary school and 11.6% of secondary principalships in 1988 (Sadker, Sadker, and Klein 1991). Corresponding figures for Canada were 17% and 6% in 1985–86 (MacLeod 1988). There are, however, provincial variations. Rees (1990), using data collected from 12 Canadian provinces and territories, reports women's percentage of principalships ranging from 15% to 38% for elementary schools and 0% to 12% for secondary schools. Provinces used different dates and reporting conventions, making comparisons and summary figures difficult.

References

Carlson, R., and P. Schmuck, 1981. The sex dimension of careers in educational management: Overview and synthesis. In *Educational policy and management: Sex differentials*, ed. P. Schmuck, W. W. Charters, and R. Carlson. New York: Academic Press.

Chessum, L. 1989. *The part-time nobody: Part-time women teachers in West Yorkshire.* Bradford: WYCROW, University of Bradford.

Cogger, D. 1985. *Women teachers on low scales.* Unpublished M.Ed. thesis. Cardiff: University of Wales.

Cunnison, S. 1989. Gender joking in the staffroom. In *Teachers, gender and careers*, ed. S. Acker, 151–67. Lewes: Falmer Press.

Department of Education and Science. 1991. *Statistics of education: Teachers in service England and Wales 1988*. London: HMSO.

Evetts, J. 1990. *Women in primary teaching*. London: Unwin Hyman.

Grant, R. 1989. Women teachers' career pathways: Towards an alternative model of 'career.' In *Teachers, gender and careers*, ed. S. Acker, 35–50. Lewes: Falmer Press.

Hughes, E. C. 1958. *Men and their work*. New York: Free Press.

MacLeod, L. 1988. *Progress as paradox: A profile of women teachers*. Ottawa: Canadian Teachers' Federation.

Middleton, S. 1989. Educating feminists: A life-history study. In *Teachers, gender and careers*, ed. S. Acker, 53–67. Lewes: Falmer Press.

Nias, J. 1989. *Primary teachers talking*. London: Routledge & Kegan Paul.

Rees, R. 1990. *Women and men in education*. Toronto: Canadian Education Association.

Sadker, M., D. Sadker, and S. Klein. 1991. The issue of gender in elementary and secondary education. In *Review of research in education*, ed. G. Grant, 269–334. Washington, D.C.: American Educational Research Association.

Inequalities in Health

31

Independent Inquiry into Inequalities in Health

Key words

Health inequalities, social class, mortality, gender, ethnicity, health-related behaviour

In general over the last century, death rates have decreased and the expectation of life has increased. Despite these general improvements, substantial inequalities in health persist in Britain.

The mortality rate amongst men of working age was, in the early 1970s, almost twice as high for the unskilled as for professionals. What is more, the gap increased in the next twenty years because mortality rates for professionals fell faster for most causes of death.

Although death rates have generally fallen over the last twenty years, there has not been a similar decrease in morbidity; the extra years of life are not necessarily lived in good health. Again, there are substantial differences between members of different social classes. In 1996, for example, seventeen per cent of professional men between 45 and 64 reported a longstanding illness, compared to forty-eight per cent of unskilled men. Other measures of ill health – obesity and blood pressure for example – follow a similar social-class gradient. There are comparable trends in health-related behaviour. For example, unskilled men smoke more and eat less fruit, vegetables and dietary fibre.

Social class is clearly not the only form of health inequality. Thus people of Caribbean, African and Indian origin have higher rates of longstanding illness than white people, while the Chinese have rates lower than the white population. Women have lower rates of mortality than men at any age. However in the last twenty years the gap has been narrowing and, furthermore, as regards healthy life expectancy women now only have a two- or three-year advantage over men.

Socioeconomic inequalities in health and expectation of life have been found in many contemporary and past societies. In England although information based on an occupational definition of social class has only been available since 1921, other data identifying differences in longevity by position in society have been available for at least two hundred years. These differences have persisted despite the dramatic fall in mortality rates over the last century.[1]

Inequalities in health exist, whether measured in terms of mortality, life expectancy or health status; whether categorised by socioeconomic measures or by ethnic group or gender. Recent efforts to compare the level and nature of health inequalities in international terms indicate that Britain is generally around the middle of comparable western countries, depending on the socioeconomic and inequality indicators used.[3] Although in general disadvantage is associated with worse health, the patterns of inequalities vary by place, gender, age, year of birth and other factors, and differ according to which measure of health is used.[4]

General trends in health

Death rates in England have been falling over the last century, from a crude death rate of 18 per thousand people in 1896 to 11 per thousand in 1996.[5-6] Over the last 25 years, there have been falls in death rates from a number of important causes of death, for example lung cancer (for men only), coronary heart disease and stroke.[6]

Life expectancy has risen over the last century,[7] but not all life is lived in good health. Healthy life expectancy – the measure of average length of life free from ill health and disability – has not been rising; the added years of life have been years with a chronic illness or disability.[8]

The proportion of people reporting a limiting long standing illness has risen from 15 per cent to 22 per cent since 1975. The proportion reporting illness in the two weeks previous to interview has nearly doubled from 9 per cent to 16 per cent. There is a slight increase in the proportion of people consulting the NHS.[9]

Measuring socioeconomic position

A number of different measures can be used to indicate socioeconomic position. These include occupation, amount and type of education, access to or ownership of various assets, and indices based on residential area characteristics. There has been much debate as to what each indicator actually measures, and how choice of indicator influences the pattern of inequalities observed. For example, measures based on occupation may reflect different facets of life for men compared to women, and for people of working age compared to older people or children.

Choice of measure is often dictated by what is available. In Britain occupational social class is frequently used, especially for data collected nationally. Table 1 shows examples of the occupations in each social class group.

| Table 1 | Occupations within social class groupings |

Social Class	Occupation
I Professional	accountants, engineers, doctors
II Managerial & Technical/ Intermediate	marketing & sales managers, teachers, journalists, nurses
IIIN Non-manual Skilled	clerks, shop assistants, cashiers
IIIM Manual Skilled	carpenters, goods van drivers, joiners, cooks
IV Partly Skilled	security guards, machine tool operators, farm workers
V Unskilled	building and civil engineering labourers, other labourers, cleaners

Source: Drever F and Whitehead M (1997)[30].

Mortality

Over the last twenty years, death rates have fallen among both men and women and across all social groups.[6,10] However, the difference in rates between those at the top and bottom of the social scale has widened.

For example, in the early 1970s, the mortality rate among men of working age was almost twice as high for those in class V (unskilled) as for those in class I (professional). By the early 1990s, it was almost three times higher (table 2). This increasing differential is because, although rates fell overall, they fell more among the high social classes than the low social classes. Between the early 1970s and the early 1990s, rates fell by about 40 per cent for classes I and II, about 30 per cent for classes IIIN, IIIM and IV, but by only 10 per cent for class V. So not only did the differential between the top and the bottom increase, the increase happened across the whole spectrum of social classes.[10]

Both class I and class V cover only a small proportion of the population at the extremes of the social scale. Combining class I with class II and class IV with class V allows comparisons of larger sections of the population. Among both men and women aged 35 to 64, overall death rates fell for each group between 1976–81 and 1986–92 (table 3). At the same time, the gap between classes I and II and classes IV and V increased. In the late 1970s, death rates were 53 per cent higher among men in classes IV and V compared with those in classes I and II. In the late 1980s, they were 68 per cent higher. Among women, the differential increased from 50 per cent to 55 per cent.[11]

These growing differences across the social spectrum were apparent for many of the major causes of death, including coronary heart disease, stroke, lung cancer and suicides among men, and respiratory disease and lung cancer among women.[10,11]

Death rates can be summarised into average life expectancy at birth. For men in classes I and II combined, life expectancy increased by 2 years between the late 1970s and the late 1980s. For those in classes IV and V combined, the increase was smaller, 1.4 years. The difference between those at the top and bottom of the social class scale in the late 1980s was 5 years, 75 years compared with 70 years. For women, the

| Table 2 | European standardised mortality rates, by social class, selected causes, men aged 20–64 England and Wales, selected years |

All causes
rates per 100,000

Social class	Year 1970–72	1979–83	1991–93
I – Professional	500	373	280
II – Managerial & Technical	526	425	300
III(N) – Skilled (non-manual)	637	522	426
III(M) – Skilled (manual)	683	580	493
IV – Partly skilled	721	639	492
V – Unskilled	897	910	806
England and Wales	624	549	419

Lung cancer
rates per 100,000

Social class	Year 1970–72	1979–83	1991–93
I – Professional	41	26	17
II – Managerial & Technical	52	39	24
III(N) – Skilled (non-manual)	63	47	34
III(M) – Skilled (manual)	90	72	54
IV – Partly skilled	93	76	52
V – Unskilled	109	108	82
England and Wales	73	60	39

Coronary heart disease
rates per 100,000

Social class	Year 1970–72	1979–83	1991–93
I – Professional	195	144	81
II – Managerial & Technical	197	168	92
III(N) – Skilled (non-manual)	245	208	136
III(M) – Skilled (manual)	232	218	159
IV – Partly skilled	232	227	156
V – Unskilled	243	287	235
England and Wales	209	201	127

Stroke
rates per 100,000

Social class	Year 1970–72	1979–83	1991–93
I – Professional	35	20	14
II – Managerial & Technical	37	23	13
III(N) – Skilled (non-manual)	41	28	19
III(M) – Skilled (manual)	45	34	24
IV – Partly skilled	46	37	25
V – Unskilled	59	55	45
England and Wales	40	30	20

Accidents, poisoning, violence
rates per 100,000

Social class	Year 1970–72	1979–83	1991–93
I – Professional	23	17	13
II – Managerial & Technical	25	20	13
III(N) – Skilled (non-manual)	25	21	17
III(M) – Skilled (manual)	34	27	24
IV – Partly skilled	39	35	24
V – Unskilled	67	63	52
England and Wales	34	28	22

Suicide and undetermined injury
rates per 100,000

Social class	Year 1970–72	1979–83	1991–93
I – Professional	16	16	13
II – Managerial & Technical	13	15	14
III(N) – Skilled (non-manual)	17	18	20
III(M) – Skilled (manual)	12	16	21
IV – Partly skilled	18	23	23
V – Unskilled	32	44	47
England and Wales	15	20	22

Source: Drever F, Bunting I (1997)[10].

| Table 3 | Age-standardised mortality rates per 100,000 people, by social class, selected causes, men and women aged 35–64, England and Wales, 1976–92 |

	Women (35–64)			Men (35–64)		
	1976–81	1981–85	1986–92	1976–81	1981–85	1986–92
All causes						
I/II	338	344	270	621	539	455
IIIN	371	387	305	860	658	484
IIIM	467	396	356	802	691	624
IV/V	508	445	418	951	824	764
Ratio IV/V : I/II	1.50	1.29	1.55	1.53	1.53	1.68
Coronary heart disease						
I/II	39	45	29	246	185	160
IIIN	56	57	39	382	267	162
IIIM	85	67	59	309	269	231
IV/V	105	76	78	363	293	266
Ratio IV/V : I/II	2.69	1.69	2.69	1.48	1.58	1.66
Breast cancer						
I/II	52	74	52			
IIIN	75	71	49			
IIIM	61	57	46			
IV/V	47	50	54			
Ratio IV/V : I/II	0.90	0.68	1.04			

Source: Harding S, Bethune A, Maxwell R, Brown J (1997)[11]

differential was smaller, 80 years compared with 77 years. Improvements in life expectancy have been greater over the period from the late 1970s to the late 1980s for women in classes I and II than for those in classes IV and V, two years compared to one year.[12]

A good measure of inequality among older people is life expectancy at age 65. Again, in the late 1980s, this was considerably higher among those in higher social classes, and the differential increased over the period from the late 1970s to the late 1980s, particularly for women.[12]

Years of life lost

Premature mortality, that is death before age 65, is higher among people who are unskilled. Table 4 illustrates this with an analysis of deaths in men aged 20 to 64 years. If all men in this age group had the same death rates as those in classes I and II, it is estimated that there would have been over 17,000 fewer deaths each year from 1991 to 1993. Deaths from accidents and suicide occur at relatively young ages and each

| Table 4 | Estimates of the numbers of lives and working man-years lost per year, selected causes, men aged 20–64, England and Wales, 1991–93 |

	Numbers of lives lost	Working man-years lost	Proportion of deaths from these diseases
Coronary heart disease	5,000	47,000	28%
Accidents etc	1,500	41,000	43%
Suicide etc	1,300	39,000	40%
Lung cancer	2,300	16,500	42%
Other neoplasms	1,700	21,000	13%
Respiratory disease	1,500	12,500	47%
Stroke	900	9,000	32%
All diseases	17,200	240,000	29%

Note: Estimates assume all men have mortality rates as for social classes I and II. Only deaths at ages 20–64 years are included in the analysis.
Source: Drever F. Unpublished analysis (1998).

contribute nearly as much to overall years of working life lost as coronary heart disease. Death rates from all three causes are higher among those in the lower social classes, and markedly so among those in class V.[13,14]

These major differences in death rates and life expectancy between social classes do not just apply to those people already well into adulthood. Infant mortality rates are also lower among babies born to those of higher social classes. In 1994–96, nearly 5 out of every thousand babies born to parents in classes I and II died in their first year. For those babies born into families in classes IV and V, the infant mortality rate was over 7 per thousand babies. As with mortality at other ages, infant mortality rates in each class have been decreasing over the last twenty years. However, there is no evidence that the class differential in infant mortality has decreased over this period.[15]

Morbidity

Although death rates have fallen and life expectancy increased, there is little evidence that the population is experiencing less morbidity or disability than 10 or 20 years ago. There has been a slight increase in self-reported long standing illness and limiting long standing illness, and socioeconomic differences are substantial. For example, in 1996 among the 45 to 64 age group, 17 per cent of professional men reported a limiting long standing illness compared to 48 per cent of unskilled men. Among women, 25 per cent of professional women and 45 per cent of unskilled women reported such a condition. These patterns were similar among younger adults, older men and among children.[9]

In adulthood, being overweight is a measure of possible ill health, with obesity a risk factor for many chronic diseases. There is a marked social class gradient in obesity which is greater among women than among men.[16-18] In 1996, 25 per cent of women in class V were classified as obese compared to 14 per cent of women in class I. For

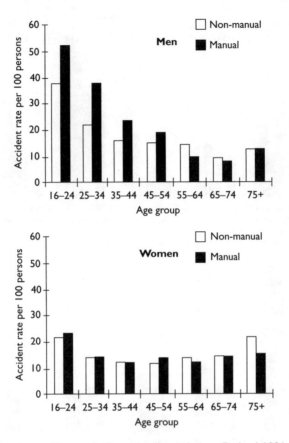

Figure 1 | Annual major accident rates, by age and social class, England 1996
Source: Prescott-Clarke P, Primatesta P (1998)[18]

men, there was no clear difference in the proportions reported as obese except that men in class I had lower rates of obesity, 11 per cent, compared to about 18 per cent in other groups. Overall, rates of obesity are rising. For men, 13 per cent were classified as obese in 1993 compared to 16 per cent in 1996. For women, the rise was from 16 per cent to 18 per cent.[18]

Another indicator of poor health is raised blood pressure. There is a clear social class differential among women, with those in higher classes being less likely than those in the manual classes to have hypertension. In 1996, 17 per cent of women in class I and 24 per cent in class V had hypertension. There was no such difference for men where the comparable proportions were 20 per cent and 21 per cent respectively.[18]

Among men, major accidents are more common in the manual classes for those aged under 55. Between 55 and 64, the non-manual classes have higher major accident rates (figure 1). For women, there are no differences in accident rates until after the age of 75 when those women in the non-manual group have higher rates of major accidents.[18]

Mental health also varies markedly by social class. In 1993/4, all neurotic disorders, such as anxiety, depression and phobias, were more common among women in

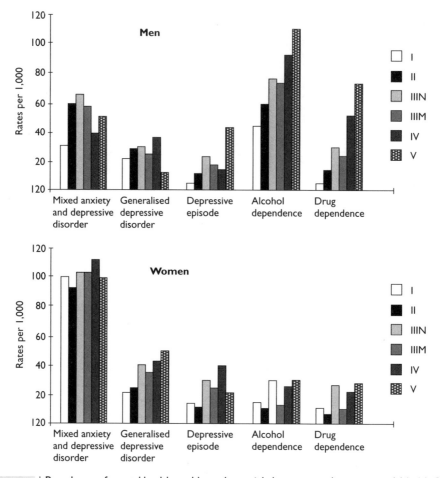

Figure 2 | Prevalence of mental health problems, by social class, men and women aged 16–64, Great Britain, 1993–94

Source: Office of Population Censuses and Surveys (1995)[19]

classes IV and V than those in classes I and II – 24 per cent and 15 per cent respectively.[19] This difference was not seen among men. However, there were striking gradients for alcohol and drug dependence among men, but not women. For example, 10 per cent of men in classes IV and V were dependent on alcohol compared to 5 per cent in classes I and II (figure 2).[19]

[...]

Health related behaviour

Over the last twenty years, the proportion of people who report that they smoke cigarettes has fallen. In 1974, roughly a half of men and two fifths of women smoked cigarettes, compared with less than 30 per cent of men and women in 1996. The trends in drinking alcohol are broadly unchanged over this period. However, the proportion of women who drank more than 14 units of alcohol a week rose from 9 per cent in 1984 to 14 per cent in 1996.[9]

There is a clear social class gradient for both men and women in the proportion who smoke. In 1996, this ranged from 12 per cent of professional men to 41 per cent of men in unskilled manual occupations and from 11 per cent to 36 per cent for women.[9] In spite of the major class differences in dependence on alcohol in men,[19] there are very small differences in the reported quantities consumed. This is not the case among women where higher consumption is related to higher social class.[9]

Among women, there are no differences in levels of physical activity across the social classes. Among men, higher proportions in the manual classes have a high level of physical activity than in the non-manual classes. However, some of this difference is due to work related physical activity. Men in non-manual occupations have higher rates of leisure time physical activity.[16]

People in lower socioeconomic groups tend to eat less fruit and vegetables, and less food which is rich in dietary fibre. As a consequence, they have lower intakes of anti-oxidant and other vitamins, and some minerals, than those in higher socioeconomic groups.[2,21–24]

One aspect of dietary behaviour that affects the health of infants is the incidence of breastfeeding. Six weeks after birth, almost three quarters of babies in class I households are still breastfed. This declines with class to less than one quarter of babies in class V. The differences between classes in rates of breastfeeding at six weeks has narrowed slightly between 1985 and 1995.[25]

Trends in health differences between minority ethnic groups

There are many indications of poorer health among the minority ethnic groups in England. For example, people in Black (Caribbean, African and other) groups and Indians have higher rates of limiting long standing illness than white people. Those of Pakistani or Bangladeshi origin have the highest rates. In contrast, the Chinese and 'other Asians' have rates lower than the white population.[26]

Although in analysing mortality rates we have to use country of birth as a proxy for ethnicity, a similar pattern emerges.[27] There is excess mortality among men and women born in Africa and men born on the Indian sub-continent and men and women born in Scotland or Ireland (table 5).

Many women from minority ethnic groups giving birth in the 1990s were born in the United Kingdom. Because country of birth of the mother, and not ethnicity, is recorded at birth registration, it is not possible to estimate infant mortality rates by minority ethnic group. However, among mothers who were born in countries outside the UK, those from the Caribbean and Pakistan have infant mortality rates about double the national average. Perinatal mortality rates have also been consistently higher for babies of mothers born outside the UK. The differences between groups have not decreased over the last twenty years.[15]

| Table 5 | Standardised mortality ratios, by country of birth, selected causes, men and women aged 20–69, England and Wales, 1989–92 |

	All causes		Coronary heart disease		Stroke		Lung cancer		Breast cancer
	Men	Women	Men	Women	Men	Women	Men	Women	Women
All countries	100	100	100	100	100	100	100	100	100
Scotland	132	136	120	130	125	125	149	169	114
Ireland	139	120	124	120	138	123	151	147	92
East Africa	110	103	131	105	114	122	42	17	84
West Africa	113	126	56	62	271	181	62	51	125
Caribbean	77	91	46	71	168	157	49	31	75
South Asia	106	100	146	151	155	141	45	33	59

Source: Wild S, McKeigue P (1997)[27]
This table was first published in the British Medical Journal, and is reproduced by kind permission of the journal.

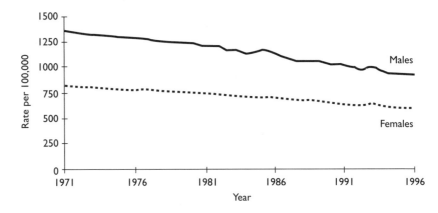

Figure 3	Standardised mortality rates, by gender, all ages, England and Wales, 1971–96
	Source: Office for National Statistics (1998)[6]

Trends in health differences between the sexes

Death rates have been falling for both males and for females (figure 3). Since 1971, these have decreased by 29 per cent for males and by 25 per cent for females, narrowing the differential in death rates very slightly. Cancers and coronary heart disease account for 55 per cent of the deaths of men and 42 per cent of the deaths of women.[6]

At each age in childhood, and on into adulthood, the age-specific mortality rates for boys is higher than for girls (figure 4).[28] For the under 5s, nearly half of the difference is due to external causes, in particular accidental drowning and submersion. For children aged 5 to 14, external causes, chiefly motor vehicle traffic accidents, account for nearly 70 per cent of the difference.[6]

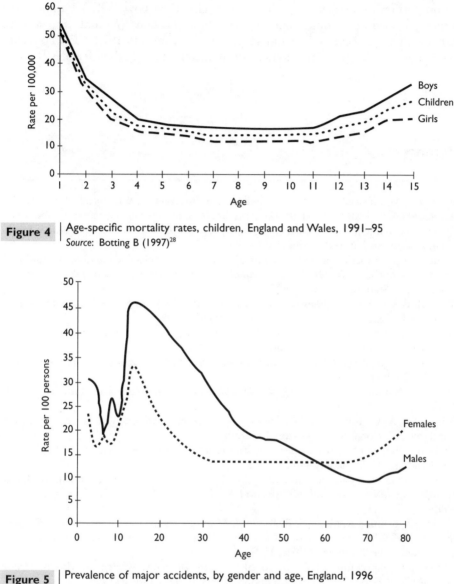

Figure 4 Age-specific mortality rates, children, England and Wales, 1991–95
Source: Botting B (1997)[28]

Figure 5 Prevalence of major accidents, by gender and age, England, 1996
Source: Prescott-Clarke P, Primatesta P (1998)[18]

Although the life expectancy gap between males and females is decreasing,[7] this is not the case for healthy life expectancy. Healthy life expectancy of females is only two to three years more than that of males.[8] Overall, there is little difference in the proportions of males and females reporting a limiting long standing illness.[20] Women report more illness of many different types than men during the reproductive years.[20]

For both children and adults of working ages, males have higher major accident rates than females (figure 5). At older ages, women have higher major accident rates than men.[18]

The proportion of smokers is higher among girls than boys.[29] By adulthood, the proportions of men and women smoking are about the same (29 and 28 per cent), compared with 51 per cent of men and 41 per cent of women in 1974.[20] For both children and adults, males are more likely to drink alcohol heavily than females.[20]

[. . .]

References

1   Whitehead M. Life and death over the millennium. In: Drever F, Whitehead M, eds. *Health inequalities: decennial supplement: DS Series no.15*. London: The Stationery Office, 1997.

2   Dahlgren G, Whitehead M. *Policies and strategies to promote social equity in health*. Stockholm: Institute of Futures Studies, 1991.

3   Whitehead M, Diderichsen F. International evidence on social inequalities in health. In: Drever F, Whitehead M, eds. *Health inequalities: decennial supplement: DS Series no.15*. London: The Stationery Office, 1997.

4   Illsley R, Baker D. *Inequalities in health: adapting the theory to fit the facts*. Bath: University of Bath, Centre for the Analysis of Social Policy, 1997.

5   General Register Office. *59th Annual Report of the Registrar General. Births, deaths and marriages in England – 1896*. London: HMSO, 1898.

6   Office for National Statistics. *Mortality statistics: cause 1996, series DH2, no. 23*. London: The Stationery Office, 1998.

7   Office for National Statistics. *English life tables, no. 15*. London: The Stationery Office, 1997.

8   Bebbington A, Carton R. *Healthy life expectancy in England and Wales: recent evidence*. Canterbury: Personal Social Services Research Unit, 1996.

9   Office for National Statistics. *Living in Britain: results from the general household survey '96*. London: The Stationery Office, 1998.

10   Drever F, Bunting J. Patterns and trends in male mortality. In: Drever F, Whitehead M, eds. *Health inequalities: decennial supplement: DS Series no. 15*. London: The Stationery Office, 1997.

11   Harding S, Bethune A, Maxwell R, Brown J. Mortality trends using the longitudinal study. In: Drever F, Whitehead M, eds. *Health inequalities: decennial supplement: DS Series no. 15*. London: The Stationery Office, 1997.

12   Hattersly L. Expectation of life by social class. In: Drever F, Whitehead M, eds. *Health inequalities: decennial supplement*. London: The Stationery Office, 1997.

13   Office for National Statistics. *Unpublished analysis*. 1998.

14   Blane D, Drever F. Inequality among men in standardised years of potential life, 1970–93. *British Medical Journal* 1998;**317**:255–60.

15   Office for National Statistics. *Series DH3 mortality statistics: perinatal and infant: social and biological factors*. London: The Stationery Office, 1997.

16   Colhoun H, Prescott-Clarke P. *Health Survey for England 1994*. London: HMSO, 1996.

17   Prescott-Clarke P, Primatesta P. *Health Survey for England 1995*. London: The Stationery Office, 1997.

18   Prescott–Clarke P, Primatesta P. *Health Survey for England '96*. London: The Stationery Office, 1998.

19 Meltzer H, Gill B, Petticrew M, Hinds K. *The prevalence of psychiatric morbidity among adults living in private households*. London: Office of Population Censuses and Surveys/HMSO, 1995.

20 Office for National Statistics. *Living in Britain: results from the general household survey 1995*. London: The Stationery Office, 1997.

21 Ministry of Agriculture, Fisheries and Food. *National food survey 1980–1996*. London: HMSO, various years.

22 Department of Health. *The diets of British schoolchildren*. London: HMSO, 1989.

23 Gregory J, Foster K, Tyler H, Wiseman M. *The dietary and nutritional survey of British adults*. London: HMSO, 1990.

24 Gregory J, Collins D, Davies P, Hughes J, Clarke P. *National Diet and Nutrition Survey: Children aged $1^1/_2$ to $4^1/_2$ years*. London: HMSO, 1995.

25 Foster K, Lader D, Cheesbrough S. *Infant feeding 1995*. London: The Stationery Office, 1997.

26 Charlton J, Wallace M, White M. Long-term illness: results from the 1991 Census. *Population Trends* 1994;75:18–25.

27 Wild S, McKeigue P. Cross-sectional analysis of mortality by country of birth in England and Wales, 1970–92. *British Medical Journal* 1997;**314**:705–10.

28 Botting B. Mortality in childhood. In: Drever F, Whitehead M, eds. *Health inequalities: decennial supplement: DS Series, no. 15*. London: The Stationery Office, 1997.

29 Office for National Statistics. *Smoking in secondary school children*. London: HMSO/The Stationery Office, various years.

30 Drever F, Whitehead M, eds. *Health inequalities: decennial supplement: DS Series no. 15*. London: The Stationery Office, 1997.

32

Public Attitudes and the NHS

Ken Judge, Jo-Ann Mulligan and Bill New

Key words

Health, National Health Service, Public Policy, State, healthcare rationing, private medicine

---

The NHS has changed considerably since the mid-1980s. Conservatives introduced the internal market and the Labour government elected in 1997 introduced and promised further changes. One of the abiding themes of the debate in the period has been the funding of the NHS. The extract that follows is from an article reviewing public attitudes to the NHS in this period of change.

The article begins with an investigation of the levels of satisfaction with various NHS services. Generally, within the last twenty years or so, the public has treated the NHS as the most urgent priority for government spending. Satisfaction over this period with the service varies between thirty-six per cent and fifty-five per cent of the population expressing satisfaction, depending, it seems, on perceptions of what the government is doing. General Practitioners consistently gain high levels of satisfaction (at around eighty per cent) while hospital services are much less well regarded. Disapproval of hospital services is concentrated not so much on the quality of treatment, or care, but on such matters as waiting times.

There is increasing public concern as to whether or not the NHS can be sustained, given the increasing cost of medical care, rising public expectations and demographic changes. In the extract, the authors test public responses to different ways of funding the service. Fewer than a third of people asked supported the idea that the NHS should be restricted to those on low incomes and almost two thirds thought that people who could afford it should be allowed to pay for better health care. These judgements indicate continued support for the traditional structure of the NHS.

Rationing, as a means of allocating scarce resources, has always occurred in the NHS. The authors investigated this issue. A significant proportion of people believe that the NHS does ration by, for example, giving preference to those who are younger or who follow a healthier lifestyle. However, very many fewer people believe that there should be rationing, at least by age or lifestyle. If there were to be rationing, the great majority believe that it should be doctors who make the decisions, not the government or NHS managers.

[. . .]

The future of the NHS

[. . .] The public seems to be increasingly worried about the government's ability to fund and run the NHS. While GPs and other health professionals continue to enjoy public confidence, there are signs that specific aspects of both the hospital service and the primary care sector are under increasingly visible strain. That being so, prioritising the NHS for extra spending remains high on the public's agenda.

Increasingly of late, concerns are being expressed as to whether the NHS can be sustained under its current funding regime, especially given the extra demands upon it from demographic changes and the growth of public expectations. Some voices, such as that of Healthcare 2000 – a group financed by the pharmaceutical industry – question the future viability of a comprehensive and universal service free at the point of use, arguing forcefully that policy makers need to consider 'raising the proportion of healthcare funding provided by individuals through options such as user charges and/or patient co-payments' (Healthcare 2000, 1995: 9). Meanwhile the new Secretary of State for Health has announced a 'no holds barred' review of health provision in the NHS.

What evidence can we glean from successive *British Social Attitudes* surveys about public opinion on these sorts of fundamental issues to do with the future of the NHS? For some years now the survey has asked searching questions about the extent to which 'free' health care might be more selectively given, leaving some to fend for themselves through private medical insurance.

A two-tier service?

To gauge the level of public commitment to the principle of a universal health service, we ask:

> It has been suggested that the National Health Service should be available only to those with lower incomes. This would mean that contributions and taxes could be lower and most people would take out medical insurance or pay for health care. Do you support or oppose this idea?

In 1996 we added a similar question on dental services:

> Many dentists now provide NHS treatment only to those with lower incomes. This means that other people have to pay the full amount for their dental treatment, or take out private insurance to cover their treatment. Do you support or oppose this happening?

As table 1 shows, opposition to both a selective NHS and selective NHS dentistry is high. In fact the proportion who favour a selective NHS has *fallen* since we first asked this question in 1983. Then, almost 30 per cent of respondents supported the idea of a selective service, compared with the 20 per cent who do so now.

Table 1

	NHS %	NHS dentistry %
Support	21	20
Oppose	77	77
Base	3,620	3,620

So, while concern about the performance of the NHS may have increased, an alternative system of provision is not at all popular. Over three quarters of the population want to retain a universal 'free at source' health service. More surprisingly, perhaps, given the actual changes to dentistry over the last few years, public feelings seem just as strong about the need for universal free dentistry.

On the other hand, although the majority of people feel that universal free care should be available, should those who can afford it have an absolute right to buy better medical care for themselves? We asked:

Do you think that health care should be the same for everyone, or should people who can afford it be able to pay for better health care?

Table 2

	%
Same for everyone	60
Able to pay for better health care	39
Base	1,221

Even more surprisingly, perhaps, a growing proportion of people, now six in ten, would ideally deny the choice to others to buy themselves out of the system. This above all suggests the extent to which the NHS is still seen by the British public as a resource to be protected and cherished. On the other hand, nearly one-third of those who oppose a two-tier NHS *also* believe that people *should* have the choice to pay for private health care. Being opposed to restricted access to the NHS does not in itself lead people to deny others the right to opt out of the system. As always, the pattern of public opinion is complex. People's views are related to their support for the welfare system in general and inevitably to their political views too. There are elements of self-interest too. People who work in the NHS, for instance, are particularly opposed to any move which might weaken it, such as restricting its access to the poor. Similarly, there are variations in response according to age, such as the comparative indifference among those under 30 towards a decline in 'free' dentistry. This might of course have something to do with the fact that this group has grown into adulthood with an increasing expectation of paying for dental care.

Rationing: old questions in new forms?

Rationing has always existed in the NHS as an inevitable consequence of wants and needs exceeding resources. The process is not, of course, confined to highly publicised cases of individuals being denied treatment, still less to whole services being threatened or withdrawn. It is far more pervasive and mundane, as the continual presence of waiting lists throughout the life of the NHS amply testifies.

It is more difficult to explain the recent explosion of interest in the subject. One possible explanation is that the size of the gap between available resources and technological potential is growing. That being so, the medical profession and the public alike are increasingly aware that what could be done in an ideal world and what can be done are growing further and further apart. Another explanation is that the 1991 NHS reforms encouraged health authorities to focus on specific strategies for rationing, rather than letting the allocation of resources 'emerge' from the interplay of a large number of independent factors. Moreover, in focusing on their resident populations, each health authority and GP fundholder is now able to specify which services should (and should not) be available for those living in their area.

Increasingly, too, the mass media have been giving a more prominent place to aspects of the rationing debate. The NHS reforms precipitated a flood of media scrutiny which has barely eased off since. This might well have contributed to a loss in public confidence.

Background to the debate

The issues involved in rationing are far too complex to be encompassed within one section of one survey. For instance, there are linked questions about who should make rationing decisions and at which level in a health care system they should be made. Such choices depend in part on bureaucratic considerations and on issues of trust and confidence. Should rationing decisions be left to clinicians who deal with individual cases and who seem to enjoy public trust, or should managers at the health authority level have a significant role, or should central government impose rules (Lenaghan, 1996)? Some, such as Mechanic (1995) argue for clinicians continuing to make the bulk of rationing decisions, but such a disaggregated system of decision-making is thought by others to lead to unacceptable variations in outcome. They prefer a national body to advise on priority setting to provide a framework within which clinicians can work (Turnberg et al., 1996).

Then there is the vexed issue of how to choose between individual candidates for treatment. Should smokers, for instance, get lower priority for certain interventions on the grounds that their likely lifespan is more limited than that of non-smokers? And, by the same token, should people get a lower priority for certain interventions as they get older? (See Underwood et al., 1993; Williams, 1997; Grimley Evans, 1997.) This principle could be extended to obese people, and so on.

Lying behind support or rejection of such criteria are different understandings of what constitutes justifiable need. Some argue that the mere existence of ill-health is sufficient reason for intervention and that other factors should be irrelevant (Harris, 1997). Indeed, it is sometimes argued that, say, elderly or overweight people are in greater need simply because their prospect of long term benefit from treatment is less good than that of younger and slimmer people. Others who interpret need more strictly as the ability to benefit, measured by concepts such as 'quality adjusted life-years', would regard the claims of smokers, the elderly and the overweight as less pressing. They view the NHS as essentially about maximising the health gain of the whole community, not only about treatment of the individual in ill health.

Others argue that smoking and weight are characteristics which, to some extent, depend on choice and lifestyle preferences. And although it is still rare for commentators to advocate openly that these lifestyle factors should lead to a lower priority for treatment, it has been suggested that smokers, for instance, should contribute relatively more to the *finance* of health care – through a tax on tobacco products (Le Grand, 1991).

What do people think about health rationing?

In view of our somewhat sparse knowledge of public opinion on health rationing (see Kneeshaw, 1997), the 1996 *British Social Attitudes* survey introduced several new questions on the topic. First, respondents were asked to consider three scenarios, each of which concerned two men on a hospital waiting list. Both men had a heart condition and both would benefit from an operation. In each scenario, the men differed on only one point:

Scenario 1 One man was a heavy smoker, the other a non-smoker;
Scenario 2 One man was aged 40, the other aged 60;
Scenario 3 One man was overweight and ate unhealthily, the other was of average weight and ate healthily.

People were asked first whether they thought each difference between the two men *would* currently be used to prioritise one over the other for the operation. In each case, a significant proportion of people believe that rationing on the basis of these criteria does occur in the NHS and that those following a 'healthy lifestyle' or who are younger will be given priority. This applies most to non-smokers: more than one half believe their claim to a heart operation would get precedence over those of a heavy smoker. As table 3 shows, smaller but still rather high proportions believe that weight-related and age-related rationing exists too.

Having established what people think actually happens, we asked what they think should happen in each case.

Table 3 | Currently, who *would* get priority, or are decisions not made on this basis?

Smoking	%	Age	%	Weight	%
– non-smoker	53	– younger man	35	– average weight	42
– heavy smoker	3	– older man	6	– overweight	4
– no difference	33	– no difference	48	– no difference	41
– can't choose	10	– can't choose	11	– can't choose	12
Base 3,085					

Table 4 | Who *should* get priority, or should decisions not be made on this basis?

Smoking	%	Age	%	Weight	%
– non-smoker	39	– younger man	20	– average weight	29
– heavy smoker	2	– older man	5	– overweight	3
– no difference	49	– no difference	65	– no difference	55
– can't choose	9	– can't choose	9	– can't choose	12
Base 3,085					

As table 4 shows, the proportions of people who support health rationing by lifestyle or age are considerably lower than the proportions who believe it happens under the present system. There is most support (four in ten respondents) for discriminating in favour of non-smokers and least support (two in ten) for discriminating by age.

This does not, of course, imply that the majority reject the idea of rationing in principle. It is quite possible that they simply reject the three criteria for rationing implied by our questions. Other criteria, such as the degree of need, whether the treatment is likely to work, or whether the candidate has a dependent family, might be more popular.

Who supports health care rationing?

As before, we used regression models to investigate which socio-demographic factors or attitudes are associated with people's beliefs about rationing. In the first place, people with pro-welfare views in general are much less likely than others to favour health care rationing on the basis of either lifestyle or age – perhaps because it is felt to constitute a challenge to the principles of equality of treatment implied by universal welfare. There are also predictable elements of self-interest in people's views on rationing. Non-smokers, for instance, are significantly more likely than smokers to favour discrimination in favour of the non-smoker. But, with respect to discrimination on grounds of age, the story is more complex. Not only those under 30 (predictably) but also those over 75 turn out to be more accepting than others of rationing by age.

Table 5 | **Where should responsibility for rationing reside?**

	%
The government	2
Managers working for health authorities	2
Managers in hospitals	4
Hospital doctors	75
Can't choose	16
Base	3,085

This may be a function of a more accepting attitude generally among older people, coupled perhaps with long experience and wisdom about the realities of life and a degree of humility about what an individual ought to expect from the state. Moreover, many of them – old enough to remember the period before the NHS – might be less likely to hold the idealistic view that the NHS is capable of doing everything.

Women are less likely than men to favour rationing, reflecting, perhaps, the widely-held stereotype that women are more 'caring' at the individual level. As for class differences, the higher one's social class and education level, the more pro-rationing one is, all other factors being equal. This could, of course, be a function of their likely greater interest in public affairs and therefore a greater familiarity with the debates. Or it could be that they are simply more likely to accept an apparent weakening of the concepts of universality and comprehensiveness in welfare provision.

Who should make the rationing decisions?

We asked all respondents:

> If decisions like this had to be made, who would you most trust to decide whether non-smokers or smokers should get the operation first?

As table 5 shows, choosing from a given list, most people wanted doctors to take rationing decisions, with little support for any of the other candidates.[1]

This represents an overwhelming vote of confidence in doctors as opposed to politicians or bureaucrats of one kind or another. It suggests too that people favour decisions based at least partly on individual circumstances rather than ones made at a political level and then implemented according to a prescribed set of 'rules'.

Conclusion

The financing and organisational structure of the National Health Service has risen in political prominence during the 1980s and 1990s, gaining in the process a high and sustained media interest. Partly deriving from this, public interest has been high too.

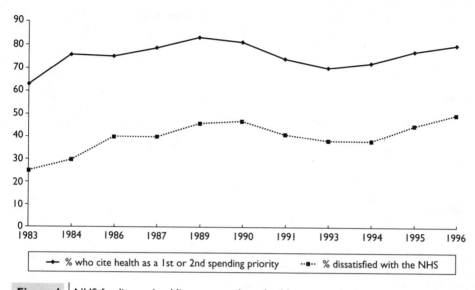

Figure 1 | NHS funding and public concern about health care services

Levels of dissatisfaction with health care provision fluctuated somewhat between 1983 and 1996, but they rose inexorably over the period and ended higher than ever. It would not be surprising if this turned out to be one of the factors contributing to the defeat of the Conservatives at the 1997 general election. Certainly a strong association exists between actual levels of government spending on the NHS, people's public spending priorities and their dissatisfaction with the NHS. As figure 1 shows, public support for higher spending and their levels of dissatisfaction with the NHS increased in tandem in the second half of the 1980s while funding increases were relatively small, then fell back somewhat in the early 1990s in the wake of the spending increases prior to the 1992 election, only to reassert themselves when spending levels faltered once again almost to a standstill in the period prior to the 1997 election.

It has been argued that cuts in health spending can precipitate increases in private insurance which would lead to a reduction in demand for increased spending on the NHS (Besley et al., 1996). But our findings offer little support for this conclusion, with only a two percentage point rise since 1991 in the number of people covered by private health insurance. On the contrary, it seems that despite growing dissatisfaction with the NHS, only a very small proportion of the public either wish to, or can afford to, abandon it in favour of private health provision.

So what of the future of the NHS? On the basis of public opinion alone, there appears to be little support for major changes in the traditional mechanism of financing the NHS through the tax system. Radical moves in the direction of promoting private health insurance or of restricting access to health care to certain social groups would risk offending public opinion at large and Labour supporters in particular. Less risky, it seems, would be to contemplate new and more explicit forms of health care rationing. But the public's willingness to embrace change in the NHS should not be overestimated. Caution will need to be the watchword in any future policy.

Note

1   These results are consistent with other surveys (e.g. Kneeshaw, 1997).

References

Besley, T., Hall, J. and Preston, I. (1996), *Private Health Insurance and the State of the NHS*, London: Institute for Fiscal Studies.

Grimley Evans, J. (1997), 'Rationing healthcare by age: the case against', *British Medical Journal*, **314**.

Harris, J. (1997), 'Maximising the health of the whole community: the case against', *British Medical Journal*, **314**.

Healthcare 2000 (1995), *UK Health and Healthcare Services. Challenges and Policy Options*, London: Healthcare 2000.

Kneeshaw, J. (1997), 'What does the public think about rationing? A review of the evidence' in New, B. (ed.) *Rationing: Talk and Action in Health Care*, London: King's Fund/British Medical Journal.

Le Grand, J. (1991), *Equity and Choice: An Essay in Economics and Applied Philosophy*, London: Harper Collins.

Lenaghan, J. (1996), *Rationing and Rights in Health Care*, London: Institute for Public Policy Research.

Mechanic, D. (1995), 'Dilemmas in rationing health care services: the case for implicit rationing', *British Medical Journal*, **310**.

Turnberg, L., Lessof, M. and Watkins, P. (1996), 'Physicians clarify their proposal for a National Council for Health Care Priorities', *British Medical Journal*, **312**.

Underwood, M. et al. (1993), 'Should smokers be offered coronary bypass surgery?', *British Medical Journal*, **306**.

Williams, A. (1997), 'Rationing healthcare by age: the case for', *British Medical Journal*, **314**.

Juvenile Crime

33

Anne Worrall

Key words

Juvenile delinquency, punishment, moral panic, gender, criminal justice system, juvenile crime

---

Worrall considers changes in the system of punishment for young offenders and the incidence of juvenile crime during the 1980s. In an earlier part of the chapter from which this extract is drawn, she suggests that there has always been a tension in penal policy between punishing in accordance with the principle of justice and consideration of the welfare of young people. In 1969, legislation was passed to decriminalize juvenile justice – young offenders were to be helped by social workers rather than controlled by probation officers. Conservative governments in the early 1980s, however, reintroduced some more punitive provisions, but nevertheless continued with social work intervention through the 'intermediate treatment' systems.

Worrall points out that most juvenile crime is not particularly serious. Public fear of crime and media reporting nevertheless create moral panics about the problem. Yet, despite the stereotypes of young offenders, the statistical evidence indicated a fall in juvenile crime in the 1980s. She discusses an increase in offending by girls. The behaviour of young women is put in the context of issues of punishment and gender differences in delinquency.

[. . .]

Facts and figures

So what happened to juvenile crime in the 1980s? Contrary to popular impression, the decade saw a sharp fall in the number of juveniles known to be committing crime. The number of juveniles found guilty or cautioned for indictable offences declined by 34 per cent between 1984 and 1994, from 206,800 to 135,800 (NACRO 1996). That decline far outstripped the 16 per cent fall in the number of juveniles in the general population and was largely consistent across age and gender. Overall, the proportion of crime known to be committed by juveniles declined from 36 per cent in 1984 to 26 per cent in 1994.

Most of the crime committed by juveniles is not particularly serious. In 1994 sexual offences and robbery each accounted for only 1–2 per cent of cautions or convictions for males, with another 11–12 per cent being for crimes of violence. Of the remaining 86–87 per cent the vast majority related to property; more than half were for offences of theft and handling stolen goods. For females, about three-quarters of all offences are theft and handling. Violence accounts for a similar proportion as it does for males but robbery and sexual offences are virtually non-existent (NACRO 1996).

Cautioning increased significantly: in 1979, 50 per cent of all juveniles were cautioned. By 1990 it was 75 per cent for males and 89 per cent for females. This varied with age (higher when younger) and geographical area (85 per cent in Surrey to 44 per cent in Durham). By 1995 the proportions had fallen slightly, especially after Home Office circular 18/1994, which restricted its use. Nevertheless, Home Office research shows that 85 per cent of offenders cautioned do not reoffend. Nor is there much evidence to suggest that large numbers are being repeatedly cautioned (Home Office Statistical Bulletin 10/1996).

Custodial sentences also fell dramatically from a peak of 12,000 in 1984 to 3,600 in 1994 (the figures for girls fluctuated between 50 and 100). The White Paper *Crime, Justice and Protecting the Public* argued that 'there is no evidence that the reduction in the use of custodial sentences has resulted in increases in juvenile crime' (Home Office 1990:45). It even questioned 'whether it is necessary to keep the sentence of detention in a young offender institution for girls under 18' (1990:45).

[. . .] The replacing of the Juvenile Court by the Youth Court was an attempt to reflect the age balance of young offenders brought to court, which was overwhelmingly in the 14 to 17 age group, while younger offenders were being successfully diverted from prosecution. At the same time, however, courts were given the 'flexibility' to impose adult sentences on 16- and 17-year-olds. In other words, the boundaries between youth and adulthood were being blurred, ostensibly to reflect the differing rates of development among adolescents.

A return to Victorian values

Such blurring both reflected and reinforced a perceived desire of public opinion to treat young criminals less and less differently from their adult counterparts. In this, a return to early Victorian values can be detected. Two emergent moral panics of the early 1990s have been joined by a third, more recent, folk devil. 'Rat Boy', the elusive persistent offender who laughed at the system, was soon accompanied by the more awful spectre of 'Child Killer' and now both have been joined by 'Tank Girl' – the new breed of 'feminist' girl criminal.

The 'Growing out of Crime' school (Rutherford 1986) taught us that many young people experiment with offending but most desist as they mature. A smaller group persists to become young adult criminals and an even smaller group commits one very serious offence. By conflating these three distinct groups, the myth is now being created that increasing numbers of juveniles are persistently committing increasing amounts of very serious crime – and increasing numbers of them are girls! We will now examine these three stereotypically constructed juvenile delinquents in more detail.

The persistent young offender

From 1991 onwards, there was increasing concern that a small number of children were committing a disproportionate amount of not-so-trivial crime, especially burglary and criminal damage. Because of their age, they could not be given custodial sentences and the option of being taken into care under section 7(7) of the 1969 Children and Young Person Act had been abolished by the 1989 Children Act. Thus was born the myth of the wild child beyond the control of any authority. Earl Ferrers gave examples to the House of Lords:

> There are reports of a 14-year-old from Tyneside who has 28 convictions and who has escaped 22 times from local authority accommodation. Another 14-year-old boy in south London has admitted taking part in more than 1000 burglaries of shops and homes in the past two years . . . He has been arrested 40 times but is too young to be given a custodial sentence for the crimes he has committed. That is pretty hot stuff.
>
> (cited in Morton 1994:2)

In response, in 1992 Michael Howard announced his intention to introduce secure training units for 12- to 14-year-old persistent offenders who were unable or unwilling to respond to supervision in the community. His definition of 'persistent' was the commission of three or more imprisonable offences, one of which must have been committed while under supervision, and the offence under current consideration must be serious enough to warrant a secure training order. In fact, although such children undoubtedly existed, their numbers were far fewer than the government and the media would have the public believe (Hagell and Newburn 1994). Despite this, and despite the very strong professional opposition to his proposals for 'prep schools of crime' (Morton 1994), the Home Secretary proceeded to include this provision in the 1994 Criminal Justice and Public Order Act. The first secure training unit was planned to open its doors in 1997. It is also worth noting that, at the same time, the Home Secretary announced (with no hint of irony) his intention to uncover the full extent of child sexual and physical abuse in local authority children's homes.

Child killers

There has always been an equivalent to a life sentence for juveniles who commit extremely serious offences such as murder, manslaughter and rape. The provision is to be found in section 53 of the 1933 Children and Young Person Act which allows courts to hold juveniles in secure accommodation 'at Her Majesty's Pleasure' and to transfer them to prison when they are old enough. The number of young people, most of them very disturbed youngsters, who have been detained in this way for murder or manslaughter, has fluctuated between 20 and 40 a year for the past 20 years and of these, only 12 in the whole 20 years have been under 14 years of age (Boswell 1996; Cavadino 1996).

What, then, was so very different about Jon Venables and Robert Thompson? Was it the fact that so many adults saw them dragging poor Jamie Bulger to his death and did nothing? Was it the blurred images on the closed circuit TV? Was it the perceived influence of video nasties? Was it just the fact that they were the youngest children to have been convicted of murder? Something about this offence was uniquely postmodern and challenging to our claim to be a civilised society. The veneer of morality seemed to be so easily and publicly stripped away and, despite all the technology, we were still unable to protect a vulnerable toddler from the violence of boys only a few years older than him (Hay 1995). Ever since William Golding's (1960) *Lord of the Flies*, we have had to confront our own knowledge of the depths of depravity that unsupervised boys are capable of, yet the only way in which we seemed able to cope with Jamie Bulger's murder was to pretend that Venables and Thompson had committed an *adult* offence and should therefore be treated like adults, subjected to the full weight of adult sentencing. 'Freaks of Nature' (*Daily Mirror*, 25 November 1993) and 'Evil, Brutal and Cunning' (*Daily Mail*, 25 November 1993) were just two of the screaming headlines that greeted the convictions for murder. The *Sun* asked its readers to fill in a coupon demanding that the Home Secretary increase the boys' sentence tariff (the minimum time they should spend in prison to satisfy the requirements of retribution and deterrence before the authorities consider their rehabilitation) from the 8 years set by the trial judge and the subsequent 10 years set by the Lord Chief Justice. The Home Secretary obliged and set the tariff at 15 years. In 1996 the High Court ruled that this decision was unlawful. The Home Secretary had the right to intervene in setting tariffs for adults but not for children. Children who kill must have their cases regularly reviewed as their personalities develop and mature – something which is inconsistent with a 15-year minimum sentence.

As a result of the Jamie Bulger case, the vexing issue of the age of criminal responsibility was reopened. The four-year zone between 10 and 14 years, when the onus is on the prosecution to produce evidence that a child *knew* that they had committed a serious wrong, was swept away by a High Court ruling in March 1994, though reinstated by the Law Lords a year later (Penal Affairs Consortium 1995).

Tank girl: the trouble with young women

If we are to believe what we read in the papers then the next moral panic, waiting round the corner, is Tank Girl, a shaven-headed, beer-swilling, feminist superheroine with her biker boots, tattoos, bright red lipstick and 'cocky, feminist, aggressive persona' (Brinkworth 1994).[1] She and her all-girl gang are menacing the streets, targeting vulnerable women (note the media tactics of divide and rule) who don't expect to be attacked by a group of young girls, some as young as 14 years. But that's not all. These girls may be devious but they are not stupid. They *know*, we are told, that the legal system is soft on them. They *know* how to work it to their advantage, dressing smartly and playing up to the magistrates.

And all this is caused by feminism. This is what happens when you loosen the controls on women. This is what happens when adolescent girls are allowed to think themselves equal or superior to boys. It is every mother's and father's nightmare – their daughter's sexuality rampant and violent. Put succinctly, 'no man is safe'.

Crime is overwhelmingly a masculine activity and the history of juvenile justice and youth social work has been the history of interest in white, working-class young men by white, working and middle-class men. The underlying philosophy has been dominated by ideals of respectable masculinity. The belief that most children grow out of crime if left alone is also based on assumptions about male adolescence: assumptions that crime is an irritating but bearable extension of normal adolescent masculinity – that 'boys will be boys'.

But crime is emphatically not an extension of normal adolescent femininity: it epitomises everything which challenges our expectations of the ways in which 'nice girls' behave. As Lees (1993) points out, the predominant feature of adolescent femininity is walking the tightrope of sexual reputation, avoiding being labelled as either a 'slag' or a 'drag'. It may be true that girls, like boys, will grow out of crime, but the possible damage to their reputations and future life prospects as respectable wives and mothers may be too great to risk radical non-intervention.

Yet our criminal courts are not filled with over-educated, ambitious young women. When girls raise their sights, broaden their horizons, increase their aspirations and self-esteem, they are less likely, not more likely to behave deviantly (James and Thornton 1980). If there is an increase in violent adolescent female delinquency, it is certainly not the result of women's liberation. On the contrary, it has far more to do with certain impoverished young women seeing no future for themselves other than lone parenthood, state dependency and social stigma and saying 'Anything must be better than that.'

The peak age for female offending is now 14 years compared to 18 years for men but at no age does offending by women remotely approach that by men. About one in five known young offenders is female. In numbers that means about 48,000 out of a total of 240,000 (Home Office 1994a). On the whole young women commit less serious crime than young men. They commit proportionately more theft and less burglary (breaking and entering a building). It is true that the second most common crime for young women is violence and its proportionate significance is increasing but we are still talking about only 190 girls (compared with 546 boys) placed on supervision for offences of violence in 1993 (Home Office 1994b).

Although cautioning rates for young offenders are high for both males and females, they are significantly higher for young women – 63 per cent for those under 21, compared with 44 per cent of men in the same age group. This is often attributed to male chivalry and an unwillingness to stigmatise young women with court proceedings. There may also be a belief that young women are more amenable to the shaming process of informal control and that more formal procedures are unnecessary.

By the time they get to court, the proportion of young offenders who are women has reduced to about one in ten. They are more likely than young men to be given a conditional discharge or a supervision/probation order and less likely to be fined or given either an attendance centre or community service order. They are far less likely than young men to receive a custodial sentence. In 1992 only 3 per cent or one in 33 young offenders (excluding fine defaulters) in prison was female (Home Office 1994a). The average prison population of young female offenders was 139, of whom fewer than 10 at any one time were juveniles. That figure represents a steady decline over the previous 10 years and, although the figures crept up again to 245 by late 1996 (National Advisory Council Newsheet Issue 2) this was not out of proportion with the rise in the prison population as a whole at that time.

At first glance, then, it may appear that young women are treated leniently by the system. However, a number of factors hidden by these statistics may cause concern. First, young women appear to be sent to custody for less serious crimes and with fewer previous convictions. Second, young women remanded in custody are only half as likely as young men eventually to receive a custodial sentence. This would appear to imply that, even though the numbers of young women remanded in custody are relatively small, they could safely be reduced further. Finally, in relation to custodial sentences, it has to be noted that 20 per cent of young women in custody are black – a figure out of all proportion to their numbers in the general population – and that increases to 30 per cent for long sentences. The currently accepted explanation for this is that many are drug couriers but that does not by any means account for the whole of the discrepancy between black and white female custody rates.

[. . .]

Although it is true that young people have always been perceived as troublesome by their elders, the assumed relationship between youth and crime seems to be stronger than ever. As Ian Loader (1996) has argued, young people are assumed to be the perpetrators of crime and are rarely constructed as victims or as consumers of criminal justice services. Yet much of the attention paid to young 'trouble-makers' may be due to their inexperience and greater likelihood of detection or to the systematic bias of criminal statistics which emphasise visible and easily counted 'street crimes' rather than the hidden crimes of the workplace and the home (Pearson 1994). In both the latter cases, young people are more likely to be the victims (for example, of employer negligence, sexual assault or child abuse) than the perpetrators.

Juvenile offenders and sex offenders have in common their experience of *exclusion* from the community. Respectable citizens and figures of authority are less and less willing to communicate with either group and are increasingly demanding that they be 'known about', watched and moved on.

Note

1   Pages 332–4 have been reproduced by kind permission of ISTD, King's College London from *Criminal Justice Matters*, No. 19, Spring 1995 pp. 6–7.

References

Boswell, G. (1996) *Young and Dangerous: the Background Careers of Section 53 Offenders*, Aldershot, Avebury.

Brinkworth, L. (1994) 'Sugar and spice but not at all nice', *The Sunday Times*, 27 November.

Cavadino, P. (ed.) (1996) *Children Who Kill*, Winchester, Waterside Press.

Golding, W. (1960) *Lord of the Flies*, Harmondsworth, Penguin Books.

Hagell, A. and Newburn, T. (1994) *Persistent Young Offenders*, London, Policy Studies Institute.

Hay, C. (1995) 'Mobilization through interpellation: James Bulger, juvenile crime and the construction of a moral panic', *Social and Legal Studies*, 4 (2):197–223.

Home Office (1990) *Crime, Justice and Protecting the Public*, Cmnd. 965, London, HMSO.

—— (1994a) *Criminal Statistics England and Wales 1993*, London, HMSO.

—— (1994b) *Probation Statistics England and Wales 1993*, London, Home Office.

—— (1996) *Summary Probation Statistics England and Wales 1995*, Home Office Statistical Bulletin 10/96, London, Home Office.

James, J. and Thornton, W. (1980) 'Women's liberation and the female delinquent', *Journal of Research in Crime and Delinquency*, 230–44.

Lees, S. (1993) *Sugar and Spice*, Harmondsworth, Penguin Books.

Loader, I. (1996) *Youth, Policing and Democracy*, London, Macmillan.

Morton, J. (1994) *A Guide to the Criminal Justice and Public Order Act 1994*, London, Butterworths.

NACRO (1996) *Criminal Justice Digest*, No 90, October.

Pearson, G. (1994) 'Youth, crime and society' in M. Maguire, R. Morgan and R. Reiner (eds) *The Oxford Handbook of Criminology*, Oxford, Clarendon Press.

Penal Affairs Consortium (1995) *Doli Incapax*, London, Penal Affairs Consortium.

Rutherford, A. (1986) *Growing out of Crime*, Harmondsworth, Penguin Books.

Moral Panics about Sex and AIDS

34

Kenneth Thompson

Key words

Moral panic, AIDS, mass media, homosexuality, deviance, representation, moral consensus

---

The concept of 'moral panic' refers to an anxious over-reaction, by the state authorities, the mass media and the general public, to a problem perceived to affect the whole of society. Recent ones include BSE, the activities of travellers and AIDS. Thompson considers the way in which AIDS was represented in the mass media. Early predictions of the likely spread of the disease were such as to cause a moral panic. This was spread by the mass media which, in their representations of the epidemic, identified unconventional sexual behaviour as its cause. In particular, gay men were demonized in the popular press. While the representations of AIDS changed in the 1990s, Thompson argues, the episode was not untypical as the mass media frequently focus on deviations from sanctioned family and sexual relationships. The media continually have recourse to a disciplinary discourse of sexual normality.

[. . .]

In this chapter we will focus on processes of representation and on mapping the discourses which the mass media use to construct a view of the events which gives rise to a sense of increasing risk and possibly moral panics, particularly panics about sexuality. A common theoretical feature of sociological analyses of these moral panics about sexuality is the focus on discourses that regulate sexuality and defend a notion of what is 'normal', 'natural' and so 'moral'. Following Foucault (1979), many of these analyses argue that we need to recognize that the image of the threatened and vulnerable family is a central motif in modern society. Familial ideology is obliged to fight a continual rearguard action in order to disavow the social and sexual diversity of a culture which can never be adequately pictured in the traditional guise of the family of cohabiting parents and children – a situation which is now occupied by only a minority of citizens at any given moment. However, familial ideology is not the only factor that might explain moral panics about sexuality. Foucault (1979) and Weeks (1985) have attempted to explain why sex itself is so important, so separate from the other human 'attributes' in modern society. They conclude that it is because our culture believes that sex speaks the truth about ourselves, that it expresses the essence of our being, and that it is for these reasons that it has become the subject of controversies and panics. Any concern about the social order is inevitably projected on to this essence, and through this sexuality becomes both an anxious metaphor and a subject of social control. Consequently, moral panics about sex are increasingly the most frequent and have the most serious repercussions in modern society.

AIDS

Susan Sontag's book *Illness as Metaphor* (1983), which was written following her treatment for cancer and analyses the imagery surrounding cancer and tuberculosis, has been influential in developing an understanding of how illnesses such as these and AIDS are constructed in the popular imagination. She identifies the metaphorical uses to which illness and disease may be put in 'making sense' of prevailing social arrangements (a theme also developed by Foucault in *The Birth of the Clinic*, 1973). An important consideration is the way in which a succession of illnesses are given a moralistic meaning that stigmatizes the victim as a pariah or social deviant. This moralizing process is increasingly accomplished through representations in the mass media.

Early reporting and newspaper comment on AIDS provide many examples of this process. In the British press, the columnist John Junor, writing in the *Sunday Express* (24 February 1985), wrote: 'If AIDS is not an Act of God with consequences just as frightful as fire and brimstone, then just what is it?' And a more elliptical leader in a similar vein in *The Times* (3 November 1984) claimed: 'Many members of the public are tempted to see in AIDS some sort of retribution for a questionable lifestyle, but AIDS of course is a danger not only to the promiscuous nor only to homosexuals.' Other papers used the device of reported speech and allusion to the views of third parties to make similar references. The *Sun* (7 February 1985), for example, carried the headline 'AIDS is the wrath of God, says vicar' and the *Daily Telegraph* (3 May 1983) used quotation marks to similar effect: ' "Wages of sin" A deadly toll.' Newspaper reporting also tended to differentiate between so-called 'innocent' and 'guilty' victims of the syndrome. Deaths of those who contracted the disease as a result of 'illicit' or 'morally unacceptable' practices (gays, bisexuals, prostitutes, drug users) were presented more negatively in the media than deaths of those infected as a result of blood transfusions or other accidental factors. In a headline story involving a schoolchild with AIDS, the *Daily Express* (25 September 1985) asked: 'AIDS: Why must the innocent suffer?' Even animals being used to test a possible cure were portrayed as 'innocent' and more deserving of sympathy than the 'guilty' victims: 'Torture of innocents: Chimps in "sex plague" tests' (*Sunday Mirror*, 4 December 1983). Another feature of reporting in the early 1980s, at least until the National Union of Journalists issued guidelines after an enquiry in 1984, was to refer to AIDS as the 'gay plague' (e.g. *Daily Telegraph*, 2 May 1983; *The Observer*, 26 June 1983; *Sun*, 2 May 1983; *Daily Mirror*, 2 May 1983). Finally, there was a constant tendency to exaggerate the numbers of people involved by extrapolating from clinical data to the wider population or by projecting forward previous rates of increase on the assumption that these are certain to be sustained. For example, a clinical study of gay men at a clinic at St Mary's Hospital, London, showing that 12 per cent of symptom-free clinic attenders had lymphocyte abnormalities characteristic of AIDS and 5 per cent also had anergy, the index combination of defects seen in AIDS, was reported under the headline: 'Thousands of British gays have symptoms of AIDS' (*The Observer*, 7 August 1983). Meanwhile the Royal College of Nursing issued a prediction that there would be 1 million cases in Britain by 1991; this was reported verbatim or as a rate of one in fifty by *The Times*, the *Sun*, the *Daily Mirror*, the *Daily Express* and the *Daily Star* (10 January 1985) (Aggleton and Homans 1988). The projections were made on the basis of assuming the continuation of the exponential growth rate of the early years of the disease, without questioning whether all the factors would remain the same, especially whether there might be changes in behaviour limiting the spread of infection.

As we saw in considering Cohen's pioneering study of moral panics, the mass media provide 'a main source of information about the normative contours of a society . . . about the boundaries beyond which one should not venture and about the shapes the devil can assume' (Cohen 1972: 17). The mass media, it is alleged, construct 'pseudo-events' according to the dictates of an unwritten moral agenda which constitutes newsworthiness. Thus, 'rumour . . . substitutes for news when institutional channels fail' (ibid.: 154), and in ambiguous situations 'rumours should be viewed not as forms of distorted or pathological communication; they make sociological sense as co-operative improvisations, attempts to reach a meaningful collective interpretation of what happened by pooling available resources' (ibid.: 154).

In an important essay on AIDS, Jeffrey Weeks draws heavily on moral panic theory, explaining how its mechanisms 'are well known':

> the definition of a threat to a particular event (a youthful 'riot', a sexual scandal); the stereotyping of the main characters in the mass media as particular species of monsters (the prostitute as 'fallen woman', the paedophile as 'child molester'); a spiralling escalation of the perceived threat, leading to a taking up of absolutist positions and the manning of moral barricades; the emergence of an imaginary solution – in tougher laws, moral isolation, a symbolic court action; followed by the subsidence of the anxiety, with its victims left to endure the new proscription, social climate and legal penalties.
>
> (Weeks 1985: 45)

Dennis Altman also discusses AIDS in terms of moral panic, but relates the form the panic takes to local and national factors. Thus:

> the Australian panic is not only a product of homophobia but is also tied to the . . . belief that they can insulate themselves from the rest of the world through rigid immigration and quarantine laws [and] a less sophisticated understanding and acceptance of homosexuality than exists in the United States.
>
> (Altman 1986: 186)

Calls for draconian legislation in such disparate societies as West Germany and Sweden lead him to conclude that 'the link between Aids and homosexuality had the potential for unleashing panic and persecution in almost every society' (Altman 1986: 187).

[. . .]

Circulation wars between the British tabloid newspapers in the 1980s led them to feature ever more gruesome stories about AIDS, and this escalation certainly led to an air of panic about morals being undermined by 'deviants' (Cohen's 'folk devils'), which, despite Watney's hesitations, seems to merit the label of a 'moral panic'. The *Sun* ran a story bringing together religion, the family, homosexuality and AIDS, under the heading: 'I'D SHOOT MY SON IF HE HAD AIDS, Says Vicar! He would pull trigger on rest of his family.' The piece featured the Rev. Robert Simpson, who 'vowed yesterday that he would take his teenage son to a mountain and shoot him if the boy had the deadly disease AIDS' (*Sun*, 14 October 1985). The vicar was pictured holding a shotgun to his son's head. The coverage managed to combine some of the most potent images of threats to normal life: family breakdown, infanticide, teenage sexuality, homosexuality and contagious disease. The Rev. Simpson was reported to have said 'he would ban all practising homosexuals, who are most in danger of catching AIDS, from taking normal communion. If it continues it will be like the Black Plague. It could wipe out Britain. Family will be against family' (ibid.).

The Press Council, the official watchdog on press standards in Britain, rejected complaints about the story that it was likely to create irrational fears about AIDS and to encourage discrimination or violence against people with the disease. The Council concluded:

> In this case the *Sun* chose a dramatic way to focus attention on the danger of Aids. Its article was not presented as medical opinion offered by the paper or as a report of medical opinion, but as a report of the strong views held by a clergyman who had already published similar comments in his parish magazine.
>
> (quoted in Watney 1987: 96)

Watney's argument is that homosexuality is constructed by the press as an exemplary and admonitory sign of Otherness, in order to unite sexual and national identifications among readers over and above all divisions and distinctions of class, race and gender. When he turns to the representation of AIDS in broadcasting, he maintains that, given the close relations between the press and broadcasting, it is not surprising that a similar situation obtains, although less so in radio because of its stronger commitment to regionalism. However, he notes that sexuality is subject to a double bind in relation to television, which is regarded as private at the point of viewing but public in its duties and responsibilities – unlike newspapers, which strongly maintain their independence of the state. Television has always been subject to official regulation, especially in relation to questions of obscenity and indecency. The BBC was founded on an assumption 'of cultural homogeneity; not that everybody was the same, but that culture was single and undifferentiated' (Curran and Seaton 1985: 179). Legislation and regulation sustained a 'consensus' orientation which excluded homosexuality. The home was regarded as a site vulnerable to moral danger, with the focus of attention fixed on the possibility of children watching adult programmes – 'adult' in this context usually meaning sexually explicit. Not surprisingly, therefore, for a long time any representation of sexual 'deviance' was either excluded or referred to in a highly coded manner. The various forms of coding included treating homosexuality as a subject of scandal, humour or humanist pathos. Alternatively, coding could involve treating it as a controversial problem in 'current affairs' programmes, which then required balancing contributions from critics, as in the case of the appearance of the 'Clean-Up TV' campaigner Mary Whitehouse when London Weekend Television ran a series of *Gay Life* magazine programmes in 1980 and 1981.

There was some change in broadcasting representations of homosexuals and AIDS when the British Government became convinced that it had to embark on a massive advertising campaign to increase knowledge about AIDS and safer sex practices. It took a long time to reach this decision and Prime Minister Margaret Thatcher is believed to have done so only with great reluctance. Her own Parliamentary Private Secretary, Michael Allison, MP, was a member of the Conservative Family Campaign, which advocated its own solution to AIDS: the isolation of all those infected and the recriminalization of homosexuality. She herself was a great supporter of Clause 28, an amendment to the Local Government Bill introduced in 1987, which forbids local councils and their schools from promoting the acceptability of homosexuality. However, there were strong reasons for going ahead with a campaign, not least the fact that the US Surgeon General Everett Koop, an ultra-conservative supporter of President Reagan, had published a report in October 1986 which painted a doomsday scenario and emphasized the importance of widespread public education. The Government announced to the House of Commons in November 1986 that it was launching a £20 million public education campaign with newspaper advertisements, posters, a leaflet to every home and a radio, television and cinema campaign. Two days after the Commons debate *The Sunday Telegraph* responded with the headline 'AIDS: The new holocaust'. The *Mail on Sunday* reported that it was the greatest danger facing Britain, and *The Sunday Times* ran a picture of the average family – two parents, two teenagers and a baby: 'They all look happy and healthy. But from what we now know about the way the AIDS epidemic is developing, all are potential victims.' The Government's television advertisements were no less ominous. The first featured an exploding mountain, a tombstone on which was chiselled the words AIDS, and a bunch of flowers; the second featured an iceberg. They did not convey much other than that something terrible was going to happen. Doctors at a Southampton hospital conducted a survey on the effectiveness of the advertisements and found that people still had little idea about the illness; one person whose first language was not English had seen the tombstone advertisement and thought that AIDS was associated with the use of pneumatic drills (Garfield 1994). However, the broadcast campaign, linked to the leafleting, did appear to have had some beneficial effects in increasing the level of expressed compassion for people with AIDS and perhaps in forestalling the victimization of homosexuals (see the Independent Television Commission research report, Wober 1991).

The Government's campaign did not completely halt the moral panic about AIDS. Religious leaders were not impressed with the campaign. The Roman Catholic Church disapproved of condom promotion and the Anglicans expressed doubts about the lack of accompanying moral guidance. The Chief Rabbi, Sir Immanuel Jakobovits, thought it 'encourages promiscuity by advertising it'. The Chief Rabbi had his own message: 'Say plainly: Aids is the consequence of marital infidelity, premarital adventures, sexual deviation and social irresponsibility – putting pleasure before duty and discipline' (Garfield 1994). Some newspaper columnists continued to denounce the deviancy and permissiveness that they blamed for the spread of AIDS, and one of them, Digby Anderson, claiming to speak on behalf of the 'moral majority', regretted bitterly that there had not been more of a moral panic about AIDS (quoted in Watney 1987: 45). However, the Government's educational campaign seemed to have taken the steam out of the moral panic and also undercut its own previous attempt, epitomized by Clause 28, to prevent the promotion of positive views of homosexuality. The National Viewers' and Listeners' Association continued to attempt to arouse public opinion against the moral permissiveness represented by AIDS and issued a report, 'Television programmes and Aids' (1992), which stated: 'We believe that the role of the media in normalising casual sex has been one of the main factors in creating this almost overwhelming and potentially most dangerous problem (Aids).' But by the 1990s this ideological position was less prevalent in the press than it had been in the 1980s. Another reaction from some parts of the press in the early 1990s was against the so-called 'AIDS industry' and an imaginary liberal Establishment for allegedly blurring the distinction between 'deviants' such as homosexuals and drug-takers, whose behaviour exposed them to risk, and 'normal' people, whose sexual behaviour did not present a risk. As the liberal columnist Neal Ascherson put it, when singling out the then editor of *The Sunday Times*, Andrew Neil, as an example of one of the representatives of this position, this was a variant on a hegemonic ideological theme of the 1980s – the populist criticism of a liberal elite who conspired against the 'aspirations of plain folk' and formed cliques described as 'industries' (Ascherson 1993). The so-called 'AIDS industry' was only the latest manifestation, following on from the 'poverty industry', the 'race relations industry', the 'Third World aid industry', the 'social work industry', and the 'Euro-industry' (allegedly devoted to abolishing Parliament and national sovereignty). In each of these cases, according to the populist ideology represented in much of the mass circulation press, the 'natural common sense' and moral healthiness of the majority of plain, ordinary folk was confronted by the machinations of a morally dubious minority. It was by playing on these contrasts that moral outrage was stirred up and sometimes gave rise to a moral panic.

The significance of AIDS for the study of moral panics is the way in which it was given a moral significance that articulated together with certain ideological themes and discourses that were contending for hegemony in the 1980s, particularly those associated with the New Right's efforts to shape a new majority. As Weeks (1985) points out, there have been three main strands in the moral and sexual shifts of the past generation: a partial secularization of moral attitudes, a liberalization of popular beliefs and behaviours, and a greater readiness to accept social, cultural and sexual diversity. The significance of the AIDS crisis has been that it could be used to call into question each of these, and to justify a return to 'normal moral behaviour'. The changes were never accepted by moral conservatives, and since the 1960s there has been a reaction against them in the form of an attempted reassertion of absolute moral values and 'social purity'. In the US a combination of television evangelism, big money and religious fundamentalism combined with New Right political forces to create the so-called 'moral majority'. Although Britain did not provide the same fertile ground for such a social movement, moral entrepreneurs were able to use the national press's interest in populist causes, especially those alleging threats to 'normal' family life from sexual promiscuity or deviance. Just as feminism could be blamed for disrupting traditional demarcations between the sexes, homosexuality could be attacked as a threat to the family and to the health of society. As Weeks puts it:

> There have been many fundamental changes in the past thirty years, but their impact has been uneven and fragmented, producing frustration as well a social progress, new tensions as well as the alleviations of old injustices. Secularization, liberalization, changes in the pattern of relationships have all taken place. But they have left deep residues of anxiety and fear, which Aids as a social phenomenon has fed on and reaffirmed.
>
> (Weeks 1985: 15)

It is within such a context of social change, anxiety and tension that moral entrepreneurs are able to promote a discourse about alleged threats to what is 'normal', 'natural' and moral with regard to sexuality. Where there is a mass-circulation popular press, as in Britain, there are ample possibilities for the amplification of deviance to give rise to a moral panic. Although Britain possessed the mass-circulation popular press conducive to the development of a moral panic about AIDS, it differed from the United States in not having a tradition of strong, grassroots social movements, including a gay and lesbian rights movement that could engage in debate with an opposed viewpoint in the form of the religious New Right. The press in America is accustomed to acting as a local forum, presenting and reporting the opinions of different pressure groups and social movements. In this respect, it might be argued, it is closer to Habermas's (1984) notion of the media as channels for rational communication, than is the British tabloid press, which corresponds more to Debord's (1970) idea of 'society as spectacle', in which the mass media excite and entertain. Perhaps the only compensation is that competition between newspapers means that the intense coverage that can create a panic can also lead to rapid exhaustion of the subject and its replacement with a new topic, especially if rival journalists cast doubt on the reports that gave rise to the panic. An example was the story abut the 'angel of death' in Dungavon, Ireland, in September 1995, when hundreds of British and foreign journalists descended on the small town after the parish priest preached a Sunday sermon claiming that a young Englishwoman had infected at least nine of the local men with AIDS in six months. By Monday the panic was such that the local health board had to set up two emergency counselling lines and, 'as every medieval morality play has to have a witch', as the *Guardian* (14 September 1995) put it, it was rumoured that the press were offering £10,000 for the name of the girl. The health authorities soon began to cast doubt on the feasibility of one woman infecting so many men in such a short space of time, and even the priest's bishop and the local mayor were said to be annoyed with the priest. Within a week the story had burned itself out and the hundreds of journalists had departed.

A further conclusion that might be drawn from this discussion of moral panics associated with AIDS is that they illustrate that although moral panics may be episodic, the discourses that construct attitudes to sexuality are deeply interwoven in the cultural fabric of a society. In a 'society of spectacles', such as where there is a national tabloid press in which newspapers vie with each other to shock and outrage readers, the incidence of moral panics may be greater and have a rapid turnover, but the underlying discourse about 'normal' and 'deviant' sexuality is more long-lasting and is part of a wider discursive formation.

References

Aggleton, P. and Homans, H. (eds) (1988) *Social Aspects of AIDS*, London: Falmer.

Altman, D. (1986) *Aids and the New Puritanism*, London: Pluto.

Ascherson, N. (1993) 'Wilful ignorance on Aids is a relic of Thatcherism', *The Independent on Sunday*, 23 May.

Cohen, S. (1972/80) *Folk Devils and Moral Panics: The Creation of the Mods and Rockers*, London: MacGibbon & Kee; new edition with Introduction, Oxford: Martin Robertson, 1980.

Curran, J. and Seaton, J. (1985) *Power Without Responsibility: The Press and Broadcasting in Britain*, London: Methuen.

Debord, G. (1970) *The Society of the Spectacle*, Detroit, Ill.: Black & Red Press.

Foucault, M. (1973) *The Birth of the Clinic*, trans. A. M. Sheridan-Smith, London: Tavistock.

—— (1976/80) *The History of Sexuality*, vol. 1, trans. R. Hurley, New York: Random House, 1978; Vintage paperback edn, 1980; London: Allen Lane, 1979; published in French as *La Volonté de savoir*, Paris: Gallimard, 1976.

Garfield, S. (1994) *The End of Innocence*, London: Faber.

Habermas, J. (1984) *The Theory of Communicative Action*, vol. 1, *Reason and the Rationalisation of Society*, trans. T. McCarthy, Cambridge: Polity Press.

NVLA (1992) *Television Programmes and AIDS*.

Sontag, S. (1983) *Illness as Metaphor*, Harmondsworth: Penguin.

Watney, S. (1987) *Policing Desire: Pornography, Aids and the Media*, London: Methuen.

Weeks, J. (1985) *Sexuality and its Discontents: Meanings, Myths and Modern Sexualities*, London: Routledge.

Wober, J. M. (1991) *Seeing into Others' Lives: The View of Homosexuals on Screen*, London: Independent Television Commission.

Index

Note: Main references to subjects are shown in **bold** print.